The Holy Spirit & Counseling

Volume II
Principles and Practice

Marvin G. Gilbert
and
Raymond T. Brock
Editors

HENDRICKSON
PUBLISHERS
PEABODY, MASSACHUSETTS 01961-3473

ISBN 0-913573-84-1

Excerpts in chapter 9 from E. Kübler-Ross, "Unfinished Business," in J. C. Hansen and T. T. Franz, eds., *Death and Grief in the Family* (Rockville, Md.: Aspen Publishers, 1969), are reprinted with permission of Aspen Publishers, Inc., © 1984.

Excerpts in chapter 13 from H. Leuner, *Guided Affective Imagery: Mental Imagery in Short-Term Psychotherapy* (New York: Thieme Medical Publishers, Inc., 1984), are adapted by permission.

Excerpts in chapter 13 from H. Malony, "Inner Healing," in D. Benner, ed., *Baker Encyclopedia of Psychology* (Grand Rapids: Baker Book House, 1985), used with permission.

Excerpts from H. Leuner, "Guided Affective Imagery: An Account of Its Development," *Journal of Mental Imagery* 1 (1977): 73-92, used with permission.

Excerpts in chapter 13 from A. Sheikh and C. Jordan, eds., *Imagery: Current theory, research, and application* (New York: John Wiley & Sons, 1983). Used with the permission of John Wiley & Sons, Inc., © 1983.

Figure 1-1 adapted from D.G. Mortensen and A.M. Schmuller, *Guidance in Today's Schools* (New York: John Wiley & Sons). Used with the permission of John Wiley & Sons, Inc., © 1966.

Library of Congress Cataloging-in-Publication Data
(Revised for vol. 2)

The Holy Spirit & counseling.

Contents: — Vol. 2. Principles and practice.
    1. Pastoral counseling.   2. Holy Spirit.
BV4012.2.H368 1985   253.5   88-195878
ISBN 0-913573-14-0 (v. 1)
ISBN 0-913573-84-1 (v. 2)

Table of Contents

CONTRIBUTORS

Larry Bass, Ph.D., is a clinical psychologist in private practice in Springfield, Missouri. As a Christian psychologist, he is active in the Missouri Psychological Association and serves on the Licensing Board of Psychologists in the State of Missouri. He wrote the chapter on "The Role of Psychology in Physical Rehabilitation."

Chuck Borsellino, Ph.D., wrote the chapter on "Group Therapy" while Director of Counseling at Evangel College in Springfield, Missouri. He is now in private practice and in training as a neuropsychologist at St. John's Regional Health Center in that city.

Raymond T. Brock, Ed.D., is an associate professor in the department of psychiatry and behavioral medicine in the Oral Roberts University School of Medicine. He is also a licensed professional counselor in the City of Faith Medical and Research Center and director of education for the Institute for Christian Living, Inc., as well as minister of education at Carbondale Assembly in Tulsa, Oklahoma. In addition to being co-editor of this volume, he wrote the chapters on "Establishing and Maintaining a Counseling Ministry," "Ministering to the Aging," "Death, Dying, and Bereavement," and "Guided Imagery and Inner Healing."

John Goodwin, Ph.D., is a professor in the department of psychology at The School of the Ozarks in Point Lookout, Missouri. He wrote the chapter on "Counseling with College Students."

Marvin Gilbert, Ph.D., co-editor of this volume, wrote the chapter on "Making Referrals" while associate professor of psychology in the behavioral sciences department at Evangel College in Springfield, Missouri. Currently he is academic dean of the East Africa School of Theology in Nairobi, Kenya, East Africa.

E. C. Hurley, D.Min., wrote the chapter on "Family Therapy." He is pastor of Mount Denson Cumberland Presbyterian Church in Springfield, Tennessee, and Director of the church's counseling ministry. He holds the rank of Lieutenant Colonel in the U.S. Army Reserve and is Chaplain for the 332nd Medical Brigade.

†David K. Irwin, D.Miss., dictated the chapter on "Cross-cultural Counseling" shortly before he was tragically killed in an automobile accident in August, 1985. A professor in the missions department of the Assemblies of God Theological Seminary in Springfield, Missouri, he was in the process of starting the Mission to the Moslems for the Division of Foreign Missions of the Assemblies of God. Dr. Irwin's royalties from this book are being designated to the Mission to the Moslems to which he was so deeply committed. His doctor of missions degree was granted posthumously by Trinity Theological Seminary in Deerfield, Illinois, in May, 1986.

John Katter, D.Min., is a professor in the practical theology department of the Assemblies of God Theological Seminary in Springfield, Missouri, where he teaches courses in pastoral counseling. He wrote the chapter on "Marriage Enrichment" in this volume.

Linda Lee Martin, M.A., wrote the chapter on "Counseling the Parents of a Handicapped Child." She is a counselor for the hearing impaired in the Montgomery County (Maryland) Public Schools. She is a deaf single parent who has adopted and is raising twelve deaf children and ministers to the deaf at Arlington (Virginia) Assembly of God.

Phil Robinette, Ph.D., is chairman of the division of social sciences and a professor of sociology at Southern California College. He directs a counseling ministry in Costa Mesa, California, which specializes in counseling ministers and missionaries and their dependents. He is also associate pastor of Newport-Mesa Christian Center. He wrote the chapter on "Marriage Counseling."

Editors' Introduction

In late 1985 *The Holy Spirit and Counseling: Theology and Theory* was published. It contained the reflections and research of fourteen theologians and psychologists. Each author was attempting to define the "fit" between the activity of the Holy Spirit and the activity of the counselor—between pneumatological doctrines and psychological theories. As the editors (and contributing authors) of that book, we have ". . . a firm conviction that what is written in these volumes needs to be written; this integration is an idea whose time has come" (from Editors' Introduction, p. iii).

We had no idea at the time how significant the reference to "time" would be; for indeed, the last three years have been extremely eventful for those who serve the Lord in a ministry of counseling. In editing that first volume, we were anticipating some reactions by non-Pentecostal scholars. Generally, however, that has not materialized. Unexpectedly, however, a strong negative reaction came from fellow Pentecostals.

In retrospect, the timing of the publication of that first book coincided with a great upheaval among evangelicals regarding the place of psychology in the church. Those who dared to suggest that psychological theories could be integrated with scriptural truth were labeled by their opponents as "deceived," at best, or, at worst, "deceivers," working hand in hand with Satan to corrupt the church and its members. In short—and quite unintentionally—we made a small contribution to Pentecostal scholarship at the very time the church was being told it should have nothing to do with such topics as the "satanically motivated" attempt to integrate psychology and theology.

Now, as this second volume is published, the situation has changed. The voices of protest against psychology were largely silenced after one of those most ardent voices admitted to years of spiritual (and undoubtedly emotional) bondage. Those who were championing this anti-psychology obsession are now, perhaps, confused and embarrassed (even as we all grieve over these unfortunate events.) The ultimate reaction of the evangelical church to all of this confusion is difficult to predict.

But it is not difficult to predict that some married couples will continue to experience severe crises and stagnant relationships. Families will still be torn by troubled children, by infants who are born with birth defects, children who become crippled by accidents and disease. Families will watch their senior members grow old, become helpless, or die. College students will always struggle to adjust to new surroundings and changing life styles. Hopefully, hurting and bruised humanity will turn to God and his church for help, relief, and healing. Caring, loving, Spirit-led counselors and pastors will still be needed as visible expressions of the love of God on earth.

For those who are ministering to these people and for those who are still in training for a counseling ministry, we present the following pages for reflection and study. Our apprehension in doing so is even greater than when the first volume was released, for now we are aware of the controversies and the divisions which "psychology in the church" has brought. But our conviction is also greater than ever before that the Holy Spirit can and does still lead, direct, inspire, convict, and heal in the counselor's office. He still desires to take our best—the theories, the years of study, the research, the helping programs—to make of them the effective tools of healing they could not possibly be without him.

The quality and extent of integration varies some from chapter to chapter, reflecting the variety of the backgrounds of the authors and their experiences with the Third Person of the Trinity in their counseling practices. But the theme of this book, as was true of volume One, is one: that God himself, in the person of the Spirit, still heals the broken-hearted and guides the counseling minister into new and creative expressions of the Spirit-empowered healing encounters. For those who dare to invite the Holy Spirit into their offices and counseling practices, we pray the following chapters will be a strong catalyst for an even more effective ministry.

Marvin G. Gilbert, Nairobi, Kenya, East Africa
Raymond T. Brock, Tulsa, Oklahoma, USA

1

ESTABLISHING AND MAINTAINING A COUNSELING MINISTRY

Raymond T. Brock

COUNSELING AS A MINISTRY

Counseling is a reflection of the very nature of Christ. In Isaiah 9:6 the prophet declared, "His name shall be called Wonderful Counselor." As Counselor, Christ is intimately involved in the ministry to hurting people, whether it be in the church or in a professional setting. It is this Counselor-Christ who has sent us the Paraclete to be alongside of the human counselor and who intervenes in caring relationships in a way that challenges the mind with the wonder of God.

Ever in tune with human need during his earthly ministry, Jesus was involved continually with people. He counseled with the woman taken in adultery in the morning (John 8:1–11); at noon he confronted the woman at the well in Samaria (John 4). The encounter with Zacchaeus was in the afternoon (Luke 19:1–10), but Nicodemus waited until the crowds had dispersed and came at night for his appointment in Jerusalem (John 3:1–17).

Lest the counselor become "weary in well doing," it should be noted that these events were spaced over several months of ministry: Jesus did not burn himself out trying to go day and night in his ministry of counseling. He met human need, but he also took care of himself.

In the post-resurrection appearances of Christ we find the direct message to go into all the world in a *counseling ministry* (Matt. 28:19–21; Mark 16:15–17), for counseling is a dimension of the Great Commission that the Lord has given to men and women of all ages. Making disciples results from counseling when the counselor is able to lead clients to a full awareness of the claims of Christ in their lives as the problems of life are faced therapeutically.

Is the counselor a Christian who counsels or a counselor who is a Christian—a Christian psychologist or a psychologist who is a Christian? Deep philosophical issues are involved in making this important distinction (Carter & Narramore, 1979; Collins, 1981; Crabb, 1977; Godin, 1965; Pattison, 1969). The individual choosing to be involved in the helping relationship must examine the issues and make a personal decision concerning this. For the editors of this book, it seems appropriate for the counselor to function as a Christian (first) who is also a helper and not to surrender to placing the roles of being a Christian and a helper in juxtaposition. The Holy Spirit will empower the Christian who is a counselor with the "power" (Gk., *dynamis*) of God as the integration of psychology and theology occur in practice during the counseling session.

COUNSELING IN THE CHURCH

Various chapters of this book highlight some of the specific counseling situations that the authors of this volume think should be considered when designing a counseling ministry. Some of the problem situations in the church necessitate a pastor who is a counselor. Others will require a multiple staff of pastors with one or more assigned the portfolio of counseling. When the congregation is growing and qualified laypersons can be trained for the counseling ministry, a lay counseling program may be warranted. In other situations, it is appropriate to refer clients to professional counselors who are in private practice in the community or assigned to one of the community's medical or educational institutions. Carr, Hinkle and Moss (1981) discussed these and other models. Attention in this chapter is directed initially to the role of the pastor as counselor.

Pastor as Counselor

As the shepherd of the flock the pastor wears many hats; one frequently worn is that of "counselor." It is a grave responsibility and a sacred privilege to be trusted by others as the burden-bearer who represents them before God. The pastor who counsels is laden with tremendous responsibilities—whether he or she wants them or not. The minister must fulfill the counseling assignment without neglecting other ministries of the church. Experience has led me to conclude that pastors who counsel should confine their case load to no more than ten counseling sessions a week. Otherwise, they will be tempted to neglect other aspects of the pastoral ministry. Administration, sermon preparation, visitation, and other essential parts of the pastoral mission must not be neglected for the one-on-one ministry to hurting souls.

All of the requisites of confidentiality, availability, and professional functioning are just as incumbent on the counseling pastor as they are on the minister's professional colleagues who are not burdened with the expectations of the congregation for pastoral care (Clinebell, 1966; Hiltner & Colston, 1961).

Counseling Pastoral Team

Within the multiple church staff, where several ministers work as a pastoral team, the portfolio of "counselor" may be assigned to one or divided among several of them. Frequently one position includes the job description "counseling pastor." This pastor assumes the major portion of counseling and planning the individual and group counseling activities of the church. He or she should also be included in curriculum planning for the various auxiliary ministries of the church so that the teaching ministries of the church can have a preventive counseling content when appropriate.

Almost certainly the youth pastor will be involved in counseling with the young people. The minister of music may also have counseling opportunities, as will the director of pastoral care. In cases of such a broad definition of the ministry of counseling, the counseling pastor should function as a coordinator of counseling ministries. Opportunities for consultation with the other staff members involved in counseling within the congregation should be scheduled. This would require the counseling pastor to serve as a supervisor of counseling activities and to conduct in-service training programs in an effort to maintain a high level of counseling efficiency (Blumenfield, 1982).

Lay Counseling

One of the new dimensions of church ministry during the past decade has been training laypersons to counsel. Many congregations are blessed with mature Christians who have skills that are appropriate to a ministry of counseling. The counseling pastor can implement training procedures to help these lay people "fine tune" their skills and become involved in the counseling ministry of the church. It is important that these individuals be carefully selected and adequately trained for their ministry within the congregation. Drakeford (1967), Crabb (1977), Collins (1976), and Wright (1977) have written extensively on this subject, as has Rozell in the first volume of this series (in Gilbert & Brock, 1985, ch. 7).

Professional Counseling

In many situations it is not feasible for the church to employ a pastor whose portfolio is primarily designed for counseling. In other situations the counseling needs of the congregation are different from the counseling abilities of the pastoral staff (Clinebell, 1966). In such instances it is advisable to make referrals to Christian professionals in the community who are specifically trained for counseling and psychotherapy (Miller & Jackson, 1985; Oglesby, 1968). The professional counselor can become a marvelous assistant to the pastor in counseling situations. This in no way suggests that the pastor is not qualified or not interested in the members: he or she has simply chosen to put major energies into other aspects of the ministry while using a support staff to strengthen the counseling ministry of the church.

In this book, preference is not given to any one of these approaches to the counseling ministry of the church; each has its own merits with attending limitations. But, the local congregation will have to determine which approach is appropriate for its situation and accept the strengths and weaknesses which accompany that decision.

Preventive-Educational Services

In addition to the formal counseling services of the church, which will be primarily rehabilitative in nature, there should be a strong educational program for preventive education. This involves distinguishing education from indoctrination and striving to teach people of all ages how to cope with life "Christianly" by using biblical principles in meeting everyday challenges (MacAlmon, 1981). Such classes will be designed for children, teenagers, and adults (both single and married). Some will be offered during the regular education hours of the church (Sunday school/family night). Depending on the age of the participants and the nature of the problems being addressed, others will need to be in the form of seminars, workshops, and symposia. Louthan and Martin (1976) have designed a workable model that can be adapted and refined to meet local needs.

Counseling in the Community

When the congregation has made the decision to establish a counseling ministry, attention must be given to the location of the service. Sometimes it is appropriate to have the counseling offices in the church; other times it is better to secure offices in a professional building in the community. Expectations of the community as well as the design of the church plant will be factors in this consideration.

Offices Outside the Church

Since some individuals are very secretive about seeing a counselor, it may be better to have the counseling functions of the church in a professional building in the community. When in private practice in Denver, Colorado, I found that there were some individuals from the church where I also served as counseling pastor who chose to drive across town to my office in a professional building in another suburb. There were non-members, however, who lived closer to the church than to my professional office who chose to come to the church office for counseling, even though they did not attend the church. Shimberg (1979) addressed some of the issues to be considered in selecting and maintaining a private counseling office in a commercial location.

I found a different situation while ministering in Dallas, Texas. Several members of neighboring churches came to my church office because they preferred a counselor who was not a staff member of their own church. In fact, there were neighboring pastors who asked me to counsel with their people so that they would not jeopardize their pastoral relationship with the parishioners by knowing too many intimate things about them.

Cooperative Counseling Involving Several Churches

In communities where several churches desire a counseling ministry, it is possible to merge efforts to sponsor a counseling service that serves the larger community. The counselors can rotate among the churches on a circuit basis, dividing their time among the facilities of the sponsoring congregations. Churches can also pool their resources and secure counseling offices in a professional complex in the community or in conjunction with one of the existing mental health facilities.

When a counseling center is a joint endeavor, each congregation financially contributes to and has a voice in its operation. This can be advantageous in a larger city; it allows a higher level of professional quality on the counseling staff while preserving the identity of the service with the sponsoring congregations. Under the right leadership this model extends to county, state, national, and even international proportions. EMERGE Counseling Center in Akron (Ohio), Narramore Foundation in Rosemead (Calif.), Link Care Center in Fresno (Calif.), Institute for Christian Living in Tulsa (Okla.), Minirth-Meier Clinic in Richardson (Tex.), and Pine Rest Christian Hospital in Grand Rapids (Mich.) are illustrations of this broad cooperative operation with in-patient and/or out-patient services designed uniquely for the Christian community. In each case, these facilities minister not only to local communities, but to lay people, ministers, and missionaries from around the country seeking therapy in a Christian setting.[1]

Another type of cooperative service develops when a Christian psychologist establishes a private practice in the community and makes his or her services available to one or more churches. The counselor frequently follows the private practice model and draws much of his or her clientele from the religious community. Browning (1982a, 1982b), Lewin (1978), and Shimberg (1979) offered suggestions to assist in establishing and maintaining a private practice as a psychologist.

It is important for the psychologist wanting to assist in a ministry of counseling to become acquainted with pastors from a variety of congregations. Establishing rapport between pastors and psychologists is a vital part of launching this strategic relationship. The pastor making a referral to a therapist must have confidence in the therapist both as a Christian and as a psychologist; Christian commitment must radiate from his or her daily and family life as well as his or her professional life.

---

[1] Details regarding services and fees may be obtained by contacting the Christian mental health services directly:

Richard D. Dobbins, Ph.D., Director, EMERGE Ministries, Inc., P.O. Box 5738, Akron, OH 44372-5738; (216) 876-5693.

Clyde Narramore, Ph.D., Director, Narramore Foundation, P.O. Box 5000, Rosemead, CA 92770; (818) 288-7000.

Stanley Lindquist, Ph.D., Link Care Center, 1734 West Shaw Avenue, Fresno, CA 93704; (209) 439-5620.

Carl R. Peterson, M.D., President, City of Faith Institute for Christian Living, Inc., 8181 South Lewis, Tulsa, OK 74137; (918) 493-8108.

Frank Minirth, M.D., Director, Minirth-Meier Clinic, 1740 North Collins, Suite 101, Richardson, TX 58080; (214) 669-1733.

Robert Baker, M.D., Executive Director, Pine Rest Christian Hospital, 6850 South Division Avenue, Grand Rapids, MI 49508; (616) 455-5000.

Making Referrals to Therapists

One of the essentials of counseling is to recognize the limits of one's training and expertise. Referrals to the appropriate helping person in the community are essential. Some people, including those who are diagnosed as neurotic individuals who require psychotherapy and chemotherapy, need the services of a psychiatrist. Others would be better helped by a psychologist who uses a variety of psychotherapeutic skills to relieve emotional stress. Technicians in biofeedback and behavior modification may also be used to deal with specific problems.

The wise pastor becomes acquainted with the various members of the community healing team (see Gilbert's chapter on "Making Referrals" in this volume). Making such acquaintances allows the minister to assess the spiritual and professional stance of the practitioner. It also provides an opportunity for the pastor to make available his or her services of spiritual ministry as a member of the community healing team. Psychology has done a good job of delineating a taxonomy of the cognitive, affective, and psychomotor domains, but as yet, little progress has been made in devising a taxonomy of the spiritual domain (Klausmeier & Goodwin, 1966). This task remains for Christians in the behavioral sciences to accomplish (Glock & Stark, 1965).

When a Christian professional has been located and a working relationship established, the pastor will then feel comfortable making referrals to that person. In many cases the therapist will want to keep the relationship between the pastor and the client intact so that the therapist and pastor cooperate in ministering to the individual. Regular meetings between the counseling pastor and professional therapist ensure that the lines of communication remain open so that the pastor is in tune with the progress of therapy at all times. Thus, he can continue to minister spiritually to the individuals in therapy. At the same time he becomes a spiritual consultant to the therapist.

Advertising

Care must be taken in announcing the opening of the counseling service and in publicizing its services. By cultivating the resources of the local media (newspaper, radio, and television), it is possible to receive good free publicity. Announcements can be sent to appropriate professionals (physicians, attorneys, dentists, and clergy), agencies (mental health, family counseling, and child guidance clinics), and educational institutions in the community. Community custom and the desired scope of the counseling services will dictate whether or not it is appropriate to put an announcement in the local newspaper. Ethical standards of the professional organization to which the counselor or psychologist belongs should be carefully observed in designing the listing in the Yellow Pages of the local telephone directory. And, it should be remembered, one of the quickest ways to become known in the community is to make oneself available to speak at service clubs and before community groups (Shimberg, 1979).

"Brochures that promote the services of a pastoral counseling center should describe them with accuracy and dignity. They may be sent to professional persons and agencies, but to prospective individual clients only in response to inquiries.'' (Code of Professional Ethics of the American Association of Pastoral Counselors, 1978, p. 25.) This same principle applies to the psychologist in private practice as well. These brochures can be distributed to local congregations, however, as part of an information service to parishioners.

DESIGNING A COUNSELING COMPLEX

Beginning a counseling ministry demands a series of decisions. Selecting the location of the service is primary. This involves the configuration of the offices and furnishings, along with the equipment and supplies necessary for conducting a functional operation. Lewis (1970) emphasized the need for privacy with a relaxed atmosphere, but added that the physical setting should reflect the personality of the counselor.

Location

If counseling is to be conducted in the church, privacy demands that the service be placed in an area other than the general offices of the building. The counseling complex should have a reception room with secretarial space, counseling office, combination play/diagnostic room, family/group therapy room, storage space, and bathroom facilities (Shimberg, 1979).

A receptionist should be on duty at all times. The presence of the receptionist ensures that the counselor is not alone in the office with a client who might act out inappropriately or need special assistance. This type of preventive protection is essential whether the counseling service is in a church or professional building. Experience has taught me that the receptionist can function as a secretary, bookkeeper, and be trained to handle the administering and scoring of selected psychological tests and inventories.

Unfortunately, some individuals will become diffident at the prospect of being seen in the reception room or counselor's office. Others may become emotionally upset during counseling. If clients have been crying or are in any way embarrassed by their appearance, they would prefer not to leave through the reception room and be observed by others who may be waiting for counseling or those who are just passing through the church offices. Therefore, it is wise to have a door in the counselor's office that leads outside or to a corridor leading to a well-marked exit.

It is desirable to have a room for group and family counseling in addition to the counselor's office. Individual therapy and couple counseling may be conducted in the office, but for families and groups, a larger area prepared with adequate seating is advisable. Another room, quiet and separate from the flow of traffic, is essential for diagnostic testing, since the atmosphere of the testing situation influences the reliability of the test results (Anastasi, 1982). This room can also be used for play therapy with children.

The storeroom should be equipped with locked files for storing case notes and shelves for organizing diagnostic materials and supplies. A small refrigerator and seating area for lunch and coffee breaks is advisable. The bathroom should be outfitted with liquid soap and paper towel dispensers, as well as a place to deposit the soiled towels. A mirror is appreciated by clients who want to freshen up before or after a counseling session. If a water fountain is not available in the counseling complex, paper cups in the bathroom will be needed.

All of the walls in the counseling area should be soundproofed for privacy. Background music provides a pleasant atmosphere and masks sounds coming from the counseling office. Music should be at a soft volume and without lyrics or heavy rhythm so as not to interfere with the thought processes of the staff or the contemplation of the clients. The console for the music should be placed beyond the reach of the clients, preferably in the storeroom.

Office Layout

The counseling office should be large enough to have both formal and informal seating areas. The counselor's desk need not be the focal point of the room, although it should have the usual professional appointments for recordkeeping and study. Since the desk forms a barrier between the counselor and the client, a less formal sitting area is needed. During the counseling session, it is often better to sit in the informal seating area with lamps and tables aesthetically placed to lend an atmosphere of relaxation to the setting. Lewis (1970) offered a variety of suggestions for placing the furniture in the counselor's office.

Furnishings

Furnishings in the counselor's office should be artistically selected. The desk area may well be formal with straight-backed chairs for clients, although an "easy chair" will attract some clients. A grouping of comfortable furniture can form a sitting area in which the counseling takes place. A recliner is appropriate if relaxation therapy or biofeedback are a part of the intervention modes. Since the counselor will spend several hours in this room each day, the furniture should be selected for comfort. The appropriate certificates, diplomas, degrees, and licenses should be displayed to enhance the professional appearance of the room.

Muted colors in wall coverings and carpets add to the restfulness of the counseling office. Shimberg (1979) recommended strong, washable wallpaper or wood paneling in preference to paint. Wall hangings should not be bold enough to distract from the conversation. A few curios from travels or interesting art objects provide a good basis for establishing rapport with new clients.

Furnishings for the reception area should be tasteful, since this is where the patient is first introduced to the counseling experience. The area should be equipped with all of the office machines essential for efficiency, with locked files placed discreetly to reflect the value of the confidential materials placed in them. The reception area should be serviceable and designed for the comfort of clients of all ages. The furniture may be covered with either fabric or plastic/leather materials, but Shimberg (1979) noted that "plastic/leather materials stand up to the wear that children can give them and are very easily cleaned. A little soap and water will remove all signs of the sticky candy bar, soiled diaper, or muddy footprints" (pp. 30, 31). He also cautioned against the use of swivel chairs and noted the importance of a place for coats, boots, and raingear for families.

A variety of reading materials appropriate to all ages should be on the tables. Devotional and informational magazines with brief articles are best so the client is not interrupted during the reading of an extended article when called for the session. The illumination of the room should be adequate for comfortable reading. It is also appropriate to have a refreshment area where hot and cold drinks are readily available to the clients, separate from the staff lunch area.

Should the counselor use bibliotherapy as a technique, there should be a good supply of books and tapes the client can purchase on the spot (Brown, 1975; Zaccaria & Moses, 1968). Otherwise, much of the assigned homework may not be done, the excuse being that the client could not find the book. It is also wise to consider having a circulating library of books and tapes that would be helpful for between-session use by the clients without adding to the cost of their counseling (Collins, 1980).

Equipment

The equipment in the counseling area is not appreciably different from that in other offices in the business areas of the church. Machines for recordkeeping, bookkeeping, and duplicating should be conveniently placed for both counselors and support staff. The kits for individual testing should be readily available with supplies replenished regularly. If biofeedback is used, the equipment should be in an adjoining room away from the counseling and reception flow of traffic, possibly in the diagnostic room.

The efficient counseling office will be equipped with a computer for word processing, billing, bookkeeping, recordkeeping, and test scoring. Care needs to be given to the selection of the equipment to make sure it is adequate for the multiple needs of the counseling office but not cost prohibitive. Sampson, Tenhagen, and Ryan-Jones (1985) found that "hardware costs may vary tremendously from a range of approximately $1,000.00 to $10,000.00" (p. 1).

A variety of software vendors are appealing to the counseling profession, so care should be taken to assess the adaptability of the systems to be used in test scoring. Sampson et al. (1985, pp. 1,2) offered some helpful criteria to be considered in software evaluation.[2]

---

[2] 1. Clear statement of the purpose of the instrument and a description of the intended client population.

2. Professional qualifications required for interpretation of the results to clients.

3. Procedures required for administration, scoring, and report generation.

4. Degree of "user friendliness" of the software, e.g., ability to change responses, response time between input and feedback, limited response set, reading level, and the availability of help options.

5. The availability of norms developed from computer-assisted administrations of an instrument as opposed to using traditional paper and pencil norms.

Supplies

Both office and testing supplies will be needed in the counseling offices. A list of the tests and inventories to be used in counseling should be drafted and the supplies purchased *before* the service begins. Additional adoptions will need to be made as the needs of the congregation change and the expertise of the counselors expands with training.

When considering testing supplies it is important to know the laws related to testing. Some commonly used psychometric instruments can be used only by a licensed psychologist, such as the *Minnesota Multiphasic Personality Inventory* (Hathaway & McKinley, 1967) and the *California Psychological Inventory* (Gough, 1956). Others, such as the *Taylor-Johnson Temperament Analysis* (Taylor & Johnson, 1984), *Prepare-Enrich* (Olson, Fournier & Druckman, 1982), *Study of Values* (Allport, Vernon & Lindzey, 1960), *Tennessee Self Concept* (Fitts, 1965), *FIRO-B* (Ryan, 1977), *Strong-Campbell Interest Inventory* (Campbell & Hansen, 1981), *Marital Satisfaction Inventory* (Snyder, 1981), and *Interpersonal Behavior Inventory* (Mauger & Adkinson, 1980) can be used by counselors with the appropriate professional training. Careful attention will need to be given to ordering supplies for the instruments that will be computer scored commercially.[3]

It is essential to know the legal ramifications of testing in the church setting and to keep the services of the church well within legal and professional guidelines. A statement from the "Code of Professional Ethics" of the American Association of Pastoral Counselors is appropriate at this point:

The use of psychological diagnostic tests by a pastoral counselor is not ordinarily expected nor encouraged. Their use must be related to appropriate supervised training and affiliation

---

6. The availability of reliability and validity data for computer-assisted versions and how they compare to traditional pencil and paper versions.

7. Approval by instrument authors/publishers to offer scoring services.

8. Clarity of all score profiles and written reports.

9. The professional qualifications of system developers and instrument authors.

10. The experience of other institutions/organizations related to the use of the software.

11. The availability of an 800 toll-free help line for assistance with software problems.

12. The options for a limited trial period of software use prior to final purchase.

13. Supplemental costs if any, e.g., special operating systems or additional hardware requirements.

14. Cost of the software and the hardware per instrument administration.

15. Adequacy: how well does the software meet the intended purpose as stated in No. 1 above ?

[3] The following test scoring services have been found to be helpful for pastoral counselors and therapists in private practice:

Consulting Psychologists Press, P.O. Box 60070, Palo Alto, CA 94306.
Institute for Personality and Ability Testing, Inc., P.O. Box 188, Champaign, IL 61820.
National Computer Systems, P.O. Box 1416, Minneapolis, MN 55440.
Western Psychological Services, 12021 Wilshire Boulevard, Los Angeles, CA 90025.

with the American Psychological Association or in conjunction with an adequately trained counseling or clinical psychologist. (1978, p. 25)

The statement of "Ethical Principles of Psychologists" prepared by the American Psychological Association offers further cautions against "the use of psychological assessment techniques by inappropriately trained or otherwise unqualified persons through teaching, sponsorship, or supervision," and notes that "the public offering of an automated interpretation service is considered as a professional-to-professional consultation. The psychologist makes every effort to avoid misuses of assessment reports" (in Anastasi, 1982, pp. 633, 634). *Unless the counselor is a licensed psychologist, the use of the term "psychologist," "psychological services" or "psychotherapy" is inappropriate—and may be illegal—in the church setting.*

LAUNCHING A COUNSELING MINISTRY

Before announcing that a counseling ministry is being established by the church, a number of decisions must be considered. A philosophy of counseling should be devised with a set of objectives established to serve as evaluative criteria. Community as well as congregational needs should be considered. (The "Personnel and Procedure Policy Manual" of the Samaritan Health and Living Center, 200 East Beardsley, Elkhart, IN 46514, is an appropriate working model.)

Staff Considerations

Selecting the staff for the counseling center may well be the most critical decision to be made. The counselor must be adequately trained and experienced as well as compatible with the church, its standards, and its leadership. In many cases ordination to the ministry as well as certification as a counselor are desirable. Support staff with lesser qualifications may be added, but some qualified person must supervise the counseling ministry and be amenable to the church and civil authorities for the functioning of the service.

Staff recruitment should proceed carefully and prayerfully. Bible colleges and seminaries as well as professional organizations are good sources for finding suitable candidates. Contact with other pastors and psychologists can lead to identification of candidates with experience and excellent training. Advertising in the *Journal of the Christian Association for Psychological Studies* is also appropriate. In screening resumes, it is important to note the professional training of the candidate as well as the spiritual qualifications. Practicums, internships, and post-graduate experiences should be noted carefully, as should membership in the appropriate professional organizations.

The *minimum* qualifications for the counseling pastor should be the M.Div. or M.A. from a seminary or university department of psychology or counseling and guidance. It is always wise for counselors with only the M.A. preparation to work under the supervision of a licensed psychologist or licensed professional counselor. Such a supervisory relationship assures the availability of a professional with whom to consult on difficult cases and who can enhance the continued development of diagnostic and counseling skills of the counselor.

Professional Considerations

In establishing fees, it will be necessary to determine if the client will pay for the clinical hour on a set-fee basis or if a sliding scale will be used. If counseling is based on a sliding fee schedule, determined by the ability of clients to pay, additional sources of revenue will need to be found. Some churches have found the use of a donation system effective. Clients are urged to pay what they can and others are encouraged to underwrite the program. Such programs have sustained themselves without having to be supplemented from the budget of the church (Money, 1984). (Robinette's treatment of fee options in his "Marriage Counseling" chapter in this volume extends the discussion of this topic.)

Remuneration for the counselor is a vital concern. Carr, et al., (1981) posed these questions for consideration:

1. To what extent will remuneration be tied to credentials?
2. To what extent will remuneration be tied to experience?
3. To what extent will remuneration be tied to sharing in the pastoral counseling center's administration?
4. To what extent will remuneration be tied to actual income generated?

(p. 99)

Carr et al. offered several remuneration models. When counselors are paid on the basis of a *negotiated salary,* they are covered with the same level of remuneration as other pastors of the congregation for "housing, travel, pension, income insurance, health and hospital coverage, etc." (p. 99). The assumption is that the church will supplement any deficiencies in fees generated from the counseling service. Another model is the *percentage salary,* which will be a proportion of fees generated from counseling. A third, "more complicated model, which provides somewhat more security for counselors, is the *salary-plus-percentage* model, in which counselors are paid a basic minimum salary for their work as counselors plus a percentage of the actual income which they generate" (p. 101).

It would be helpful if a study of fees charged to clients and salaries paid to counselors in the community could be made so that the church can function appropriately in relation to other similar services in the community. Certainly counselors are worthy of the considerations given to other members of the pastoral staff, with additional attention being given to the professional training brought to this specialized ministry.

Client Considerations

For whom will the counseling service be designed? The answer to this question will reflect the philosophy of counseling adopted by the congregation along with the goals and objectives announced in the purposes of the counseling service.

These purposes will influence the kind of services offered and types of counselors recruited. Community needs as well as the professional training of the counselors must be considered in designing a ministry of counseling.

SERVICES OF A COUNSELING MINISTRY

Varied approaches to counseling will need to be maintained by a counseling ministry. Both individual and group counseling will need to be provided. Individual counseling should vary in intensity, depending on the needs of the clients. Group counseling should be designed to meet the needs for pre-marital, marital, and family counseling, as well as provide special support groups for unique problems faced by the clients (e.g., grief, divorce, unemployment).

Individual Counseling

It is helpful to note that individual counseling varies in depth and breadth, depending on the unique needs of each client. In the educational setting, Mortensen and Schmuller (1966) described the developing intensity of a therapeutic model progressing from the simple interview to advisement to counseling into psychotherapy. In the pastoral setting, the process develops from pastoral conversation to pastoral advising to pastoral counseling and into psychotherapy by professionally trained therapists who may or may not be on the pastoral staff.

Pastoral conversation. This term was suggested by Pruyser (1976) to describe the initial pastoral intervention on an informal basis. It occurs in the aisles and corridors of the church and in the parking lot. It is the beginning of a counseling relationship where issues are presented in such a way that rapport is established and an appointment can be made for further dialogue.

Pastoral advising. Advising was used by Mortensen and Schmuller (1966) to describe the direct intervention of a counselor in a counselee's decision-making process. In this phase of interaction a direct question is met by a direct answer. This form of pastoral intervention deals with immediate situations and surface issues. It is a good way to establish rapport, but care must be taken not to offer quick solutions that deal with symptoms masking deeper problems. Again, this activity may occur in places other than the counseling office; it may occur informally in social and semi-public settings.

Pastoral counseling. This is the heart of the service offered by the church and should be conducted in a professional setting. It is an in-depth involvement with a parishioner and deals with the vital issues of life. It requires training—both academic and supervised internships—because of the delicate relationship that evolves between the counselor and parishioner-client. Counseling is more than conversation and advisement, but is not as intense as psychotherapy, which demands specific professional training (Mortensen & Schmuller, 1966). It involves choice-evaluation and decision-making with resolution of mild behavior problems. If a sufficiently trained member is not on the church staff to conduct such a counseling ministry, referral to appropriate community personnel must be made. Meier, Minirth and Wichern (1982) offer the following guidelines for pastoral referral:

1. Refer anyone suicidal, including severely depressed individuals.
2. Refer anyone homicidal.
3. Refer anyone with an obvious physical problem.
4. Refer psychotics and some severe neurotics.
5. Refer anyone who cannot be handled adeptly because of limited time in the counselor's schedule.
6. Refer anyone with a problem beyond the counselor's ability to handle or that the counselor feels uncomfortable handling (p. 334).

Mortensen and Schmuller (1966) noted that counseling and psychotherapy are closely related, both in process and content, so that it is difficult to differentiate between them. In the pastoral setting, however, this differentiation is essential. They initially quoted Tyler (1961) to help clarify the distinction between counseling and psychotherapy according to outcomes and aims:

"The aim of therapy is generally considered to be personality change of some sort. ...Counseling [is used] to refer to a helping process the aim of which is not to change the person but to enable him to utilize the resources he now has for coping with life" (p. 12). Counseling helps in *constructing* a plan, for example, whereas psychotherapy will be concerned with *reconstructing* ways of behaving. (p. 343)

Psychotherapy. Psychotherapy, based on the definition given above, requires professional training and skills in diagnosis and treatment and can only be conducted by a trained professional, usually a clinical or counseling psychologist or psychiatrist who is certified by a professional association and licensed by the state in which he or she practices. It is on the level of psychotherapy that personality and character issues are treated. Pastors usually focus on counseling, while psychotherapy is the province of a trained Christian professional who may be on the pastoral staff or in private practice in the community.

Figure 1-1, adapted from Mortensen and Schmuller (1966), illustrates the deepening ego-involvement of the counselor and counselee in the therapeutic relationship. It is evident that the counseling pastor needs to be acutely aware of the limitations of his or her training and experience and stay within the boundaries of expertise. Establishing a good referral procedure with local professionals is essential in giving quality service to the congregation (Oglesby, 1968).

In recruiting staff for the counseling service, care should be taken to ensure that a variety of skills are represented and each member of the counseling team is conversant with the various levels of expertise needed for a well-rounded counseling ministry. Experience not only in counseling but also in making and receiving referrals is essential in staff recruitment. Both Drakeford (1967) and Collins (1977) have addressed this point.

Group Counseling

Group counseling is effective in assisting the counselor to make maximum use of counseling time. Many problems experienced by individuals in the congregation

DEGREES OF COUNSELING INTERACTIONS

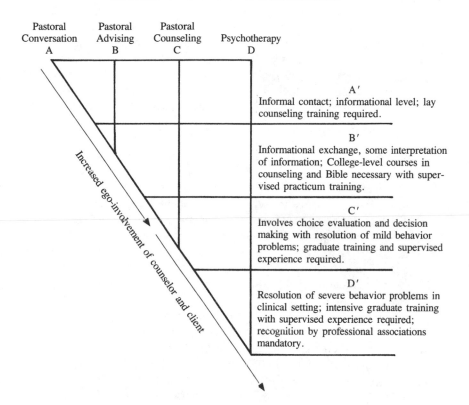

Figure 1-1: *Continuum of Therapy*. Line A to D represents a continuum that illustrates the growing development and deepening of the therapeutic relationship from pastoral conversation and advising to counseling and psychotherapy. The A' to D' column illustrates the need for increased skill to move to the deepening levels of involvement. (Adapted from Mortensen & Schmuller, 1966.)

can be handled in a group setting (Corey, 1981; Hansen, Warner & Smith, 1976; Yalom, 1975). Some groups will exist primarily for sharing and giving opportunity for catharsis in a loving community. Other groups are of such a nature that instruction plus interaction are appropriate. Support groups fall into this category and can deal with problems of children of specified ages, grief, divorce, job loss, addictions, eating disorders and other unique problems. (See Borsellino's discussion of the varied foci of groups in his chapter on "Group Therapy" in this volume).

Clinebell (1966) suggested that there are several advantages to using group counseling in the pastoral setting. He observed that many of the problems faced in the congregation can be addressed more effectively in a small group setting.

It also represents a better stewardship of pastoral time if the groups contain from six to eight members. He sees the group approach as a way to stimulate growth individually as the clients reach out to be supportive of each other. And, "the small group is a natural milieu for *short-term educative counseling*" (p. 208). He illustrated this in pre-baptismal counseling in which the participants are "nurtured by the group's *esprit de corps*" (p. 208). Davis (1984) pointed out that the Sunday school can also be used effectively in group counseling activities. In the educational setting, groups of up to 12 members have been effective.

Couple Counseling

Counseling of couples in both pre-marital and marital settings is a primary function of pastoral counseling. This involves preparing couples for marriage and assisting them after they have returned from the honeymoon. Preventive in nature, *pre-marital counseling* helps to forestall some of the pitfalls that are common in establishing a relationship as intimate as marriage. Wright (1977a) addressed this topic with specific suggestions for planning the counseling sequence for an individual couple as well as for groups of couples. He also offered suggestions in using the *Taylor-Johnson Temperament Analysis* (Taylor & Johnson, 1984) in the sessions. Attention should also be given to the use of *Prepare* for singles and *Prepare MC* for marriages involving children (Olson et al., 1982).

Marital counseling may be either educational or rehabilitative and is usually the result of crisis intervention. Again, Wright (1981) and Sholevar (1981) have written specifically on this issue. The *Taylor-Johnson Temperament Analysis* (Taylor & Johnson, 1980) is as useful in marital counseling as it is in pre-marital counseling. The *Enrich* portion of the *Prepare-Enrich* inventories (Olson et al., 1982) is helpful as are the *Marriage Satisfaction Inventory* (Snyder, 1981), *Interpersonal Behavior Survey* (Mauger & Adkinson, 1980) and *Couple Pre-counseling Inventory* (Stuart, 1983).

Family Counseling

Marriage and family counseling are unique forms of group counseling in which pre-marital, marital, and family issues can be dealt with from both *educational* and *therapeutic* points of view. Wynn (1982) dealt extensively with this approach from a pastoral perspective. The family approach was well presented by Barnard and Corrales (1979). Use of the family systems approach by such theorists as Ackerman (1958), Bell (1975), Bowen (1978), Haley (1967), Haley and Hoffman (1967), Minuchin (1974), Minuchin and Fishman (1981), Satir (1964), Satir, Stachowiak and Taschman (1975), and Whitaker (1970, 1976) can be effective in the church setting. Gilbert elaborated on the "fit" of such systems theories with the theology of the Holy Spirit in Gilbert and Brock (1985, ch. 14).

Clinebell (1966) indicated that the family may be seen in its entirety or in subgroups. Parents and children may be seen as a nuclear family. If necessary and feasible, the grandparents may be invited to participate for extended family counseling. Bernard and Corrales (1979) emphasized the importance of seeing the family as a unit for the initial interview to allay all fears that the therapist and the parent making the appointment might be in collusion. They also discussed effectively the methods of terminating the family counseling sequence.

Intensive Counseling/Therapy

Even when the needs of the client exceed the training and expertise of the pastor and a referral is made, the pastor is still a vital member of the healing team. The minister is needed to keep the spiritual concerns of the client in focus in the therapeutic interaction.

The pastor should become familiar with the testing instruments commonly used by psychologists and psychiatrists. He or she should study these from an academic point of view and in consultation with a therapist to become knowledgeable of the implications of findings from the testing. To illustrate the benefit of this effort as well as the benefit of the team approach, I recall one of the effective counseling pastors I know who established a close working relationship with a clinical psychologist. This pastor would administer the *MMPI* in the church office and take it to the psychologist for interpretation and diagnosis. By establishing this type of consultation arrangement with the therapist, the pastor benefited greatly; the psychologist would not only interpret the test, but would also design a sound treatment plan to be implemented in the pastoral setting.

This form of ongoing consultation can be effective for the clients and also provide continuing professional development for the pastor. The effectiveness of this cooperative procedure is measurable in changed lives. The psychologist makes the diagnosis, sets up the treatment plan, and involves the pastor in the interventions; however, the counseling is conducted in the church setting with spiritual variables constantly in focus. In the process, the client gains a new respect for the pastor and his or her ministry as a true shepherd with extraordinary helping skills.

THE HOLY SPIRIT IN THE COUNSELING MINISTRY

Everything about the counseling ministry needs to be conducted with the awareness of the sovereignty of the Holy Spirit as the Chief Counselor. No part of the counseling ministry should be planned or implemented without seeking divine guidance in the entire program. Prayer and meditation are essential in planning, implementing, and perpetuating a counseling service in the community (Foster, 1978).

Planning

Planning for a counseling ministry in any community begins in the heart of a pastor who is striving for excellence in being the undershepherd of the flock God has entrusted into the pastor's care. As the pastor carries the burdens of the congregation to the Lord in prayer, the Holy Spirit is available to indicate situations that require more than the preaching and teaching ministries of the church. It may become evident that an added ministry of counseling is needed.

As this happens, a burden for individuals and their unique needs allows the potential for a ministry of counseling to emerge. Prayerful pursuit of this burden leads to planning how these special needs—both individual and corporate—can be met. A program of counseling thus begins to form in the heart of a pastor who is in tune with the varied needs in the congregation. This has been true throughout the history of the church, but the needs are accentuated in the technological society in which we live (Clebsch & Jaekle, 1964).

Realization of this burden should lead to an examination of the church facilities and the staff—both lay and pastoral. If staff members must be added, seeking the will of God in selecting the counselors and support staff is essential. But, the Holy Spirit, the Paraclete, is ever present to guide (John 16:13), illumine, and caution when human ingenuity would be inclined toward divergent directions. The same divine presence guides in examining the facilities of the building and exploring the options for locating the service in the community setting. How marvelous it is to know that the Spirit of Truth can lead the searching pastor into all the truth necessary for planning and implementing a ministry of counseling as an evangelistic outreach into the community!

Implementing

As the plans move from the inspiration stage to the practical level, the Holy Spirit leads the seeking pastor in making decisions, appointing feasibility study groups, and selecting committees to do the "fine tuning" of the program. Again the prayer, intercession, and meditation that enliven other facets of the ministry are functional in the implementation activities of opening the counseling service. They must be balanced by spiritual leadership that bears the mark of the Holy Spirit on other facets of the pastor's personal life and ministry; the pastor's example lends credibility to pastoral planning.

Selecting the right location to serve the most people is a primary step, but of even more importance is selecting the right individuals to be involved in staffing the counseling center. This will include both professional staff and laypersons who will be involved in the daily operation of the service. Everyone involved, from the receptionist to the therapist, should be a born-again, Spirit-filled believer with appropriate training for the task assigned. The counseling ministry will be no more spiritual than the members of the counseling team. Those involved in the ministry cannot afford to offer less than Spirit-filled living and a total commitment to the ministry of counseling if the service is to be a truly Pentecostal/charismatic ministry to the congregation and to the community.

Spiritual guidance should be sought in (a) designing the facilities; (b) determining the types of services to be offered; (c) establishing the methods to be used in testing, interviewing, diagnosing; and (d) carrying out the counseling mission. This also includes budgeting, public relations, and recordkeeping. If all of this seems somewhat overwhelming and foreign to the reader, again we are reminded that the Holy Spirit is available to guide and direct. Further, Spirit-filled psychologists are available to serve as consultants. They can assist with the detailed planning and staff interviewing that are necessary for beginning a counseling program.

Figure 1-2 contains a flow chart illustrating the process of designing a counseling service in the church. The pastor responds to the personal burden given by the

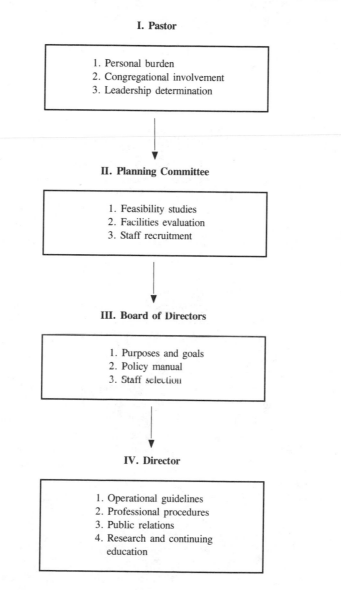

SEQUENCE FLOW CHART FOR LAUNCHING A COUNSELING SERVICE

I. Pastor

1. Personal burden
2. Congregational involvement
3. Leadership determination

II. Planning Committee

1. Feasibility studies
2. Facilities evaluation
3. Staff recruitment

III. Board of Directors

1. Purposes and goals
2. Policy manual
3. Staff selection

IV. Director

1. Operational guidelines
2. Professional procedures
3. Public relations
4. Research and continuing education

Figure 1-2

Holy Spirit and invites the congregation to share the burden and provide leadership for establishing the counseling service. Next, a planning committee launches feasibility studies, evaluates the facilities, and initiates staff recruitment. As plans materialize, the purposes and goals of the counseling service are devised by a board of directors; the director of the service should be selected early in the process so he or she can be involved in defining the purposes and goals, as well as in writing a policy manual. The board is then ready to select the remaining professional and support staff for the service. The director functions under the board of directors and the pastor to finalize the guidelines for operation and professional procedures to be followed. In launching the counseling program, the director will be involved in public relations and should at all times be alert to the needs for research and continuing education of the counseling staff.

Perpetuating

Perpetuating the counseling ministry is uniquely the province of the Holy Spirit. If he has been invited to overshadow the total program from the beginning of planning through the implementation of each phase of the function, the obvious blessing of his presence will be upon the daily operation of the ministry. His presence will be seen in the results that accrue from the counseling sessions. Human ingenuity must be utilized to its maximum, but daily there will be unique situations that can be handled adequately only through the constant overshadowing of the Spirit of Truth who functions in the life of the counselor and the personality of the clients.

When God's counseling service is designed to meet the needs of his hurting people, the Holy Spirit will make the counseling team more than conquerors in wrestling against the powers that impinge on the human personality and the carnal spirits of those who have not yet submitted themselves to the scrutiny of the Holy Spirit (Rom. 8:37; Eph. 6:12; Gal. 5:19–21; Col. 3:5–9).

In my personal experience, it has been amazing to see how many times the Holy Spirit makes himself known in the daily operation of a counseling ministry. Insights have been given into business dilemmas, relationship conflicts with professional colleagues, and personal problems in the lives of clients. There are times when counselors must stand in awe when they realize how the Holy Spirit has intervened in the lives of the clients and has used the counselor to be God's hand extended to reach out to people who are hurting. Yes, Christ's name is Counselor and he is a *Wonderful Counselor*. He has extended this dimension of his grace through the Holy Spirit to function in the life of the counselor who allows himself to be filled with the Holy Spirit and motivated by his power.

SELECT BIBLIOGRAPHY

Ackerman, N. (1958). *The psychodynamics of family life: Treatment of family relationships.* New York: Basic Books.

Allport, G. W., Vernon, P.E., & Lindzey, G. (1960). *Study of values.* Boston: Houghton Mifflin.

American Association of Pastoral Counselors. (1978). *AAPC Handbook* (rev. ed.). Washington, D.C.: American Association of Pastoral Counselors.

Anastasi, A. (1982). *Psychological testing* (5th ed.). New York: Macmillan.

Barnard, C. P., & Corrales, R. G. (1979). *The theory and technique of family therapy.* Springfield, IL: Charles C. Thomas.

Bell, J. E. (1975). *Family therapy.* New York: Aronson.

Blumenfield, M. (Ed.). (1982). *Applied supervision in psychotherapy.* New York: Grune & Stratton.

Bowen, M. (1978). *Family therapy in clinical practice.* New York: Aronson.

Brown, E. F. (1975). *Bibliotherapy and its widening applications.* Metuchen, NJ: Scarecrow.

Browning, C. H. (1982a). *How to build a practice clientele using referral sources: A sourcebook.* Los Alamitas, CA: Duncliffe's International.

_____. (1982b). *Private practice handbook: The tools, tactics and techniques for successful practice development* (2nd ed.). Los Alamitas, CA: Duncliffe's International.

Campbell, D. P., & Hansen, J. (1981). *Manual for the SVIB-SCII Strong-Campbell Interest Inventory* (3rd ed.). Stanford, CA: Stanford University Press.

Carr, J. C., Hinkle, J. E., & Moss, D. M., III. (1981). *The organization and administration of pastoral counseling centers.* Nashville: Abingdon.

Carter, J. D., & Narramore, B. (1979). *The integration of psychology and theology: An introduction.* Grand Rapids: Zondervan.

Clebsch, W. A., & Jaekle, C. R. (1964). *Pastoral care in historical perspective.* Englewood Cliffs, NJ: Prentice-Hall.

Clinebell, H. J. (1966). *Basic types of pastoral counseling.* Nashville: Abingdon.

Collins, G. R. (1976). *How to be a people helper: You can help the others in your life.* Ventura, CA: Vision House.

_____. (1977). *The rebuilding of psychology: An integration of psychology and Christianity.* Wheaton, IL: Tyndale.

_____. (1980). *Christian counseling: A comprehensive guide.* Waco, TX: Word.

_____. (1981). *Psychology and theology: Prospects for integration.* Nashville: Abingdon.

Crabb, L. J., Jr. (1977). *Effective biblical counseling: A model for helping caring Christians become capable counselors.* Grand Rapids: Zondervan.

Davis, B. (1984). *Teaching to meet crisis needs.* Springfield, MO: Gospel Publishing House.

Drakeford, J. W. (1967). *Integrity therapy: A new direction in psychotherapy.* Nashville: Broadman.

Fitts, W. H. (1965). *Tennessee Self Concept Scale: Manual.* Nashville: Counselor Recordings and Tests.

Foster, R. J. (1978). *The celebration of discipline.* San Francisco: Harper & Row.

Gilbert, M. G., & Brock, R. T. (Eds.). (1985). *The Holy Spirit and counseling: Theology and theory.* Peabody, MA: Hendrickson.

Glock, C. Y., & Stark, R. (1965). *Religion and society in tension.* Chicago: Rand McNally.

Godin, A. (1965). *The pastor as counselor.* New York: Holt, Rinehart & Winston.

Gough, H. G. (1956). *California Psychological Inventory: Manual.* Consulting Psychologists Press.

Haley, J. (1976). *Problem solving therapy.* San Francisco: Jossey-Bass.

Haley, J., & Hoffman, L. (1967). *Techniques of family therapy.* New York: Basic Books.

Hansen, J. C., Warner, R. W., & Smith, E. M. (1976). *Group counseling: Theory and process.* Chicago: Rand McNally.

Hathaway, S. R., & McKinley, J. C. (1967). *Minnesota Multiphasic Personality Inventory: Manual.* New York: The Psychological Corporation.

Hiltner, S., & Colston, L. G. (1961). *The context of pastoral counseling.* Nashville: Abingdon.

Klausmeier, J. J., & Goodwin, W. (1966). *Learning and human abilities: Educational psychology* (2nd ed.). New York: Harper & Row.

Lewin, M. H. (1978). *Establishing and maintaining a successful professional practice.* Rochester, NY: Professional Development Institute.

Lewis, E. C. (1970). *The psychology of counseling.* New York: Holt, Rinehart & Winston.

Louthan, S., & Martin, G. (1976). *Toward better families.* Newberg, OR: Barclay.

MacAlmon, E. L. (Ed.). (1981). *Essential Christianity: The Christian in contemporary society.* Springfield, MO: Evangel College Press.

Mauger, P. A., & Adkinson, D. R. (1980). *Interpersonal Behavior Survey (IBS): Manual.* Los Angeles: Western Psychological Services.

Meier, P. D., Minirth, F. B., & Wichern, F. B. (1982). *Introduction to psychology and counseling: Christian perspectives and applications.* Grand Rapids: Baker.

Miller, W. R., & Jackson, K. A. (1985). *Practical psychology for pastors.* Englewood Cliffs, NJ: Prentice-Hall.

Minuchin, S. (1974). *Family therapy techniques.* Cambridge: Harvard University Press.

Minuchin, S., & Fishman, H. C. (1981). *Family therapy techniques.* Cambridge: Harvard University Press.

Mortensen, D. G., & Schmuller, A. M. (1966). *Guidance in today's schools.* New York: John Wiley & Sons.

Oglesby, W. B., Jr. (1968). *Referral in pastoral counseling.* Englewood Cliffs, NJ: Prentice-Hall.

Olson, D. H., Fournier, D. G., & Druckman, J. M. (1982). *Prepare-Enrich: Counselor's manual.* Minneapolis: Prepare-Enrich.

Pattison, E. M. (1969). *Clinical psychiatry and religion.* Boston: Little, Brown & Company.

Pruyser, P. W. (1976). *The minister as diagnostician: Personal problems in pastoral perspective.* Philadelphia: Westminster.

Ryan, L. R. (1977). *FIRO-B: Manual.* Palo Alto, CA: Consulting Psychologists Press.

Sampson, J. P., Jr., Tenhagen, C. A., & Ryan-Jones, R. (1985). Guide to microcomputer software in testing and assessment. *AMECE Newsnotes, 20* (4), pp. 1–24. Iowa City, IA: Association for Measurement and Evaluation in Counseling and Development.

Satir, V. (1964). *Conjoint family therapy.* Palo Alto, CA: Science and Behavior Books.

Satir, V., Stachowiak, J., & Taschman, H. A. (1975). *Helping families to change.* New York: Aronson.

Shimberg, E. (1979). *The handbook of private practice in psychology.* New York: Bruner/Mazel.

Sholevar, G. P. (Ed.). (1981). *The handbook of marriage and marital therapy.* New York: SP Medical & Scientific Books.

Snyder, D. K. (1981). *Marital Satisfaction Inventory (MSI): Manual.* Los Angeles: Western Psychological Services.

Stuart, R. B. (1983). *Couple's Pre-Counseling Inventory: Counselor's Guide.* Champaign, IL: Research Press.

Taylor, R. M., & Johnson, R. H. (1984). *Taylor-Johnson Temperament Analysis: Manual.* Los Angeles: Psychological Publications.

Tyler, L.E. (1961). *The work of the counselor.* New York: Appleton-Century-Crofts.

Wise, C. (1980). *Pastoral psychotherapy: Theory and practice.* New York: Jason Aronson.

Whitaker, C. (1970). *Marital and family therapy.* Chicago: Instructional Dynamics (cassette audiotapes).

_____. (1976). The hindrance of theory in clinical work. In P. Guerin (Ed.), *Family therapy: Theory and practice.* New York: Gardner.

Wright, H. N. (1981). *Marital counseling: A biblically based behavioral cognitive approach.* Denver: Christian Marriage Enrichment.

_____. (1977a). *Premarital Counseling.* Chicago: Moody.

. (1977b). *Training Christians to counsel.* Eugene, OR: Harvest House.

Wynn, J. C. (1982). *Family therapy in pastoral ministry.* San Francisco: Harper & Row.

Yalom, I. D. (1975). *The theory and practice of group psychotherapy* (2nd ed.). New York: Basic Books.

Zaccaria, J. S., & Moses, H. A. (1968). *Facilitating human development through reading: The use of bibliotherapy in teaching and counseling.* Champaign, IL: Stipes.

2

MAKING REFERRALS

Marvin Gilbert

INTRODUCTION

The increasing complexity and changing nature of the world in which we live has been the subject of sermon and secular documentary alike. This evolution of modern culture and modern humanity is clearly and somewhat frighteningly detailed by Alvin Toffler's best seller, *Future Shock*. One aspect of the future world in his vision is the prominent role of the specialist, the expert in a narrow field. In contrast to the specialist, Oates (1978) and others continue to advocate the concept of the generalist pastor. Oates implies that the parish pastor must continue to hold a generalist perspective, even though clerical specialists continue to arise in such roles as the professional pastoral counselor or therapist.

The meeting of the generalist pastor and the specialized helping professional can be a disturbing experience for both. The pastor may be awed by the knowledge and expertise of the specialist, particularly when the culture values specialization. The specialist, on the other hand, may distrust the pastor, view the pastor as unnecessary or, like a border guard trying to communicate with a foreigner seeking entrance into the country, may not be able to find a common language with the generalist.

Some generalist pastors attempt to convince themselves that the specialist is not needed. This is probably most frequently the case when the mental or spiritual health of parishioners is involved. The literature in the field of pastoral care is, however, increasingly critical of such beliefs. If the specialist is needed, insofar as the pastor (and parishioner) is concerned, then bridging the educational, methodological, and philosophical gaps between the two is essential.

The pastor needs the specialist for consultation, education, and referral. This chapter is designed to help bridge the gap between the two by educating and equipping the pastor to refer hurting, needy people to sources of specialized help.

Although most of the literature in the pastoral care field dealing with pastoral referral focuses upon referral to mental health professionals, the number of potential specialized helpers is much larger and more varied. A basic assumption communicated throughout this chapter is that "referral" is a broad concept not limited to psychiatric or psychological referral. The types of possible referral targets are presented in a later section of this chapter; they reflect the wide scope of possible referral activities.

What Is Referral?

The definition of "to refer" in *Webster's Seventh New Collegiate Dictionary* is "to send or direct for treatment, aid, information or decision." This definition adequately encompasses the behavior of pastors who actively encourage parishioners to seek any form of help (treatment, aid, information, or decision) from other professionals and experts; however, it does not adequately define the struggle some pastors have when considering how best to serve people seeking help. Neither does it specify the role of pastoral referral within the total framework of pastoral ministry.

The pastoral care literature has discussed almost every conceivable helping strategy. One of the themes echoed throughout this body of books and journals is that referral is part and parcel of pastoral counseling in particular and pastoral care in general. In recent articles, Lee (1976) and Toekle (1977) both conveyed the idea that good pastoral referral is good pastoral counseling. In this regard, Klink (1962) stated: "referral is not a pastoral failure. It is a subtle and important helping art. Help often begins with the process of referral, . . . helping people to focus their needs and clarify their feelings" (p. 11).

Pastoral referral necessarily involves both a parishioner-focused process in the pastor's office and an interprofessional communication process, by phone or in person, between the pastor and the referral professional. Pruyser (1976), in reference to the latter process, stated that referral should be a professional process by professionals who hold different perspectives. This sounds good, but on the basis of the studies reviewed later in this chapter, it actually appears to be more theoretical fancy than fact. Thus, although those writing about this subject are highly supportive of pastoral referral, it is the individual pastor's personal definition of referral which largely determines the scope of his or her referral activities.

What Pastoral Referral Is Not

As a pastor seeks to understand what referral is and what role it has in ministry, what referral is *not* must be evaluated. My perspective is that referral is not:

1. A reduction or elimination of pastoral responsibility for the parishioner. Whether the referral target is a psychiatrist or an attorney, the pastor remains the pastor. He or she must continue to love, support, and care for the referred person(s) while not interfering with the professional-client relationship.

2. A violation of pastoral ethics. Any case-specific communication between the pastor and the referral professional must be with the parishioner's permission. The ethical guidelines for referral have been developed and widely used in other professions and are readily adapted to pastoral referral.

3. A decision made unilaterally by the pastor and forced upon the parishioner as the only alternative. If the pastor experiences serious resistance to the idea of referral, the parishioner must know the pastor's door remains open, despite the pastor's honest evaluation.

4. An extremely complicated, risky process. Any helping procedure, including referral, requires practice and mastery of certain principles and techniques. The principles of referral are relatively straightforward, and the average pastor will, in a short period of time, have ample opportunity for practice.

5. Limited only to mental health referrals. The list of potential sources of "treatment, aid, information, or decision" is quite long and varied. Many sources of special help are available even in small communities.

THE PERSONAL DEFINITION

Referral may be personally viewed by a pastor as (a) a "last ditch" effort by an increasingly frustrated pastor; (b) a desperate, crisis intervention effort; (c) a necessary evil; or (d) another technique of good pastoral care. How a pastor views referral will depend upon a large number of variables: some of these are theological position, education, counseling training, previous referral experiences, and availability of competent referral resources.

The purpose of this chapter is not to "sell" referral; books of that type are already available. Its purpose is to enable those pastors who already believe referral *is* or *may be* appropriate behavior to make referrals effectively.

REVIEW OF PASTORAL COUNSELING AND REFERRAL RESEARCH

Referral is lauded in the pastoral counseling literature as an extension of effective pastoral counseling and pastoral care. The available data indicate, however, that more is being written about the subject than is being done. Gurin, Veroff, and Feld (1960) reported that 42% of all people seeking mental health help go to clergy first for that help. This Gurin et al. finding is reported in almost every pastoral counseling text. The finding less frequently quoted, however, is that on the average, only 9% of the 42% are ever referred to a mental health professional. Gurin et al. compared this finding with the referral data for nonpsychiatric physicians, and stated:

> Ministers . . . apparently see themselves as the final therapeutic agent much more often than physicians do since they do not so often refer the people that come to them to more specialized therapeutic resources. (1960, pp. 314–315)

They further stated that of the parishioners and nonparishioners who seek initial help from clergy, an additional 25% might be referred if pastors were better diagnosticians or could overcome their own resistance to referral.

Bell, Morris, Holzer, and Warheit (1976) examined the records of 17,723 patients of psychiatrists in private practice and two community mental health centers in order to determine who referred them. Bell et al. found only 11% of this large sample had taken a problem to a pastor during the previous 12 months. They also reported that between 75% and 80% of this 11% who had sought pastoral counseling were never referred; 10% of this 11% were referred directly to a mental health professional, and an additional 10% were referred after some counseling with a minister. These data indicate that clergy were more active in referral activities than Gurin et al. (1960) reported, but both studies illustrate the general lack of referral activity by ministers.

Both of the studies reported above were large scale mental health projects not specifically focused on clergy as referral sources. Larson (1965), in a study of 422 clergy in New England, found that of all Protestant clergymen in his study, 29% made three or more referrals in one year, 38% made one to two referrals, and 33% referred no one. This variability in referral activity is also supported by Kevin's (1977) data. Kevin reported the average number of referrals by the 90 pastors in his study was 10.2 during a one-year period, but the standard deviation was 16.5—indicating some pastors were very active in referral while many others never referred. In another study conducted over a one-year period, Moore (1976) found that 70 pastors referred 375 parishioners, for a 5.3 annual referral rate. Moore analyzed his findings by categories, and reported the following: (a) 67.2% of the pastors referred 0 to 4 parishioners, (b) 15.7% referred 5 to 9 parishioners, and (c) the remaining 17.1% referred between 10 and 45 parishioners each during the one-year period.

Eaton, Speth, Goldberg, and Todd (1963) found that the 34 clergy in their study referred 144 clients during a three-month period. These referrals went beyond mental health professions, however, to include Alcoholics Anonymous, physicians, and social welfare agencies. Thus, the 4.2 referrals per minister over the three-month period would presumably have been lower if only mental health professionals had been considered as referral targets, and presumably would have compared closely with Larson's (1965) data reported above.

The overall lack of referral activity by clergy is further supported by Mannino, Rooney, and Hassler (1967), who examined the referral records of a community mental health center in Maryland over a 10-year period. During this period, there were 228 Protestant churches of all major denominations, 34 Roman Catholic churches, and two Jewish synagogues active in the community. Despite ongoing efforts by the center's staff to solicit referrals from community professionals, only 60 pastors contacted the center during the 10-year period, and only 14 of these made more than one referral. These data are consistent with findings by Bell et al. (1976), who found that referrals by pastors composed only 1.0% and 2.2% of all referrals received at a large and a small community mental health center, respectively.

The Referral Patterns of One Group of Evangelical Pastors

In order to further illustrate the lack of actual contact between pastors and referral professions, the results of a study I conducted are reported and briefly discussed. A total of 111 Assemblies of God pastors living in the southwestern United States were surveyed in 1979; 74 usable forms were returned. Among the questions on the form, one asked how many people the pastor had referred to mental health professionals in the preceding 12 months and another asked what percentage of people seen in a formal or informal counseling setting were referred during the same 12 months. The results are presented in Table A.

Question #	Min.	Max.	Range Mdn	M	SD
1. People Referred in 12 months	0	12	.4	1.2	2.1
2. Percentage of People Counseled and Talked to Who are Referred	0	99	.4	6.5	13.8

Table A

The average referral rate was very low in comparison with findings previously reported in the literature. The mean of 1.2 referrals per pastor indicated only slightly more than 74 referrals to mental health professionals had been made in one year by the pastors. The standard deviation was almost twice as large as the mean, indicating most pastors made no referrals. Of all of the people counseled by the pastors or talked to regarding mental health concerns, only 6.5% were ever referred.

Neither this study nor the others reported in the first part of this review answers all of the questions regarding pastoral referral. The trend is clearly evident, however: the average pastor, across denominations, is rarely involved in referral —this, despite the apparently obvious benefits to the pastor and parishioner of an occasional referral. That a few pastors are moderately involved in referral, however, provides evidence that referral *is* a workable expression of pastoral care for those pastors who know how to communicate with referral professionals and how to prepare parishioners for referral.

TYPES OF REFERRAL POSSIBILITIES

The number of potential referral professions is large, as evidenced by the length of this section; however, this large number of professions can effectively be categorized: (a) medical professions, (b) the legal profession, (c) social service professions and agencies, (d) general mental health professions, and (e) mental health specialists.

Mental health professions are discussed last because the other professions tend to be deemphasized or ignored as potential referral professions in the literature. The broader the scope of potential referrals, the more effective the pastor can be in aiding parishioners spiritually, emotionally, and tangibly during times of stress, change, and crisis. This "holistic" concept of pastoral care is discussed later in this chapter.

MEDICAL PROFESSIONS

Family Doctor

Referral to a parishioner's family physician is in order whenever a pastor suspects *any* type of medical problem or when the parishioner complains of physical difficulties. There are times when such referral can be difficult, e.g., when the parishioner suspects or fears major illness. The pastor may need to counsel with the person for some time before such a referral is accepted.

All physicians hold both a bachelor's and M.D. degree. In the case of osteopaths, a bachelor's and D.O. degree is required. The intensity and duration of training is similar for both. Each has completed at least one year of internship/residency, and has passed some form of state qualification to practice the profession.

Medical Doctor: Specialist

In most cases, the specialist accepts referrals only from other M.D's or D.O.'s. Therefore, referral to these professionals is generally at the discretion of the family doctor.

Addresses. The American Medical Association, 535 N. Dearborn St., Chicago, IL 60610.

The American Osteopathic Association, 212 E. Ohio St., Chicago, IL 60611.

LEGAL PROFESSION

Attorneys are appropriate referral professionals for a wide range of legal problems. Many lawyers specialize in one or more areas of legal practice: criminal law, corporate law, tax law, estate law, family (domestic) law, bankruptcy, etc. The pastor should be aware of the type of clients and cases a particular attorney normally handles before making a referral.

Lawyers generally are required to graduate from college and complete a three-year program in law school. They are further required to pass a state bar exam before being allowed to practice law in a given state.

Address. The American Bar Association, 1155 East 60th St., Chicago, IL 60637.

SOCIAL SERVICE AGENCIES AND PROFESSIONALS

Agencies

State-operated social welfare agencies. These agencies represent the state's welfare insofar as the living conditions and family life of its citizens are concerned. The functions of these agencies are varied, but generally involve supervision of child placement and foster care, providing education and guidance for troubled families, and serving as agents of the courts regarding all aspects of individual and family life.

Private social welfare agencies. These agencies provide a variety of educational and material services to people in a community. Often, the agencies are sponsored by a church organization and provide services primarily to those in a given denomination.

Salvation Army. Many Salvation Army centers provide clothing, housing, and food for people on a limited, temporary basis.

The American Red Cross. The Red Cross plays a vital role in emergency relief of all types and social services in hospitals and the armed forces.

Alcoholics Anonymous. This service is a volunteer, lay-directed, self-help group devoted to obtaining and maintaining sobriety for its members. It serves all people on a no-charge, donation basis through support meetings, educational programs, counseling, and family support.

Veteran's Administration. The V.A. provides counseling and assistance for a wide range of needs for veterans and their families. The V.A.'s services include job rehabilitation, medical treatment in in-patient and out-patient facilities, burial services, home financing, etc.

Drug and alcohol rehabilitation centers. These centers are operated by state and private means. They provide counseling, rehabilitation and "drying out" services for alcoholics, drug abusers, and their families.

Y.M.C.A./Y.W.C.A. These agencies provide a wide range of services beyond the stereotypical physical fitness programs. They operate youth camping programs, provide specialized training programs from assertiveness training to classes on childbirth preparation and parenting, and provide services to physically and mentally handicapped children and adults.

Senior citizen centers. These agencies provide a variety of educational, recreational, and transportation services for older adults in the community. Services often include hot meal programs and limited in-home medical care.

Personnel

Generally, the staff members of the various social service agencies have at least a bachelor's degree in psychology, sociology, or social work/social welfare. In some cases, however, volunteers and paraprofessionals are used who have received some training, but who are not qualified as "professional" staff. These dedicated people often make the difference between an agency's success or failure, especially so in the A.A. and Red Cross programs.

In some agencies, a master's degree in one of the helping disciplines (e.g., psychology, social work, counseling, or rehabilitation) is required for staff positions. Social welfare agencies and some governmental agencies will often establish a master's degree as a minimum qualification.

General Mental Health Professions

The mental health field is a broad one, with a variety of professional titles and degrees included. There are, however, four basic titles, with specialization generally occurring subsequent to recognition as a psychiatrist, psychologist, social worker, or counselor.

Psychiatrists

A psychiatrist is a medical doctor (M.D.) who has specialized in the diagnosis and treatment of mental and emotional dysfunction. Psychiatrists are able to prescribe medication and to hospitalize, as appropriate to the patient's condition. They also provide conventional counseling or psychotherapy, as do other mental health professionals.

A referral to a psychiatrist in private practice may require an intermediary referral by a family physician, though some will accept direct referral from clergy. Depression, sleep and eating disorders, nightmares, inappropriate behavior and emotions, suicidal thought, paranoia, and delusions and hallucinations are all symptoms that would indicate the need for a referral to a psychiatrist.

Address. The American Psychiatric Association, 1700 185th St. N.W., Washington, D.C. 20009

Psychologists

Psychologists in private practice can generally be categorized as clinical or counseling psychologists, though occasionally an educational or industrial-organizational psychologist will work in private practice. As a rule, psychologists in private practice will hold a Ph.D., a Psy.D., or Ed.D. degree in psychology. They tend to see the same types of clients as psychiatrists, or clients with somewhat less debilitating problems. They cannot prescribe medication, except through cooperation with a medical doctor. In all states in the U.S., psychologists must be licensed in order to practice psychology in private practice.

Psychologists work in a variety of settings in addition to private practice. In some mental health agencies and counseling centers, psychologists might hold only a master's degree and are active in psychological test administration, interpretation, and diagnosis, in addition to direct counseling services.

Address. The American Psychological Association, 1200 17th St. N.W., Washington, D.C. 20036.

Social Workers

Social workers are employed in social service agencies, as discussed above, in mental health clinics and centers, in hospitals, and in private practice. Those social workers who specialize in helping emotionally and mentally disturbed clients may be termed psychiatric social workers.

Generally, a direct referral to a social worker would be made only when the social worker is in private practice. Such professionals tend to limit their practice to marriage and family therapy (as discussed below), child therapy, and group counseling, though this varies with the professional.

It is possible to be employed in a social service agency with only a bachelor's degree in social work. However, a master of social work degree (M.S.W.) is the minimum educational requirement for full professional social work status, especially in private practice. The M.S.W. degree is a full two-year graduate training program. Beyond this degree, highly experienced and competent social workers may be awarded certification by the Academy of Certified Social Workers and include the letters A.C.S.W. following their name.

Address. National Association of Social Workers, 15th and H St. N.W., 600 Southern Building, Washington, D.C. 20005.

Counselors

The profession of counseling is very broad; counselors work in a variety of settings with varying degrees of professional training. In general, they seek to help relatively "normal" people understand themselves better, make decisions, and obtain a more satisfying life adjustment.

Counselors tend to specialize, depending upon their work setting. Counseling specializations include school counseling, rehabilitation counseling, career development and employment counseling, alcohol and drug abuse counseling, marriage and family counseling, and pastoral counseling. These latter two are discussed in the following section.

A referral to an employment counselor can benefit a parishioner who is entering the work world for the first time or who is deciding upon a mid-life career change. Rehabilitation counselors are generally employed by agencies; they work with physically, mentally, or socially disabled people to adjust to life, find employment, develop employable skills, etc. (see also Bass's chapter on Rehabilitation Therapy). Drug and alcohol rehabilitation counselors provide needed support, hope, and challenge in rehabilitation centers and agencies.

Most counselors employed by public schools have at least a bachelor's degree, and many schools and almost all colleges require a master's degree as a minimum qualification. An internship lasting from a few months to as long as one year is also common in both master's and doctoral-level training programs.

Only a few states in the U.S. have licensing laws governing the practice of counseling. Most counselors, however, are members of one or more professional organizations, including the one listed below. These organizations provide ethical guidelines, training opportunities, and referral services for their members—as do the other organizations listed in this chapter.

Address. The American Association for Counseling and Development, 5999 Stevenson Ave., Alexandria, VA 22304. The A.A.C.D. has 13 subdivisions for counseling specializations, including school, rehabilitation, mental health, and career and college student personnel counseling.

SPECIALIZED MENTAL HEALTH PROFESSIONS

Many types of counseling disciplines and approaches could be discussed in this section. Two such specializations, however, will be of broad interest to the referring pastor: marriage and family counseling, and pastoral counseling.

Marriage and Family Counseling

This professional specialization is practiced by psychiatrists, psychologists, social workers, and counselors specially trained in this field. The professionals may work alone or in two-person teams (co-therapy). Generally, they meet with a couple or entire family, with the goal of improving communication and family relations.

As a distinct professional field, marriage and family counseling is young—as is true of pastoral counseling. A master's degree is rapidly becoming the accepted minimum for professionals, especially for those in private practice.

Address. The leading professional organization is the American Association for Marriage and Family Therapy, 1717 K. St. N.W., Suite 407, Washington, D.C. 20006. The A.A.M.F.T. is an interdisciplinary organization which has an effective member-training program that leads to the category of clinical membership. Professionals who advertise themselves as clinical members of A.A.M.F.T. have demonstrated competence in this area of counseling.

Pastoral Counseling

As a distinct counseling profession, pastoral counseling has existed for only a few decades. Under the leadership of the American Association of Pastoral Counselors, this field has developed rapidly. A majority of A.A.P.C. members—in the categories of Member, Fellow, and Diplomat—work in settings other than parish pastoral ministry, including mental health centers, Christian and/or pastoral counseling centers, and private practice.

Pastoral counselors are trained to deal not only with traditional counseling issues and concerns, but also with spiritual and doctrinal-type struggles. Extensive training in counseling has marked this field from its inception. The basic level of training for membership in A.A.P.C. normally includes graduation from college and from seminary with the three-year Master of Divinity degree, ordination, some structured and supervised training in counseling, and at least one quarter (three months) of Clinical Pastoral Education in a hospital or other setting.

Address. The American Association of Pastoral Counseling, 3000 Connecticut Ave. N.W., Suite 300, Washington, D.C. 20008.

WHEN TO REFER

A Pro-Active Model of Referral

The pastor has one of the most enviable roles and positions, as far as having access to people's lives is concerned (Adler, 1965). The minister does not need to wait, indeed should not wait, for an invitation to visit parishioners. He or she need not wait for a knock at his or her office door to engage hurting people in healing dialogue.

A pro-active model for pastoral intervention includes the following functions: (a) look-out sentry, (b) city directory, and (c) first-aid specialist. As a look-out sentry, the pastor constantly scans his people for indicators of problems and dysfunction. Subtle indicators will be noted, such as absence from church services, unusual behavioral problems with a child during church school, etc.

As a city directory, the pastor will know what services are available in the community, where they are located, who the contact person is, and what type of reception the parishioner is likely to experience there. Having this information readily at hand will create confidence in both the pastor and the contact person.

Many problems encountered by a pastor do not require referral; his skills in counseling, consultation, and spiritual/emotional intervention are sufficient. Like a skilled first-aid provider, the pastor provides immediate aid and comfort, and will only direct the more serious "injuries" to a "physician," whether literal or figurative.

Indicators of Needed Referral

One of the most challenging tasks faced by the pastor is distinguishing between those problems the minister can help resolve and those which require referral. In this regard, much of the pastoral referral literature has focused upon referral to mental health professions.

Dicks (1960) and Jackson (1964) proposed that the pastor must have enough knowledge of psychiatric symptoms and psychopathology to know when a referral is indicated. Bentz (1967) pointed out that it is often the less educated pastors who fail to make the most effective use of referral.

The symptoms which Dicks (1960) identified as requiring referral include psychosis, neurosis, manic-depressive syndrome, and paranoia—pathological symptoms which presumably would require some degree of sophistication or knowledge to identify accurately.

More specific guidelines for determining whether referral is needed appear frequently in the literature. Waterman (1960) stated that a parishioner who displays an acute, severe emotional disturbance should be referred. Wygant (1971) warned, however, that the suggestion of referral should not be made unless the parishioner's anxiety level is low enough to allow the client to accept a referral suggestion or until the bond of trust between pastor and parishioner is strong. Thus, even when the pastor is faced with a severe emotional problem, immediate referral may not be the most effective approach.

A useful approach for determining when some form of pastoral intervention may be needed is presented by Steward (1979) and others who view crisis periods in an individual or family as coinciding with predictable family life-cycle changes. When a person marries, divorces, gives birth to a child, or loses children to college, work, or marriage (the "empty nest"), then the status quo or "homeostasis" is upset and adjustment is needed. The greater the quality and quantity of personal and social resources available to the person at such crisis points—including the pastor—the less probable the need for referral.

Not only do parishioners experience life-cycle crises, they also experience situational crises via loss of a job, death of a family member or friend, serious illness or injury, moving, etc. As with life-cycle stress, the greater the support resources available to the person, the less probable the necessity of referral.

Other authors have approached the issue of referral from the pastor's perspective. The pastor should refer when (a) the parishioner's problem goes beyond his experience and training, (b) when the time demands of a given case exceed the time the pastor can realistically devote to it, and (c) when the parishioner is a friend, relative, or person in a power position within the congregation (Clinebell, 1966; Farber, 1973; Hulme, 1955; Lee, 1976; Toekle, 1977). Farber (1973) stated that referral is in order when the parishioner is attempting to avoid psychiatric treatment; a statement consistent with Klink's (1962) position on the positive benefits of referral counseling.

The trend noticeable throughout the referral literature is that referral should be made in direct, positive correlation to the amount of stress and disruption of a person's life. Parishioners are most open to intervention and change during such times of high stress.

The more sophisticated the pastor is in understanding mental health problems and symptoms of stress, the more intelligently he or she will be able to refer and communicate with the referral professional. The same principle holds for medical, legal, and social welfare referrals. Thus, the tasks before the pastor are to (a) accurately identify personal or family dysfunction, (b) evaluate honestly the pastor's own ability/willingness to provide the needed intervention, (c) know who is available as referral professionals, and (d) sensitively time the presentation of the need for referral to the parishioner. Obviously, such tasks are not mastered overnight; experience and confidence must be gained in knowing both personal limitations and abilities, and when the parishioner's problems demand help beyond that available through pastoral counseling/consultation.

SEEKING REFERRAL POSSIBILITIES

Once it has been decided that a referral would be the best helping strategy, the pastor must select the best available person as the referral professional. In some communities, the under-availability or over-availability of referral personnel makes this a challenging task. The following simple guidelines for locating these personnel can make the task more manageable.

Where to Look

Yellow Pages. The yellow pages in the local telephone directory is an excellent listing of referral professionals from a variety of disciplines. This is, for many pastors, the logical beginning point. In searching the yellow pages, persistence is the key. In large communities, most of the job or service (profession) titles discussed previously will have a separate listing. The smaller the community, the fewer the specific titles listed. Most common titles will be cross-referenced at the beginning of the yellow pages section. For instance, the yellow pages in the telephone directory in a city in which the author lived for two years did not have a separate listing for "mental health clinics"; however, these clinics are cross-referenced, and the reader is directed to "clinics." The information is usually available for the pastor who wants to find it.

Community directories. Most communities print directories of all health, mental health, and social services available in a given geographic area. The directories may be available through a variety of agencies. The most probable starting place for obtaining this type of information is the local Welcome Wagon or other community welcoming services.

Professional organizations. The organizations listed earlier in this chapter are excellent sources of referral information. Upon request, most, if not all, will provide a list of certified, licensed, or approved member professionals within a given geographic area. This source of information may be particularly helpful in identifying those referral professionals who do not, for a variety of reasons, list themselves in the telephone directory white or yellow pages. A letter of inquiry to the organization director on church letterhead will generally receive excellent cooperation.

Parishioner's recommendations. The parishioners in a local church can be excellent sources of information about who is available and the quality of the various professionals' work. The pastor who is new in a community and parish should question parishioners about the medical, legal, and social services and the mental health personnel available in the community; a list of recommended professionals can then be developed.

Fellow ministers' recommendations. Formal organizations such as local ministerial alliances, as well as informal discussions with other clergy, can provide valuable information about referral possibilities. Although a pastor may not fully appreciate the doctrinal position of a pastor from another denomination, that pastor's positive or negative experience with a given referral professional can provide invaluable information to the referring pastor.

Beyond Name and Title: Referring Yourself

The need for knowing one's referrals. Clinebell (1966) and others have consistently found a very positive relationship between the pastor's personal knowledge of the referral professional and the successful outcome of the referral; therefore, it is imperative for the pastor to become acquainted with the referral professional. While this can be accomplished to a degree during community service meetings and social gatherings, the opportunities are limited and in-depth conversations are not generally conducted.

The strategies for self-referral. Self-referral, that is, contact with the referral professional initiated by the pastor, can be accomplished in several ways.

1. The pastor can initiate a luncheon or coffee meeting in a restaurant. In such an informal setting, the pastor can learn much about the professional's approach to working with people, fees charged, openness to receiving referrals from the pastor, etc.

2. The pastor can simply call a prospective referral professional and become acquainted with him or her by phone. Although face to face meetings are preferable, a "telephone acquaintance" is far superior to a "blind referral."

3. The pastor can also refer by making a 30-minute appointment with the professional in the professional's office. This allows the pastor to see the professional "at work" and thus allows the pastor to speak from experience about what a parishioner can expect. The disadvantage is that the pastor may be charged

for the visit, although many professionals are willing to donate time to prospective referral sources.

Obviously, these strategies are time-consuming; a pastor cannot make such close contact with all professionals in the telephone book or directory. Developing a list of recommended referral professionals is a necessary first step in developing acquaintance with referral professionals.

What to Look for

The time spent with the referral professional will generally be brief, due to mutually busy schedules. The pastor, therefore, must make maximum use of that time by bearing in mind what he or she needs to find out. The following list of questions is suggested as a topic organizer to guide the conversation.

1. How does the professional describe his or her method of working with people?

2. Does the professional have a specialization of preferred clientele?

3. Does the professional consider religious/spiritual issues important in practice? Would the professional have difficulty with people who present concerns over spiritual or moral issues?

4. What fee is charged? Is there any provision for low income people such as donated time or a sliding fee scale?

5. Would the professional be willing to accept referrals from a pastor? Would he or she be willing to confer with the pastor (with client approval), in providing for the client/parishioner's total well being?

6. What actual procedure would the professional prefer the pastor to follow in making a referral?

A direct question from a pastor regarding the referral professional's personal religious or spiritual condition may not be advisable. If the pastor perceives the referral professional is not a Christian, the person should not be automatically eliminated as a referral possibility. The professional's response to Question 3 above, however, should be a crucial determinant of the professional's acceptability, particularly in sensitive areas such as mental health counseling. The pastor must take care not to create standards for referral professionals that are so strict that no one can qualify, nor so lax that he refers to professionals who might harm parishioners spiritually.

PREPARING YOURSELF FOR THE REFERRAL

A crucial aspect of successful referral is the manner in which the pastor presents to the parishioner the need for and benefit of a referral. Before this can be done, however, the pastor must personally prepare by carefully examining what the pastor's role should be. Often, the pastor experiences role conflict; this is especially true in the referral process.

In preparing for referral, therefore, the pastor must honestly evaluate personal, subjective personality factors and must face the possibility of conflicting feelings and roles in the referral process. (Even experienced mental health professionals struggle with similar feelings when referring a client with whom they have been unsuccessful.) The pastor, in honestly facing his personal limitations, must recognize the practical impossibility of being "all things to all men" in today's complex world. He then can embrace both personal strengths and weaknesses, and acknowledge that he cannot help everyone on every occasion. If this attitude of humility pervades all that the pastor does, those parishioners who are referred will not be confused by the pastor's unvoiced, inner conflict when talking about referral. They will perceive, instead, genuineness (congruence), even if the pastor's personal feelings of regret for not being able to help more directly are expressed.

PREPARING THE PARISHIONER

The task of preparing the parishioner for a referral is a logical extension of the pastor's personal preparation in that the same process of honest evaluation is involved. In a clear, concise treatment of how to prepare parishioners for referral, Clinebell (1966) provided the following nine-step outline.

1. Create the expectation of referral whenever the pastor's role of counselor is discussed publicly or is published in the church bulletin.

2. Mention the possibility of referral early in any relationship in which it is likely to occur.

3. Start where the parishioner is in perception of the problem and the type of help that is needed.

4. Work to bring the parishioner's perception of the problem and its solution close enough to the pastor's perception to permit the referral to "take," i.e., to be successful.

5. Help the person resolve emotional blocks with reference to the particular helping professional or agency recommended.

6. Interpret the general nature of the help which the person may expect to receive, relating it to the person's own sense of need.

7. Establish strong enough rapport with the person so that the relationship with the minister may serve as a bridge over which the person may walk into another helping relationship.

8. Attempt to motivate a person to try a recommended professional, even if the counselee is only mildly willing to seek such help.

9. Let the person know that pastoral concern and care will continue undiminished after the referral.

Although Clinebell lists nine steps and other authors provide similar lists, I see three basic ingredients involved in preparing a parishioner to accept and follow through with a referral suggestion. These basics are timing, honesty, and the creation of hope.

Timing Is Crucial

A general guideline detectable in the preceding list of nine steps is: The more emotionally "loaded" the parishioner's problem, the more the pastor should avoid attempting a quick referral. Conversely, when a parishioner is in need of legal advice or other forms of specialized guidance or information, a referral should be made quickly. Good referral, therefore, requires sensitivity to the parishioner and a willingness, if necessary, to provide counseling for some time in order to facilitate a successful referral.

Honesty Is a Virtue

One of the functions a counselor provides is that of reality-tester. This is especially true of the pastor-as-counselor. Sharing an honest evaluation of the parishioner's problems can facilitate a deeper self-examination by the parishioner. Bell (1975) and others have emphasized the narrowing of vision, the reduction of perceived alternatives, and the increase in the frequency of ineffective coping mechanisms, such as denial, which people experience during stressful crisis situations. A trusted pastor who has good rapport established with a parishioner and who does not overwhelm people with "the truth" can provide a badly needed reflection of reality. The greater the denial and the more severe the problem, the longer the pastor may need to take, however, before gently "confronting" the parishioner with his perspective of reality.

Creating Hope

This subtle task is perhaps the most important one the pastor must master if referral is to be effective. This hope must be realistic, not wishful thinking or fantasy. A parishioner will perceive unrealistic hope as being either deceptive, with disasterous consequences later, or as factual.

Hope, for the parishioner, means that the problem(s) will be resolved or lessened in intensity. In creating hope, the pastor can (a) point out the positive coping strategies already being used by the parishioner (they are always there if you look hard enough); (b) express confidence in the referral professional—and personal acquaintance with him if possible; and (c) discuss the benefits to be derived from referral, including receiving competent, specialized care, confidentiality, and (if available) cooperation and a team spirit between the professional and the pastor.

In creating hope, the pastor can and should stress God's care and investment in the parishioner's life. Many verses of Scripture provide sound justification for a theology of hope and trust in God for the future (e.g., Rom. 8:18–39). These can be effectively integrated into referral counseling. Of course, the pastor's attitude and behavior must also convey hope. A pastor's frustration with the parishioner for not improving or despair over the magnitude and severity of the problem can easily dash all hope within the parishioner. Therefore, the pastor's theology must be consonant with his or her words, attitude, and action.

STRATEGIES FOR SUCCESSFUL REFERRAL

After self-preparation and preparation of the parishioner has been accomplished (at least to some extent), the pastor must initiate specific referral strategies. Four specific strategies will be discussed in this section: (a) contacting the referral professional, (b) determining who calls first, (c) deciding how far to go, and (d) continuing contact with the professional.

Contacting the Professional

The pastor should contact the referral professional before mentioning the name of that professional to the parishioner. This will enable the pastor to know if the referral will be accepted, it will allow the professional to know from whom the referral is coming, and it will add to the pastor's confidence when later discussing the possibility of referral with the parishioner. It is generally unethical at this point to discuss the parishioner by name with the referral professional; do not mention a name until the parishioner is willing for you to do so; however, the parishioner's problem can be described and a brief history can be shared (if desired by the professional).

Determining Who Calls First

After the parishioner has expressed willingness to be referred, a decision must be made regarding who will call or visit the professional to make an appointment. Most authors stress the importance of leaving the responsibility for contacting the professional with the parishioner. This is important in that it communicates to the parishioner that he or she must assume personal responsibility for improvement, and it assures the professional that the parishioner is genuinely motivated to seek help.

An alternative to this total parishioner responsibility is to have the person call the professional for an appointment while in the pastor's office or presence. This strategy would be appropriate for parishioners who evidence shyness, procrastination, or who are openly fearful or anxious. The reassuring, quiet presence of the pastor may make the difference between calling and not calling. The pastor should, however, actually require the parishioner to dial the number and speak with the professional or secretary. If the parishioner chooses to make the appointment in person, the pastor, in some instances, may wish to accompany the parishioner, but should allow the person to speak for himself. The pastor should not discuss the parishioner with the professional in the parishioner's presence.

Deciding How Far to Go

There are times when a parishioner will neglect or openly refuse a referral, despite the pastor's best efforts and skills. As with issues of involvement in the church, the pastor must recognize that the success or failure of the referral is ultimately dependent on the parishioner. The old saying about leading a horse to water is still true.

A parishioner's refusal—whether active or passive refusal—to follow through with a referral recommendation must not automatically be interpreted as disinterest in receiving help. When the pastor learns that the parishioner has done nothing about contacting the professional, the pastor should use that opportunity to explore further the parishioner's world and problem. Gentle confrontation, modeling the Holy Spirit's confrontation of sin in our lives, can lead to positive results if the pastor makes it explicitly clear during discussion of referral that the parishioner can and should come back to visit with the pastor—at least a few times.

As long as the parishioner expresses a desire for help, the pastor must provide it, while at the same time honestly sharing his or her own "reality" with the parishioner. Out of such "round 2" discussions and counseling can emerge another plan for referral. In some cases, the parishioner may have actually attempted to work with the professional, but something prohibited the development of rapport between the two. The pastor needs to know this before suggesting a referral to that professional again.

In other cases, the parishioner's attachment to the pastor may have been stronger than either realized, thus subtly prohibiting a successful referral. In such cases, the pastor will have to help the parishioner "detach" from him and "attach" to the other professional. This is a process requiring close communication between the pastor and the professional, and may require some time of concurrent meetings (individual counseling with both professional and pastor) before the parishioner feels comfortable in seeing the professional alone. This situation is most common when the problem is an emotional one and the professional is in the mental health field.

Continuing Contact with the Professional

A common practice among many professionals, especially those in the medical profession, is for the professional making the referral to maintain contact with the referral professional regarding the client's or patient's condition and progress. Many referral professionals, therefore, anticipate ongoing consultation with the person making the referral. This is particularly true in those cases where both will continue to provide some form of care or support.

With the parishioner's (hopefully written) approval, the pastor is ethically free to discuss the person with the referral professional. Often the pastor can provide needed background information in this way, and can receive "up-to-date" information about the parishioner's progress. Such consultation will not only benefit the parishioner, but it will strengthen the relationship between pastor and professional.

Other Referral Strategies

A chapter on pastoral referral is, of necessity, written in rather general terms; general strategies for successful referral have been discussed. Hopefully, as the general strategies are practiced, each pastor will also develop a personal style and method of referral that works in a given community and with a given professional. Experimentation and practice will lead to increasingly effective referral strategies. As a by-product, the pastor will develop an effective inroad into the professional community as his care, love, and concern for people are clearly demonstrated.

SELECT BIBLIOGRAPHY

Adler, M.D. (1965). An analysis of role conflicts of the clergy in mental health work. *Journal of Pastoral Care, 19,* 65–75.

Bell, J. E. (1975). *Family therapy.* New York: Aronson.

Bell, R. A., Morris, R. R., Holzer, C. E., & Warheit, G. J. (1976). The clergy as a mental health resource: Parts I and II. *Journal of Pastoral Care, 30,* 103–115.

Bentz, W. K. (1967). The relationship between educational background and the referral role of ministers. *Sociology and Social Research, 51,* 199–208.

Clinebell, H. J., Jr. (1966). *Basic types of pastoral counseling.* Nashville: Abingdon.

Crawford, K. (1967). The minister's self image and pastoral counseling. *Pastoral Psychology, 18,* 49–54.

Dicks, R. L. (1960). *Pastoral work and personal counseling* (rev. ed.). New York: Macmillian.

Eaton, J. W., Speth, E. W., Goldberg, A., & Todd, M. A. (1963). Pastoral counseling in a metropolitan suburb. *Journal of Pastoral Care, 17,* 93–105.

Farber, H. (1973). Is the pastor a psychotherapist? *Journal of Pastoral Care, 27,* 100–106.

Gilbert, M. G. (1980). Variables in the decision by Assemblies of God pastors to counsel or refer. *Dissertation Abstracts International, 40,* 4410A.

Gurin, G., Veroff, J., & Feld, S. (1960). *Americans view their mental health.* New York: Basic Books.

Hulme, W. E. (1955). *How to start counseling.* New York: Abingdon.

Jackson, G. E. (1964). The pastoral counselor: His identity and work. *Journal of Religion and Health, 3,* 250–256.

Kevin, R. C. (1977). Factors influencing the judgment and referral of mental health presenting problems by clergymen and psychologists. *Dissertation Abstracts International, 37,* 4989A–4990A.

Klink, T. (1962). The referral: Helping people focus their needs. *Pastoral Psychology, 13,* 10–15.

Larson, R. F. (1965). Attitudes and opinions of clergymen about mental health and causes of mental illness. *Mental Hygiene, 49,* 52–59.

Lee, R. R. (1976). Referral as an act of pastoral care. *Journal of Pastoral Care, 30,* 186–197.

Mannino, F. W., Rooney, H. L., & Hassler, F. R. (1967). A survey of clergymen's referrals to a mental health clinic. *Journal of Religion and Health, 6,* 66–73.

Moore, P. L. (1976). Mental health consultation and the clergy: The place of values and other factors. *Dissertation Abstracts International, 37,* 1176B.

Minuchin, S. (1975). A conceptual model of psychosomatic illness in children. *Archives of General Psychiatry, 32,* 1013–1038.

Oates, W. E. (1978). Some common sense about the minister as counselor. *Journal of Minister's Personal Library 1,*10–12.

Olson, D. H. (1974). Marital and family therapy: Integrative review and critique. In W.C. Nichols, Jr. (Ed.), *Marriage and family therapy.* Minneapolis: National Council on Family Relations.

Pruyser, P. W. (1976). *Minister as diagnostician.* Philadelphia: Westminister.

Steward, C. W. (1979). *The minister as family counselor.* Nashville: Abingdon.

Toekle, C. H. (1977). Referral in pastoral mental health counseling. *Currents in Theology and Mission, 4,* 39–42.

Toffler, A. (1970). *Future shock.* New York: Bantam Books.

Wygant, W. C. (1971). The problem of mental health referral. *Pastoral Psychology, 22,* 41–45.

3

MARRIAGE COUNSELING

Phillip D. Robinette

INTRODUCTION

Recent statistics on marriage and remarriage confirm that marriage is still the most popular form of social organization in the United States. An article in *Newsweek* (May 15, 1975) computed that in contemporary America: 96% will marry, and 38% of those will divorce; 79% of those divorced will remarry, and 44% of those remarried will divorce again. This means that approximately 62% of those marrying stay married and that 56% of those remarrying will stay remarried. If we add the total percent staying married (96% × 62% = 60%) to the percent of those originally married who divorced, remarried and stayed remarried (96% × 38% × 79% × 56% = 16%), then we have 76% (60% + 16%) of the marriageable population who choose marriage over alternative lifestyles. Much attention has been directed at the growing number of unmarried couples living together. Duvall and Miller (1985) point out that although the number of cohabiting couples tripled between 1970 and 1981, they only comprised 3.5% of all couple households in 1981.

Quest for Marital Satisfaction

Despite the popularity of marriage, marital partners often find satisfaction and continuing growth in the marital relationship to be elusive. Persons engaged in marriage counseling observe quickly that many marriages still intact are in reality as bad off or worse than those which have terminated in divorce. Couples continue to go through the motions of a relationship, but their hearts are not in it. At some time in the past they stopped believing that their present marriage would be able to fulfill their personal expectations and needs.

It naturally follows that when people cannot find fulfillment within a marriage relationship they may eventually look outside of it to find either solutions or alternatives to that relationship. This search outside of the relationship often becomes complicating and confusing.

Arthur Stinchcombe (1965) observed that at any point in time, members of a given society are generally restricted to selecting a lifestyle from those currently available. Certainly most people imitate the significant others in their lives by organizing their lives in similar forms and functions, but in today's society, the available choices can hardly be described as restricted. Indeed, it is the very multiplicity of alternate lifestyles and the flexibility of societal norms that places such a strain on marital longevity.

Pressures on "Christian Marriage"

From the Christian perspective, there are basically two places to look for answers to marital frustrations: within the organized church and outside of it. It would be nice if this choice were as discrete as it should or could be. Unfortunately, it appears that the church has permitted itself to "drop the ball" of needed leadership at a time when its ministry to marriages may be needed the most.

Organized evangelical Christianity has ignored the impact of modern societal change on the marriages of its members. The passage of time has widened the gap between the more traditional biblical view of marriage and its secular alternatives. In general, it appears that the struggle between influencing and being influenced by society has been won by the secular society. The "salt" of Christianity, at least as it is applicable to the preservation of the sanctity of marriage, has "lost its savor."

As churches have become increasingly composed of members with failed marriages, many leaders have felt compelled to abandon their more idealistic beliefs about marriage in favor of more realistic ones. Although most leaders would deny lowering the formal standards regarding married life, many have revised membership and leadership requirements to accommodate the marital casualties in their congregations. The point being made is not to criticize the adaptation efforts of organized religion; rather, it is only to highlight the enormous need for marriage counseling within the church as well as within the society as a whole. The primary function of marriage counseling, therefore, is to provide a relatively protected neutral zone for couples to enter temporarily where their marital relationship can safely and constructively be diagnosed and treated.

COMPONENTS OF MARRIAGE COUNSELING

Marriage counseling requires three basic components—a counselor, a married couple, and a counseling relationship.

A Counselor

That a counselor is an essential component of a counseling situation may sound obvious, but let me explain. Persons with problem marriages may interact with numerous individuals about their feelings and perceptions in an effort to solicit helpful responses. Unfortunately, this may result in ameliorated emotions and a premature conclusion that something potentially helpful to the repair of the marriage is taking place. Such discussions often merely serve to perpetuate popular myths about marriage such as those discussed by Stinnett and Walters (1977):

1. Marriages have problems galore.
2. Marriage is a down-hill experience.
3. Marriage is a 50-50 proposition.
4. Sex role differences are fixed and non-negotiable.
5. Children will cure a bad marriage.
6. Marriage is a solution for problems and unhappiness.
7. The successful marriage has no conflict.
8. Marriage is more important to women than to men.
9. All psychological needs should be fulfilled by marriage.
10. Good communication eliminates all conflict.
11. All troubled marriages can be improved by improving the sexual relationship.

It is strategically important that conversations about marital problems take place with a qualified and objective third person trained in marriage counseling. If they do not, two counterproductive consequences are likely to be experienced. First, the more troubled partner will become confused and bewildered by the array of contradictory advice collected. Second, well-intended yet inaccurate opinions may be acted upon leading to unnecessary disillusionment.

The Marriage Counselor with the Married Couple

It is a misnomer to label sessions with an individual marital partner as marriage counseling. An individual can be counseled about his or her marriage, but marriage counseling can only be done with the conjugal couple together (Miller & Jackson, 1985). Marriage is a relationship constructed out of the blended contributions of two separate individuals. As in all social relationships, the whole is greater than the sum of its parts. It is impossible to understand the structure and function of a marriage simply by examining the personality traits of two partners. Each marital relationship has its own unique characteristics.

The proper way to assess and treat a relationship is to deal directly with both individuals simultaneously. This enables the counselor to economize the potency of intervention (i.e., not to have to repeat what took place with one spouse to the other) and to observe the dyadic interaction firsthand. This helps to avoid the pitfalls encountered by assuming that the perceptions of one spouse regarding the marriage are necessarily shared by the other. It also eliminates the time-consuming effort of simulating interactions between the present and absent spouse.

When both members are present, all the events occurring within the therapeutic sessions are *mutually* experienced. Reactions are immediately observable and can serve as catalysts in determining the direction that the next step of therapy will take. Decisions can be mutually agreed upon "on the spot," and strategies for their implementation can be enacted without delay. Conflicts encountered during the session can immediately be confronted and the resolutions process inaugurated. See Leslie (1976, pp. 60–68) for a good discussion of the advantages and limitations inherent in the use of conjoint marriage counseling. It takes two to make a marriage. It follows that it also takes two to be involved in saving a faltering one.

The distinctiveness of marriage counseling is emphasized by Stahman (1984, p. 1):

> Marital and sex therapy (counseling) is the systematic application of techniques or interventions that are intended to modify the maladaptive or maladjustive relationships of married couples. The marriage counselor, regardless of discipline (marriage and family counselor, physician, psychiatrist, psychologist, pastoral counselor, social worker, and the like), serves as a counselor-consultant to the marriage relationship, not to one spouse or the other. Thus, the focus of change is the marital relationship. Usually, and preferably, both partners are actively involved in the counseling sessions and, since the marital relationship or system is the focus, both partners are the objects of the therapy and behavioral change.

The goal of marriage counseling, according to Clinebell (1984, p. 248) is "to help each couple co-create a relationship where both partners are enabled to discover and develop their maximum gifts as individuals in mutually enhancing ways."

Some marriage counselors prefer other approaches to structuring the counselor-client relationship. For example, Meier, Minirth, and Wichern (1982, pp. 363, 364) clarify that:

> In individual counseling only one member of a couple comes in for counseling, hoping to find healthier ways to cope. In collaborative marital counseling the two members of a couple see different counselors. The counselors may get together at times to discuss the case. In concurrent marital counseling one counselor sees both members but at separate times. In conjoint and combined marital counseling both partners are separately seen at times by one counselor, but they also may be seen together.

A Counseling Relationship

For counseling to be effective, the relationship between counselor and couple must change from a secondary to a primary one. *Secondary* relationships (Thio, 1986) tend to be impersonal and formal. They are the consequence of required interactions resulting from the societal and organizational positions we occupy. *Primary* relationships, on the other hand, are characterized by common interests and goals, conversational intimacy, and feeling secure enough to risk self-disclosure. It may take several counseling sessions for this to occur.

The establishment of a counseling relationship does not occur automatically. Some couples come to talk and to ventilate their feelings, but are really not open to being influenced by the counselor. Others briefly present their problem(s) to the counselor and expect to obtain the solutions in the same session. Still others test the counselor with minor issues before deciding whether or not to tell the whole story.

The purpose of the counseling relationship is a unique one. It is not friendship. Nor is it to model how relationships should be (e.g., the therapist taking on the role of one spouse or the other to demonstrate what a good one is like). It is intended to be a problem-solving relationship; that is, one in which problems pertaining to the couple-relationship are diagnosed and treated. It is both unethical and valueless to the couple for the counselor to convince them that they would be better off if they would have married someone more like the counselor than their spouse!

Herbert and Jarvis (1959, p. 53) pointed out that "the counselor and the client use the relationship that has been developed between them to enable the client to see himself and his behavior within his marriage more clearly." The welfare and relational healing of the client couple must always be the counselor's paramount concern.

ISSUES RELATED TO THE MARRIAGE COUNSELOR
Generalist or Specialist?

Time constraints force every counselor to choose between career and professional objectives. People doing or intending to do marriage counseling must decide whether this counseling specialty will be a minor or major part of their professional practice.

Often, people in the helping professions or those holding ministerial positions find themselves doing some marriage counseling as a part of their overall responsibilities. Many professional counselors with general counseling practices also find themselves with a limited share of their clientele needing marriage counseling. Such persons obviously cannot expect to be as knowledgeable or experienced as those clinicians who specialize in marriage counseling. As generalists, they are required to keep up with the developments in all aspects of their vocations; this necessitates a great deal of reading and continuing education.

Being a generalist has both negative and positive aspects. The negative ones pertain to the constraints of limited preparation and expertise. The major positive aspect is accessibility. The reason the generalist does marriage counseling in the first place is because his or her position identifies the generalist as a logical resource to couples experiencing marital difficulties. Considering the enormous difficulty of linking together the needy marriage and the marriage counselor, the generalist's proximity fulfills a very important function.

The specialist is one whose preparation and practice deal primarily with marital dysfunctions. Normally, specialists have (a) graduate degrees (at least at the master's level) related to marriage counseling, (b) supervised experience and (c) either a state license to practice or a clinical membership in the American Association of Marriage and Family Therapists (Fretz & Mills, 1980).

The specialist generates clients through advertising or referrals. Specialists may be employees of organizations (e.g., a minister of counseling or family life in a large church or a member of a community counseling clinic), or they may be in private practice. Unlike generalists, the specialist will carry the occupational title of marriage counselor or therapist.

Advising, Counseling or Therapy?

Ironically the least qualified are generally the quickest to give advice. Advice-giving is presumptuous for several reasons:

1. It assumes an accurate knowledge of the surface and underlying causes of the marital problems.

2. It concludes that a particular course of action (solution) is superior to alternative ones in this specific instance.

3. It implies a successful outcome (the resolution of marital deficiencies if the advice is followed).

4. It elevates the counselor to the level of a god in the eyes of the counselees and fosters counselor-worship and client-dependency (e.g., return to the source with future problems).

The goal of counseling is not for the counselor to solve the couple's problems. Rather, it is to assist the couple in learning how to solve their own problems. If the counselor is really successful, the couple will not only learn to deal with its present difficulties but will be equipped to handle future ones as well.

L'Abate and McHenry (1983), pp. 190–191) discussed at length the differentiation in terms between "marriage counseling" and "marital therapy." The essential difference pertains to how severely disturbed the recipients of treatment are. The less severely disturbed require *counseling* and the more severely disturbed need *therapy*. Note that the focus is not on the seriousness of the marital relationship dysfunctions, but on whether or not one or both of the marital partners are mentally disturbed.

It follows that in cases where mental disturbance exists, individual therapy as well as marital counseling is necessary. This fact, along with professional competitiveness between clinical psychologists and marriage counselors over the qualification of marriage counselors to do individual psychotherapy, led to a name change by the American Association of Marriage, Family and Child Counselors in 1978. The new name—American Association for Marriage and Family Therapists—constituted a declaration that their members were qualified and ready to treat all marital relationships—those with or without severely disturbed individuals. The change was also aimed at improving the ability of members of the association to receive third-party reimbursements from health insurance companies for their services.

It should be noted that although treating a severely disturbed individual is not technically marriage counseling, it may be indispensably concomitant to it!

Theoretical Framework

Until the mid-1970s graduate programs specializing in marriage counseling were rare. Most practitioners were trained in the disciplines of psychology, sociology, or social work. Despite the proliferation of professional two-year master's degree programs recently in marriage and family counseling, the field still possesses an interdisciplinary character.

The consequence for the student of marriage counseling has been a large and diversified collection of theoretical perspectives from which to choose. For an overview of these theoretical approaches see Burr, Hill, Nye, and Reiss (1979), Corey (1982), and Gurman and Kniskern (1981).

Although the scope of theoretical frameworks is too large to address here (see section three of Gilbert & Brock, 1985), it is important to note that the counselor's perspective is inextricably connected to his or her conceptualization of problem causation and the intervention strategies utilized to improve them. For example, the psychologist may scrutinize the couple's minds (*psyche*) for problem antecedents, whereas the sociologist would examine the couple's connections with its environment (*socius*).

It is sometimes more confusing than enlightening to realize that the same symptomology may be interpreted to have a large number of even contradictory meanings depending upon the theoretical perspective utilized to view it. This poses a strong argument for counseling to be offered by an interdisciplinary team of professionals.

An examination of psychological and sociological theory-building verifies that at the present time neither discipline purports to have developed a grand theory of personality development or social behavior. A grand theory would be defined as one that comprehensively explains all aspects of some component of human behavior that are applicable to all persons at all times and in all places.

Clearly the opposite phenomenon is true. The professional workplace has a multitude of competing theories. The wise counselor should have a basic respect for several approaches and prayerfully, with the guidance of the Holy Spirit, select the one most appropriate to each client couple's particular set of relevant factors. Some marriage counselors subscribe so wholeheartedly to a single theoretical perspective that they insist on counseling every couple in exactly the same way, regardless of their personal/social history, presenting problems, or demographic and environmental variables. They are in danger of employing a form of counselor manipulation and client abuse.

Competence and Referral

Working with interns who have completed all of their graduate academic requirements for state licensure as marriage counselors and who are accumulating hours of supervised counseling to qualify to take the licensing exams has convinced me that academic training alone does not produce competency. One of the interesting forms of resistance encountered during therapy sessions sometimes come from spouses who have had a few psychology courses in college and who presume the therapist cannot offer them any ideas they do not already know. This, of course, is a shallow excuse, especially in view of the fact that the most productive professionals consistently continue their education by attending professional meetings and workshops and by reading scholarly journals.

Furthermore, directing a multi-staffed counseling center for the past 12 years has also demonstrated to me that counseling experience does not always translate into a feeling of competence. Periodically therapists will share with me their frustration of feeling clinically bankrupt of ideas to help particular couples make progress toward improving their marriages. Fortunately, in a multi-staff setting, staff meetings can be used to present perplexing cases to professional peers for review and the generation of alternative approaches. If some or all of the counselors are born-again and Spirit-filled, praying and ministering in spiritual gifts to each other can supernaturally rejuvenate the therapist both personally and professionally.

Competency is a matter of self-evaluation and peer review; that is, in order to be competent, a therapist must *feel* competent and have that feeling confirmed systematically by others. Competency is not an all-inclusive characteristic. No one is competent with all couples, at all times, and with all problems. Everyone is a mixture of strengths and weaknesses. Competent counselors are those who recognize their strengths and admit their weaknesses to themselves and to others.

We are practicing in an age of professional specialization; it is no longer demeaning to state the limitations of one's services or to refer clients to others more adequately prepared to serve them. (See Gilbert's chapter on "Making Referrals" for a discussion of referral strategies.)

Diagnosis and Treatment Goals

Diagnosis usually originates from the counselor's theoretical framework (previously discussed), the couple's presentation of their problems, and/or some form of diagnostic testing. Some counselors prefer using diagnostic measures and argue that they economize time (i.e., they can generate a diagnosis quickly and begin treatment sooner) and are more accurate than the client's idiosyncratic perspective.

In practicality, all three diagnostic sources—theory, client presentation, and testing—are valuable and essential. The critical issue is one of sequence. If a particular theoretical framework is used in the diagnostic procedure, the tendency is to force the factors into a particular mold of terminology, variables, and hypotheses to be tested. This results in an amazing (and perhaps artificial) similarity of diagnoses over time!

On the other hand, if a counselor always begins with a set of standardized diagnostic tests, he or she may prematurely conclude that he or she has diagnosed the problem before even meeting with the client for the initial session. It is better to use initial test data as a starting point from which to gain some idea about the nature of the problems and use the first meeting to confirm or deny this hypothesis. However, many counselors have found it more appropriate to delay use of the testing data until after the initial interview is over.

I have found the following sequence to be most useful. I begin by giving both members of the couple an opportunity to express their problems in their own way, checking for agreement or disagreement between the spouses. Much can be learned by listening to them and observing their attitudes, emotions, organization, and reactions. I am more apt to observe how they treat one another while they are in control of the dialogue than when they are responding to a more structured interview.

Next, I discuss with the couple some of the available diagnostic tests and, together with them, decide upon one(s) we feel will be most helpful. The reasons for soliciting their cooperative compliance are to reduce test anxiety and to get more correct results, since most assessment instruments are based on self-reporting techniques.

The final step of the diagnostic process is to select the most relevant theoretical perspective considering the information obtained from the initial interview and the diagnostic tests. (Fischer [1978, pp. 311–316] has developed a very helpful and comprehensive framework for analyzing clinical theories.) Sensitivity to the leadership of the Holy Spirit is strategic at this point as the counselor must decide on at least a tentative choice of treatment which will preclude other useful ones. In actual practice, most counselors tend to rely on approaches that have worked successfully for them in the past for various presenting problems. The crucial value of the Holy Spirit is to enable us to transcend the limitations of the past while still respecting its utility for treating certain dysfunctions.

The end result of the diagnostic process is the formulation of a treatment plan. The treatment plan should include:

1. Goals of the therapeutic intervention mutually agreed upon by the counselor and the couple.

2. A delineation of what part the counselor will do and what part the couple is to do.

3. An estimate of the length of time the treatment should take.

Client morale is important during the treatment phase. However, it is the counselor's responsibility not to create expectations that are unlikely to be fulfilled. Promising or inferring success as the result of marital therapy is both unethical (i.e., it violates most professional codes of ethics) and damaging to the reputation of the marriage counseling field for the clients when such predictions fail.

I have found one successful way to maintain morale is to communicate to the couple that there are several different ways of treating its problems. If the first alternative is productive, fine. If it is not, then we will select another—and still another if necessary. This approach seems to generate positive cooperation in trying each alternative without fostering unnecessary frustration and depression if one or more of them are unsuccessful. This method seems compatible with the perspective of a creative God who encourages his spiritual offspring to anticipate more solutions to problems than may first appear in a given set of circumstances.

Session Length and Cost

A 1984 survey report by Psychotherapy Finances (Ridgewood Financial Institute, 1984) indicates that the length of individual sessions varies from 45 minutes to 60 minutes, with the majority of therapists having 50-minute sessions. Fees for marriage counselors nationwide range from under $40 to over $80 per session. The distribution of fees is bi-modal with fees of $50 and $60 per session having the highest frequencies: 22% each.

Some people wonder why private (non-public) counseling is not usually offered for free. The answer is fourfold. First, there is normally an overhead cost for the facilities (e.g., rent, utilities, malpractice insurance) in which the counseling takes place. Second, unless the counselors are salaried employees of an organization, they depend on the fees for personal income. Third, most practitioners operate on a fee-split basis, meaning that they usually retain only 50-70% of the fees they collect. A percentage of zero is zero! Fourth, clients who do not pay for their counseling services tend to miss appointments more frequently, do not follow through with agreed-upon assignments, and generally experience less improvement during the treatment process than fee-paying clients. For a comprehensive treatment of issues related to charging fees in the context of a Christian community, see Carr, Hinkle, and Moss (1981).

Termination or Transfer

The major connotation associated with terminating a couple from therapy is that the contribution of the intervention has either been completed or exhausted. The first outcome implies that the goals of counseling have been achieved and the marriage is stable enough to continue on its own. The second outcome implies that at least some aspects of the marital problems are still unresolved, but continued counseling is not expected to make a significant difference. It could mean that, for various reasons, one of the spouses has decided to stop participating in the counseling efforts to improve the relationship.

Negative aspects of termination. There are at least two possible negative aspects to terminating the counseling relationship. One is that the counselor is relieved of responsibility for the case and redirects attention to the remaining cases. This translates into the cessation of direct influence on the marriage by the one most knowledgeable about it. Often, therapists do not initiate contacts with previous clients even if they discover new resources that might aid a given relationship. However, the withholding of important information could involve a legal or ethical issue. (See Van Hoose & Kottler [1985] for an up-to-date treatment of these issues as they pertain to the responsibility of the counselor.) The second negative aspect is that clients tend to stop their systematic efforts at marital improvement when their counseling is discontinued. As long as clients are paying for counseling and are accountable to meet and interact with the counselor, they tend to be motivated at least to attempt constructive change.

Post-counseling motivation. This presents an interesting challenge for the counselor: namely, how to perpetuate counselor-influence and client-motivation during the post-therapy period. I have used two methods with some success. One involves suggesting that the couple return periodically for a "check-up" to determine how well they are following through on their therapeutic gains and whether they have encountered any additional difficulties. Having this future deadline may prevent regressive behaviors and may encourage the couple to continue working for the marriage in anticipation of the follow-up sessions.

Another method is to communicate to the couple that instead of terminating therapy they are being transferred over to the ministry of their local church. They are instructed that if they regularly attend and participate in the services and activities of their church they will be in a constructive environment that can continue to support the progress they have made in counseling. In my own counseling experience, I have discovered that the local church can offer the following supportive mechanisms:

1. Inspiration to motivate couples to improve themselves and their relationships with God and others.

2. The accumulation of informative ideas that answer questions and provide positive direction for life.

3. A responsive and caring community in which needs can be expressed and prayer can be offered.

4. Opportunities to serve others and share ideas that have been found to be healing and restorative.

5. An ongoing form of social structure to plug into at any time to alleviate loneliness, depression, and boredom.

In this regard, religious clients are advantaged inasmuch as few other social organizations provide such a complete collection of supportive assets.

Issues Related to the Marital Couple

Problem Categories

The etiology of marital problems can often be attributed to one of four classifications. It will be noted that each of the problem categories solicits a different type of interventive response.

Mental illness. The first category is mental illness. The counselor must examine the mental status of each partner to assess the presence or absence of mental pathology. If pathology is detected, its degree of influence on the marital problem must also be ascertained. If mental disorder is suspected and the marriage counselor is not trained in psychometry (psychological testing and diagnosis), a referral for this information should be made. (Wright [1981, pp. 404–417] gives an annotated listing of tests and inventories to use in marriage counseling.)

In situations where mental illness does exist, it must often be treated on an individual basis *before* the actual marital (relationship) counseling can be effective. In such cases, patience and cooperation by the spouses are needed. Many counselors and couples have endured unnecessary frustration at the apparent lack of progress in couple counseling because individual mental dysfunction has gone untreated.

It should be noted that some counseling scholars firmly reject the reality of the entire concept of mental illness. They believe it is a myth created by self-seeking professionals who have the need to control and manipulate ignorant victims for personal gain and professional advancement. The most outspoken advocate of demythicization is Szasz (1970).

Deviant Behavior. The second category is deviant behavior. This classification refers to behaviors that violate societal, religious, or family norms. Norms are not limited to expectations, but also refer to the standards and conduct of living of either the majority of people or the persons holding official or legal positions. Examples of deviance that affect marital relationships are abortion, homosexuality, extramarital sex, unemployment, alcoholism, and the violation of specific statements made by the couple in their wedding vows.

Deviant behavior can influence the marital relationship either directly or indirectly. It is easy to realize how the examples cited above can directly disrupt the equilibrium of a relationship. In such cases, therapy must accomplish two objectives.

First, it must aim at the termination of deviant acts that threaten the continuation and growth of the relationship. However, cessation must be more than a temporary intermission; it must be final. Obviously, this is easier said than done and requires the willing effort of the offending spouse. As our criminal rehabilitation system testifies (Arnold & Brungardt, 1983), overcoming and eradicating patterns of habitual deviance is difficult even in a constructive counseling context.

Second, therapy must work through the task of repairing the damage already done to the marriage by the deviant acts. These two objectives may call for two different forms of counseling. The norm violator may need individual therapy while simultaneously participating in marital therapy to deal with the restoration of the damaged relationship.

Knowledge and skill proficiency. The third classification category focuses on knowledge and skill proficiency. Naisbitt (1982) has concluded that we are living in an "information society." (The current demand for marriage and family literature and seminars is perhaps greater than at any previous time in history.) Often couples experiencing marital dysfunctions have not had extensive premarital counseling and actually lack the requisite information and relational skills for building a viable marriage. For example, some couples experiencing sexual problems may be totally ignorant of information contained in an ordinary college textbook on human sexuality. In some cases, the primary function of the counselor is to allow the couple to ask questions and seek the answers (see Katter's chapter on "Marriage Enrichment").

The counseling approach in this instance is more of an educative one. It might be argued in such cases that counseling is not really needed (L'Abate & McHenry, 1983), and that providing a recommended reading list and seminar information is all that is necessary. For many, however, the personal encounter with the counselor is essential to answer questions, to plan for change, and to monitor the process of problem-resolution. A case in point is a deficiency in communication skills. Excellent reading resources and even brief interventions like Marriage Encounter are often insufficient catalysts to produce totally new patterns of couple communications (Doherty, Lester & Leigh, 1986). There is no substitute for the weekly tutoring during marriage counseling to point out destructive modes of communication and to replace them systematically with more constructive ones.

Crisis.   The fourth classification category pertains to the critical nature of the marital problems. Usually this has reference to immediate danger to one or another of the marital partners themselves or to the relationship. The former might be precipitated by threatened or attempted suicide or spouse abuse and the latter by verbal threat of divorce. Such circumstances require immediate crisis counseling; the couple cannot wait until the next available appointment slot. Normally, the crisis problems must be addressed before actual marital therapy can begin. If the crisis intervention is unsuccessful, actual marital counseling can rarely commence.

Problem Location

The genesis of marital problems generally can be located either within or outside of the *relationship* or a combination of both. Problems originating within the partners' personalities and within the dyadic connection were discussed above. But, what if the contributing causes are located in the couple's social environment? Counseling directed at the individual or couple would be limited to learning ways to cope successfully with their external circumstances. It would be preferable to focus on the environmental factors producing the irritation (e.g., in-laws, neighborhood, employment, religious affiliation). In such cases it may be necessary to examine and alter the couple's relational links with these aspects of its social structure. For example, a husband employed as a traveling salesman may lack the time at home necessary to build a stable relationship with his wife. If efforts at adjusting to this employment constraint fail, changing employers or occupations may become a prerequisite to restoring marital health. If so, the counselor would aid the couple in investigating alternatives, assessing the strengths and weaknesses associated with each of the alternatives and in formulating strategies for disengagement and replacement. The counselor, in conjunction with the Holy Spirit, plays a significant role as an anchor, refuge, and resource during this often traumatic transition period. Following this alteration stage, more traditional forms of couple-centered therapy can take place.

Temporal Focus

Almost every couple asks the same question in the initial counseling session: "Where should we begin to describe our problems?" The counselor's response requires serious thought and will dictate the temporal focus the couple will make. There are three fundamental choices—the past, the present, and the future.

Focusing on the *past* could mean retracing the couple's relationship from the time the partners met or could even include selected recollections from childhood. Concentrating on the *present* usually means starting where the couple is right now (e.g., asking, How would you describe your marriage right now? What do you see as its strengths and weaknesses?). Giving attention to the *future* generally means addressing the couple's expectations, goals, and dreams for the marriage. It assumes constructive changes are preferred, and the issue is the direction and substance of the desired changes. All three foci are certainly meritorious and have potential for improving marital harmony.

Leslie (1964, p. 914) stated his own preference regarding this temporal focus issue:

> Marriage counselors focus on present relationships as much as possible and work backward through the client's development only as far as necessary to resolve the present relationship problems. Thus, rather than stressing the analytical notion of regression to the stage of greatest pre-oedipal weaknesses, marriage counselors assume that most clients need not work through all early developmental problems in order to be helped to cope with current interactional difficulties.

Marital Life-Cycle

Another crucial area to investigate in order to understand marital clients properly is their current stage in the developmental life-cycle of marriages. A description of the typical sequence of stages is reprinted by Duvall and Miller (1985).

1. Married couples (without children).
2. Childbearing families (oldest child birth to 30 months).
3. Families with preschool children (oldest child 2½ to 6 years).
4. Families with school children (oldest child 6 to 13 years).
5. Families with teenagers (oldest child 13 to 20 years).
6. Families launching young adults (oldest or first child gone to youngest or last child leaving home).
7. Middle-aged parents (empty nest to retirement).
8. Aging family members (retirement to death of both spouses).

A couple's location on the life-cycle influences its relationship in many areas, including marital satisfaction, frequency of coitus, financial pressure, and propensity for extramarital affairs. It follows that astute marriage counselors will thoroughly familiarize themselves with the details of life-cycle factors and will recognize the need to develop different intervention strategies for each one. For example, it is not likely that middle-aged, previously unmarried newlyweds would be counseled in the same manner as a middle-aged couple encountering the "empty-nest" syndrome for the first time.

Reflections on Marital Problems

Based on years of clinical practice, the following statements can be made about marriage problems:

1. Causation is complex and continuous.
2. Realization by spouses is not uniform.
3. Solutions are not standardized.
4. Personal problems can cause marital problems and vice versa.
5. Societal and religious normlessness often results in conditions of individual and dyadic *anomie*.
6. Marital failure does not necessarily imply personal failure.
7. Marital change is unavoidable.
8. Being equally yoked doesn't guarantee success.
9. The raw material necessary for marital satisfaction and continuity varies considerably among couples.

10. Hidden agendas complicate spousal assessment.

11. Unrealistic expectations produce frustration and futility.

12. The absence of good communication patterns is more a function of defeat than skill.

13. Marital relationships are like living organisms—they are either growing or dying.

14. The decision to end a marriage is usually one-sided.

15. Many couples delay marriage counseling until it is too late.

ISSUES RELATED TO THE COUNSELING RELATIONSHIP

Rapport

Since counseling is sometimes called "talking therapy" (i.e., improving cognition and behavior through a process of verbal interaction), it follows that not much can be accomplished until the client is willing to begin sharing openly and honestly. The establishment of rapport usually must be initiated and earned by the counselor. I have identified several obstacles:

1. Forced counseling against the client's will.

2. Embarrassment about the details of self-exposure.

3. Feelings of powerlessness in relation to the therapist.

4. Fear of punishment for wrong or illegal behaviors.

5. Fear of manipulation by the therapist to say things they do not want to reveal.

6. Therapist attitudes of judgmentalism or supervision.

7. Lack of privacy from potential interruptions or eavesdropping in the counseling office.

8. Client's state of mental disorientation or autism.

9. Anticipated emotional pain of reliving past traumas.

10. Negative experiences with previous therapists.

11. A personality trait characterized by suspiciousness and distrust.

12. Intentional lying and deception by the client.

13. A client "martyr complex" wherein he or she feels unworthy to make progress in therapy.

It is the counselor's responsibility to overcome any of these obstacles which may impede the development of a sympathetic relationship with the client. If this does not occur in the first session, the client will often not return to that therapist for counseling. I have found that genuine rapport—a conscious willingness to reveal all—sometimes does not occur until months into the therapeutic process.

Confidentiality

Professional codes of ethics require that the information divulged during counseling sessions be treated as confidential material. Generally, this means that the counselor is constrained from sharing that information with anyone without signed consent of the client. The therapist is responsible for informing the client (preferably in writing) of those particular behaviors not included under the normal umbrella of confidentiality prior to actually beginning the counseling process.

For example, there are some exceptions to the normal rules of confidentiality:

1. Discussion regarding aspects of the case with professional associates may occur to serve the client better; however, in such cases, the actual identity of the client should be disguised as much as possible. In situations where disguise is impossible, confidentiality is not actually broken as the professional colleagues are also under ethical rules of confidentiality.

2. Reports of child, spouse, or self-abuse to designated authorities for immediate protective action are often mandated by local, state, or federal law.

3. Marriage counselors will occasionally be ordered by the courts to be an expert witness in a legal litigation or to deliver over to the courts specified confidential records that are within their jurisdiction to request. The counselor should keep this possibility in mind when recording information into the case narrative. Hammar (1983, pp. 61–80) provides an extended discussion of this topic.

Duration of Therapy

The need for marriage counseling is usually a response to some crisis in the relationship in which the couple feels powerless to cope successfully. The mediation, then, serves a twofold purpose. First, it assists the couple in surviving and recovering from the elements and consequences of the crisis. Second, it utilizes the therapeuic interaction to teach new and more successful ways to strengthen the dyadic connection so that future problems will not need to escalate to a critical point. In my own counseling practice, marital *therapy* is short-term therapy. Ordinarily it can be completed in 4 to 13 sessions; however, subsequent sessions may be needed from time to time when new crises emerge.

From this view, marriage counseling is an instance of crisis intervention. Helping couples to grow in their relationship and to add mental resources is actually a form of marriage enrichment that focuses on *preventing* irreconcilable differences from developing between spouses (see Katter's chapter on "Marriage Enrichment"). Marriage *enrichment* should be an ongoing process within normal marriages.

"Long-term marital therapy" may be a misnomer. Lengthy marriage counseling often deals more with mental or characterological disorders in one or both of the partners that preempt the possibility of developing the initial viable counseling relationship. In most cases, a condition of individual normality is a prerequisite for establishing a lasting interpersonal relationship such as marriage. Therefore, long-term marital counseling might be better depicted as a condition where *marital* therapy is temporarily suspended until the goals of *individual* therapy are completed.

Directive or Nondirective Counseling

The issue of initiative and momentum during the therapy sessions is highly correlated with the theoretical perspective utilized by the therapist. Each perspective suggests an appropriate role and division of labor for therapist and client. Conceptually, if the therapist controls the direction of therapy, it is considered a directive approach; if the client is the primary influence, the therapy is generally labeled nondirective.

In reality, it can be argued that all therapy is directive. Even in instances where the client sets the pace and provides his or her own direction (e.g., Rogers's client-centered therapy), the therapist actually controls what does and does not take place. It only *appears* that the client can provide direction for the counseling because the therapist has decided that the nondirective approach is the best way to get the client to "open up" and reveal information strategic to solving the problems.

It seems plausible that for therapeutic progress to be made, direction must emanate from the therapist. Clients have already verified their inability to organize and manage their own recovery by the antecedent act of engaging a counselor.

PRAYER, SCRIPTURE, AND THE HOLY SPIRIT

Prayer, Scripture, and the Holy Spirit are three essential elements of Christian marriage counseling that can be utilized in three basic ways by the counselor.

The Exclusive Approach

One approach might be to use prayer, Scripture, and the Holy Spirit as the *exclusive* elements in the counseling program. In such a program, prayer is a central part of every session; it facilitates rapport between the couple and counselor by having them agree together in prayer for the marriage. Identified problems arising during the sessions are treated with *prayer therapy*—each specific need would be verbalized before each other and God (Parker & St. Johns, 1957). Such a method of problem-resolution implies that the couple does not believe the dysfunctions in the marriage can be successfully treated by their efforts alone. Furthermore, it implies that couples do not expect the counselor to be their primary source of help. They require the help of God to change and to stay changed in a constructive and growing way.

The Scriptures, as used in the exclusive approach, become the standard for determining the right and wrong attitudes and behaviors associated with the conjugal relationship. Thus, problems are defined as deviations from scriptural principles. Solutions involve realigning the couple's conduct and lifestyle according to the scriptural model. This approach assumes that mutual scriptural compliance will result in marital permanence and satisfaction. This is not to say that couples adhering to the Bible will not be subject to problems; however, it does imply that the methods for dealing with such problems probably have biblical precedence. Thus, the proper response to problems should be searching the Scriptures for information and then explicitly following its ameliorating methodology.

The role of the Holy Spirit in the exclusive approach is one of facilitator. Prayer is initiated and executed by entering into and receiving the anointing of the Holy Spirit. The guidance of the Holy Spirit is imperative in locating and understanding relevant Scripture portions. Diagnosis is dependent upon spiritual discernment from the Holy Spirit. Treatment essentially involves the Holy Spirit's ministry of spiritual gifts both during and after the therapy sessions. This approach is more likely to be employed by nonprofessional helpers who must rely more heavily upon God than education and clinical experience.

The Incidental Approach

A second way that prayer, Scripture, and the Holy Spirit might be utilized in marriage counseling is as *incidental* elements. Christian therapists who choose this approach intentionally subordinate these spiritual ingredients to the social-scientific theoretical framework they employ to treat couple dysfunctions. Prayer might be used as a prefunctory act to signal that it is time to get down to the business of working through the problem areas. Or prayer might be used as a benediction, concluding sessions by asking God to bless the efforts already expended during the session.

Scripture, from the incidental view, is relegated to a position of supplementary resource. The application of Scripture to ailing marriages is not deemed essential to the healing process; nevertheless, if the couple feels better by hanging on to a Bible promise or imitating an Old or New Testament character, then, by all means the Scripture should be included.

Likewise, the view of the role of the Holy Spirit is ancillary. He provides an auxiliary anointing upon the therapist's professional tools primarily obtained through academic preparation, professional affiliation, and experience.

The Integrated Approach

A third way to utilize prayer, Scripture, and the Holy Spirit is *integrated* with other resources available to the marriage counselor. This approach removes the competition between sacred and secular assets. It assumes that *all* helpful resources should be applied when they will benefit the marriage. Thus, the issue changes from one of *which* to one of *when* and *how*.

The integrated method shares characteristics with the marriage it is attempting to mend. Both wedded life and spiritual-professional integration involve the careful blending of two separate yet compatible entities. Both can function separately or symbiotically. The frequency and conditions of mutuality can vary with time, location, and environment.

This is to say that there is no set pattern or form that the integration usually takes. Considering the variety of ways that different religious groups interpret and apply Scripture and the range of theoretical types within the social sciences, it follows that efforts at integrating the two will only increase the number of possible permutations.

The *integrated* approach, then, avoids the problems associated with an *under-* or *over*emphasis on prayer, Scripture, and the Holy Spirit found in the *exclusive* and *incidental* approaches. Furthermore, one may have experienced difficulty in personally embracing the written integrative efforts of other theorists and practitioners. There were probably some parts with which agreement was possible but other parts that just did not seem to fit. The phenomenon addressed here is similar to the one that pushes many marital therapists into becoming theoretical eclectics.

Ideally, integration can also be approached eclectically. This means that the integrative therapist probably will not have a standardized way of using prayer, Scripture, and the Holy Spirit during every counseling session and with every category of marital abnormality. Prayer will be a respected form of communicating with God about the details of the counseling encounter. It will be practiced at the times most appropriate to the entire treatment strategy. It will occur at a time of reciprocal consent and participation.

Likewise, the use of Scripture will be very carefully managed to maximize its potency and helpfulness to the particular couple being treated. For example, the introduction of the idea in Romans 8:28 that "All things work together for good" must take place at the acceptable moment for the clients—not the therapist—in order to be truly effective.

The integrative view sees the Holy Spirit as an essential and implicit influence in every session. The Spirit-filled counselor submissively places talents, tools, and self under the Spirit's leadership. The Holy Spirit becomes an integral part of everything the therapist thinks and does. The therapist will often talk introspectively with the Spirit during the counseling session, while asking for insight and understanding, and when making difficult decisions. The therapist will sometimes be aware that what is happening in the session is attributable more to the Spirit's input than that of the therapist.

Every Christian counselor must decide between the exclusive, incidental and integrative approaches when applying prayer, Scripture, and the Holy Spirit in therapy. In my own view, the *exclusive* approach prevents the utilization of the vast resources of literature and research on marriage and family relationships. It also might lead to the impression that the practitioner is judgmental, prejudiced, and "holier than thou." It could also easily promote a condition of separatism between the counselor and other mental health professionals in the community.

The *incidental* approach, on the other hand, appears to me to constitute a position of negligence for the genuine Christian counselor. It may communicate to the couple being treated and to the community that secular professionalism is more important than submission to biblical guidelines and the influence of the Holy Spirit. Operating in such a role model is unnecessary, although it may be the approach of choice by some Christian counselors.

Personally, I regard the *integrated* approach as both plausible and preferable. It conforms to the biblical injunction that "the sons of God are led by the Spirit of God" (Rom. 8:14). It seeks to blend the best of the therapist's spiritual relationship with the Lord and his or her academic and clinical training and experience. In such an integration, it is important to achieve balance between the two and to maintain the proper priority of keeping prayer, Scripture, and the Holy Spirit in the preeminent position. I attempt to accomplish this by never consciously applying any concept or method that is contradictory to any scriptural truth. During counseling sessions I often have biblical illustrations and quotations come to mind to amplify concepts communicated in the session. At other times I find myself quietly asking the Holy Spirit for direction and insight during the counseling interaction, and I have been very much aware that his help surpasses my own human rationality.

The integrative approach makes plausible the view of perceiving the Holy Spirit as a *co-therapist*. In a Christian context, this idea has positive ramifications for both the counselor—there is a Paraclete alongside to help—and for the couple who can have confidence that God is part of the solution process.

CONCLUSION

Marriage counseling is a serious responsibility. Often a couple in trouble only gives it one try. The circumstances are usually not optimal for a positive and constructive intervention to take place. Many couples wait until the relationship is already dead before seeking specialized outside help. In such cases, the solution often falls more under the categories of miracle and resurrection than marital repair.

This is why the Christian counselor who is accustomed to utilizing the resources of prayer, Scripture, and the Holy Spirit has a decided advantage over the secularist. Earthly life is characterized by the co-existence of the limitations of humanity and at the same time faith in the supernatural. This is precisely the position of the practicing Christian marriage counselor.

Therefore, the challenge of contributing to the salvation of relationships is very similar to the many other objectives given by Christ to his willing disciples. Marriage counseling, then, is another of the valid and needed ministries of the Holy Spirit to the church and the world.

SELECT BIBLIOGRAPHY

Arnold, W. R., & Brungardt, T. M. (1983). *Juvenile misconduct and delinquency.* Boston: Houghton Mifflin.

Burr, W. R., Hill, R., Nye, F. I, & Reiss, I. L. (Eds.). (1979). *Contemporary theories about the family.* (Vol. II.) New York: Free Press.

Carr, J. C., Hinkle, J. E., & Moss, D. M., III. (1981). *The organization and administration of pastoral counseling centers.* Nashville: Abingdon Press.

Clinebell, H. (1984). *Basic types of pastoral care and counseling.* Nashville: Abingdon.

Corey, G. (1982). *Theory and practice of counseling and psychotherapy.* Monterey, CA: Brooks/Cole.

Doherty, W. J., Lester, M. E., & Leigh, G. (1986). Marriage Encounter weekends: Couples who win and couples who lose. *Journal of Marital and Family Therapy, 12,* 49–61.

Duvall, E., & Miller, B. C. (1985). *Marriage and family development* (6th edition). New York: Harper & Row.

Fischer, J. (1978). *Effective casework practice: An eclectic approach.* New York: McGraw-Hill.

Fretz, B. R., & Mills, O. H. (1980). *Licensing and certification of psychologists and counselors.* San Francisco: Jossey-Bass.

Gilbert, M. G., and Brock, R. T. (Eds.). (1985). *The Holy Spirit and counseling: Theology and theory.* Peabody, MA: Hendrickson.

Gurman, A. S., & Kniskern, D. P. (Eds.) (1981). *Handbook of family therapy.* New York: Brunner/Mazel.

Hammar, R. R. (1983). *The pastor, church, and law.* Springfield, MO: Gospel Publishing House.

Herbert, W. L., & Jarvis, F. V. (1959). *The art of marriage counseling.* New York: Emerson Books.

L'Abate, L. (1983). Prevention as a profession. In D. R. Mace (Ed.). *Prevention in family services.* Beverly Hills: Sage Publications.

L'Abate, L., & McHenry, S. (Eds.). (1983). *Handbook of marital interventions.* New York: Grune & Stratton.

Leslie, G. R. (1976). Should the partners be seen together or separately? In R. H. Klemer (Ed.), *Counseling marital and sexual problems* (pp. 60-68). New York: Robert E. Krieger.

_____. (1964). The field of marriage counseling. In H.T. Christensen (Ed.) *Handbook of marriage and the family* (pp. 912-943). Chicago: Rand McNally.

Meier, P. D., Minirth, F. B., & Wichern, F. B. (1982). *Introduction to psychology and counseling: Christian perspectives and applications.* Grand Rapids: Zondervan.

Miller, W. R., & Jackson, K. A. (1985). *Practical psychology for pastors.* Englewood Cliffs, NJ: Prentice-Hall.

Naisbitt, J. (1982). *Megatrends: Ten new directions transforming our lives.* New York: Warner Books.

Parker, W. R., & St. Johns, E. (1957). *Prayer can change your life.* Englewood Cliffs, NJ: Prentice-Hall.

Ridgewood Financial Institute. (1984). Fee and practice 1984 survey report. *Psychotherapy finances.* Vol. 2, No. 8 (August). Ridgewood, NJ: P.O. Box 509.

Spitzer, R. L. (Chairperson). (1980). *Diagnostic and statistical manual of mental disorders* (3rd edition). Washington, D.C.: American Psychiatric Association.

Stahman, R. F. (1984). Treatment forms for marital and sex counseling. In R. F. Stahman, & W. J. Hiebert (Eds.), *Counseling in marital and sexual problems: A clinician's handbook* (3rd edition). Lexington, MA: Lexington Books.

Stinchcombe, A. L. (1965). Social structure and organizations. In J. G. March (Ed.), *Handbook of organizations.* Chicago: Rand McNally.

Stinnett, N., & Walters, J. (1977). *Relations in marriage and family.* New York: Macmillan.

Szasz, T. S. (1970). *Ideology and insanity: Essays on the psychiatric dehumanization.* New York: Anchor Books.

Thio, A. (1986). *Sociology.* New York: Harper & Row.

Van Hoose, W. H., & Kottler, J. A. (1985). *Ethical and legal issues in counseling and psychotherapy* (2nd edition). San Francisco: Jossey-Bass.

Wright, H. N. (1981). *Marital counseling: A biblically based, behavioral, cognitive approach.* Denver: Christian Marriage Enrichment.

4

MARRIAGE ENRICHMENT

John C. Katter

DEFINITIONS

This chapter focuses on the relationship between husband and wife, the marital dyad, which is the primary axis of all family relationships. Marriage enrichment should lead to family enrichment. Our concern here is to focus upon the philosophy and methods of enriching the heterosexual marriage relationship.

Marriage enrichment is a concept which is pregnant with optimism. The word *enrichment* speaks of improvement, development, or growth in a positive, healthy direction. Applied to marriage, it means that the relationship between husband and wife can flourish; their individual lives and their relationship together can become richer and more satisfying.

Thus, marriage enrichment is an experience of growing, rather than stagnating, and its purpose is to make marriage good and better—not simply permanent. There are no perfect marriages because there are no perfect people. Enrichment assumes the belief that all couples have room to improve their marital relationship throughout their entire lives.

Underlying the relationship of marriage is the foundational concept of *commitment*. In fact, if I could choose only one word to say about marriage, it would be commitment—to God and to each other. From a biblical perspective, the pledge of spouses to each other is to be fulfilled as long as both parties live. Marriage is a covenant relationship. It is sacred and special. Christ's relationship to the church is the model for the marriage relationship (Eph. 5:21–33). Just as Christ is committed to the church, husbands and wives are to be committed to each other and ought to manifest that commitment by loving, submitting to, communicating with, and caring for one another. Husbands are to love their wives *as Christ loved the church* and wives are to be subject to their husbands *as the church is subject to Christ*. The stresses of life and the pressures of our secular culture do not lessen the need for living out the commitment of marriage in such a way that growth will result.

HISTORICAL DEVELOPMENT AND PROGRAMS OVERVIEW

The roots of the process and dynamics of marriage enrichment may well stem from our earliest ancestors, Adam and Eve. No doubt, throughout human history many married couples have experienced in some sense what we now call marriage enrichment. They learned to improve marital communication, resolve conflicts, express feelings, forgive each other, and adjust to various changes and circumstances in their lives. For example, Sarah took the initiative to talk with Abraham and a conflict was resolved (Gen. 21:9–14). Also, the Mosaic law allowed a man who took a wife to be excused from military and civic duty for one year to give happiness to his wife (Deut. 24:5). This may be viewed as an early means of marriage enrichment.

Influencing Factors

The use of the term *marriage enrichment,* however, is of recent origin. The enrichment movement in the United States began in 1961; various individuals and groups began developing marriage enrichment programs to stimulate and to improve married life in our contemporary society. Some of the factors which led to this development include the following: (a) a rising divorce rate (even among Christians); (b) the reluctance of married persons to seek counseling prior to a time of crisis when their marriage was actually threatened; (c) the women's liberation movement with its emphasis upon assertiveness and equality of the sexes; and (d) the human potentialities movement which has promoted group experiences and the fulfillment of the individual (whether single or married) (Hof & Miller, 1981, p. 4; Otto, 1976, pp. 14–15).

It is commonly recognized that many couples receive little or no formal training in preparation for marriage (Wright, 1977). They do not learn those communication skills necessary to deal with the realities of married life, except by informal observation of their parents' communication style. The myth that "love will see us through and solve all our problems" explodes, and the false conclusion is sometimes drawn, "I guess I married the wrong person." The problem is that they have not learned how to *be*—not find—the right person. Marriage enrichment, then, is purposed to start where people are and improve their *being* and *becoming* as spouses.

Early Pioneers

It is noteworthy that the early movement of marriage enrichment endeavors involved couples as its leaders. Herbert and Roberta Otto began conducting programs of marriage and family enrichment in 1961. Their work developed into the *More Joy in Your Marriage* program, which is typically presented in a two-day (Saturday and Sunday) schedule with a variety of activities planned (Otto, 1976).

Also in 1961, David and Vera Mace began their work in marriage enrichment among the Quakers. In 1973 they founded the Association of Couples for Marriage

Enrichment (ACME) as a national organization for married couples (Mace & Mace, 1974). Member couples commit themselves to specified objectives, involve themselves in ongoing efforts to better their marriages, pay dues, and receive mailings and newsletters. Couples of any religion, race, age, class, or vocation are welcome candidates for ACME membership. ACME has grown to the point where it now has members in all 50 states and in a number of foreign countries (Hof & Miller, 1981).

Leon and Antoinette Smith developed the Marriage Communication Lab in the mid 1960s. They conducted their first leadership training program for couples in 1966. Their "typical" training program, sponsored by the United Methodist Church, requires full participation in activities beginning with a noon meal on Monday and concluding with the noon meal on Friday. Prerequisites for becoming a leader couple are more specific than for most other enrichment programs; "one of the partners must be a professional in the helping field" (Otto, 1976, p. 243). Couples completing this intensive week of training are then prepared to lead the Marriage Communication Lab Enrichment experiences.

The Marriage Encounter movement began in Spain in 1962 under Father Gabriel Calvo and first appeared in the United States in 1967 (Hof & Miller, 1981). Originally this was a Roman Catholic phenomenon, but a number of Protestant and Jewish groups—have since been organized. This program involves presentations by leader couples, individual writing, and private, couple dialogue. It is conducted over a weekend from Friday evening through early Sunday evening.

Continued Development

During the 1970s a dramatic proliferation of locally developed enrichment programs emerged. Concerned individuals—some qualified and many unqualified—sensed the need for marriage enrichment and developed their own programs to meet this need. Some programs became nationally known. For example, H. Norman Wright developed the Christian Marriage Enrichment Seminar program in 1974. This two-day seminar is designed to train pastors and their wives and selected lay couples. It deals with communication, marriage goals, roles and responsibilities, decision making, and conflict resolution.

Larry Hof and William Miller (1981) originated and refined the Creative Marriage Enrichment Program. This model has been used with nonclinical and clinical couples at the Marriage Council of Philadelphia and in church and community settings elsewhere. Various experiential exercises are included in this program with the primary focus on *inclusion, control,* and *affection* needs. Inclusion means being and experiencing oneself as a unique, important, and significant person. Control involves being competent and able to cope in interpersonal relationships with respect to power, authority, submissiveness, etc. Affection connotes intimacy, love, and emotional closeness.

The national YMCA promotes the Positive Partners program for ordinary couples. It originally was developed by a YMCA staff member in Los Angeles in the early 1970s. This widely available marriage enrichment opportunity is inexpensive and was designed to be led by nonprofessionals who have some training and who feel good about their own marriage (Otto, 1976).

Some locally developed programs grew out of academic settings. Sherod Miller, Elam Nunnally, and Daniel Wackman developed the Minnesota Couples Communication Program (MCCP) based on their doctoral studies in the late 1960s. This program, now called the Couples Communication Program (Hof & Miller, 1981), focuses on developing communication skills and sensitivity to couple processes. Groups of five to seven couples meet for twelve hours—usually three hours a session for four weeks—with one or two certified instructors.

Bernard Guerney (1977) developed the Relationship Enhancement program using elements of Rogerian psychotherapy (e.g., expression and acceptance of feelings—both positive and negative), behavior modification (operant learning theory), and social learning theory (e.g., conflict management can be taught to married couples). This is a highly structured, systematic, educationally oriented, short-term program. It may be used with one couple or a group of couples, and may be scheduled for a weekend or series of weekly one-hour sessions. The leader of the Relationship Enhancement program is not encouraged to disclose his or her personal feelings, experiences, or moods. This is in contrast to other leadership styles, such as Marriage Encounter and ACME leader couples; the latter are required to be vulnerable and share personal feelings and experiences.

I began teaching classes in marriage enrichment in 1978. The classes grew out of the project for my doctoral dissertation (Katter, 1978). In these classes I emphasize that communication based on commitment is the key to marital growth and conflict resolution. I deal with topics such as roles, identity, building esteem for oneself and one's spouse, relating to parents and in-laws, couple devotions, financial matters, sexual intimacy, and planning for the future. Small group discussions and couple communication are interspersed with class lecture and large group activities. For a number of years I have also conducted weekend marriage enrichment seminars in churches and retreat settings, focusing on these and other issues in a structure and orientation suitable for the particular group or church.

Summary

Many individuals and married couples have developed and conducted various programs in marriage enrichment; I cannot name or discuss them all in this chapter. Perhaps the most commonly known organizations in the field include Marriage Encounter, the Association of Couples for Marriage Enrichment (ACME), the Couple Communication program, the Marriage Communication Labs, the Christian Marriage Enrichment, and the Relationship Enhancement program.

According to Hof and Miller (1981), "Marriage enrichment programs are not limited to the United States, but this country does appear to be the leader in the field at present" (p. 6). Programs in marriage enrichment have proliferated in recent years, and it seems reasonable to expect that this trend will continue.

THE NEED FOR MARRIAGE ENRICHMENT

A cartoon in the introduction to Wright's (1974) book, *Communication: Key*

To Your Marriage, depicts a woman seated in a marriage counselor's office saying, "When I got married I was looking for an Ideal—then it became an Ordeal and now I want a New Deal." For many couples, the American dream of marriage has become a nightmare. Often, this is a result of unrealistic expectations, unbiblical considerations, and depersonalization.

Unrealistic Expectations

First, let us look at some unrealistic expectations. Many people are blinded when they get married. They are like the girl who grew up next door to me. When she was about to be married, she said she had found "Mr. Perfect." She could find no fault in him whatsoever. Some erroneously believe that they have found the perfect mate, and they will have no problems. However, marriage always involves a clash between an unreal image of the other person—or of the marriage relationship in general—and the actual person—or marriage. Adjustments must be made to differences and problems that come along. Some look for a utopia (a word meaning literally, "no place") in marriage. They expect something magical to happen. But good marriages must be built by two people working together step by step. Unrealistic expectations are exemplified in the following statements: (a) "he will never be attracted to another woman"; (b) "she will always want to meet my every need"; or (c) "we know that *we* won't have any major problems."

Unbiblical Considerations

Second, unbiblical considerations abound in our secular culture. Some of these are listed here: (a) "If it doesn't work, get a divorce"; (b) "Sex is the basic substance of love"; (c) "I'm going to please myself" (Romans 15:3 says, "even Christ pleased not himself"); (d) "It's wrong to share negative feelings with your spouse"; (e) "A Christian should never get angry" (Jesus did!); (f) "I have the right to demand a certain material standard of living"; and (g) "Everything I want I really *need.*" All of these statements above can be refuted with Scripture.

Depersonalization

Third, unfulfilling depersonalizations can negatively affect the marriage relationship. Gangel (1972, pp. 13–21) discussed ten of the more pressing problems faced in Christian family living: organization, industrialization, high mobility, divorce and separation, substitute parents and fatherless children, low moral standards, pressured schedules, secularization and materialism, strained family relations, and sociological detraction (i.e., other social groups fulfill roles and responsibilities formerly carried out by the family). These and other factors can depersonalize an individual's view of self and/or spouse. The marriage relationship can suffer as wives feel unfulfilled and husbands feel demasculinized. For many, watching television (even together) reduces communication between husband and wife and promotes living in fantasy worlds. There is a real need for spouses to talk and to listen to each other, reveal themselves, and understand the other in order to avoid those depersonalizing influences that are so common in our culture.

Crises of the Family Life-cycle

Although most couples report that the first year of their marriage was very happy, there is usually a gradual decline in happiness to the late thirties and then an upward trend again. Often there are waves of reported higher and lower happiness throughout the life-cycle. Every marriage relationship has its transitions, changes, crises, turning points, or passages. Some of these are predictable; others are not. Evelyn Duvall (Duvall & Miller, 1985, p. 26) developed an eight-stage family life cycle in reference to normal family functioning with the following designations and descriptive qualities: (1) married couples (without children); (2) childbearing families (oldest child birth–30 months); (3) families with preschool children (oldest child 2½–6 years; (4) families with school children (oldest child 6–13 years; (5) families with teenagers (oldest child 13–20 years); (6) families launching young adults (first child gone to last child leaving home); (7) middle-aged parents (empty nest to retirement); and aging family members (retirement to death of both spouses). Howard and Charlotte Clinebell (1970) stated,

> Each stage in the marital cycle has its unique demands, frustrations, worries, joys, and satisfactions. At every stage, the demands on each partner are different. The pattern of needs changes from stage to stage, altering the nature and intensity of the will to relate. . . . The periods of transition from one stage to another can be occasions of pressure and crisis as the couple struggles to let go of the familiar, comfortable past and master the demands of a new stage. Old methods of gaining need-satisfaction, and of relating, no longer work as they have in the past. Such periods of transition can be opportunities for discovering new ways of relating, new joys and satisfaction which can give new depth and height to intimacy. (pp. 103–104)

Thus the concept of family life-cycle is helpful for marriage enrichment. It is important for couples to know how typical families change over the course of time. There are variations to be sure. For example, some couples never bear or rear children. Others have children in sets of two's that are 10 to 12 years apart. Wherever there is more than one child, the stages of the family life-cycle overlap and are somewhat repeated. Obviously, what is going on in the family at a particular time affects the marriage relationship, and marriage enrichment can occur at any stage. In fact, those of us who have conducted marriage enrichment seminars/classes have received many reports of marriage enrichment occurring in every stage of the family life-cycle.

ASSUMPTIONS OF MARRIAGE ENRICHMENT

I have previously outlined five important assumptions which underlie marriage enrichment (Katter, 1978, p. 27):

1. Almost any marriage can be improved. There is untapped potential.
2. Communication, within the context of commitment, is the key to problem solution and growth in marriage.

3. Every couple is unique. No two marriages are exactly alike.
4. God wants people to have growing, healthy marriages.
5. Knowledge, understanding, and action properly directed can lead to the prevention of marriage problems.

Prevention

Preventive ministry to couples in the form of marriage enrichment is at least as important as counseling couples in times of crisis. Marriage enrichment attempts to correct communication patterns in order to avoid deterioration and the eventual dissolution of marriages. There are a number of couples who are functioning adequately now who will drift apart as the years pass unless they realize the need for continued growth and communication. "Building sound, healthy, growing marriages does not occur by accident. This takes insight and effort. The old adage is still true, 'An ounce of prevention is worth a pound of cure' " (Katter, 1978, p. 9). Preventing problems from developing in a marriage is like using a weed killer on the lawn. It is designed to keep weeds from growing by killing them when they are small.

Growth

The need for marriage enrichment goes further than the *prevention* of problems. *Growth* potential exists in each person and in every marriage. As stated earlier in this chapter, there are no perfect marriages because there are no perfect people. Yet both individuals *and* marriage relationships can grow. The alternative is stagnation which leads to deterioration. According to David and Vera Mace (1974),

> Studies have shown that the average American marriage, as perceived by husbands and wives, grows progressively less satisfactory as the years pass. A marriage that is allowed to drift, therefore, is more likely to drift downward than upward. (p. 107)

One book of the Bible, the Song of Solomon, devotes a great deal of attention to the marriage relationship. It is very descriptive and picturesque. Chapter 2, verse 15, states "Take us the foxes, the little foxes, that spoil the vines: for our vineyards are in blossom." This indicates that the presence of negative and destructive forces in a marriage relationship must be recognized and properly dealt with before they ruin the relationship or limit its fruitfulness. Thus there is a need for marriage enrichment.

THE NATURE OF MARRIAGE ENRICHMENT

There is a great deal of variety in the procedures used in marriage enrichment programs, but the nature of enrichment includes several things which virtually all proponents emphasize. It is like fertilization; desirable nutrients are added to the soil of marriages which have either been depleted or were never present. One important "nutrient" is effective communication.

Often, good communication behaviors and effective ways of relating can be increased in frequency or intensified in quality to create greater marital satisfaction. For example, a couple may have quality conversations at times and discuss some issues at a deep level, yet such times may occur infrequently. This is like a one ounce, juicy, top quality steak—delicious, but you want more of it! Both quality and sufficient quantity are necessary. Planning for regular, continuing marital communication is part of marriage enrichment. This involves listening as well as talking. Sharing of feelings as well as ideas, thoughts, hopes, dreams, hurts, memories, goals and life's experiences is an ongoing *privilege,* while listening to one another is a *responsibility.* It is part of the nature of marriage enrichment to encourage couples to listen more carefully to each other. Marriage enrichment also enables persons to share more tactfully or speak the truth in love (Eph. 4:15, 25). A commonly accepted principle of communication is that *how* something is said, including important nonverbal messages, may be more crucial than *what* is said (Mehrabian, 1971). Improving marital communication, both verbal and nonverbal, is part of the nature of marriage enrichment.

ACKNOWLEDGING AND DEVELOPING ASSETS

Recognizing and developing personal and couple strengths is another ingredient in enrichment. Affirming the good qualities of one's self and one's spouse is helpful. Every couple has strengths which can be built upon to increase its confidence and courage in overcoming crises and weaknesses. Weaknesses are like the Slough of Despair in John Bunyan's *Pilgrim's Progress;* concentrating upon them and dwelling within them causes a person to sink deeper into the quagmire.

Bridges of compensation can be built over weak areas when the pillars are grounded firmly in the strengths of the marriage (Wright, 1979). Every marriage has weak spots, but couples can build upon their strengths to grow beyond them. For example, a strength such as a good sense of humor can do much to alleviate the tension of a weakness like indecision when it comes to buying clothing or having the dishwasher repaired.

Building Esteem

Marriage enrichment encourages the building of self- and spouse esteem. Many people struggle to feel a sense of self-worth. They have anxieties and neurotic complexes which need to be worked through. Finding a realistic picture of one's self in Christ and learning to accept and love one's self appropriately is a prerequisite to loving one's spouse and building his or her esteem.

Marriage enrichment does not provide individual psychotherapy; rather, it teaches couples who have normal, healthy marriages to recognize and stop behaviors which hinder the development of self-esteem, and it calls for actions which build self- and spouse esteem. In our culture, two words which destroy self-esteem are "dumb" and "ugly." They should never be used in reference to a spouse (or a child). On the positive side, "smart" and "beautiful" enhance self-esteem. Marriage enrichment promotes "catching" people doing or being good and complimenting them for it. Praise for good qualities and even for completing routine tasks builds self-esteem.

Conflict Management and Resolution

Communication which aims at conflict resolution is advocated by many proponents of marriage enrichment (e.g., Mace & Mace, 1974; Wright, 1977a; Carter, 1983). A given program may examine several styles of handling conflict; individuals identify which styles they use in dealing with conflict in their marriage relationships. Practice sessions then give couples the opportunity to try alternate methods of resolving their disagreements. The presence of other couples doing the same thing gives them support, even though couple conversations are generally private. Opportunity may be given for some couples to share with others how they worked through a problem in the past or in the present session. In this way, couples can learn much from each other; they may learn more from their peers than from a seminar leader (or leader couple) by seeing the principles of conflict management and resolution in practice.

Forgiveness

Forgiveness needs to be stressed in marriage enrichment too. When wrongs have been done, confession and appeal for forgiveness are in order. Here, differences between secular and religious programs are evident. Secular enrichment programs often avoid or say very little about the subject of forgiveness. Wrongdoing is socially defined, and apologizing for making a mistake is in order only if one gets caught. Church enrichment programs acknowledge the reality of sin and the violation of the personal relationship with God and the other person involved when wrongdoing occurs. Forgiveness is not cheap; it is costly. Hof and Miller (1981) deal with what they call the "experience of forgiveness" and provide handouts for couples in their Creative Marriage Enrichment Program. They actually have three different formats: nonreligious focus; religious focus; and Christian focus (pp. 151–157).

Wright (1979) in his book *The Pillars of Marriage* devotes the last chapter to "Learning to Forgive Completely." He stresses the fact that a person who is "in Christ" and forgiven by God has the capacity to forgive others. Forgiveness is biblical and is necessary for personal and couple growth. Identifying specific personal offenses and asking one's spouse for forgiveness can be done verbally or in writing. This requires openness and vulnerability. Such communication should be meaningful, not mechanical; *it is the heart to heart talk.* Recognition of the seriousness of sin in producing distance and disruption of fellowship in personal relationships accompanies a repentant spirit. Sometimes this process includes the shedding of tears. Often, both persons can find something for which they need the other's forgiveness. And both are encouraged to *forgive genuinely* their spouse. This means not holding the offense committed by the other person any longer.

Such forgiveness may be very hard for some to give. Extreme cases may need to be dealt with by qualified counselors. However, many normal people can be helped by marriage enrichment and come to learn how they can forgive their spouse completely. The lack of forgiveness may be a more serious problem than the original offense. Genuine forgiveness is truly a healing process.

Balancing Individual-Couple Tensions

Marriage enrichment promotes the growth of both the individuals and the marriage. Most programs place the emphasis upon the marital entity. Some focus more on the individual person at first to provide a basis for the enhancement of the marital relationship (Hof & Miller, 1981). Many strive to achieve a balance, fostering the continued growth of both the marriage relationship and the persons in it. In my judgment, this combined emphasis is the best. However, in contrast to our individualistic-oriented culture, a commitment to enriching the marriage relationship takes precedence in marriage enrichment.

Marriage enrichment encourages mutually desirable fulfillment in the spiritual, social, and sexual aspects of marriage. This involves accepting and dealing with changes and common adjustments that accompany the stages of marriage (Clinebell & Clinebell, 1970; Singer & Stern, 1980; Wright, 1982). Both individual and couple interests change over time. New roles and responsibilities are assumed, and role reversals sometimes occur. Life is dynamic not static, and it brings new opportunities, failures, and successes.

MacDonald (1976) stated, "Marital success begins with *commitment,* is sustained by *discipline,* and is evaluated by its productivity *in making human beings something better than what they were when they entered into the relationship*" (p. xviii). Smalley and Scott (1982) added,

> that there are some wives so content in their personal relationships with God, their husbands, and their families that they are able to live happily in circumstances as they are with the philosophy, "What you've got is not nearly as important as who you've got" (p. 149).

With this kind of attitude, spouses endeavor to be sensitive to and understanding of each other as needs arise and are expressed. They sincerely try to meet one another's needs.

Couple devotions can be developed to add enriching spiritual vitality to the marriage (Katter, 1978). In recent years, I have placed more emphasis upon this subject in my own enrichment programs, and couples say it has been helpful. Regular Bible reading and prayer together are growth-producing. Times of praise and petition for the needs and concerns of others will draw the couple closer to each other and to God. Listening to worshipful music and singing together are also enjoyable.

Sexually, couples can experience growth, mutual understanding, and fulfillment of one another's needs in biblical and personally satisfying ways. The book, *Intended for Pleasure,* by Ed and Gaye Wheat (1977) is excellent in its treatment of enriching the sexual relationship in marriage. Clifford and Joyce Penner's teaching guide, *Sexual Fulfillment in Marriage* (1977), and other helpful resources can be used to promote a better sexual relationship. Since this is a sensitive area, some marriage enrichment programs do not deal directly with the sexual dimension of married life. Other programs do focus on sexuality to some degree, and couples have reported that their sexual relationship has improved as a result (Hof & Miller, 1981).

Many marriage enrichment programs also give couples opportunities to discuss other topics such as finances, roles and relationships, and relations with parents and in-laws. Mini-lectures, role playing, case studies, small group discussions with three or four couples in a group, and couple communication may be utilized to assist couples in making common adjustments to the real life situations they face now or may face in the future.

Positive, Reality-Oriented Emphasis

The nature of marriage enrichment is largely positive. It may include expressions of problems or complaints, but emphasis is placed on turning a *problem* into a *project*. Making positive use of the negative is stressed. Alternate ways of responding to one another are considered. Brainstorming without initially rejecting any ideas is promoted. Finding solutions to problems is seen as a process which may be somewhat painful but is well worth the effort.

Life is viewed holistically. An improvement in one area will affect other areas of the marriage relationship. In Christian marriage enrichment, a biblical, balanced lifestyle is encouraged. Attention must be given to the spiritual, mental, social, and physical dimensions of married life.

A reality orientation is essential to marriage enrichment. There is only so much that can be done to improve beauty, brains, or bank accounts. Being realistic means accepting one's spouse and one's self with limitations as well as with capacities for growth and change. We can learn to accept the weak and frustrating characteristics, along with the strong and fulfilling ones, in ourselves and our spouses. We can learn to grow and improve in our marriage relationships without unrealistic expectations of perfection.

RESEARCH ON MARRIAGE ENRICHMENT

Several years ago Mace (1975) identified the following nine areas of research on marriage enrichment: (1) obstacles to participation; (2) couple group process; (3) retreat patterns; (4) leadership patterns; (5) effectiveness of procedures; (6) marital growth and potential; (7) therapeutic interaction between couples; (8) the love-anger cycle; and (9) the preventive approach. Although Mace, an early pioneer in marriage enrichment, called for such research, neither he nor others have adequately researched all these areas. Most published research on enrichment has appeared in professional journals within the past ten years; it is clearly a new and undeveloped research area.

Mace (1975) stated, "Our experience of twelve years in marriage enrichment convinces us that couples can be highly therapeutic to each other, a fact hitherto obscured by the intermarital taboo" (p. 172). In this context, he recognized four facilitating mechanisms:

> *reassurance* when couples are able to share openly with each other; *cross-identification,*

> when two couples find that they are or have been involved in closely similar adjustment processes; *modeling,* when a couple struggling with some difficulty sees another who has resolved the difficulty; *support,* as couples develop lasting friendships arising out of shared marriage enrichment experiences. (Mace, p. 172, emphasis is the author's)

These mechanisms seem to be at work in marriage enrichment programs. Actual research on them, however, has been slow in coming.

GENERAL RESEARCH CONSIDERATIONS

Hof and Miller (1981), while emphasizing the infancy of research on marital enrichment programs, summarized data from forty different studies of various types of marriage enrichment experiences. They proposed that

> The most basic question to be addressed by outcome research is whether the intervention procedure is followed by specific affective, attitudinal, cognitive, or behavioral changes. . . . most of the outcome studies reviewed do report positive changes on at least some measures following a marital enrichment experience. Furthermore, significant changes are not restricted to any particular type or class of variables. (p. 57)

Hof and Miller (1981) also discussed some of the attitudinal and methodological problems involved, such as the negative view of research among many in the field of marriage enrichment and the difficulty in selecting appropriate measures of change which can demonstrate growth in a quantitative fashion. "Subjective responses are not sufficient for the *scientific* demonstration of the effectiveness of marriage enrichment programs. Good science requires that the outcome of a marriage enrichment experience be publicly verifiable and replicable, and therefore, measurable" (p. 53). They also dealt with randomization, control groups, and specific measurement considerations. They expressed cautious optimism concerning recent research in marriage enrichment and stressed the need for additional, more objective research.

Research of Marriage Encounter

One form of marriage enrichment, Marriage Encounter, has been examined by a number of researchers. Research of Marriage Encounter is important because it is the largest marriage enrichment movement in the world (Doherty & Walker, 1982). More than two million couples have experienced one of these weekend programs. Research reports to date indicate that most participants' responses to Marriage Encounter weekend are positive. Milholland and Avery (1982) note significant short-term increases in marital satisfaction and levels of trust, but not in self-disclosure. Marital self-disclosure scores were already quite high at pretest; it would be difficult to increase such scores to demonstrate a significant increase. Also, the scale used (Jourard Self-Disclosure Scale) "may not be sensitive to changes in self-disclosure as taught in Marriage Encounter experience" (Milholland & Avery, 1982, p. 88).

Lester and Doherty (1983) studied 129 couples in eastern Iowa who had experienced a Marriage Encounter weekend between 1970 and 1980. The couples averaged four years since their Marriage Encounter weekend. The authors found that 84% of the husbands and 75% of the wives felt that Marriage Encounter had a positive impact on their marriage relationship. "However, almost one in ten couples in our sample may be classified as negatively affected by the program, based on three or more reported problems associated with participation in Marriage Encounter" (p. 187). The dialogue technique was the most frequently mentioned positive aspect. The chief negative factor was that needs were identified but not later fulfilled.

James Stedman (1982), in his article entitled, "Marriage Encounter: An 'Insider' Consideration of Recent Critiques," observed:

> No critique of the Marriage Encounter experience can ignore the theological dimension, and it appears to me that behavior science professionals interested in the weekend need a rather clear understanding that a theology of marriage is central to all Marriage Encounter expressions. It also seems to me that professionals need to know something of the nature of that theology. (p. 124)

Outcomes for Communication-Based Programs

Joanning (1982) summarized a study of seventeen couples who had completed the Couple Communication Program:

> Couples increased significantly on all measures at immediate posttest. Marital adjustment returned to pretest levels by five month follow-up. Couple perceived communication quality and rater judged communication quality maintained posttest levels. The findings suggest a need for more skills training in the program, an increase in length of the program, and consideration of program improvements designed to enhance generalization. (p. 463)

Joanning also mentioned that "sixteen [of the seventeen] couples reported feeling much closer during and immediately following training" (p. 466).

Similar results were reported in my dissertation study (Katter, 1978). Fourteen of fifteen student couples indicated that participation in a seven-week marriage enrichment seminar improved communications in their marriage relationship. Bienvenu's *Marital Communication Inventory* (MCI) was used as a pretest and posttest measure of change. The results were statistically highly significant, indicating there was a positive change in the quality of couple communication from pretest to posttest.

Brock and Joanning (1983) conducted a comparative effectiveness study of the Relationship Enhancement Program (RE) and the Minnesota Couple Communication Program (CC). This study involved 26 couples in the RE group, 20 couples in the CC group, and 8 couples in a control group. Four testing times were utilized: pretest, midtest, posttest, and follow-up test. Three measuring devices were used at all four testing times: The Marital Communication Inventory (Bienvenu, 1970), the Dyadic Adjustment Scale (Spanier, 1976) and the Communication Rapid Assessment Scale (Joanning, Koval & Brewster, 1982).

They reported that "Results at posttesting showed that RE was more effective in increasing marital communication (both behavioral and self-report) and marital satisfaction than CC. A three-month follow-up showed that RE couples' outcome remained superior to CC couples'. Additional analyses revealed that couples' experiencing low marital satisfaction prior to training were best helped by the RE program'' (p. 413)

Various factors that might explain the different outcomes of RE and CC training are given in the study. One factor is that the population involved was not a true marital enrichment population. A number of couples had below normal scores in marital satisfaction on the pretest. Such couples may have been more suited to treatment by RE than by CC. Guerney (1977) stated that RE can be used as a therapy strategy for couples who have low marital satisfaction. This would be an advantage over CC training which is for couples who have marital satisfaction ''at and above the population norm'' (Brock & Joanning, 1983, p. 420). A second factor, then, is that RE is effective for more than enriching normal, healthy marriages, whereas CC is designed only for the couples who have normal marital satisfaction prior to treatment. A third factor mentioned in the study is that the CC leader role is more complex and demands more experience than the RE leader role. Further research is called for as to leadership training for effectiveness in conducting such programs.

Cautions

Stedman (1982) cautioned against sending couples to Marriage Encounter indiscriminately. If they are in the early stage of marital therapy, the weekend may result in either a very negative experience or an intensely positive but short-lived experience. In either case, they may leave therapy.

It is important to note that marriage enrichment is not for every couple at any time. Hof and Miller (1983) concluded that, ''Many couples and individuals simply cannot benefit from marriage enrichment experiences, or benefit from them as much as from conjoint or individual therapy'' (p. 557). This cautious view is clearly supported by many researchers (e.g., Doherty & Walker, 1982).

Apparently, more objective scientific research is necessary to examine both positive and negative results of various marriage enrichment programs on couples. We should not simply rely on mean scores of pre- and posttests. Alternate treatment groups and control groups (without treatment) should be utilized. The use of existing tools and the development of new ones for research and evaluation is essential, despite the noted difficulties associated with conducting marriage enrichment research (Hof & Miller, 1983).

Summary

Obviously, more research on marriage enrichment is needed. What programs are most effective and with whom? How does a weekend experience compare with a series of weekly sessions? What definitions can be given to terms such as ''marital growth,'' ''increased ability to resolve marital conflicts,'' and ''improved functioning in building spouse esteem''? How can such variables be measured more objectively? Studies are also needed to compare the effectiveness of various patterns of program leadership—individual, married couple, or man and woman co-leaders. These are a few among many concerns for further research.

Most of the research which has been done in this area is highly subjective or flawed in basic research design. Thankfully, marriage enrichment experiences, as reported by most participants, are much more positive than negative.

THE HOLY SPIRIT AND MARRIAGE ENRICHMENT

In reviewing the literature to date, I found a strange silence with regard to any specific mention of the work of the Holy Spirit in connection with marriage enrichment. However, some Christian writers do speak of the Holy Spirit at work in the marriage relationship and in the home. For example, Louis and Colleen Evans (1976) believe that "the Holy Spirit gives to each spouse some gift or gifts of the Spirit for the common good, that is, for the functioning of the home, both for its own sake and for the sake of the world" (p. 34). Later, they stated that

> One of the first steps in putting gifts of the Spirit to work in a marriage is to *believe* in such a thesis and to enter into the process of becoming aware, sensitive, and on the lookout for indications of your own and others' gifts. (p. 38)

Marriage enrichment in a biblical and Christian perspective requires an integration with the Holy Spirit. I firmly believe that the Holy Spirit can be vitally involved in marriage enrichment. Several years ago an unmarried couple who had two children attended a marriage enrichment seminar I was conducting in New York. Halfway through the weekend they came to me and said that they felt they should get married. The Holy Spirit had dealt with them during the seminar, and they were moved to make a personal response in a biblical way.

The Activities of the Spirit

Some of the basic functions of the Holy Spirit's ministry referred to in the Gospel of John include teaching (14:26), guiding into truth (16:13), glorifying Christ (16:14), and reproving of sin, righteousness, and judgment (16:8). These activities can have practical implications for marriage enrichment. The Spirit may well be involved in inspiring, anointing, and directing the conversation of the marriage enrichment leader(s), the small group discussions, and the couple communication. Sometimes the Spirit may work through peer couples in stimulating an attitude of hope and confidence. One person put it this way, "I know now we can work through whatever problems come our way in life." During times of constructive criticism, the Holy Spirit may actually be at work reproving a husband or wife and aiding him or her to receive kind corrections and suggestions for improvement.

The Holy Spirit guides into truth by sharpening memories of past experiences and by opening channels of change. Fresh applications of biblical truth brighten the marital pilgrimage. In response to one of the marriage enrichment seminars that my wife and I conducted one woman said, "My husband and I are doing new and neat things together that we've not done before and it's great!" The Holy Spirit is at work glorifying Christ as spouses edify one another, forgive one another, communicate openly and deeply with each other, resolve conflicts together, discuss the Scriptures and pray together, and plan for the future together.

In response to a couple communication exercise, an emotional husband said to his wife, "I remember what you did that I thought I couldn't forgive you for, but now the deep hurt is gone—I've forgiven you!" The Holy Spirit helps heal the hurts and the heartaches, and gives hope for tomorrow.

Fruit of the Spirit

It is my conviction that one of the key functions of the Holy Spirit is to produce growth in the lives of believers that will be evident in their interpersonal relationships. In Galatians 5:22–25, Paul says:

> But the fruit of the Spirit is love, joy, peace, long-suffering, gentleness, goodness, faith, meekness, temperance: against such there is no law. And they that are Christ's have crucified the flesh with the affections and lusts. If we live in the Spirit, let us also walk in the Spirit.

The qualities of the fruit of the Spirit do not originate in the husband or wife. The source is God. In Christian marriage enrichment, the Holy Spirit helps couples grow in biblical and mutually fulfilling ways. The Spirit is incarnationally at work in believers to manifest *his* love, *his* joy, *his* peace, etc. in and through husbands and wives. At the same time, he can be "lived in" and "walked in" as believers are continually "filled with the Spirit," as Paul admonished in Ephesians 5:18. Such a relationship in and with the Holy Spirit greatly enriches the marriage relationship! This is only possible when the flesh is crucified—not coddled—and when persons are filled with the Spirit—not drunk with wine.

Gifts of the Spirit

The gifts of the Spirit (1 Cor. 12 and 14, Rom. 12, Eph. 4) may also operate in ways which enrich marriage relationships. A word of wisdom or discernment may be given by the Holy Spirit to a husband or wife to clear up a difficulty they face together. The leader of a marriage enrichment seminar may be directed by the Holy Spirit to say something which is actually a word of knowledge— information which is supernaturally imparted, not derived through human effort or ingenuity. The Holy Spirit may give special faith or mercy to a husband or wife and thus enrich a marriage. For example, an unemployed husband remained stable and strong as God imparted faith to him to trust for needed finances and a new job. In these and in many other ways the Holy Spirit works to enrich marriages through the gifts of the Spirit.

Summary

The Holy Spirit is at work in Christian marriage enrichment. We may not always be aware of his presence, but he is with us constantly. I believe we need to heighten the awareness of couples during a marriage enrichment experience, so that they sense the Spirit's presence. He is the best facilitator of effective communication. In his presence there is freedom for us to be ourselves, and there is love that liberates our loved ones. The Holy Spirit promotes acceptance, understanding, listening with empathy, courage to change ourselves, kindness in dealing with the faults of our spouse, and faith in God and in each other. His power is unlimited. Producing and nurturing growth are delightful activities to him. The Holy Spirit as Paraclete stands *alongside* to help us love our spouse as a real person. He also works *within* the lives of believers. I see the Holy Spirit as a very important Person who is intimately involved in the process of Christian marriage enrichment.

SELECT BIBLIOGRAPHY

Bienvenu, M. J. (1970). Measurement of marital communication. *The Family Coordinator, 19,* 26–30.

Brock, G. W., & Joanning, H. J. (1983). A comparison of the Relationship Enhancement Program and the Minnesota Couple Communication Program. *Journal of Marital and Family Therapy, 9,* 413–421.

Carter, W. L. (1983). *The push-pull marriage: Learning and living the art of give-and-take.* Grand Rapids: Baker Book House.

Clinebell, H. J., & Clinebell, C. H. (1970). *The intimate marriage.* New York: Harper & Row.

Doherty, W. J., & Walker, B. J. (1982). Marriage encounter casualties: A preliminary investigation. *American Journal of Family Therapy, 10,* 15–25.

Duvall, E. M., & Miller, B. C. (1985). *Marriage and family development.* New York: Harper & Row.

Evans, L., & Evans, C. (1976). Gifts of the Spirit in marriage. In G. Collins (Ed.), *Make more of your marriage.* Waco: Word.

Gangel, K. O. (1972). *The family first.* Minneapolis: HIS International Service.

Guerney, B. G. Jr. (1977). *Relationship enhancement.* San Francisco: Jossey-Bass.

Hof, L., & Miller, W. R. (1981). *Marriage enrichment.* Bowie, MD: Robert J. Brady.

_____. (1983). Marriage enrichment. In D. H. Olson & B. C. Miller (Eds.) *Family studies review yearbook* (Vol. 1). Beverly Hills: Sage Publications.

Joanning, H. (1982). The long-term effects of the Couple Communication Program. *Journal of Marital and Family Therapy, 8,* 463–468.

Joanning, H., Koval, J., & Brewster, J. (1982). *Development of a rapid measure of assessing dyadic communication.* Lubbock: Texas Tech University, Family Resource Center.

Katter, J. C. (1978). *Ministry to married couples.* Unpublished doctoral dissertation, Midwestern Baptist Theological Seminary, Kansas City, MO.

Lester, M. E., & Doherty, W. J. (1983). Couples' long-term evaluations of their Marriage Encounter experience. *Journal of Marital and Family Therapy, 9,* 183–188.

MacDonald, G. (1976). *Magnificent marriage.* Wheaton: Tyndale.

Mace, D. R. (1975). Marriage enrichment concepts for research. *The Family Coordinator, 24,* 171–173.

Mace, D. R., & Mace, V. (1974). *We can have better marriages if we really want them.* Nashville: Abingdon.

Mehrabian, A. (1971). *Silent messages.* Belmont, CA: Wadsworth Publishing Co.

Milholland, T. A., & Avery, A. W. (1982). Effects of Marriage Encounter on self-disclosure, trust, and marital satisfaction. *Journal of Marital and Family Therapy, 8,* 87–89.

Otto, H. (Ed.). (1976). *Marriage and family enrichment: New perspectives and programs.* Nashville: Abingdon.

Penner, C., & Penner, J. (1977) *Sexual fulfillment in marriage.* Omaha: Family Concern.

Singer, L. J., & Stern, B. L. (1980). *Stages: The crises that shape your marriage.* New York: Gosset & Dunlap.

Smalley, G., & Scott, S. (1982). *For better or for best* (rev. ed.). Grand Rapids: Zondervan.

Spanier, G. B. (1976). Measuring dyadic adjustment: New scales for assessing quality of marriage and similar dyads. *Journal of Marriage and the Family. 38,* 15-28.

Stedman, J. M. (1982). Marriage Encounter: An insider consideration of recent critiques. *Family relations. 31,* 123-128.

Wheat, E., & Wheat, G. (1977). *Intended for pleasure.* Old Tappan, NJ: Revell.

Wright, H. N. (1974). *Communication: Key to your marriage.* Glendale: Regal.

_____. (1977a). *Communication and conflict resolution in marriage.* Elgin, IL: David C. Cook.

_____. (1977b). *Premarital counseling.* Chicago: Moody.

_____. (1979). *The pillars of marriage.* Glendale: Regal.

_____. (1982). *Seasons of a marriage.* Ventura: Regal.

5

FAMILY THERAPY

E. C. Hurley

The accomplishments and failures of humanity have historically and theologically involved more than individuals; they have generally occurred within the context of family organizations. The original fall of humanity was a family affair with both Adam and Eve participating. God promised Abraham that he would bless his seed, thereby blessing a nation through the father of the Jews. Jacob and Esau's struggles for power and blessings were a family phenomenon. Such accounts appear again and again; many biblical events occur within a family context. Family negotiations are as ancient as history itself; therefore, it should not be surprising that the church has a vested interest in ministering to the family. In addressing this subject we will begin with a discussion of the contemporary family therapy movement.

Historical Development

No one individual can be credited as the father or mother of the family therapy movement. A number of therapists began the practice of seeing several family members during the same therapy session during the decade of the 1950s. The professional community viewed this practice with a jaundiced eye since individual therapy had been the traditional, accepted approach. Reputable therapists sometimes welcomed clients through the back door in order to see the entire family in a therapy session. New York, Philadelphia, Washington, D.C., Atlanta, and Palo Alto, California, became centers of development for the family therapy movement.

Ackerman

Nathan Ackerman was one of the early pioneers in family therapy (hereafter FT). Ackerman, working in New York City, developed a FT theory based on a psychodynamic (i.e., psychoanalytic) view of the individual and the family integrated into a social psychology framework. Ackerman's work represented 25 years of clinical and research experience as a practicing psychiatrist. He was certainly ahead of his time in suggesting the relationship of family and community networks with psychosomatic illness. *The Psychodynamics of Family Life* (1958) is a compilation of the late therapist's creative approach to families.

Bowen

Another psychiatrist, Murray Bowen (1978), of Topeka and later in Washington, D.C., was also focusing on providing therapy with families during the 1950s. Bowen served on the staff of the Menninger Clinic in Topeka; there he treated schizophrenics by hospitalizing as many of the family members as possible. He developed a "three generational" hypothesis for schizophrenia, which included the grandparents, the parents (whom he viewed as extremely immature), and the children (with the schizophrenic child having a symbiotic attachment to the mother).

Bowen's major contributions to FT are represented in his concepts of "triangulation" and "undifferentiated ego mass." *Triangulation* is a process that occurs in all families and social groups. A two-person emotional system will expand to a three-person system (i.e., one person is added) when under stress. This triangulation may take the form of an extra-marital affair or an attachment to activities outside the home such as work, civic organizations, or church involvement. Such attachments are made to avoid difficulties within the family system, especially the marital system. *Undifferentiated ego mass* represents a family composed of members who were emotionally stuck together, lacking their own identity. Such family members cannot exist independently of each other; they are fused together. Bowen's work is best represented in his book entitled *Family Therapy in Clinical Practice* (1978).

Whitaker

No discussion of FT contributors could be complete without a discussion of Carl Whitaker. Whitaker has maintained a leadership role throughout the development of FT. John Neill and David Kniskern (1982) have provided an excellent description of Whitaker's development as a therapist in the book *From Psyche to System: The Evolving Therapy of Carl Whitaker*.

Whitaker's professional pilgrimage spans 40 years of psychotherapy. He moved from the field of obstetrics and gynecology to psychiatry. He worked in Syracuse, Louisville, Oak Ridge (Tennessee) and Atlanta. While in Atlanta, he and his staff founded the Atlanta Psychiatric Clinic where they investigated schizophrenia. Whitaker became convinced of the interaction between the psychotic and the family. He saw himself, the therapist, as temporarily replacing the mother as a symbiotic partner with the schizophrenic patient. Later, Whitaker relocated to Wisconsin, where he presently serves as professor of psychiatry at the University of Wisconsin Medical School.

Whitaker has not drawn from a specific school of FT; one of his major contributions to the field has been his eclectic, existential approach to therapy. He will not do therapy with a family if one of the nuclear family members is absent from the session. It is not unusual for him to have three generations of the family in therapy at the same time, even including parents from both sides of the marriage. Whitaker believes the therapist should use himself or herself to assess (a) the family's quality of intimacy and (b) the family's sense of itself as a continually developing unit. *The Family Crucible,* by Augustus Napier and Whitaker (1980) is a classic description of the FT process performed by Whitaker and Napier.

The MRI Group

The Mental Research Institute (MRI) of Palo Alto, California, has contributed to the growth of a number of pioneers in FT. In the 1950s, Gregory Bateson led a research project staffed by Don Jackson, Jay Haley, John Weakland, Paul Watzlawick, John Bell, and Virginia Satir (Gurman & Kniskern, 1981; Hoffman, 1981). The MRI group was studying the classification of communication in terms of various levels of meaning. Among other areas of interest, the group looked at patterns of schizophrenic transactions. They came to view the family as the primary learning context for schizophrenia. Jackson termed the family's mechanism for maintaining *equilibrium* within its system as "family homeostasis," while his idea regarding the family's *deviation process* in establishing a new setting for the family system was termed "runaway" or "amplifying feedback" (Gurman & Kniskern, 1981; Hoffman, 1981). Both processes are vitally important to family life.

This same group developed the "double bind" theory of communication, which described a context of habitual communication impasses imposed on one member of the family by another member of the system. The "double bind" presents a no-win situation for the member; no matter how he or she answers the message-sender, disapproval will be expressed.

Bateson moved the MRI group beyond the double bind theory to the study of family coalitions. He coined the phrase "the infinite dance of shifting coalitions" to describe the behavior the MRI group observed in numerous schizophrenic families where no two persons seemed to be able to get together for direct, open communication, either to agree or disagree.

Haley and His Associates

Another member of the MRI group, Jay Haley, was influenced by the work of the medical hypnotist Milton Erikson (Haley, 1973). Erikson, who held both a medical degree and a graduate degree in psychology, introduced a new approach to psychotherapy that was cultivated at MRI. This approach focused on brief, short-term therapy, which came to be called "Strategic Therapy."

The influence of MRI spread as Jay Haley moved in 1967 to join Salvador Minuchin and Braulio Montalvo at the Philadelphia Child Guidance Clinic (Guerin, 1976). These three persons worked together in the development of another approach to FT called "structural family therapy." This approach, attributed primarily to Minuchin, focuses on changing the family by changing the family structure. The family's structure can be changed through challenging the family's symptoms, boundaries, or sense of reality. This approach is outlined in the books *Families and Family Therapy* (Minuchin, 1974) and *Family Therapy Techniques* (Minuchin & Fishman, 1981). Structural family therapy has been one of the most popular approaches to FT in recent years.

In 1976 Haley left the Philadelphia Child Guidance Clinic and moved to Washington, D.C., where he joined the faculty of the University of Maryland Medical School and established his own FT practice with his wife, Cloé Madanes. They identified their therapeutic approach as "strategic family therapy." The strategic family therapist focuses on the presenting problem while assessing the heirarchial structure of the family. A family symptom is viewed as being the result of a confused organizational hierarchy within the family. Therapeutic intervention is directed toward changing the interactional processes that perpetuate the family's organizational and hierarchial problems. The contributions of this wife-husband team are documented in Haley's (1976) *Problem-Solving Therapy* and Madanes's (1981) *Strategic Family Therapy*.

The Milan Group

A European approach to FT at the Milan Center for Family Studies, located at Milan, Italy, was influenced in its early development by the MRI group (Gurman & Kniskern, 1981). This is the fourth force within the field of strategic family therapy (the other three being Erikson, Haley, and the MRI group). The Milan group has made a major international contribution to the field of strategic therapy. In Europe the term "systemic" has been used to describe this unique form of therapy.

This therapeutic approach developed with the use of a four-person team, with a male-female therapy team meeting with the family and another female-male team observing behind a one-way mirror (screen). Their treatment usually consists of about ten sessions at intervals of one month or longer.

The Milan group identifies their treatment as a "long, brief therapy" because the number of hours with the family is small, but the duration of time required for family reorganization can be very long. The Milan approach focuses on the neutral stance of the therapist. A manner of circular questioning is used to elicit information; that is, the therapist might ask the father about which child in his family is closest to the mother. Rituals, tasks, and paradoxical prescriptions are used to intervene in the family's destructive interaction. The systemic approach to therapy is described in Palazzoli, Boscolo, Cecchin and Prata's (1978) book, published under the English title *Paradox and Counterparadox*.

INFLUENCES OF THEORIES

It becomes apparent from the previous discussion that numerous individuals and therapeutic teams have made significant contributions in the historical development of the family therapy movement. Their theoretical orientations have included psychodynamic, behavioral/social learning theory, as well as general systems theory.

Psychodynamic Theory

The number of early therapists who possessed medical degrees is indicative of the early contributions of psychodynamic theory to the family therapy movement. Psychodynamic contributions continue to be made specifically in the areas of *object relations theory* (see Bass, in Gilbert & Brock [1985] chapter 8) and family of origin work. Psychodynamic theory views the union of husband and wife in a dyadic relationship as a process in which both persons bring with them the psychological heritage that has contributed to their own individual development. Each marital relationship then is seen as being inextricably bound to the parent-child relationship in the two families of origin (Bowen, 1978; Pearce & Friedman, 1980). The same strengths and weaknesses that existed in the parent-child relationship in the family of origin are likely to exist in the marital relationship. The successful attachment or bonding of the infant to the significant parent (object constancy) will later determine the success of uniting with a spouse in marriage. The child's ability to separate from his or her parents and develop a capacity for separateness (separation-individuation) will then allow the mature adult to enjoy marriage and family life without being overly dependent on other family members.

While Sigmund Freud was responsible for the development of individual psychodynamic theory, his successors have transported the concepts into the realm of the family. Leaders such as Adler, Anna Freud, and Sullivan have allowed the psychodynamic approach to focus on the individual's interaction with the environment. Ackerman (1958) integrated psychodynamics into the family structure. Presently, family therapists fall along a spectrum ranging from subscribing to all of Freud's theories to applying only object relations theory to their practice of FT. Psychodynamic theory is appealing to the practitioner since it is the only theory (in revised form) that offers both an intrapsychic and interactional perspective for individuals and families. *Family Therapy: Combining Psychodynamic and Family Systems Approaches* (Pearce & Friedman, 1980) provides an example of how a psychodynamic paradigm can be integated into a family systems approach.

Social Learning Theory

Social learning (behavioral) theory has not made the contribution to FT that it has to the marriage therapy field (Jacobson & Margolin, 1979). It is briefly discussed in this chapter since what oftentimes begins as FT eventually involves marital therapy; and, what may begin as marriage counseling can lead to FT. The major distinction between marital therapy and family-oriented therapy is simply the number of people in the counseling room.

The social learning approach is based primarily on the concept of positive and negative reinforcements, either to affirm behavior or to extinguish behavior.

Generally, punishment is not effective in changing behavior, since its effects are of a short duration and it often creates a retaliatory attitude. Immediate reinforcement is effective in maintaining desired behavior or changing undesired behavior. As a result, behavioral therapy is more suited for individual or couple counseling; it is somewhat unwieldy to use with an entire family. I believe a social learning approach is the treatment choice in doing FT with aggressive children. Gerald Patterson and his colleagues at the Oregon Research Institute have developed an excellent social learning approach for families with children whose behavior is considered aggressive or out of control. *A Social Learning Approach to Family Intervention* (Patterson, 1975b) is a step-by-step treatment manual prepared for the family therapist. Another book entitled *Families: Applications of Social Learning to Family Life* (1975a) has been written and revised by Patterson for the families to read when entering therapy.

Since marital therapy is often intertwined with FT, the reader is referred to Robinette's chapter in this volume dealing with marital therapy. Additional reading in this area should include the basic text for behavioral marital therapy by Jacobson and Margolin, entitled *Marital Therapy* (1979). *Helping Couples Change* (Stuart, 1980) is recommended reading for understanding the social learning approach to therapy.

Systems Theory

The most significant theory to impact upon the family therapy movement has been borrowed from general systems theory and cybernetic epistemology. General systems theory is the development of Ludwig von Bertalanffy's (1968) concepts, which addressed a number of major dilemmas that had been arising in the field of the biological sciences. Today, a systems view is seen as a new and very different model of the world.

A full discussion of systems theory is included in Gilbert and Brock (1985). Since this chapter is describing FT, systems theory is only briefly discussed here in order to provide the reader with an understanding of the practical application of the systems paradigm to FT.

General systems theory is applied to family theory and therapy by defining a system as a group of interacting objects whose group membership is established and maintained by a boundary. The family is viewed as a collection of elements with a relationship between the elements that operates in a somewhat predictable manner. Each unit in the family is constrained by and dependent upon each of the other members. Members within the family system can be seen as subsystems (spousal, parent-child, or sibling) or as individuals. The interactions within the family system are viewed in a descriptive manner rather than with a cause-and-effect perspective.

The system's boundaries keep necessary things within the system, while the boundaries function to keep out things that would threaten the family. Healthy, functional boundaries have permeability. The *permeability* of the boundary determines how easily others can enter the family system. The *clarity* of the family's boundary is proportional to the clarity in the family's relationship. If the boundary becomes unclear or inappropriate, the family system can become dysfunctional. The importance of this concept is seen in the typical stepfamily. Stepfamilies usually have extremely open, permeable boundaries (Sager, et al., 1983) that provide little structure for the newly-formed stepfamily.

The addition or deletion of a family member can create tremendous stress on the family system. A family controls its system's stability and change process through *homeostasis* (Burr, Hill, Nye, & Reiss, 1979). A thermostat that regulates the heating and cooling system is an example of a homeostatic mechanism. The thermostat keeps the temperature from falling too low by turning on the heat; when the room's temperature reaches a certain point the heat is turned off. The same procedure works for the cooling system. It is thought that families handle change in a similar manner. Each family has a specific amount of stress it can handle. When the family reaches the apex of its toleration, symptoms are produced by individual members (referred to as *scapegoats*). For example, a couple experiencing marital problems may also see personal problems develop in their child. The child may exhibit school problems or personal problems in a covert—perhaps unconscious—attempt to keep the focus off the parents' marital difficulties. Family therapists interested in the entire family system would not focus on the child's individual problem exclusively, but would bring in the entire family to gain an understanding of how each family member perceives the difficulty within the family.

A cause-and-effect approach would attempt to find the contributors to the child's problem and intervene; however, the family therapist views the family system as operating in a process of reciprocity. Pathology is not an individual experience; each family member contributes to the ongoing family process. Most family difficulties develop when families are unable to handle the change required of the family system.

Many difficulties are the result of families becoming "stuck" in developmental points in the family's life. For instance, the birth of a new child, the last child's beginning school, or the last child's leaving home can create levels of stress that challenge the stability of the family system. When the family system seems overwhelmed, outside intervention is often needed for successful coping. Family therapy provides such intervention.

Family systems are maintained by *feedback loops* (Keeney, 1983a). These loops are similar to the circuit wires that allow the thermostat to control heating/cooling mechanisms. A *negative feedback loop* dampens the control to keep the change from getting out of hand. A *positive feedback loop* amplifies the deviation until some change occurs. For example, an ill child could be part of a negative feedback loop that keeps the parents' marital problems from exploding. A positive feedback loop could be an extra-marital affair, which increases the intensity of the marital dissatisfaction until the problems explode, resulting in some form of change in the family.

Family members have their own rules for handling the family's day-to-day interactions. These collective family rules are called "rules of transformation," and are often simply called "family rules." They prescribe how a family can respond to any given situation. As the therapist assesses a family, an understanding of the family's rules of transformation becomes important to the therapy process. In understanding the family rules, the therapist begins to understand the alternatives the family members perceive among themselves.

The family therapist assists the family to become "unstuck" by introducing change into the system. Such intervention by someone outside the family system is called *second order* change. This second order change is frequently unplanned and uncontrollable. It is a quantum leap in a new, unfamiliar direction, usually occurring during a state of crisis. The *first order* change is the family's controlled, conscious attempt at solving its problem by alleviating the symptom. A *second order* approach to the family's difficulties regards the family's attempted solution (the symptom) as actually part of the problem itself.

THE PRACTICE OF FAMILY THERAPY

Family therapy begins with the therapist joining with the family. This basically is aimed at getting the family to accept the family therapist into its system during therapy. Generally the therapist, utilizing any model of therapy, is careful to recognize each member of the family as he or she enters the therapy session (Keeney, 1983b). The views of each family member are openly solicited during the sessions.

The theory to which the therapist subscribes largely defines the therapist's function. The structural therapist initially defines a social subsystem that can be changed within the family, then formulates a solvable problem. For example, the therapist might identify the parental subsystem as needing a more intact boundary. The father could be withdrawn, using his business as a reason for not being home to interact with the wife and children. When this happens, the mother quite naturally assumes a greater share of responsibility in management of the home. The therapist might select to intervene by instructing the parents to conduct joint decision-making tasks, while the father is directed to spend a Saturday morning sharing his expertise with the children. On the other hand, the Milan group would study the sequence of behaviors, that is, what happens among the parent and child subsystems when the father spends time at home and away from home? The Milan group might suggest that although mother is spending a lot of time with the children, such time spent together is serving an important need, therefore mother is encouraged to be *overinvolved* with the children (in hopes that she will really back off from her overinvolvement). Feedback from the family would be continually monitored as such paradoxical interventions are used.

Family assessment requires the therapist to join with and intervene within the family system. The family's power-influence hierarchy and interactional sequences are noted in the assessment, and an understanding of the family's view of things is gained. This is called understanding the "family map" (Minuchin & Fishman, 1981). The family mentally maps out its view of the world at large and how its social unit relates to this world. This map is often not addressed by the family until a therapist describes his or her perception of it.

The First Session

In most models of FT the therapist sees the entire family together during each session. However, the model developed by Bowen (1978) does treat individual members of the family rather than the entire family constellation.

In general, therapy begins when a family member seeks professional help for a family problem. Typically, the family therapist schedules an initial interview with the entire family. At the first interview the therapist begins by learning about the family's interactions, while becoming better acquainted with each family member. Each member should have an opportunity to describe his or her own opinions about the family. The therapist should note such things as how the family handles agreement/disagreement, how flexible it is in generating alternatives in solving problems, the type of boundaries within its system and subsystems, and the strength of its hierarchy.

It is normal for the therapist to conclude the first session by explaining his or her perception of the family and proposing a treatment procedure that includes how long the therapy is expected to take. Often the therapist will contract for five to eight sessions with the understanding that the length of therapy may be mutually renegotiated later.

Pragmatic Issues

In actual practice a family will normally spend 50 minutes in each therapy session. The number of therapists involved in therapy is determined by both the therapeutic model and economic constraints. Structural family therapy (Minuchin & Fishman, 1981) can be practiced by one or more therapists in the session. The Milan (systematic family therapy) group likes to use a therapy team consisting of a male and female therapist (Keeney, 1983b). Institutions that are funded for education and research can usually afford the use of therapy teams. Their income is not dependent on the number of clients seen. However, a therapist in private practice knows that income is correlated with the number of clients/families seen. As a result, when two or more therapists in private practice work with the same family, they are actually losing money despite what may seem to be a high fee.

The number of sessions required by a family therapist is also dependent on the therapeutic orientation. A psychodynamically focused therapist may continue to treat a family for several months, viewing the clients' relationships as the fundamental building blocks of mental life (Nichols, 1984). Such therapists will attend to the expression of affect in relation to other people. Family therapists who practice systematic family therapy often plan on terminating family treatment within ten sessions (De Shazer, 1982). They are concerned more with changing interaction patterns than the expression of emotions.

Studies conducted by membership within the American Association for Marriage and Family Therapy indicate that the average cost for FT in the United States ranges between $55.00 to $60.00 per session (personal communication with the national office, August 16, 1984). Many church, community, and state-funded counseling centers offer therapy on a sliding fee scale; that is, a family pays according to its income. Such scales range from $5.00 to $100.00 per therapy session.

Applying Theoretical Assumptions

Family therapy is an orientation, not a method, which focuses on both the content and process within the therapy session. The therapist follows the family's sequence of interactions, looking for recurring patterns, while studying the family's boundaries with each of its subsystems.

The family therapist enters therapy with the belief that problem families usually stabilize around one family member who becomes the problem patient (Satir, 1967). The family, then, usually resists change, attempting to maintain a homeostatic balance within the family. The problem patient, sometimes identified as the *scapegoat,* presents his or her problem as an unconscious representation, or analogy, of the family interaction. While the family may really want the presenting problem solved, the therapist usually intervenes into the family interaction expressed by the presented problem. In other words, the therapist's view of what is the true problem is broader than the individual's perspective. Therapists from both the structural and strategic models regard the individual's problem as the family's attempted solution to the real underlying problem. A structural therapy approach would go beyond the presented problem, while Haley's problem solving therapy would focus only on mobilizing the family to solve the presented problem.

For an example, let us discuss a family who enters therapy with an adolescent who is the identified patient (IP) in the family. The adolescent is having problems in school with truancy and poor grades. The structural approach to intervention would be based on what the therapist perceives as the problem. The structural family therapist might expand the therapy to possibly include marriage counseling; however, the strategic therapist, focusing on the family's definition of the presenting problem, might reframe the child's activities, giving his actions a new meaning to the parents. Often, changing the meaning of the IP's act (by reframing) allows the family to change enough to become "unstuck" in its process. The Haley approach would intervene directly with the problem adolescent unless the family identifed a new problem during the therapy process. Typically, this strategic approach is met with less family resistance than is the structural approach.

CURRENT STATUS OF THE FAMILY THERAPY MOVEMENT

Research Issues and Findings

The maturation process of any discipline includes its ability to examine its own effectiveness in service delivery. This discipline has developed slowly due to the scattered work of many individuals and therapy teams from numerous disciplines. Such development has included the morphogenesis of the therapy techniques as well as therapeutic paradigms. The family therapy movement has only recently arrived at the point in its development where serious research is being conducted.

The early approaches were primarily psychodynamic in orientation. Psychodynamically orientated therapies are difficult to evaluate by research. It is difficult to measure change in such intrapsychic dynamics as regression and transference. While family therapists have been pragmatic in using whatever works in family treatment, "whatever works" is not necessarily easily measured by researchers.

On the other hand, research involving the entire family is both cumbersome and expensive. The best attempt at researching the entire family is represented in Kantor and Lehr's (1975) book, *Inside the Family*. This research was conducted with 19 normal families, and used a participant observer technique of data collection. Their model focuses on the distance-regulation of the family and its individual members. This research model is difficult to replicate due to its financial expense and the large number of individuals needed to record the observations.

A young spokesperson for the family therapy movement is Bradford P. Keeney. Keeney, an epistomologist in the FT field, suggests that much of the existing FT research has measured an individual level and applied the results to the family level as a social unit (1983b). His argument for research measurements that contain systems validity is an important point for contemporary researchers. Totaling individual scores and averaging them as a family score is not an accurate measure of a family. Further psychometric development is certainly needed in this area.

The early pioneers in FT were generally more interested in blazing new trails than in providing scientific measurement for outcome studies. The emphasis was on conducting therapy rather than research. This remained true until the past decade. Particularly in the last ten years a substantial number of empirical research studies have emerged. Numerous reviews providing critical evaluation of the earlier research literature have been published (Beck, 1975; Gurman, 1971, 1973, 1975; Kniskern & Gurman, 1975). The reviews conclude that both marital and family therapy are effective. In fact, Bergin (1971) reported that FT improvement rates are surprisingly akin to those reported for individual therapy. This is a significant report, since only a few years ago FT would not have been compared to individual psychotherapy.

It should be noted that many of the early outcome studies contained methodological errors which plagued their reliability. However, Garfield and Bergin (1978) reported that the major forms of FT (nonbehavioral) provided overall improvement rates of 73% (27% did not improve). It is believed that 5-10% of clients in FT experience a deterioration or worsening in the family's relationships because of FT. Due to the methodological shortcomings in the research designs, however, it is impossible to determine an accurate deterioration rate.

An examination of five nonbehavioral family outcome studies revealed that all treated families emerged as superior to the no treatment control groups (Gurman & Kniskern, 1981).

Training

Training for family therapists is available in free-standing institutes (which typically do not offer graduate degrees) where the emphasis is on the development or enhancement of FT skills (Liddle, 1982). The Marriage Council of Philadelphia, the Philadelphia Child Guidance Center, and the Family Therapy Institute of Washington, D.C., are examples of free-standing training programs.

Training alternatives to the free-standing institute are universities that offer graduate degrees in FT along with experience in the practice of FT through practicums and internships (Nichols, 1979). Texas Tech University, Purdue University, and Eastern Baptist Seminary are representative of the secular and church-related institutions that offer graduate degrees in FT. The number of graduate programs accredited by the nationally recognized American Association for Marriage and Family Therapy (AAMFT) continues to grow each year (Johnson, 1984).

The clinical membership requirements outlined by the AAMFT emphasize the graduate degree programs. Current membership requirements in AAMFT include specific coursework that must be taken in areas of theory, therapy models, and the application of marriage and family therapy under supervision. The academic institutions emphasize both FT research and therapy in their curriculum.

A number of states currently have licensing laws for the practice of marriage and family therapy. Arkansas, California, Connecticut, Florida, Michigan, North Carolina, New Jersey, Nevada, Texas, and Utah license the professional who provides marriage and family therapy. Such licensure maintains a level of quality control, since each state determines the qualifications a psychotherapist must meet in applying for public recognition as a marriage and family therapist.

Summary

We may therefore conclude that previous literature has supported the efficacy of FT. The movement's growth as a discipline is reflected by the improved research designs which are exhibited in current FT literature.

INTEGRATION WITH THE HOLY SPIRIT

The Generative Functions in Family Therapy

A skilled family therapist has: (a) mastery of therapy techniques (he or she knows *how* to do family therapy); (b) a good theoretical foundation (he or she knows *why* he or she is doing a specific intervention); and (c) sensitivity to the therapy process (he or she knows *when* to intervene). Therefore, the effective therapist has learned to evaluate continually both the content (what is said) and the process (the direction) of the therapy session.

The Christian family therapist is not only sensitive to the therapy process, but is also sensitive to the presence of the Holy Spirit within the lives of those persons in the therapy session. The Holy Spirit is the generative agent of God whose ministry is to execute the will of God the Father and Son (Gen. 2:7; Rom. 8:9; Acts 17:28). The therapy session can provide the context for God's Spirit to work

creatively in the family's interaction; the therapist is mindful that the family is
God's creation, not the therapist's. The therapist must trust God to execute his
creative acts within the therapy sessions, knowing that Christ in us is the hope
of glory (Col. 1:27). It is good theology and systems theory to view God's presence
in the therapy session as forming the isomorphic structure of the treatment system.

Through the spiritual dynamics of the session, faith in the Holy Spirit's ministry
can enable the family's system to provide *negative feedback* when the family needs
stability and *positive feedback* when the family needs change. During the positive
feedback loop, the therapist must recognize the ministry of the Holy Spirit in
what seems to be a "deviation amplification process." In other words, what
appears to be an intense move toward change can be viewed in light of the potential
of God to work among his people—therapist and family alike! What may appear
as a "dark night of the soul" for the family can be reframed by the Christian
therapist as an opportunity for the generating/regenerating power of the Holy
Spirit to move the family system (morphogenesis) to a new, better level of relating
and interaction (Rom. 8:11).

Scripturally, from Genesis to Revelation, the work of the Holy Spirit has been
to bring things and people together. Family therapy is a process where people's
lives (and families) are brought together. The ministry of the Holy Spirit in the
process of FT is the ultimate in second order change, that is, the use of an outside
agent to bring about change in the family.

The Hope Factor

The Christian family therapist trusts the ministry of God's Spirit to create hope
and positive anticipation within the context of FT. Such hope transcends both
the limits of the therapist's skills and the family's dilemma. Hope allows the Spirit
who brought forth Jesus Christ from the tomb of death to resurrect dead
relationships and energize the celebration of new life.

The therapist has many opportunities to acknowledge the Holy Spirit's
contributions to the therapy session through the use of prayer with the clients
and through the Spirit's involvement in the therapist's task assignments and
directives during the sessions. *Positive connotation* (Hoffman, 1981) is the
therapeutic technique of pointing out the good in what is perceived to be a bad
situation. In essence, it is the shining of light into darkness. It is the seeing of
opportunity in a crisis. Since, "without a vision the people will perish" (Prov.
29:18), the family therapist must assist the family to gain a vision; to allow the
light of hope to shine into the darkness of a hopeless situation.

The Family Therapist's Function as "Seelsorger"

"*Seelsorger*" is a German title used for clergy, meaning "the one who cares
for the soul." The Christian family therapist is one who cares for the whole person:
body, soul, and spirit. He or she occupies a privileged position within the family's
inner sanctum. There are times when the therapist makes intercession between
family members. The therapist hears the innermost secrets of individuals and

families; the therapist witnesses the wounds and scars of the family's mistakes, sins, and failures and then prescribes healing in the name of Jesus the Christ.

The therapist needs to be empowered by the Holy Spirit (Acts 1:8; Eph. 5:18) and must walk in the Spirit in order for the Comforter to guide him or her and the family into all truth (John 16:13). In this manner one can be a spiritual counselor and guide to individuals and families. Ultimately, the mission of the church, as the body of Christ, is to deal redemptively with people. A family therapist has an opportunity not only to deal redemptively with people (in relation to God), but, also to instruct family members to deal redemptively with *each other* in all aspects of their lives. In this manner the family therapist is indeed a *"Seelsorger."*

CASE STUDIES

The reader should note that the names and geographical locations of the following cases have been altered in order to protect the identity of those persons involved in the case studies.

Case 1

Mrs. Bentley was referred to the family therapist by her pastor. She had recently moved into the area from another state. The move offered her husband an opportunity to go into business for himself. Mr. Bentley was not a professing Christian, but he was supportive of the wife's church involvement. The move occurred while the youngest child was preparing to get married. Mrs. Bentley's presenting problem was that she no longer enjoyed being around her husband. In fact, she indicated that the one thing that kept her sane was listening to the audio tapes of a well-known evangelist. The more she disliked being around her husband, the more time she spent listening to her religious tapes.

After the initial assessment with the husband and wife the therapist saw the difficulties revolving around the following issues. (1) The family's relocation forced the spouses into a closer proximity to each other than they had previously experienced. (2) The parents were dreading the "empty nest" syndrome. The intervention consisted of structuring the wife's activities in a manner that gave her some interpersonal space within the marriage. In other words, getting her out of the house and involved in some church and community activities broke up the marital withdrawal pattern. At the same time, several therapy sessions were conducted with the engaged daughter present. The agenda in these sessions was the preparation for their daughter's leaving home and the father and mother's learning once again to live together without children.

The wife's initial escape into the world of her religious tapes was a triangulation of her marriage with the tape objects. The more involved she became with the tapes the less she could relate with her husband; however, the obvious danger lay with the potential damage to the marriage and the husband's increasing animosity toward the religion that was pulling his wife away from him. The prescribed intervention (a) unbalanced the wife's triangulation, (b) allowed the husband to give her some emotional space, and (c) allowed the couple to begin the new phase of their life together without children.

Case 2

Joe and Mary entered FT identifying three presenting problems: (a) two of Joe's grown children had moved back home, (b) they were having financial problems (including Mary's overuse of credit cards), and (c) Joe, age 60, was experiencing sexual impotence. Mary, twelve years younger than Joe, complained they were living together "like brother and sister." Joe's sexual impotence seemed to be symbolic of his lack of potence within the entire family. Mary clearly controlled the power within the family. Mary complained that the more she attempted to get Joe to listen to her, the more he withdrew from the family by becoming involved in various church activities and meetings.

The therapist approached this family with a structural intervention. First, he joined with the family in order to establish his acceptance by the family members. Next, both Joe and Mary were assisted in arriving at *their* joint decision to tell the children that they must find another place to live. (Both children had good employment and were mature enough to be on their own.) Also, the therapist gave a paradoxical injunction to the couple that they were to engage in physical intimacies, but under no circumstances were they to engage in sexual intercourse. This injunction interrupted the performance anxiety which Joe was experiencing in attempting to "be a man" to Mary. Over the course of several weeks the couple privately viewed the film series *Sensate Focus* to develop their sense of sexuality without the pressure to perform. During the following weeks the couple began to improve in their sexual functioning, even though the therapist had instructed the couple not to consummate their physical intimacy.

An obvious pattern between the couple was Mary's "nagging" and Joe's withdrawing. This pattern was interrupted with the therapist's directing the therapy sessions; he encouraged Joe to share more of himself while the therapist controlled Mary's talking. This was basically an enhancement of the couple's communication. This intervention in the old communication pattern stopped the nagging-withdrawal sequences, allowing Joe and Mary to reorganize their relationship. As this reorganization occurred, Joe's overinvolvement in church activities diminished; however, he and his wife continued jointly to support the church worship and social activities.

Often the therapist and pastor can assist each other with consultation. With Joe and Mary's consent, the therapist consulted with their pastor regarding their overinvolvement in church activities. This step ensured the pastor's support in Joe's withdrawal from certain church activities. The pastor's consultation can provide an important additional view of the family's functioning.

While doing FT, I often invite the pastor (who has referred the family) to join me as a co-therapist. This invitation is extended with the family's consent, of course. Co-therapy allows the pastor to enhance personal counseling skills while participating in the therapy ministry. This procedure generally strengthens the family's relationship with the pastor.

SUMMARY

The discipline called "family therapy" is continually changing. This chapter has focused on both the theory and application of FT within a Christian context. Some models are better known and more often utilized. For example, many family service agencies utilize Minuchin's (1974) structural family therapy. It is a standard "work horse" model with a theoretical structure that is easily understood by most beginning therapists. This model does not continue to change, like those of the systematic therapies. And, as a therapist continues to mature professionally, the structural family therapy model can be used to compare and contrast with other models of therapy.

As with the Samaritan woman (John 4:1–42) deeper issues sometime underlie problematic interpersonal relationships. Jesus Christ, in relating to the needs of humanity, was able to see through the surface issues in people's lives in order to deal with the real problems. Such is the duty of the family therapist, regardless of his or her theoretical orientation. May we as therapists be sensitive to the leadership of God's Spirit in dealing redemptively with people, meeting them where they are in the name of Jesus Christ and in the power of the Spirit.

SELECT BIBLIOGRAPHY

Ackerman, N. (1958). *The psychodynamics of family life.* New York: Basic Books.

Beck, D. F. (1975). Research findings on the outcomes of marital counseling. *Social Casework, 56,* 153–181.

Bergin, A. (1971). The evaluation at therapeutic outcomes. In S. Garfield & A. Bergin, *Handbook of psychiatry and behavior change.* New York: John Wiley & Sons.

Bertalanffy, L. von. (1968). *General systems theory.* New York: Braziller.

Bowen, M. (1978). *Family therapy in clinical practice.* New York: Aronson.

Burr, W. R., Hill, R., Nye, F. I., & Reiss, I. L. (1979). *Contemporary theories about the family.* (Vols. 1–2). New York: Free Press.

De Shazer, S. (1982). *Patterns of brief family therapy.* New York: Guilford Press.

Garfield, S., & Bergin, A. (1978). *Handbook of psychotherapy and behavior change* (2nd ed.). New York: John Wiley & Sons.

Gilbert, M. G., & Brock, R. T. (1984). *The Holy Spirit and Counseling: Theology and theory.* Peabody, MA: Hendrickson

Guerin, P. J., Jr. (Ed.). (1976). *Family therapy: Theory and practice.* New York: Gardner Press.

Gurman, A. S. (1971). Group marital therapy: Clinical and empirical implications for outcome research. *International Journal of Group Psychotherapy, 21,* 174–189.

_____. (1973). Marital therapy: Emerging trends in research and practice. *Family Process, 12,* 45–54.

_____. (1975). Some therapeutic implications of marital therapy research. In A. S. Gurman & D. G. Rice (Eds.), *Couples in conflict: New directions in marital therapy.* New York: Aronson.

Gurman, A. S., & Kniskern, D. P. (Eds.). (1981). *Handbook of family therapy.* New York: Brunner/Mazel.

Haley, J. (1973). *Uncommon therapy.* New York: Norton & Co.

_____. (1976). *Problem-solving therapy.* New York: Harper & Row.

Hoffman, L. (1981). *Foundations of family therapy.* New York: Basic Books.

Jacobson, N. S., & Margolin, G. (1979). *Marital therapy.* New York: Brunner/Mazel.

Johnson, S. (1984, May-June). AAMFT profile: Growth and opportunity. *Family Therapy News,* p. 20.

Kantor, D., & Lehr, W. (1975). *Inside the family.* San Francisco, CA: Jossey-Bass.

Keeney, B. P. (1983a). *Aesthetics of change.* New York: Guilford Press.

_____. (1983b). *Diagnosis and assessment in family therapy.* Rockville, MD: Aspen Systems.

Kniskern, D. P., & Gurman, A. S. (1975). Research on training in marriage and family therapy: Status, issues, and directions. *Journal of Marital and Family Therapy, 1,* 83-94.

Liddle, H. (1982). Family therapy training: Current issues, future trends. *International Journal of Family Therapy, 4*(2), 81-97.

Madanes, C. (1981). *Strategic family therapy.* New York: Jossey-Bass.

Minuchin, S. (1974). *Families & family therapy.* Cambridge, MA: Harvard University Press.

Minuchin, S., & Fishman, H. C. (1981). *Family therapy techniques.* Cambridge, MA: Harvard University Press.

Napier, A. Y., & Whitaker, C. A. (1980). *The family crucible.* New York: Bantam Books.

Neill, J. R., & Kniskern, D. P. (1982). *From psyche to system: The evolving therapy of Carl Whitaker.* New York: Guilford Press.

Nichols, M. (1984). *Family therapy: Concepts and methods.* New York: Gardner Press.

Nichols, M. (1979). Education of marriage and family therapists: Some trends and implications. *Journal of Marriage and Family Therapy, 5,* 19-28.

_____. (1984). *Family therapy: Concepts and methods.* New York: Gardner Press.

Palazzoli, M.S., Boscolo, L., Cecchin, G., & Prata, G. (1978). *Paradox and counterparadox.* New York: Aronson.

Patterson, G. R. (1975a). *Families: Applications of social learning to family life* (rev. ed.). Champaign, IL: Research Press.

_____. (1975b). *A social learning approach to family intervention.* Eugene, OR: Castalia Pub. Co.

Pearce, J. K., & Friedman, L. (1980). *Family therapy: Combining psychodynamic and family systems approaches.* New York: Grune & Stratton.

Sager, C., Brown, H., Crohn, H., Engel, T., Rodstein, E., & Walker, L. (1983). *Treating the remarried family.* New York: Brunner/Mazel.

Satir, V. (1967). *Conjoint family therapy.* Palo Alto, CA: Science & Behavior Books.

Stuart, R. B. (1980). *Helping couples change.* New York: Guilford Press.

6

COUNSELING THE PARENTS OF THE HANDICAPPED CHILD

Linda L. Martin

Parenting has never been easy. There are always many questions regarding the best thing to do in a given situation. There are always frustrations, heartaches, and sorrow that cause the Christian parent to seek wisdom from the Lord. Along with this, however, there is also the joy and pride of being a parent. When the problems of rearing a handicapped child are added to these "normal" problems of parenting, parents have a much more difficult task; they often have no idea of how to cope with this situation. The diagnosis of the handicapping condition may be given at birth or later; the handicap may be present at birth or it may occur later as the result of an illness, injury, or accident. In any event, at the time of the diagnosis the parents will often seek assistance from a minister or Christian counselor while attempting to adjust to the change that has occurred within their family.

THE "DREAM" CHILD

One of the first matters that needs to be understood by both the counselor and the parents of the handicapped child is the way in which the discovery of a child's handicapping condition affects the parents. *All* expectant parents have a mental image of how they would like for their child to be. Huber (1979) stated that this mental image reflects the parents' perceptions of themselves and of other significant individuals in their lives. This mental image also includes attributes that will enable the child to assume successfully the role assigned by the cultural stereotypes of society. We dream about how the child will look, sound, feel, and behave; we also dream about the teenager and the adult he or she will become (McCollum, 1984). Will the child be an athlete . . . a doctor . . . an artist . . . or perhaps a missionary, or a brilliant lawyer? The possibilities are almost endless.

The special event of the birth of a child invites the interest and excitement of the parents' friends, family members, and the religious community to which the parents belong. Usually as a child begins to grow, the parents' expectations and dreams are gradually modified as they begin to recognize their child's actual capabilities. As the reality of day-to-day living helps the parents to discard the fantasy of the dream child, they begin to accept their child for who he or she is and wants to become. When a baby is born handicapped or a child later becomes handicapped, however, the parents are abruptly and harshly confronted with the reality that there is little or no hope for the fulfillment of their dream for the child (Ball, 1983). A child with Down's Syndrome will not win a Nobel prize; a deaf child is not likely to become a famous concert pianist; a child having no use of the lower limbs will not become a pro football player. When the fantasy is lost, the parents are filled with a deep sense of bewilderment, and the process of grieving begins (McCollum, 1984).

THE KÜBLER-ROSS MODEL OF LOSS AND ADJUSTMENT

The model of loss developed by Elizabeth Kübler-Ross (1969) applies to the parents who are dealing with the experience of having a handicapped child (Huber, 1979). The Kübler-Ross model consists of five stages: *denial, anger, bargaining, depression,* and *acceptance.* It is important for the minister or Christian counselor working with parents of handicapped children to understand these five stages of dealing with loss and how they apply to the parent of a handicapped child. These stages and their application are outlined below.

Denial

This first stage usually occurs after the parent has been informed that the child has a handicapping condition. In some cases the handicap is so physically obvious that the parents either do not experience this stage or the denial is only a fleeting thought that passes quickly through the parents' minds. In other cases the handicap is so hidden that the parents tend to remain at this stage for a long period of time. This stage may be illustrated when the parents are confronted with the diagnosis and reply, "No, not my child; this cannot be happening to us, and this cannot be the true diagnosis." They may go to great lengths in their search for proof that the child is normal. They may take the child from one professional to another in a long process of trying to find what they consider to be the "right" diagnosis. Such parents may be entirely unable to face the reality that the child *is* handicapped and might never meet their parental expectations. They may have great difficulty expressing their feelings during this initial stage of the grieving process (Huber, 1979).

It is normal in this stage for the parents to attempt to behave in a strong, stoic manner. If the pastor or counselor is aware of the situation, and the parents seem to show no need to discuss it, it would help a great deal if the pastor or counselor could sit down with the parents privately and acknowledge that while their ability to function well in a very difficult situation is admirable, he or she would admire them no less if they, at times, found it very rough to handle and wanted to share it with someone (Ball, 1983). If the pastor addresses the situation in this way, this might be the push the parents need to begin to deal with their feelings.

Denial is usually a temporary defense and will soon be replaced by a partial acceptance. Most parents do not use denial extensively. They may briefly talk about the reality of their situation and then suddenly indicate their inability to look at it realistically any longer (Kübler-Ross, 1969).

During this period, dialogue about the situation should take place at the convenience of the parents, that is, when *they*—not the listener—are ready to face it. This dialogue must also be terminated when the parents can no longer face the facts and resume their previous denial (Kübler-Ross, 1969). The counselor used by the Holy Spirit should be encouraged by realizing that the Spirit is an expert in helping each of us to face a sometimes painful reality.

Anger

When denial cannot be maintained any longer it is replaced by feelings of anger, rage, resentment (Kübler-Ross, 1969), and envy towards parents with normal children. The parents begin to ask, *Why?* Why has this happened to us? What have we (or I) done wrong? Why is God punishing us (me)? Why *our* child? Why *us*? Why *me*? Such anger may be directed toward God, the professionals who made the diagnosis, parents of normal children, relatives, the handicapped child, or themselves.

Punishment. As parents search for a reason why their child is handicapped, the condition may be interpreted as punishment for past behavior. Some have an almost obsessive need to find the ''cause'' of the handicap and to be able to affix the blame for their child's problem to someone or something other than themselves. The parents may blame each other: ''*You* are the one who ran around with other girls before we were married.'' ''If *you* had taken better care of yourself while you were carrying this child this would not have happened.'' These kinds of accusations place a difficult strain on the marital relationship. Parents often devote enormous amounts of energy and time in seeking an answer to the question of causation. Many times this question cannot be answered accurately; even if an answer is forthcoming it rarely resolves anything on the emotional level (Luterman, 1979).

Death wish. A fundamental and destructive form of anger may be directed at the child for being sick, different, and handicapped and, therefore, for violating the parents' expectations for a normal child (Huber, 1979). Put quite starkly, a parent may ''wish'' the child were dead, because of the way the disability has disrupted their lives (McCollum, 1984). They will only rarely (if ever) express this wish and anger to another. Such anger is totally unacceptable to them, and they feel it will be totally unacceptable to others; therefore, they generally keep this secret to themselves. Murphy (1977) stated that most parents of handicapped children would not be surprised at other parents making such statements; they know how other parents feel because they have been there themselves.

Fear. Fear is another immediate response. We often fear the unknown more than we fear the known. With the parents of the handicapped child, fear of the future is a common emotion: What is going to happen to this child when he or she is an adult? What will happen to this child when I am gone? Will the child ever learn to be independent? Memories return of the handicapped persons they have seen before. There is fear that society will reject the child, fear about how any siblings will be affected, questions about whether to risk having any more children, as well as concerns about whether the other parent (husband or wife) or grandparents will love the child. This fear can become overwhelming and lead to increased anger (Smith, 1984).

Powerlessness. Another source of anger is the feeling of helplessness. This feeling causes great frustration and anger, especially for those parents who have believed they were in control of their lives up to this point. Suddenly as a result of having a handicapped child, they have lost control. Now others— professionals—who normally would have no control over them are making decisions that will change their lives radically. They often react with anger and rage when forced by circumstances to give up the control they have had over their own lives. Plans and dreams for the child and for their own future may now have to be abandoned. There is also the feeling of utter helplessness because they cannot *do* anything to make their child better. The inability to help a hurting child is one of the most devastating feelings a parent can ever experience (Luterman, 1979). Powerlessness to change what is happening is very difficult to accept (Smith, 1984) and leads to exasperation and rage.

Guilt and self-esteem. When anger is turned inward it often manifests itself as guilt (Huber, 1979). All too easily we find reasons to accuse ourselves, since we are all imperfect. This leads to a loss of self-esteem. For the parents of a child with a handicap, this loss of self-esteem comes from many sources. Most parents expect to contribute unflawed genes to the embryo, causing it to develop into a healthy child (McCollum, 1984). If unable to do this, they feel guilty. The mother especially may feel guilty if something that occurred during the pregnancy caused the disability, since she was responsible for carrying the child. Both parents expect that they will be able to surround their child with such loving care and protection that a happy, healthy development will be insured and at least some of their dreams about the child fulfilled. The child's disability, whether inherited or acquired, confronts the parents with a sense of failure. They have failed to live up to the expectations of others and themselves, and they are helpless to undo the child's faulty development. The parents' sense of self-esteem and competence is often drastically shaken (McCollum, 1984).

Thus, the loss of self-esteem is frequently fed by guilt. Most parents experience periods of time when they will review any acts of commission or omission that they feel might have led to the child's disability. They may review their thoughts and feelings as well. Any negative feelings about the pregnancy or about the child before the handicapping condition developed can seem unforgivable (McCollum, 1984). Some parents may view the child as punishment for past sins. This can lead to an inability to relate to the child or to love the child; such parents view the child as a constant reminder that they have somehow displeased God. Sometimes the parent who perceives the child in this manner will begin to neglect or abuse the child in an effort to "get even" with the child or with God for daring to punish them in this way. Other parents may attempt to find ways to punish *themselves,* reasoning that if they punish themselves enough, God will perhaps be satisfied and will cease to punish their child.

Another frequent manifestation of the guilty feelings of the parents is displayed in the form of parental overprotection of the handicapped child. The parents' attitude toward the child becomes, "Now that one unfortunate thing has happened to you, we are not going to let you ever experience another." The parents who feel this way will often determine to "dedicate" themselves to the child in order to protect the child and see that he or she has the very best possible life. This dedication may exclude everyone else, including the child's siblings and even the other parent if he or she does not feel the same sense of "dedication." Obviously this reaction can be very unhealthy for all family relationships (Luterman, 1979).

Parents who feel destructive, hostile, or embittered towards their handicapped child will at some point experience guilt about these feelings and thoughts. Guilt can lead to further resentment of the child; the parents may begin to feel guilty about being resentful. At this point they may begin to wonder if there might be something wrong with them for feeling so much resentment toward a child who is their own flesh and blood (Luterman, 1979).

When the parents' sense of guilt reaches the place where it is unbearable, it may be expressed as hostile blame of others—doctors, nurses, God, their own parents, very often their spouses (McCollum, 1984), and perhaps even the minister or counselor working with them. This stage of anger is very difficult for the family and close friends to cope with because the anger may be displaced in many directions and randomly projected onto anyone in the parents' proximity. When the family members and friends react personally to the parents' anger and respond with their own anger, the parents' hostile behavior continues (Kübler-Ross, 1969).

It is a real tragedy when we do not understand the actual reasons for the parents' misplaced anger and react to it personally. Family members and friends may shorten their visits in order to avoid the expressed anger or even the general feeling of tension caused by unexpressed anger. Few people choose to confront the situation by placing themselves in the parents' position. If we did, perhaps we would see that we too would be extremely angry if our life was so rudely and abruptly interrupted. Viewing the situation from the parents' perspective we might ask ourselves, "what else could we do with our anger but to vent it on those people who can still enjoy the things we are no longer able to enjoy?" (Kübler-Ross, 1969). The parents feel very vulnerable and lose trust that the world—their own home in particular—is a safe place where nothing bad is going to happen to them. They will never again be able to approach living with the same carefree trust that they had before they became parents of a child with a handicap (Luterman, 1979); they are angry at those individuals who can still experience this "safe" environment.

Parents who are respected, listened to without judgment, and understood, who are given attention and time to adjust, will soon respond and begin working through their anger. They must know that they are still valuable human beings and that they will really be heard.

Bargaining

Often when the parents see that their angry demand for God to remove this disability from their child—and from their own lives—is not answered, they will decide to try bargaining with him. They reason: If God has decided to do this to me (us) and he did not respond to my (our) angry pleas and demands, maybe he will be moved to answer us favorably if I (we) ask him nicely and do something nice for him. Kübler-Ross (1969) stated that most bargains are made with God and are usually kept a secret or are only mentioned "between the lines" of conversation or in a minister's private office.

Most of us can remember times during our childhood years when we asked our parents to allow us to participate in some kind of special activity. When our request was met with a negative reply, we might have stormed around in an angry temper tantrum or locked ourselves in our room temporarily. We were expressing our anger by rejecting them, but after a while we began to have second thoughts. We may have then tried another approach: being extremely nice and cooperative, even volunteering to do some chores around the house that under normal circumstances our parents would have never succeeded in getting us to do. Then we asked our parents, "If I am very good all week and do these chores every day without your asking me, then will you let me do this?" (Kübler-Ross, 1969). We were engaged in the process of bargaining.

The parents of the handicapped child often try using the same type of maneuver with God. They know from life experience that there is always a slim chance that they may be rewarded for good behavior and be granted a wish in return for special services (Kübler-Ross, 1969), and so the parents in desperation seek to gain God's favor in this manner.

Kübler-Ross (1969) also stated that promises may be associated psychologically with quiet guilt and as such should not be brushed aside by the counselor. If the parents make such a statement, the counselor may wish to find out if they feel guilty for some omission, such as not attending church regularly, or if there are deeper unconscious hostile wishes that precipitated such guilt. An example of this might be the parent who did not want to have another child and who, during the pregnancy, wished that enough harm would befall the fetus to cause a miscarriage to terminate the pregnancy.

The attempts at bargaining are continually followed by further bargaining when the original promises are found to have no effect on the situation (Kübler-Ross, 1969). Feelings of inadequacy, blame, helplessness, guilt, hostility, and failure at bargaining combine to unravel further the parents' faltering self-regard; as a result, depression begins to enfold them (McCollum, 1984).

Depression

When the parents finally realize that the situation is real and unchangeable—that the handicap is not going to go away—they usually enter a state of deep depression. At this point parents may find themselves lacking energy for anything except the barest essentials of living. One parent when speaking about this stage of grief stated: "Every time I looked at or even thought about my child I would burst into tears. I could not do anything except stay in my house; I did not want to see or talk to anyone." The numbness, stoicism, anger, and rage are replaced by a great sense of loss (Kübler-Ross, 1969).

Reactive depression. The parents may go through two different types of depression. The first type could be labeled as reactive depression and is associated with grieving for the loss of the dream child and the guilt the parents may feel in the course of the search for the "cause" of the child's handicap. An understanding person will have no difficulty in eliciting the cause of this type of depression and in helping the parents to relieve some of the accompanying unrealistic guilt or shame.

Most of us initially react to sad individuals by trying to cheer them up and by telling them to not look at things so grimly or so hopelessly—to not be so very negative about the situation. We encourage them to look at the more positive side of the issue, in this case all the things that the child *can* do. We do this because of our own needs, that is, our own inability to tolerate another's depression for an extended period of time. *After* allowing the parents truly adequate time to mourn, this intervention can be very useful in helping them to deal with this type of depression (Kübler-Ross, 1969).

Anticipatory depression. The second type of depresson does not occur as a result of past loss but because the parents are considering *impending* losses. It could also be labeled preparatory depression (Küblcr-Ross, 1969). The parents do feel genuine sorrow for the handicapped child, but they also grieve for themselves (McCollum, 1984) in anticipation of the losses in their own lives. They have faced the fact of the child's handicap and their own inability to do anything to change it. They understand that they will have to face the pain of their loss and accept their situation and thus modify their lives. They are now taking time to rethink their plans and regroup their resources.

While the problems associated with the birth and/or rearing of a handicapped child were superficially obvious to them before, it is only now that the far-reaching implication of the problems in terms of the future effect on their family is beginning to become clear. This often results in parents experiencing this type of depression. For example, parents who love to ski and who have a child confined to a wheelchair may become depressed when they realize that they will never again be able to enjoy skiing down a mountain slope as a whole family. Music-loving parents of a profoundly deaf child may be depressed when they realize that never again can they enjoy a musical concert together as a family. The family that enjoys a fun day at the amusement park may experience depression when its members discover that one of their children has a severe seizure disorder that prohibits *any* amusement rides; the parents realize that never again can the whole family know the joy of plunging down the roller coaster together and hearing *all* the children scream with delight.

In addition to these realities, the family of the handicapped child must deal with many demands and frustrations that are not part of the lives of most families. These include the thoughtless ridicule or curiosity and questions by others. Other Christians make such inconsiderate remarks as, "There must be something wrong with your faith or you must have some sin in your life because if you had enough faith and no sin then your child would be healed." Added to these are the long, expensive, frustrating, and sometimes painful experiences with hospitals and various health professionals (Paul, 1983).

Acceptance

When parents have had enough time and have been given enough help in working through the previously described stages, they will reach a stage in which they are neither depressed nor angry about their personal "fate" or the "fate" of the family as a whole (Kübler-Ross, 1969). They will have mourned their loss and will be ready to allow the Holy Spirit to begin to pour in the comfort and healing of the self-esteem that can come only from him.

Need to mourn. It should be noted that the parents should never be denied the right to mourn. There are some individuals who would have the parents reach immediate acceptance, stating that if the parents really believe that "All things work together for good to them that love God" (Rom. 8:28), this immediate acceptance would be possible. While it is true that in the long run—and in God's perspective—everything will work together for the good of the entire family, it is highly unrealistic to expect the parents to embrace this truth overnight. The individual who counsels with the grieving parents needs to realize that the grieving process takes time—from several weeks to several years. It is very important to allow the parents to have the opportunity to mourn without condemnation from those who should be assisting instead of hindering this necessary healing process. The counselor should also remember that a death has occurred—the death of the dream child; the parents must be allowed the same right to mourn as those who experience the actual physical death of a loved one. The Scriptures reflect the right to this mourning process: "To everything there is a season and a time ...a time to mourn" (Ecc. 3:1,4). Jesus also said: "Blessed are they that mourn for they shall be comforted" (Matt. 5:4). When the parents have been allowed enough time to mourn, they will be ready to receive the comfort that Jesus promised. Neither the parents' character nor faith is weak simply because they need time and counsel to adjust to what can only be described as a very difficult situation (Ball, 1983).

Characteristics of acceptance. Parents reaching this final stage of acceptance seem to accept their handicapped child for who—and what—he or she is. They have learned to appreciate the child's strengths and to tolerate the weaknesses. They may have even learned to take pleasure in the child and what the child *can* do, with little or no emphasis on things that the child may be unable to do. The child may be viewed as having a unique, vital place within the family and the household (Huber, 1979).

It is sometimes difficult to recognize when parents have passed into this stage. Wortis (1966) suggested two indicators of acceptance: the degree to which the mother functions in her usual manner and the degree to which both parents meet the needs of their normal children as well as those of the handicapped child.

Non-acceptance dynamics. Some parents seemingly never reach the stage of acceptance. Even after the child is grown and independent, the parents may continue to struggle severely with anger and depression about the child's disability. They may have become bitter toward God and other people. Perhaps they did not receive enough support to take them through the grief stages, or perhaps they simply would not allow the Holy Spirit to minister to their needs. Whatever the cause of such nonacceptance, I still believe that the vast majority of parents will eventually reach the acceptance stage when given enough support. This requires an atmosphere where both the counselor and the parents allow the Holy Spirit to minister.

There are those individuals who would state that the parents should never reach this acceptance stage; to do so would be to decide that God is not going to heal the child and would, therefore, reflect lack of faith "preventing" God from doing a healing work. To even present such an idea to the grieving parents is to place an unnecessarily cruel burden on their shoulders. We must never set ourselves up as being able to command or demand that God do anything. He is the one who is sovereign, not we. We must learn to accept that sometimes in his great wisdom he does not do things exactly as we, with our human understanding, think that he should do them. His ways are not like ours: "For my thoughts are not your thoughts, neither are your ways my ways, saith the Lord. For as the heavens are higher than the earth, so are my ways higher than your ways, and my thoughts than your thoughts (Isa. 55:8, 9). We need to let God *be* Lord even in this painful and hard-to-understand area of our lives. For the parents to live in a state of continuous emotional turmoil, refusing to allow the Holy Spirit to bring the acceptance and comfort that they so desperately need, does not bring any glory to God. The parents need to be assisted to reach the stage where they can accept both the child and the handicap as if the child will always be like this while, at the same time, never closing their minds to the fact that God has the ability to heal the child if in *his* wisdom it is the best thing to do. For the parents to come to this place of acceptance while still believing in God's sovereign love and wisdom requires more faith than to believe continuously that God is going to "fix" things so that the child will be perfectly normal.

THE COUNSELOR'S PERSPECTIVE
Stage Diagnosis and Sensitivity

When the minister or counselor is attempting to deal with the parents of the handicapped child, it is important for him or her to be aware of these loss stages and to be able to determine in which stage the parents are. The counselor should work differently with parents in the denial or anger stage than with parents in the stage of acceptance.

It is also important to realize that the parents may not stay in one stage as long as expected or may not move neatly from one stage to another but may move back and forth between stages. This is especially true of the middle three stages—anger, bargaining, and depression. The parents may go through these three stages in an almost cyclic manner for a period of time before moving into (and remaining in) the final stage of acceptance. Huber (1979) stated that parental adjustment to a child's handicap can be a slow learning process; few parents know instinctively how to handle the intense feelings of loss that result from the realization that their child is handicapped.

These stages that the parents go through in learning how to deal with the child's handicap are normal. They are a *healthy* way to react to a shocking reality. The adjusting parents are *not* behaving in a disturbed or pathological manner—their feelings of loss are to be expected. Such feelings should be recognized in this light and even be encouraged as much as possible (Huber, 1979).

Parents should not be pushed, urged, or reasoned out of an early stage. They should be allowed to proceed at their own pace and helped to discover their own resources. The style they use in handling the situation should be accepted because what may seem unorthodox to the counselor may be successful for many parents. The parents should be allowed to share their ideas and encouraged to use them. If they deny the reality of the situation their denial should not be reinforced; *neither* should their defenses be stripped. Some parents experiencing these feelings may just need more time. The counselor should try to sense where the parents are and move at their speed (Huber, 1979).

Adopted Children

The minister or Christian counselor also needs to be aware that this grieving process can also occur in the case of a healthy adopted child. Many individuals think that when the parents have chosen to adopt a child there should be no depression or angry feelings. After all, the child has become a member of the family by the choice of the parents, not because the child just happened to be born into the family. Nothing could be further from the truth. Adoptive parents *also* dream of what the child will be like during the period when the home study is being done and during the waiting period which occurs before the child is placed in their home. The amount of time that the adoptive parents have to dream about their child is usually longer than a pregnancy—in some cases it can stretch into several years. Prospective adoptive parents are asked specifically and in detail which handicapping conditions they are willing to accept and work with and are informed before the adoption about any known handicaps the child may have. Still there have been cases where the adopted child turned out to have handicaps of which no one was aware at the time of placement. Also the adopted child is as equally prone as any other child to accidents, injuries, and illnesses that might result in a lifetime handicapping condition. When either of these situations occur, the adoptive parents will need to go through the mourning process like any other parents.

GUIDING PARENTS THROUGH THE ADJUSTMENT PERIOD

Roos (1973) described how parents have a variety of feelings to deal with, including loss of self-esteem, shame, ambivalence, depression, self-sacrifice, and defensiveness. He stated that although parents have common emotional reactions and conflicts, the way that they handle the situation varies considerably. Buscaglia (1975) identifies stages through which parents progress and includes grief, anguish, hurt, shock, disbelief, helplessness, and frustration. Many parents report feelings of grief, disbelief, or anger after living with a handicapped child for 20 years or more.

Vernon and Ottinger (1980) propose that coping constructively cannot begin until parents accurately understand the irreversibility of the condition and its implications. If this understanding and acceptance are not accomplished, and if the parents are not guided wisely through the emotional turmoil of this period, the mourning that should be experienced is chronically repressed, and chronic denial is substituted for realistic understanding and effective coping. The resultant inability to cope adequately causes further frustration and anxiety as the parents and child struggle through the years to deal with the realities of their mutual communication and emotional needs.

All of these authors have pointed out the need of parents of the handicapped child to work through various stages and feelings in learning how to deal effectively with their child and his or her handicap. How can the parents be assisted to do this? Burggraf (1979) stated that such stages are developmental: when parents have an opportunity to develop a human relationship with a counselor (or other helping professional), and when such a relationship is characterized by caring, respect, dignity and openness, they can learn to think in terms of stages and the feelings that accompany each stage. They can and will learn to deal with the here-and-now feelings of guilt, denial, anger, and resignation in this atmosphere.

How can the counselor help the parent learn how to parent more effectively the child with a handicapping condition? Norton (1979) cautioned that counselors must have worked through their own feelings about handicapped children and must be able to accept and love the handicapped as they are. Counselors must never try to hide the truth from parents. Instead they must be truthful, helping parents to understand their child's handicap and the full implications of it, and their feelings about coping with the child. This is necessary because, as Buscaglia (1975) pointed out, you cannot give another person what you do not have yourself.

FAMILY RELATIONSHIPS

Dinkmeyer and Muro (1971) stated that the family is the most significant single influence on the child's growth and development. Buscaglia (1975) added that it is within the security of the family that the handicapped child first learns that he or she is a person who can trust, love, and be loved, and where—even with severe limitations—it is permissible to be oneself.

Families today are often under great stress, even without such additional problems as having a handicapped child. Grandparents and other relatives are frequently not available to "help out" because of geographic (if not emotional) distance. Neighbors often know very little about each other and consider it improper to inquire. Close friends may live across town or just as far away as the grandparents (Paul, 1983). There is, therefore, often no one to help regularly, other than the professionals. This makes it more likely that parents will turn to the church family for the support they need, rather than to their own families.

There is no "typical" family with a handicapped child. The only things that various families of handicapped children have in common are the additional pressures imposed on the family life by the presence of the child (Paul, 1983). However, some of the relationships that may occur within any family having a handicapped child merit consideration by those in the helping professions.

Husband/Wife Relationships

The relationship between the parents of the child will certainly be affected. Problems emerge as a consequence of the parents' attempting to find the "cause" of the child's handicap. Further problems are created indirectly by the educational program in which the child is placed. Many programs for educating parents of the handicapped child meet during the day; often only the mother can attend the meetings regularly. This can and does place an enormous amount of strain on the husband-wife relationship, since the mother is on the receiving end of the information and passes it on to the father. The father therefore often finds himself in a passive role and may begin abdicating decision-making concerning the child. His wife, however, may not want to have this level of responsibility. A mother under the weight of educational decision-making and child management responsibilities may begin to press the husband for assistance. The husband, who may not be well informed, may find it difficult to accept direction from his wife, since it often seems like criticism. This can lead both to become defensive and argumentative. Many men reared in a traditional family setting, where the man is expected to make all the important decisions, cannot cope with this reversal of roles. With all these factors added to the normal stress of the marriage relationship, many relationships complicated by special-needs children end in divorce (Luterman, 1979). The counselor may have to help the husband realize his need to become more involved and should be prepared to do marriage counseling in addition to counseling the parents with regard to their feelings about the handicapped child.

Parent/Grandparent Relationships

The relationship between the parents and the grandparents of the handicapped child also suffers a role-reversal. Grandparents not living in the same town as the child can—in cases where the handicap is not physically visible—become fixated in the denial stage. For those grandparents who do begin to go through their own grieving process, there is the double pain of having a handicapped grandchild and knowing that their own child is suffering. This is often very difficult for them to deal with emotionally.

The grandparents lack knowledge and information about the handicapping condition; the parents, however, perhaps through their contacts with professionals or a parent education group, may rapidly acquire the information and the emotional support they need to work through the mourning stages faster than the grandparents are able to move. Since the parents know more about the handicap than their own parents do, they are thrust into a teaching role; they often have to "parent" their own parents by providing them with emotional support and information. Therefore, when the parents of the handicapped child are in greatest need of support from their own parents, it is often not forthcoming and they may begin to resent their parents (Luterman, 1979). The counselor should include the grandparents in some counseling sessions when this is possible, or arrange with a minister or counselor in the area where the grandparents live to provide some assistance to them.

Siblings

The siblings of the handicapped child may also have their own problems adjusting. If the situation is not handled properly the presence of a handicapped child can cause emotional problems for the normal siblings. The parent may give normal children much less parental time and energy because the handicapped child demands so much of both. The siblings need to have some attention in their own right, not just during the time when they may be helping the parents care for the handicapped child. The non-handicapped sibling is often asked to assume more responsibility at a much earlier age than would be the case if the family did not have a handicapped child (Luterman, 1979).

Parents need to be reminded that although their lives within the family circle may be difficult, they can learn to cope with these difficulties and can, in turn, help other family members achieve some degree of acceptance. There may also be problems regarding future siblings. While parents may have been planning to have a larger family, the birth of a handicapped infant will often cause them to change their mind. They become fearful that having produced one handicapped child they may, should they have any more children, produce another. When possible, if the siblings are old enough, they need to be included in some type of counseling sessions also.

Parent/Child Relationship

One of the most important goals in parenting any child is to facilitate the development of the capacity for self-direction. This goal has special significance for the handicapped child. It is tragic when a physically dependent child becomes an adult burdened with the additional handicap of being emotionally dependent on external direction and control. Such psychological reinforcement of a physical handicap is extremely destructive to the spirit of the handicapped person. It is not easy to develop in adult life if the individual has not been allowed to develop gradually while growing up. The individual cannot remain an obedient child without any self-direction for twenty years, then suddenly be transformed into a responsible adult on his twenty-first birthday.

The two most common ways that parents block their child's development are through *pushing* and *overprotection*. Both of these extremes of parental behavior express the parents' underlying lack of faith in the child's inner resources. On the one hand, when parents *overprotect* a child they prevent the child from developing initiative; they thereby take away the child's courage. On the other hand, when parents *push* a child they interfere with the child's initiative by taking away the child's opportunity to find personal motivation. Yet it is extremely difficult for parents to allow the child gradually to develop the capacity for self-direction until they themselves have learned how to handle their own feelings regarding the child and the handicap. During some of the final sessions the counselor has with the parents, they should be made aware of how crucial it is to allow the child to develop gradually as much independence as possible—at least emotionally—even if physical independence is not possible.

THE COUNSELING SESSIONS

The Counselor and the Community

One of the most helpful things the counselor can do for the parents is to put them in touch with other parents facing a similar situation. It is helpful for the parents to have contact with both those who are currently trying to adjust to being parents of a handicapped child and also with those who have successfully coped for some years. There are different insights to be gained from these two perspectives.

It would be especially helpful if the counselor could put Christian parents in touch with other Christian parents with handicapped children. This would provide the parents with the special opportunity to share with fellow believers and to pray with someone who really knows what it means to face a handicapped child daily.

Session Guidelines

The following suggestions are offered to help the Christian counselor facilitate the counseling session with the parents of the handicapped child:

1. Begin each session with prayer, inviting the Holy Spirit to take control of the session and to accomplish what he would like in the lives of those present.

2. Do much more listening than talking. The parents will often reach conclusions by themselves if they are simply allowed to talk their feelings out.

3. Do not be judgmental or opinionated.

4. Do not try to cheer the parents. They need to express their negative feelings openly so they can deal with them. The counseling session is a good place to do this.

5. Plan sessions with an open agenda. Allow the parents to lead the way, to decide when they are ready to deal with the various issues.

6. The parents will not be able to adjust instantly to the burden of the handicap. For the purpose of solving immediate problems, it may be helpful to guide them to approach the situation in stages.

7. Allow the parents time to talk with each other and to make plans. It is vital to encourge the parents to communicate with each other and to encourage them to begin making their own plans, instead of relying on others to make plans for them.

8. Do not use out-dated terminology to refer to the child or to the handicap. Parents of a deaf child can be deeply offended when obsolete terms like ''deaf and dumb'' or ''deaf-mute'' are used. Also parents having a child with a seizure disorder can be offended by the use of the term ''fits.''

9. Pray with parents at the end of the session, encouraging them to verbalize in prayer also. Some parents hesitate to tell God how they really feel for fear that he will be angry and ''do something else to us.'' They may feel safe to do this in the presence of the counselor, reasoning that God could not possibly be angry with the counselor and so would be more kindly disposed toward the parent in his or her presence.

10. Encourage parents who have been baptized in the Holy Spirit to pray in tongues if they have difficulty expressing themselves in English. Being able to do this often brings a feeling of great release to the stressed parent.

SUMMARY

Parents with a handicapped child face a much more difficult task as they try to assist the child, within the limits of the particular handicap, to grow into an independently functioning adult. This task is further complicated by the parents' struggle to accept the child, the handicap, and the implications of that handicap. It is also difficult because, as Buscaglia (1975) and Dinkmeyer and Muro (1971) have pointed out, the future for the handicapped child will depend on the dynamics of the home situation and the parents responsible for creating and maintaining the home situation in which the child finds himself or herself.

We have examined ways in which the professional counselor may be of assistance to the parents in the struggle to complete this task successfully. We have seen that the feelings that the parents experience are normal for parents of a handicapped child.

Leigh (1975) pointed out that many of the research studies done with handicapped children and their parents indicate that parent counseling may be more beneficial in many situations than direct therapy or remediation with the child. Parents of handicapped children have a long difficult road to follow as they learn to cope. They need all the help they can get; those having the skills, training and ability to give this assistance should be doing everything possible to meet that need.

The parent should also be encouraged to find that help which comes only from the Lord through the power of the Holy Spirit as they believe his Word: "Be strong and of a good courage, fear not, nor be afraid . . . for the LORD thy God, He it is that doth go with thee; he will not fail thee, nor forsake thee" (Deut. 31:6).

SELECT BIBLIOGRAPHY

Ball, J. R. (1983). Pastoral help for families of handicapped children. In J. L. Paul (Ed.), *The exceptional child.* Syracuse, NY: Syracuse University Press.

Burggraf, M. Z. (1979). Consulting with parents of handicapped children. *Elementary School Guidance and Counseling, 13,* 214–221.

Buscaglia, L. (Ed.). (1975). *The disabled and their parents: A counseling challenge.* Thorofare, NJ: Charles B. Slack.

Dinkmeyer, D. & Muro, J. (1971). *Group counseling: Theory and practice.* Itasca, IL: F. E. Peacock.

Huber, C. H. (1979). Parents of the handicapped child: Facilitating acceptance through group counseling. *Personnel and Guidance Journal, 57,* 267–269.

Kübler-Ross, E. (1969). *On death and dying.* New York: Macmillan.

Leigh, J. (1975). What we know about counseling the disabled and their parents: A review of the literature. In L. Buscaglia (Ed.), *The disabled and their parents: A counseling challenge* (pp. 39–63). Thorofare, NJ: Charles B. Slack.

Luterman, D. (1979). *Counseling parents of hearing-impaired children.* Boston: Little, Brown, & Company.

McCollum, A. (1984). Grieving over the lost dream. *The exceptional parent.*

Murphy, A. T. (1977). Counseling way: Lessons parents have taught me. *Volta Review, 79,* 145–152.

Norton, F. H. (1976). Counseling parents of the mentally retarded child. *School Counselor, 23,* 201–205.

Paul, J. L. (1983). Families of handicapped children. In J. L. Paul (Ed.), *The exceptional child.* Syracuse, NY: Syracuse University Press.

Roos, P. (1973). Parents of mentally retarded children—misunderstood and mistreated. In A. Turnbull & H. Turnbull (Eds.), *Parents speak out.* Columbus, OH: Charles E. Merrill.

Smith, P. (1984). For parents when they learn that their child has a handicap. *The NAD Interstate* (newspaper), p. 6.

Vernon, M. & Ottinger, P. (1980). Counseling the hearing-impaired child in a mainstreamed setting. In L. Benjamin & G. Walz (Eds.), *Counseling exceptional people.* Wash., D.C.: The National Institute of Education.

Wortis, J. (1966). Successful family life for the retarded child. In *Stress on families of the mentally handicapped: Proceedings of the Third International Conference of the International League of Societies of the Mentally Retarded,* Paris.

7

MINISTERING TO THE AGING

Raymond T. Brock

Age is a state of mind. A man may feel old while the calendar says he should be aging; or, he may remain young while his body visibly ages. Such an observation no doubt led Solomon to write: "For as he thinketh in his heart, so is he" (Prov. 23:7). We can see a Christian attitude toward the secret of aging gracefully in a beautiful statement by Paul:

> Your attitude should be the kind that was shown us by Jesus Christ, who, though he was God, did not demand and cling to his right as God, but laid aside his mighty power and glory, taking the disguise of a slave and becoming like men. And he humbled himself even further, going so far as actually to die a criminal's death on a cross (Phil. 2:5–8, LB).

Aging is the process of growing old. It begins with birth and culminates with death. In this chapter, aging refers to the third phase of life, following childhood and adolescence. Robert Browning (1961) celebrated the process of aging in his famous poem, "Rabbi Ben Ezra"

Grow old along with me!
The best is yet to be,
The last of life, for which the first was made. . .

It is helpful for the Christian counselor, no matter what his personal age, to be aware of research concerning the aging process. *Gerontology* is the science of studying the old and *geriatrics* is the study of the medical problems of the aged. *Ageism* is used to describe the prejudice to which the aged population is frequently subjected (McKenzie, 1980).

In *Aging and Vitality*, Fries and Carpo (1981) reported that the data suggest that lifestyles of activity and moderation are associated with relative longevity. They suggest that even in the absence of disease, a natural life span and a natural death are intrinsic in our biology (p. 22). As a result, they offered a "new syllogism"

1. The human life span is fixed.
2. The age at first infirmity will increase.
3. Therefore, the duration of infirmity will decrease (p. 7).

They affirmed that there is a natural limit to life, a point beyond which medical science cannot extend it. They established the biological limit for human life at about 114 years and attributed rumors of longer life in the mountainous regions of Abkhazia in Russia, the Huinza province of Pakistan, and the isolated village of Vilcabamba in Ecuador to inaccurate records and errors in oral reporting (pp. 13–17).

At the turn of the twentieth century, death occurred at an average age of 47 years, after a brief terminal illness which accounted for less than one percent of the life span. With increasing medical technology, however, this latter figure has increased so that currently 10% or more of the life span may well be spent in terminal illness.

Today the life expectancy is an average of 73 years—26 years longer than at the beginning of the twentieth century. Specifically, the white female can expect to live 78 years, while the normal life span for the white male is 70 years, at least in Western countries (Fries & Carpo, 1981). It is a challenge to the Christian counselor to help clients come to grips with the inevitability of aging and lead them into making the kinds of decisions that will prolong active involvement in life and forestall the diseases and accidents that either shorten the life span or contribute to spending the latter years in a lingering terminal illness.

PROLONGING NATURAL LIFE

The body's aging process is called *senescence*, defined as "an accumulation in cells and organs of deteriorating functions that begins early in adult life" (Fries & Carpo, 1981, p. 4). Studies indicate that various cells, organs, and connective tissues of the body age at different rates; some organ systems are more critically impaired by aging than others. This is known as *molecular aging* and is influenced by the "Hayflick limit" (Hayflick & Moorehead, 1961), which is the barrier to indefinite replication of healthy cells in the body. This reminds us that "it is appointed unto men once to die, but after this the judgment" (Heb. 9:27).

In our life time, society has almost eliminated premature death. Death from tuberculosis, smallpox, polio, diphtheria, tetanus, typhoid and paratyphoid fevers, and whooping cough have been reduced 99% or more. Even syphilis is limited almost entirely to those older individuals who contracted the disease before the introduction of antibiotics. The major exception to this trend of eradicating premature death because of major infectious diseases has been the respiratory problems of pneumonia and influenza. The eradication here is only about 85%, but deaths from respiratory diseases occur almost exclusively among the infirm, the very old, or those who are already ill with another disease (Fries & Carpo, 1981).

A new disease, at least in Western countries, is the acquired immune deficiency syndrome (AIDS). The death rate from AIDS is estimated to be 100% because no adequate medical intervention has yet been discovered. Fortunately, this new scourge affects only a small proportion of the total population, although the incidence is rising in some metropolitan centers (Fries & Carpo, 1981).

The chronic diseases that continue to represent a major health threat continue to be atherosclerosis, cancer, emphysema, diabetes, osteoarthritis, and cirrhosis. These diseases account for 80% of all premature deaths and 90% of all disability among the aged segment of our population (Fries & Carpo, 1981). The evidence points to the fact that personal health habits are the main risk factor in the lethal power of these diseases. The counselor will want to remember that preventive approaches to healthful living hold more promise than medical interventions for improving human health and prolonging active life in the aged.

PERIODS OF AGING

Hurlock, quoted by Troll (1975), said, "The adult is an individual who has his growth and is ready for his status in society with other adults." Then she added, "We can now look at adulthood as the middle of life, a long-lasting time that blends into an equally long old age" (p. 2). The process of aging has been divided into various periods of time by researchers to simplify discussion of the trends noted in the general population. Sheehy (1976) divided the adult years into ten-year periods and referred to the transitions between the decades as *Passages*.

> During each of these passages, how we feel about our way of living will undergo subtle changes in four areas of perception. One is the interior sense of self in relation to others. A second is the proportion of safeness to danger we feel in our lives. A third is our perception of time—do we have plenty of it, or are we beginning to feel that time is running out? Last, there will be some shift at the gut level in our sense of aliveness or stagnation. (p. 21)

Levinson (1978) used an overlapping strategy to note that the demarcation of transitions in aging is not discrete and varies from individual to individual. He suggested that *younger adulthood* spans 17 to 45 years and set *middle adulthood* between ages 40 and 65. *Later adulthood* falls between 60 and 85; however, a new period has evolved in this century for the increasing number of individuals who fall into *late late adulthood*, which Levinson stated begins about age 80. Each of these periods is reviewed and discussed in some detail.

YOUNG ADULTHOOD

This is the most dramatic period of life. Levinson (1978) called these "the peak years" for biological functioning, noting that "full height and maximum strength, sexual capacity, cardiac and respiratory capacity, and general biological vigor" (p. 21) are attained in these years. Intellectual skills "such as memory, abstract thought, ability to learn specific skills and to solve well-defined problems are near their peak in early adulthood" (p. 21).

Intimacy vs. Isolation

The seminal work that has been extremely helpful to therapists in describing the development sequences of the life span was written by Erikson (1968). The final three of his "Eight Ages of Man" were devoted to the adult years. Each age represents a unique set of challenges for the maturing individual. The process of developing mature relationships in early adulthood lies in completing the tasks of the earlier years, which Erikson postulated as developing *trust* rather than *mistrust*, *autonomy* rather than *shame* and *doubt*, *initiative* rather than *guilt*, *industry* rather than *inferiority*, and ego *identity* rather than *role confusion*.

The chief challenge facing young adults, Erikson said, is to achieve *intimacy*, the ability to trust, share, and give oneself emotionally, spiritually, and mentally to another without the compulsion for sexual performance. Failure to make the adjustments leading to intimacy leads to *isolation*, the avoidance of life's opportunities. Evidence of isolation is the development of character problems. Isolation involves a repudiation of life in which a person attempts to destroy seemingly dangerous forces and becomes isolated from the mainstream of life.

Success in the quest for intimacy requires the capacity to enjoy intimate, nonerotic relationships with both men and women as a single person before attempting to establish and maintain a happy marital relationship. Erikson quoted Freud in saying that the essential task of a man at this age is to develop the capacity "leiben und arbeiten," to love and to work—and in that order.

Marriage does not necessarily indicate intimacy has been achieved, as is illustrated by those who married with the expectation of solving their problems, only to be disillusioned and unhappy in their marriage. Menninger (1976) suggested that promiscuous sexual behavior is evidence of a lack of emotional intimacy and is an indicator of isolation, with its attending loneliness within the disturbed individual. The isolated young adult feels alone in the crowd, unfulfilled on the job, and unsatisfied in bed with another person.

Actualization

Intimacy offers the potential for developing what Maslow (1968, 1971) called *self-actualization*. It is attainable in young adulthood. If it is not achieved in the early adult years, however, the individual is likely to remain less than fulfilled in the remaining years of life. Maslow's research led him to describe the "self-actualizer" as a man or woman who has achieved wholeness in life with a balanced integration of physical, emotional, and spiritual dimensions of personality.

People in the process of self-actualization live close to reality and can tolerate ambiguity. They accept themselves and others, and experience little guilt or anxiety. They display an effervescent spontaneity in thought and behavior. *Problem-centered* rather than *ego-centered*, they become involved in broad social issues while at the same time maintaining a need for privacy, and they enjoy solitude that allows them to hold an objective point of view. As a result, they maintain a relative independence from their culture; yet, they do not flaunt convention just for the sake of being different.

The self-actualizing individual enjoys a deep appreciation for life and sees beauty in the mundane. He or she enjoys mystical, ecstatic experiences more than others, and seems to see limitless horizons. A deep social interest allows the self-actualizing person to identify sympathetically with people in general while maintaining intimate and satisfying interpersonal relations with only a few selected individuals. Democratic in orientation, the self-actualizing person is void of the prejudices that fragment society. He or she has the ability to discriminate clearly between means and ends, and enjoys the process of reaching goals.

A special gift of the actualizing person is a good sense of humor; this allows this person to be philosophical in thinking, but his or her jokes are nonhostile. Zimbardo (1980) noted that the person in the process of actualizing enjoys a "primary creativeness that comes out of the unconscious" and produces truly original, new discoveries" (p. 312). This gift of creativity allows the self-actualizing person to be resistant to enculturation; this individual fits into culture but remains independent of it. He or she does not respond with blind compliance to culture's demands. "With all of these characteristics," Zimbardo (1980) concluded, "self-actualized persons are particularly capable of loving and of being loved in the fullest way" (p. 312).

Maslow believed that self-actualization is available to all adults of every culture. In his studies of Western cultures, however, he found that less than 2% of the college-age population attained this status, and less than half of the adults had attained it by age 40. Herein lies a challenge for the Christian therapist: the most normal, adjusted persons in the community should be the Spirit-filled Christians who have the guidance of the Holy Spirit to assist them in exploring the dimensions of their God-given potential. Guidance in how to pursue the processes of self-actualization is found in the Beatitudes (Matt. 5:1–22); learning to think as Jesus thought brings forth the fruit of the Spirit enumerated by Paul (Gal. 5:22, 23).

Christ-Actualization

In *The Emotional Side of Men* (Schmidt & Brock, 1983), I have noted that:

> some Christians have difficulty with the concept of *self*-actualization, suggesting that it by definition represents behavior that is self-centered. To overcome this semantic drawback from what appears to be a healthy Biblical concept I have coined the word Christ-actualization. I believe this is the meaning of Galatians 2:20, where Paul says, "I am crucified with Christ: nevertheless I live; yet not I, but Christ liveth in me; and the life which I now live in the flesh I live by the faith of the Son of God, who loved me and gave himself for me." (pp. 58, 59)

For two decades now I have been exploring the actualization concept from a Christian perspective. I have become convinced that a Christian can go beyond the world's concept of adequacy or authenticity to actualize in Christ—to move beyond *self-actualization* to *Christ-actualization*. By way of theoretical background, Maslow (1968) said that the actualization process is developmental; the person must first meet his or her D-motive needs (D for *doing*), which progress in hierarchical order from physical, safety, love and belongingness to achieve self-esteem. Above this he placed self-actualization as a B-motive (B for *being*). I envision *Christ-actualization* as an even higher step. It connotes the transcendence that results from a personal walk with Christ—as the individual is being led by the Holy Spirit into all the truth God wants to reveal.

Shostrom and Montgomery noted in *Healing Love* (1978) that it "is not that he or she is perfect, but rather that he or she is *being perfected* by the healing love and power of God. The process of being made whole involves gradual transformation of one's entire being'' (p. 82). While I agree, I have also come to believe that the power of the Holy Spirit can streamline the process; some new Christians may move more quickly and easily into actualization experiences than many who have been in the church all of their lives but who have not grown toward Christian maturity. Thus, I emphasize that *Christ-actualization* is a process and not a state to be attained. Actualizing Christians enjoy this experience more frequently than their Christian peers. This is consistent with Paul, who said:

> Brethren, I count myself not to have apprehended, but this one thing I do: forgetting those things which are behind and reaching forth unto those things which are before, I press toward the mark for the prize of the high calling of God in Christ Jesus (Phil. 3:13, 14).

The work of the Holy Spirit in the life of believers, then, does not relieve them from responsibility for their own behavior; rather, the Spirit empowers them to face needs realistically and to grow into the Christian maturity that God has made available through the incarnation of his Son, Jesus Christ. Wagner (1975) is helpful to Christians who are striving to develop such a healthy self-esteem, as is Narramore (1985) in his discussion of condemnation and how to distinguish between wholesome guilt ('constructive sorrow') and neurotic guilt.

Kolb and Brodie (1982, p. 75) use the term ''mature adult'' to describe the person who:

> 1. Has developed a clear personal identity, demonstrated by the ability to form an intimate, satisfying, and loving relationship with a mature member of the opposite sex and take on the responsibilities of rearing children.
>
> 2. Is able both to assume personal responsibilities when necessary and to accept the decisions of those with competent authority for the general good.
>
> 3. Independently pursues his own goals, with recognition of his limitations and with willingness to seek advice from others when indicated.
>
> 4. Is able to maintain and enjoy his personal relations with others, making due allowances for their deficits with an understanding tolerance.
>
> 5. Is absorbed and satisfied in achievement relative to his family, vocation, and avocations rather than in personal self-assertions.
>
> 6. Functions well at home and at work in terms of developing gratifying relations with others as well as in being generally free of symptoms of illness.

It is apparent that the processes of self-actualization and mature adulthood can begin in the young adult years and continue throughout the sequence of aging through the declining years. The unique tasks of young adults in the process of becoming all they have been created to be have been enumerated by Havighurst (1953). The process begins with the decision of whether or not to marry and if so, when. For it must be remembered: marriage is a choice—it is not a mandatory course in life. Although ''married'' is usual, ''single'' is, nonetheless, *normal*. Current census data indicate a significant portion of the adult population (reportedly 4% to 8%) never marry.

For the person who elects marriage, there are the tasks of selecting a mate and learning to live with a marriage partner. Then comes the decision of whether or not to have children. If the choice is for children, the tasks of child rearing and managing a home are significant. To sustain the family unit, the launching and perpetuating of a career are vital concerns. It is also important to take on civic responsibility and to function in a congenial social group. Although Havighurst neglected to mention the point, it is vital for the Christian young adult to identify with a Christian community and become active in spiritual endeavors.

MIDDLE ADULTHOOD
Generativity vs. Self-Absorption

Between 40 and 65, the adult is said to be middle aged. This is the time of optimal development in the home and workplace. The groundwork laid earlier in life bears fruit in these challenging years. In Erikson's (1968) model, if the earlier ages have been traversed successfully, the result will be *generativity* which is productiveness—not only for oneself, but also for succeeding generations. The emphasis is on the motivation behind the work effort, not the amount of time or energy expended in the pursuit of a career. Generativity involves being productive and creative for others more than self. It also involves pride and pleasure in one's children and grandchildren, and enjoying the privileges of guiding the next generation into a full life. For instance, if a man is working hard and producing well for the benefit of his wife and children, he is involved in generativity. Generative Christians are excellent examples or models who can take 1 Corinthians 11:1 literally: "Follow my example, as I follow the example of Christ" (NIV).

Erikson used the term *self-absorption* to describe the person who is caught up in the quest for ego satisfaction and personal fulfillment—one who thrives on the limelight or accolades that come from compulsive workaholic behavior. Self-absorption is the antithesis of generativity and represents failure to reach optimal middle adulthood. Such a person is egocentric and nonproductive, and has experienced early personal impoverishment, self-indulgence, and self-gratification. Too often this approach to life leads to the addictive life-controlling problems of alcoholism, drug abuse, sexual infidelity, and eating disorders.

Havighurst (1953) indicated that the developmental tasks of middle adulthood involve achieving adult civic and social responsibility, plus establishing and maintaining an appropriate economic standard of living. For the married couple, the added tasks are assisting teen-age children to become responsible, happy adults, and discovering that there really is "life after children." At the same time middle adults must adjust to the declining vigor of their own aging parents. Even more important is the challenge of relating appropriately to one's own spouse as a dynamic, vital person. Developing adult leisure-time activities while at the same time adjusting to the physiological changes that occur in middle age complicates these tasks.

Again, Havighurst did not mention the necessity for identifying with Christ and his church, but spiritual fellowship and ministry are important issues which

Christian adults in middle life should place high on their list of priorities. The fruits of generativity are so much more rewarding than self-absorption that the aging process becomes exciting, especially to the Spirit-filled Christian.

Mid-Life Crisis

A relatively new phenomenon that has occurred in this century, especially in the technological societies, is the *mid-life crisis*. Jim Conway (1978), writing from personal experience, observed that a mid-life crisis influences both marriage and career. It demonstrates itself in depression, anger, frustration, and rebellion, which are seen in seeking to restore lost youth, taking early retirement, becoming a workaholic, or becoming involved in an emotional or sexual affair. This crisis is a pervasive experience that involves the total person—physically, socially, culturally, spiritually, and vocationally.

Although the mid-life crisis has traditionally been attributed to men, women also become subject to it as the distinction between job descriptions blurs and the workplace is shared equally between the sexes. Jim Conway's wife Shirley (1980), in analyzing what Jim's mid-life crisis had done to their marriage, discovered that her own aging process was entwined in her husband's experiences and influenced his period of discontent.

A mid-life crisis may happen anywhere between ages 21 and 99 but the first unsettling period usually comes about age 30 as a person is launching a career. If it is determined one is headed in the wrong direction, however, there is time for change. The next unsettling period, and usually a more severe one, strikes between ages 35 and 55, but usually in the fourth decade of life (Conway, 1978, p. 142).

Levinson (1973) noted that this upheaval "may take the form of a crisis, in the sense of turmoil, disruption, and dramatic changes. . . . [Or] it may go more smoothly. But at the end of it, the man will be different from what he was at the beginning" (p. 14). To this Conway (1978) added: "The mid-life crisis demon loses its terror as we understand the normal developmental stages of life, and our understanding gives good reason for hope" (p. 143).

"Burnout" as a symptom of mid-life crisis was first described by Freudenberger in 1974. He coined the word to describe the depletion of energy, dampened enthusiasm, and loss of idealism he had observed in the workplace. Additional insights have been contributed by Lazarus (Lazarus, Averill, & Opton, 1974), who discussed general ways of coping with stress, and Pines, Aronson, and Kafry (1981), who added active and inactive dimensions to the strategies of Lazarus, devising a "coping grid" of four types. In his seminars, Dobbins (1984) deals with specific ways of coping with burnout which are useful to the Spirit-filled psychologist and counselor. His findings are the result of research and practice in both Christian and secular settings. (For additional reading, see my chapter on "Burnout" [Gilbert & Brock, 1985]).

It should be noted, however, that burnout and the other expressions of mid-life crises are not terminal. They arise because of inadequate coping mechanisms.

Insight and therapy can divert, delay, and/or prevent them. The person who falls victim to a crisis profits most readily from a combination of spiritual, cognitive, and emotional interventions. The Spirit-filled therapist is uniquely qualified to minister to the adult in mid-life who is struggling with the tasks of aging. Even when a crisis sneaks up inadvertently, it need not be considered fatal. The victim can and usually does recover as therapeutic resources are activated.

LATER ADULTHOOD

The goal of later adulthood, which spans the years between 60 and 80, is a maturity that integrates the emotional and spiritual dimensions of *being* with the physical state of the aging person. Brink (1985) estimated that "the percentage of elders in America has increased from 4% in 1900 to 11% today. By the year 2015 that figure could rise to the 15–20% range" (p. 462).

Integrity

The crisis of this age is choosing between *integrity* and *disgust* or *despair*. Erikson (1968) described integrity as "the ego's accrued assurance of its proclivity for order and meaning—an emotional integration faithful to the image-bearers of the past and ready to take, and eventually to renounce, leadership in the present" (p. 139). Integrity involves the acceptance of a person's one and only life-cycle as uniquely his or her own and the contribution of others to that life as adequate with no substitutions demanded. This involves a new and different way of remembering parental love which is now free from the wish that things in the family of origin had been different. It also demands an acceptance of life and taking responsibility for one's own behavior. It also incorporates being connected to the stream of life with men and women of the past who established order, created objects, and communicated sayings that convey human dignity and love. "Although aware of the relativity of all the various lifestyles which have given meaning to human striving, the possessor of integrity is ready to defend the dignity of his own life style against all physical and economic threats" (Erikson, 1968, p. 140).

Success in this stage of adulthood is represented by an appreciation of continuity with the past, present, and the future. The cardinal goal of later adulthood is *wisdom*, which Erikson defined as a "detached concern with life itself, in the face of death itself" (1964, p. 133). The person who is aging gracefully accepts the life-cycle and is content with his or her lifestyle. This person cooperates with the inevitabilities of life and, when the time comes, can accept death with dignity. Oates (1973) noted that:

> The recent concern of pastoral psychologists and physicians with the issues of death and dying focus on the importance of the virtue of wisdom as growing out of facing matters of life and death. Of course, the young who have to go to war come to terms with life and death much earlier. (p. 80)

Havighurst (1953) indicated that the tasks of this age include adjusting to decreasing physical strength as well as to living on the reduced income that comes with retirement from career involvement. Establishing an explicit affiliation with one's age-mates is important, as well as the continued meeting of social and civic obligations. Establishing satisfactory physical living arrangements frequently involves leaving the family home and being uprooted from familiar environmental and social surroundings. But, the hardest task of all is adjusting to the death of a spouse and learning to live again as a single adult after years of companionship and fellowship. The incidence of widowhood begins in young adulthood and increases through the years. It is estimated that two-thirds of the females in late adulthood have been widowed (Brink, 1985). With unresolved problems rooted in loneliness, self-concept, limited income, and declining health, they represent a unique counseling challenge.

Spiritual Needs and Religious Involvement

Spiritual resources are vital in meeting spiritual needs on an individual and group basis. Havighurst did not address the value of maintaining active involvement in a Christian community in one's later years of life. But the Christian counselor will want to include this essential task when working with aging clients and their children. According to McKenzie (1980), it is a myth to assume that people will generally become more religious as they grow older; rather, she observed that those who appeared to be more religious in later adulthood had "received more religious training as they grew up, and have continued upon a religious path established during the early or formative years of their lives. Differences in religious orientation appear to be generational rather than age-related" (p. 16).

Although age does not seem to influence either an increase or decrease in religiosity, Moberg (1965) noted that there is a tendency toward decreased church attendance in old age. It is obvious that church attendance cannot be equated with religiosity but it is also evident that lack of transportation, declining health, and changes in living arrangements influence frequency of church attendance. McKenzie (1980) concluded that "there is no evidence suggesting that as people grow older they become more involved in religious activities, gain increased satisfaction from religion, or devote more time and attention to religious concerns" (p. 16).

Brink (1985) found that older people have more traditional religious beliefs, including scriptural literalism and obedience to the commandments, and that they read their Bible more frequently and pray more often. They are also more likely to listen to more religious radio programs and watch more television ministries. Further, he noted, "Most measures of adjustment correlate positively with most measures of religion. The happiest elders attend church the most often" (p. 464). It also appears that prayer and religious belief provide solace for the elderly, especially in concerns with death and bereavement. The Christian counselor will want to find ways to stimulate religious faith among believers and offer hope to unbelievers that will allow them to put their trust in the Lord as their life-cycle approaches its inevitable end. A Christian conversion is possible at any point in life, as many late-in-life conversions testify.

It is evident that attention to spiritual needs of the older adult population should be a high priority for the Christian therapist. Previous spiritual experiences and religious involvements need to be analyzed and modified to conform to the restrictions of the aging process. It is also essential to remember that the next phase of existence has to do with eternity; a personal relationship with Christ must be stabilized in order to move realistically into the inevitability of death.

Retirement

Retirement has long posed a challenge for the aging adult. It has been my observation that unless a person has previously experimented with recreational and leisure activities that require less energy than contact sports, he is apt to be discontented when he has more time and less money. Retirement needs to be anticipated in young adulthood if it is to be entered smoothly in the later years (Coleman & Glaros, 1983).

> Retirement is a difficult transition for some elders, even those who looked forward to it. After a few weeks of what seems like an extended vacation, life can get boring unless there are absorbing outside interests. A phasing out of one's career is preferable to an abrupt end. Serious difficulties in coping with retirement are more likely when the individual has few interests apart from work, when there are financial problems, or when the wife resents the post-retirement frequency of contact. (Brink, 1985, p. 462)

It is also true that many people begin to discover and develop special abilities and talents for the first time in old age. This fact led McKenzie (1980) to coin the new word *recareering*, which denotes that retirement allows for disengaging from previous career restrictions and allows for experimentation with new pursuits.

> Although the majority of older individuals are not engaged in formal remunerative employment, it is erroneous to equate productivity and creativity with "holding down a job." Regardless of employment status, many older citizens continue to be productive, contributing, and creative members of society well into later maturity. If the creative potential of the 65-and-over population is denied, ignored, or suppressed by society, all members of that society will suffer a significant loss. (McKenzie, 1980, p. 13)

Numbers of older adults remain in the workplace past retirement, such as Senator Claude Pepper and J. C. Penney; others, such as Grandma Moses, discovered hidden talents even in the late late adult years. But, change is inevitable: wise is the aging person who prepares adequately for it.

Despair–The Bleak Alternative

If the older adult does not approach life with integrity, he or she becomes the victim of *despair*. Erikson (1968) used this term to describe the aging person who finds that time is slipping by, who discovers no meaning in human existence, and who has lost faith in self and others. This person wishes desperately for a second chance at the life-cycle with more advantages than were enjoyed in the younger years. Unfortunately, there is no feeling of world order or spiritual sensitivity. As a result, he fears death. Erikson noted that the person who has not accepted that life has its limits feels that life is too short and wants another opportunity to seek integrity.

His despair is often hidden behind a show of disgust, a misanthropy, or a chronic contemptuous displeasure with particular institutions and particular people—a disgust and a displeasure which, where not allied with a vision of superior life, only signify the individual's contempt for himself. (p. 140)

Remorse and regret over lost opportunities, compounded by a fear of death, plague the life of the aging individual who has not successfully resolved the first seven of the "Eight Ages of Man" (Erikson, 1968) so integrity can be experienced in life's final stage. Despair shows on the face, is revealed in attitudes, and leads to a life of loneliness. The Christian counselor can deal with this loneliness creatively by distinguishing between loneliness and solitude. Aloneness is not loneliness for the person who pursues creative activities and who maintains warm relations with others. Some of the world's great literature, art, and music were created in solitude. Bible study, prayer, and meditation are creative ways of exploring integrity rather than despair.

LATE LATE ADULTHOOD

Late late adulthood is the label created by Levinson (1978) for life that begins at 80. Individuals at this age frequently suffer from various infirmities and at least one chronic illness. The territory of the life space is smaller; the circle of relationships is diminished; there is a preoccupation with immediate bodily needs and what few comforts of life are still available. But, it is important to understand that along with senescence, psychosocial development continues in this advanced period of life.

What does such development at the end of the life-cycle mean? McKenzie (1980) asserted: "It means that a man is coming to terms with the process of dying and preparing for his own death" (p. 38). Rather than focusing on the demands of life, a person in his or her eighties must prepare for death and the transition into an unknown eternity. Whether it will come in a few months or in twenty years, death is imminent, so the aging adult lives in the shadow of death. One must make peace with dying in order to be involved creatively in life.

The person who believes in the immortality of the soul must prepare for afterlife. This process lends meaning to life and death in general, as well as to one's own life and death in particular. As a result, the aging individual remains vital and continues to engage actively in social life. In the process, the aging individual provides an example of wisdom and personal nobility to others who will follow down the path of life. This dynamic represents the ultimate involvement with one's own self in the quest for integrity. What matters most now is the aging person's final sense of what life is about, his or her "view from the bridge" at the end of the life-cycle. "He must come finally to terms with the self—knowing it and loving it reasonably well, and being ready to give it up" (McKenzie, 1980, pp. 38, 39). The Christian who recognizes that Jesus is the Good Shepherd in the "valley of the shadow of death" is adequately prepared to make this transition with dignity because of personal integrity (Ps. 23).

The patriarchs of biblical times as well as the older giants of history and contemporary life set an example for people of all ages to consider. We can profit by examining the successes and failures of those who have been permitted to live into this later period of life. Their example can challenge younger people to rise to the heights of their God-given potential.

Prolonging Vitality While Aging

Since old age is not a disease (Brink, 1985), the elimination of premature disease discussed at the beginning of this chapter enhances the potential for extending life longer than any previous generation of modern times has experienced. Fries and Carpo (1981) have suggested that it is now possible to extend the end of natural human life to an average of 85 years without disease. They concluded: "the increase of life expectancy results from the elimination of premature death rather than by extension of the natural life span" (p. 75). In interpreting their statistical data they reported:

> The best projections we can develop indicate that the median natural human life span is set at a maximum of 85 years with a standard error of less than one year. Making the assumption of a biological bell-shaped distribution, and taking account of the known frequency of individuals living into their second century of life, one can calculate the standard deviation to be slightly less than 4 years. In other words, one in 10,000 individuals reaches the age of 100; this age is approximately 4 standard deviations from the mean. By the statistical rules of normal distribution, in the ideal setting two-thirds of natural deaths would occur between the ages of 81 and 89, and 95% of natural deaths would occur between the ages of 77 and 93. (Fries & Carpo, 1981, pp. 76, 77)

Fries and Carpo (1981) hypothesized that postponement of chronic disease is dependent on removing the risk factors that are part of contemporary life, factors that are directly under the control of the adult at any age. These include:

> cigarette smoking, excessive alcohol consumption, excessive body weight, excessive consumption of fatty foods, inadequate exercise, exposure to environmental toxins, inadequate use of mature psychological defense mechanisms, and living in the psychological state of helplessness, without options. (Fries & Carpo, 1981, P. 86).

It is in dealing with the excesses and addictions of aging that the services of Spirit-filled clinicians can be invaluable, both in prevention and habit-changing interventions. These include the decision to take charge of life and develop a support system in the Christian community which encourages positive resolution of life's problems. Group therapy and Bible study groups are useful as are other outreach ministries of the church. I have observed many such changes occurring among in-patients in a psychiatric unit as well as in out-patient settings under the guidance of Spirit-filled psychotherapists and trained counseling pastors.

Ultimately, then, the quality of the aging life is a product of personal choice because the aging person is the only one who can take charge of the risk factors which bring on disease or weaken the immune system. Fries and Carpo (1981) used the term *plasticity* to suggest that:

> deterioration of a function with age is not preordained, except in very broad statistical terms. An individual can alter the rate of aging in most of the important variables. . . . postponement of chronic illness is a form of plasticity; it represents the ability of the

individual, by personal decisions, to delay the onset of infirmity.'' (Fries & Carpo, 1981, p. 91).

INTEGRATION

No human being had a choice in being born. This decision was made by others and sanctioned by God, or death would have occurred in the interuterine or postnatal environments. Having been born and then reaching adulthood, we are faced with choices that determine the quality of life. In this chapter, attention has been given to the developmental stages through which the normal human being progresses and some of the tasks that need to be considered in the aging process. Ways of making these choices and controlling behavior have been suggested. It remains for us, then, to make those personal choices, to face the transitions, to cope with the challenges, and to plan for creative resolutions of unforeseen problems.

The Holy Spirit is available to adults to guide them into truth. This involves discovering the facts that are revealed in the natural and behavioral sciences as well as the truths of Scripture. If all truth is God's truth (Holmes, 1977)—and I believe it is—then the challenge before the Spirit-filled psychologist and counselor is to study the "tools of the trade" from both disciplines (psychology and theology) and to function at "the state of the art" (Stocks, 1985). The integration of psychology and theology is a demanding on-going task that requires study and perseverance (Carter & Narramore, 1979; Collins, 1977; Collins & Malony, 1981).

Carter (1983) has summarized the findings of psychology related to adult maturity and compared them to biblical perspectives. He concluded that psychologists focus on five basic dimensions:

(a) having a realistic view of oneself and others; (b) accepting oneself and others; (c) living in the present but having long-range goals; (d) having values; and (e) developing one's abilities and interests and coping with the tasks of living. (Carter, 1983, p. 184)

A biblical perspective, Carter noted, also has five dimensions based on the assumptions that the mature person should "have a realistic or objective view of himself and others."

1. To perceive the self, others, and world from the divine perspective (1 Cor. 12:14–15; Rom. 13:1–3; Eph. 4:4);
2. Biblical maturity involves the accepting of oneself and others (Matt. 22:39);
3. Living in the present with long-term goals is basic in the Scriptures (1 Cor. 5:9, 10);
4. Having values which are self-chosen (Josh. 24:15);
5. Developing one's abilities and interests in everyday living (Eph. 4:7, 12; 2 Tim. 1:6). (Carter, 1983, pp. 189, 190)

Certainly all of the data are not yet in, but the Spirit-filled therapist has an inside track on utilizing the data available to bring wholeness to his or her own life and relationships as well as those of his or her clients. Study, prayer, meditation, and praying in the Spirit are essential methods of the counselor who would devise preventive as well as rehabilitative methods of dealing with the normal processes of aging and the conditions that arise when the aging person is out of synchronization with either natural or spiritual laws. A personal devotional life that fortifies the counselor to diagnose problems and devise therapeutic interventions is essential for effective ministry to the aging. The operation of the Holy Spirit in the process is assured (John 16:13).

Oh, Holy Spirit: reveal to us all that the Father has available to us and free us from the lethargy that would impede our progress in exploring all of the dimensions of truth available to us in this universe created by the Triune God expressly for your most exalted creation—humankind. Teach us to mark the measure of our years, enjoy them to the full, and prepare us for the mystery that is to be revealed to us when death transports us into the higher realms of reality you have prepared for us!

SELECT BIBLIOGRAPHY

Brink, T. L. (1985). Gerontology. In D. G. Benner, (Ed.), *Baker encyclopedia of psychology*. Grand Rapids, MI: Baker Book House.

Brock, R. T. (1985). Avoiding burnout through spiritual renewal. In M. G. Gilbert & R. T. Brock (Eds.), *The Holy Spirit and counseling: Theology and theory*. Peabody, MA: Hendrickson Publishers.

Browning, R. (1961). Rabbi Ben Ezra. In O. Williams (Ed.), *The centennial edition of F. T. Palgreave's the golden treasure of the best songs and lyrical poems*. New York: New American Library (Mentor Books).

Carter, J. D. (1983). Maturity. In H. N. Malony (Ed.), *Wholeness and holiness: Readings in the psychology/theology of mental health*. Grand Rapids, MI: Baker Book House.

Carter, J. C., & Narramore, S. B. (1979). *The integration of psychology and theology: An introduction*. Grand Rapids, MI: Zondervan.

Collins, G. R. (1977). *The rebuilding of psychology: An integration of psychology and Christianity*. Wheaton, IL: Tyndale Publishers.

Collins, G. R., & Malony, H. N. (1981). *Psychology and theology: Prospects for integration*. Nashville: Abingdon.

Coleman, J. C., & Glaros, A. G. (1983). *Contemporary psychology and effective behavior* (5th ed.). Glenview, IL: Scott, Foresman & Company.

Conway, J. (1978). *Men and mid-life crisis*. Elgin, IL: David C. Cook Publishers.

Conway, S. (1980). *You and your husband's mid- life crisis*. Elgin, IL: David C. Cook Publishers.

Dobbins, R. D. (1984). *Crisis counseling: A professional seminar for pastors and counselors*. Akron, OH: Emerge Ministries.

Erikson, E. H. (1964). *Insight and responsibility*. New York: W. W. Norton.

———. (1968). *Identity: Youth and crisis*. New York: W. W. Norton.

Freudenberger, H. J. (1974). Staff burnout. *Journal of Social Issues, 30*, 159–165.

Fries, J. F., & Carpo, L. M. (1981). *Vitality and aging*. San Francisco: Wm. H. Freeman & Co.

Havighurst, R. J. (1953). *Human development and education*. New York: McKay.

Hayflick, L., & Moorehead, P. S. (1961). The serial cultivation of human diploid cell strains. *Experimental Cell Research, 25*, 585.

Holmes, A. (1977). *All truth is God's truth*. Grand Rapids, MI: Eerdmans.

Hurlock, E. B. (1968). *Developmental psychology* (3rd ed.). New York: McGraw-Hill.

Kolb, L. C., & Brodie, H. C. H. (1982). *Modern clinical psychiatry* (10th ed.). Philadelphia: W. B. Saunders.

Lazarus, R. S., Averill, J. R., & Opton, E. M., Jr. (1974). The psychology of coping: Issues of Research and assessment. In V. G. Coelho, et al. (Eds.), *Coping and adaptation*. New York: Basic Books.

Levinson, D. J. (March 1, 1973). The normal crises of the middle years. Symposium sponsored by the Menninger Foundation at Hunter College, New York City.

_____. (1978). *The seasons of a man's life*. New York: Ballantine Books.

Maslow, A. H. (1968). *Toward a psychology of being* (2nd ed.). New York: Van Nostrand.

_____. (1971). *The farther reaches of human nature*. New York: Viking.

McKenzie, S. C. (1980). *Aging and old age*. Glenview, IL: Scott, Foresman & Company.

Menninger, W. (1976). *Happiness without sex*. Kansas City: Sheed, Andrews & McMeel.

Moberg, D. O. (1965). Religiosity in old age. In *Gerontologist, 5*, pp. 78–87.

Narramore, S. B. (1984). *No condemnation: Rethinking guilt motivation in counseling, preaching, and parenting*. Grand Rapids, MI: Academie Books (Zondervan).

Oates, W. E. (1973). *The psychology of religion*. Waco, TX: Word Books.

Pines, A., Aronson, E., & Kafry, D. (1981). *Burnout: From tedium to personal growth*. New York: The Free Press.

Schmidt, J., & Brock, R. (1983). *The emotional side of men*. Eugene, OR: Harvest House Publishers.

Sheehy, G. (1976). *Passages: Predictable crises in adult life*. New York: E. P. Dutton & Co.

Shostrom, E. L., & Montgomery, D. (1978). Healing love: How God works within the personality. Nashville: Abingdon.

Stocks, M. (1985). Personal and spiritual growth. In M. G. Gilbert & R. T. Brock, (Eds.). *The Holy Spirit and counseling: Theology and theory*. Peabody, MA: Hendrickson Publishers.

Troll, L. E. (1975). *Early and middle adulthood: The best is yet to be—maybe*. Monterey, CA: Brooks/Cole.

Wagner, M. E. (1975). *The sensation of being somebody: Building an adequate self-concept*. Grand Rapids, MI: Zondervan.

Zimbardo, P. G. (1980). *Essentials of psychology and life* (10th ed.). Glenview, IL: Scott, Foresman & Company.

8

THE ROLE OF PSYCHOLOGY IN PHYSICAL REHABILITATION

Larry Bass

HISTORICAL PERSPECTIVE

The vocational rehabilitation arm of psychology has been actively involved in contributing to the understanding, treatment, and subsequent adjustment of persons who develop or acquire through accident or injury various types of physical disabilities. The first conference on psychology and rehabilitation was conducted in 1958 at Princeton University. A second conference was held in Monterey, California, in 1970, and the publication that resulted from that conference (Neff, 1971) demonstrates the increasing role psychology has taken in the rehabilitation process of individuals with physical disabilities.

The role of psychology in the rehabilitation of persons with physical disorders or conditions has dramatically changed over the years. For many years, theorists in psychology and psychiatry have pointed to the influences of emotional and perceptual factors on the development, maintenance, and treatment of a variety of physical disorders and conditions. For instance, traditional psychoanalytic literature has suggested the influence of certain emotional disturbances on the development of specific physical disorders (Alexander, 1950; Grinker, 1973). The more current theories in psychology have expanded these early concepts into a deeper appreciation and understanding of the rather complex interaction of emotions, lifestyle factors, and physical disorders. This chapter is, in part, an exploration of some of this current thinking.

Current Emphasis

The present emphasis in psychology is on understanding the physically disabled person as a "whole person" and appreciating how factors such as emotions, lifestyle, family environment, attitudes, and perceptions impinge on and contribute to the development of a physical disorder. In addition, psychologists try to assess how these factors either aid or inhibit the adjustment and rehabilitation process following a physical injury or illness.

The earlier emphasis in vocational rehabilitation was on contributions psychology could make in testing. Of immediate concern was the measurement of various intellectual abilities, personality strengths and weaknesses, etc. to help the person make appropriate vocational choices, given the physical limitations. Psychology continues to make this very important psychometric contribution, but the role of psychology in the rehabilitation process has been greatly expanded to include helping the patient and the patient's family adjust to the physical disability so that the patient is able to function as well as possible, given the physical limitations. The psychologist often is directly involved in the rehabilitation process *with* the patient and the patient's family to help them cope with *any* emotional, psychological, or social influence that might block the process of rehabilitation. The psychologist, thus, functions as a facilitator to the patient, family, and rehabilitation team to help insure that the rehabilitation process continues to provide the greatest possible benefit.

BEHAVIORAL MEDICINE AND THE MEDICAL "TEAM" APPROACH

An outgrowth of this involvement of psychology in the rehabilitation process is a greater appreciation for the complicated interaction between psychological and emotional reactions and chronic physical disabilities. As a result, an entirely "new" field of psychology has emerged: *behavioral medicine*.

Behavioral Medicine

Behavioral medicine has grown to include a multifaceted area of psychology that attempts to treat the "whole person." Behavioral medicine encourages the concept that the mind and the body interact so closely and intricately that treatment of disorders must include aspects of *all* of the following factors: (a) intrapersonal, (b) situational, (o) environmental, (d) perceptual, (e) emotional, (f) psychological, (g) spiritual, and (h) physical. Behavioral medicine has especially been helpful in better understanding the role of stress factors in physical illness and the more effective management of persons with chronic pain.

The Medical Team

Increasingly, psychologists are being included as an important part of the "medical" team in a hospital setting. The perspective brought by the psychologist to the treatment of physical disorders is now being recognized as an extremely important one. The psychologist possesses skills to assess and evaluate various factors or influences which may be operating to produce, maintain, or exacerbate a medical illness or condition. For example, the psychologist may point out to the medically ill person how the person's lifestyle may be contributing to the medical problem. A patient with chronic migraine headaches may be living in a "pressure cooker" manner which takes its toll on the body. The psychologist's helpfulness, then, need not be limited to those situations where the physician suspects mental disease or emotional turmoil, such as hysterical functioning or any one of the psychotic disorders.

A good working relationship with the physician can be most helpful in making the referral to the psychologist a smooth process. The physician may say, "I can find no positive medical results on your tests; the problem must be in your head. I'm going to have you see a psychologist." Such a statement can cause the patient to become defensive and resist the consultation with the psychologist. The physician would be wiser to include the psychological consultation as part of the *usual* evaluation of a patient with a known stress-related medical problem. Even if definite medical problems are discovered, the psychological/emotional factors no doubt play a role as well; treatment of the medical problems is very likely to proceed more smoothly if all of these issues are addressed in the treatment program. Consequently, the integration of psychological issues with physical treatment is often the best way to insure the greatest response to treatment. If the psychological issues are ignored or dealt with separately, the prognosis for lasting symptom change is not as good.

Consultation with Medical Staff

Another important service a psychologist can provide in a medical hospital setting is consultation with the staff who work to diagnose and treat persons with medical problems. The staff personnel often experience their own unique reaction to the patients they work with on the units. It is not possible (nor desirable) for the staff to remain dispassionate and emotionally uninvolved while working with chronically ill patients. The patient with cancer, chronic obstructive pulmonary disease, multiple sclerosis, spinal cord injury, cerebral vascular accident (stroke), brain injury, or amputation (to name only a few impairments and illnesses) represent some extremely difficult challenges in treatment. Negative reactions among the staff personnel to the multiplicity of issues presented by these patients are inevitable. In addition, the families of these patients also experience a wide range of reactions to the medical issues, and the staff sometimes experiences strong reactions to the family members.

The psychologist can become invaluable in helping the staff deal therapeutically with these issues so that the effective rehabilitation of the patient can continue. The psychologist can help the staff personnel be aware of their *own* feelings of anger, hurt, fear, overprotectiveness, hostility, etc., which may interfere with the therapeutic treatment of the patient or family member. The patient, in addition to the staff, can benefit greatly from this consultation service.

Biofeedback in Rehabilitation

An additional treatment modality which has emerged over the past two decades and which is frequently used by psychologists as well as other rehabilitation professionals is biofeedback. Biofeedback has been found to be helpful in a variety of ways in the rehabilitation of chronic physical disability. Biofeedback involves the use of instrumentation to measure various physiological responses in the body. Three modalities are most frequently used in rehabilitation work. An electromyograph (EMG) is used to measure muscle activity; an electroencephalograph

(EEG) measures electrical activity in the brain; and a thermal unit is used to measure skin temperature, which reflects changes in the cardiovascular system.

EMG biofeedback. EMG biofeedback is valuable in muscle re-education work with spinal cord injuries and stroke patients. Muscle activity that is out of the awareness of the patient can be recorded by the machines. The patient can sometimes work with the muscles to increase the readings, thus increasing the muscle activity and, consequently, increasing the strength of the muscle. These same patients sometimes experience muscle spasms, which means there is spontaneous muscle activity that can be quite dysfunctional and annoying. For example, an arm or leg will move or straighten out and the patient cannot control this action or prevent it. The patient can, through EMG feedback, learn to decrease the spasmodic muscle activity and learn to achieve some control over the spasms.

EEG biofeedback. EEG biofeedback applications include measuring and controling brain wave activity, especially the *alpha* wave. Alpha brain waves accompany deep relaxation states characterized by a sense of well-being and inner calm. Alpha wave training has been used with patients who experience chronic pain; EEG biofeedback training has been associated with decreases in pain for these patients (Melzak, 1975; Melzak & Chapman, 1973).

Thermal biofeedback. Thermal biofeedback has been shown to be helpful for patients suffering with chronic migraine headaches and various other cardiovascular disorders such as Renaud's disease (chronic cold hands and feet which can become quite painful), and chronic high blood pressure (Basmajian, 1979). The patient with these disorders learns to increase the skin temperature in the fingertips. Typically a thermistor is taped to a finger of each hand and the temperature is recorded. The patient then learns to increase and decrease the measured temperature. Learning to *control* the temperature is what appears to be important.

Biofeedback effectiveness

Biofeedback training as a treatment modality has met with extreme, mixed reactions. Many researchers continue to assert that biofeedback treatment is primarily a placebo (Bakal, 1979). A placebo is effective when changes occur because of what the patient *expects*; changes are *not* due to *real* changes in the ability to control (through biofeedback) the undesired physiological processes.

In spite of the controversy, results with biofeedback treatment in rehabilitation patients continue to be promising, especially in the areas of relaxation and control of spasticity in spinal cord-injured patients and stroke victims (Basmajian, 1979).

It is not known at this time whether biofeedback treatment *per se* is the important element of treatment, or if learning deep relaxation with the consequent "shutting down" of the muscular and cardiovascular systems is important for symptomatic relief. It is no doubt greatly encouraging for a patient with a flaccid extremity, which the patient cannot voluntarily move, to see muscle activity occurring in that extremity through the use of biofeedback instrumentation. These recordings certainly help to maintain an optimal motivational level in the patient so that the patient continues to cooperate with appropriate physical therapy and occupational therapy programs. If the patient cannot see any direct benefit for a period of time in therapy, then it is difficult to sustain the needed cooperation and motivation. Therefore, the value of biofeedback is seen, at this point, primarily as an adjunct to the other treatment modalities involved in the rehabilitation process. (For more information see: Bakal, 1979; Goldenson, 1978; Moos, 1977; Strain & Grossman, 1975; Wittkower & Warnes, 1977).

TREATING BIRTH DEFECTS

We have noted the general contributions a psychologist can offer in the rehabilitation process for various medical problems. Now the focus will turn to a more specific discussion of various medical problems requiring rehabilitation and what some of the specific concerns are for the psychologist who provides services to these patients, families, and the various health service professionals who work with them. Physical disabilities resulting from birth defects comprise a large group of disorders. In this group falls such medical problems as: spina bifida, cerebral palsy, blindness, deafness, congenital absence of extremities, congenital heart problems, etc. Children with such disabilities can profit from psychological consultation to aid in adjusting to the physical limitations.

Family/Parental Issues

It is important to consider the effects of the physical limitation not only on the patient but also on the parents and other family members (see L. Martin's chapter, "Counseling the Parents of the Handicapped Child"). Parents often struggle with feeling that they are responsible in some way for the handicap of the child. The father may wonder if the handicap was somehow transmitted genetically through him. The mother may fear that she caused the handicap because of something she did wrong (or something she failed to do correctly) during the term of her pregnancy. Sometimes these fears are not openly acknowledged by the parents but are "secret thoughts" that are not brought out and discussed openly.

As a result of these unspoken fears and guilt, parents may deny the child's handicap or reject the child by placing the child in an institutional setting where they will not have to deal with the issues regularly. Parents may also react in the opposite extreme and develop an overprotective or hovering attitude in raising the child. The child may then develop a sense of being so damaged and handicapped that "normal" functioning and survival apart from the parents is not possible. The child then experiences many separation problems and identity problems as he or she becomes older. A more complete discussion of these and other issues involving the parent-child interactions can be found in Goldenson (1978), Moos (1977), and Marinelli and Dell Orto (1977).

The psychologist can be extremely helpful to the family as each member deals with the various effects experienced because of the child's birth defect. The psychologist's therapeutic task is to identify and accept various fears, anxieties, feelings of anger, depression, guilt, etc. and work *through* these issues so the child and the family can reach the best levels of functioning given the reality of the physical handicap.

Self-Concept/Body-Concept Issues

The child must be encouraged to accept the physical limitations realistically while focusing on those abilities which can be developed so that functioning can be maintained at the highest appropriate level possible. The child must be encouraged to define self-worth not only in terms of production or what one can *do* but also in terms of *who* one is as a person. This is difficult because so much of our society is focused on production and the value of *things* as opposed to the value of *persons*. Here, the worth of each person to God, as affirmed by the gospel, can be important to both the psychologist and to the child and family as a means of maintaining a clear understanding that value lies in personhood, not in productivity. Cultivating in the child a healthy sense of self- worth is a primary goal of the psychologist as a member of the rehabilitation team.

In addition to focusing on the importance of a healthy "inner person," the psychologist must also be aware of body image issues. How the particular handicap affects the child's attitudes, perceptions, and feelings toward the body becomes very important. Once again, our society holds out a certain body image as ideal: young, healthy, sexy, and pretty/handsome. Any deviation from this ideal can contribute to feelings of unattractiveness or inferiority and to a tendency to remain isolated and alone or in the protective environment of the family.

Social Initiation

The child can be encouraged and trained to talk with others about the obvious physical aspects of the congenital problem. The child also needs to learn to become an initiator in social situations. Many people who are not accustomed to physical disability are unsure of whether to talk about the handicap or not. Consequently, they may remain at a distance or engage in other avoidance tactics so as to avoid an embarrassing situation. The child with the handicap must learn how to break through these barriers appropriately in order to cultivate meaningful relationships with others outside of the family.

The parents must also learn to let the child take some of these social risks. The loving parent may find it difficult to let go of the child, knowing the possibility that the child might be socially rejected. The therapist can help the parents deal with their overconcern and overprotective attitudes and encourage the child to separate appropriately from the parents.

Vocational and Lifestyle Choices

Another issue with which the psychologist can be helpful in the full rehabilitation of the child with a congenital physical handicap is in assisting the child to choose an appropriate vocational career. The psychologist can assess the person's interests, intellectual and emotional strengths and weaknesses, and functional limitations of the physical disability in an attempt to narrow the choices for an appropriate career. A careful assessment is required so the person can explore and develop the natural abilities and potentials which are needed for appropriate and gainful employment. A thorough knowledge of vocations and their physical demands and requirements is obviously needed by the psychologist.

There are many lifestyle issues that are also important to consider in working with a child who has a handicap. There are certain activities which may not be possible for the child to attempt. For example, the child may be able to attend sports events but may not be able to participate in the sports activity. In addition, there may be some leisure-time activities that may not be open to the child. It is important for the person with a congenital physical handicap to develop hobbies, appropriate physical exercise programs, appropriate social friendships, religious activities and involvements, and other activities which will facilitate the development of a lifestyle that is as full and as rich as possible.

Sexual Functioning

A final area of concern for the psychologist working with persons with congenital physical problems is sexual functioning. Too often the assumption is made that persons with physical disabilities are not interested in sexuality or they do not have sexual feelings and desires. It is important to remind the rehabilitation team members and the family members that sexuality *is* an appropriate and important issue for the child with a congenital physical handicap. Sexuality issues tend to emerge for the handicapped child just as they do with any child. The rehabilitation staff needs to be trained how to respond to these issues, as do the parents. The child should *not* be given the message that sexuality is not an option or that it is wrong or inappropriate to feel sexual or to desire sexual activities. Some excellent resources for the professional rehabilitation staff as well as parents is *Not Made of Stone: The Sexual Problems of Handicapped People* by Heslinga, Schellen and Verkuyl (1974) and *Toward Intimacy* by the Task Force on Concerns of Physically Disabled Women (1978).

TREATING SPINAL CORD INJURY

Spinal cord injury presents another unique challenge to the rehabilitation team. With the increase in the incidence of automobile accidents, sports activity accidents, and recreational activity accidents, the numbers of patients requiring these services have rapidly increased. Consequently, many rehabilitation units in hospital settings have expanded their psychological services to treat such injuries.

The Stages of Adjustment

Patients who experience a spinal cord injury often do not realize immediately the extent of the physical damage. They frequently verbalize that they are "just temporarily" unable to feel or move their extremities. They feel that after a few days everything will return to normal. Ruge (1969) and Trieschmann (1980) describe the psychological process patients with spinal cord injury experience.

The psychologist who functions as a member of the rehabilitation team hopefully can help the patient through this adjustment process so that little interference with the demands of the physical rehabilitation program will occur. It is important to communicate to the patient that these emotional reactions are normal and to help the patient experience and work through various feelings.

Shock. The first stage in the emotional adjustment process following a spinal cord injury can be labelled "shock." During this period, the patient frequently experiences a slowing down of thoughts and the flow of ideas. Emotions appear flat, and vagueness, confusion, and isolation characterize interaction with others. It is as if the person does not comprehend completely what has happened. This reaction may serve to help the patient not to become overwhelmed emotionally and thus protects him or her from having to deal with the trauma and tragedy of the injury. This stage may last from a few hours to a few days.

Partial recognition. The shock phase gives way to the stage of partial recognition, which may last from a few days to a few weeks. The patient is able to focus thoughts more than during the shock phase. It is as if the patient is gradually beginning to deal with the reality of the traumatic injury. He or she begins to ask more questions. Typically, however, the patient still defends against expressing or experiencing personal *feelings* about the injury. The patient also tends to avoid thinking about the future; more attention is given to dealing with present issues.

Initial stabilization. As the injured person continues to recognize more and more of the reality of the injury, a period called initial stabilization is entered. This period may last for months or years, provided it is not disturbed or confronted by the demands of reality. The patient during this stage may appear to have accepted what has happened and even may seem comfortable with the medical routine and procedures. He or she is cooperative and somewhat passively compliant. That is, he or she does what is expected in nursing, occupational therapy and physical therapy regimens. It is important to remember, however, that the patient has *not* yet dealt with his or her *feelings* about what has happened. Consequently, the stabilization is only *apparent*; it does not represent a final and genuine acceptance of the injury.

The stage of initial stabilization ends as the patient is continually confronted with the demands of reality which ultimately disturb the comfortable, compliant attitude that has developed. Also, the stage may end when the patient begins to think about and brood over what is happening. As the patient experiences how his or her body does not move, function, and feel as it did prior to the injury, it becomes increasingly difficult to remain comfortable and cooperative. In some cases, this stage may end when the patient begins to go home on the weekend, leaving the safe, protective environment of the hospital unit. Most frequently, the stage of initial stabilization ends as a result of the rehabilitation staff continually placing greater demands on the patient to work in therapy and to learn new ways to care for him or herself independently. These demands disrupt the previously developed equilibrium.

Regression. As the initial stabilization dissolves, it is replaced by emotional turmoil and/or a return to the denial and emotional blandness similar to that which occurs during the shock phase. This becomes a critical period in the rehabilitation process and is a point at which psychological consultation can become helpful to both the patient and the staff.

The staff members may need help in dealing with their own reactions to the patient as they experience frustration, irritation, guilt, or a mixture of all of these feelings as the once cooperative, compliant, pleasant patient becomes resistive (passively or actively) to therapeutic requests and demands. Further, the patient can often profit from psychological consultation at this point. It can be frightening to begin experiencing some of the powerful emotions associated with the stage of regression. Prior to this point in the emotional adjustment process, the patient is generally not receptive to psychological intervention since there is a sense of "comfort" in focusing more on the physical issues associated with the injury. At the regression stage, however, the patient may be experiencing significant distress and may be willing to explore personal feelings with the psychologist.

It should be mentioned again, however, that psychological consultation occurs much more smoothly and easily at this point if the psychologist is perceived by the patient as an integrated member of the rehabilitation team. If the psychologist has made rounds with the physician, has been visible on the rehabilitation unit in physical therapy, occupational therapy, or in group sessions held on the unit, the consultation is accepted more readily. If, however, the psychologist meets the patient for the first time at this point, the patient is more likely to feel that the physician and rehabilitation staff now think he or she is "going crazy" and needs to see the "shrink." It may take several therapy sessions to work through these fears and anxieties; the patient may refuse to meet with the psychologist altogether.

(a) Denial. The regression stage has various manifestations; one common expression of regression is denial. This expression is similar to the earlier stage of shock. The denial at this point, however, is often mixed more with ego defense mechanisms of projection and displacement. There may even be a sense of "magical thinking." As an example, one patient refused to attend physical and occupational therapy or cooperate with intermittent catheterization. When confronted with this and asked why he no longer wanted to cooperate with his rehabilitation program, he asserted, "Well, why should I? I know that within a few years or months the doctors will have perfected a spinal cord transplant like they have for other parts of the body. I'll just wait for my transplant instead of working so hard in therapy." If this person cannot be helped out of this severe state of denial, he may remain with a hostile, projecting attitude where he expects things to be done for him and given to him without him accepting personal responsibility. He may also come to believe that other people are responsible for his difficulties. This attitude is potentially extremely dangerous. Lack of self-responsibility can quickly lead to severe physical consequences, such as pressure sores or bladder difficulties, which may eventually lead to death.

(b) Depression. Through a combination of reality constantly confronting the

patient with what must be done every day for survival and the patient's own process of working through personal feelings of being injured, the denial diminishes, and a second manifestation of the regression stage is likely to emerge. This can be described as a type of realistic depression. The patient may feel helpless, frightened, lost, moody, doubtful of personal abilities, and, in the extreme, he or she may become suicidal.

Many patients become frightened at this point since they feel they not only have a damaged body but they are losing control over their mind as well. Patients should be encouraged to accept the depression as a part of the natural process of working through the reactions to being injured. The rehabilitation staff must also try to accept the depression without giving messages of "Now, don't feel that way. It will all work out." The staff personnel generally do not enjoy working with a patient who is discouraged, doubtful, and uncooperative. The psychologist can help the staff to understand and to accept the patient's feelings as normal and necessary in order to adjust to life as a spinal cord injured person.

Realistic self-acceptance. The final stage of the adjustment process subsequent to spinal cord injury is reaching a point of realistic self-acceptance. The patient will have experienced and worked through many feelings associated with being injured; the patient will have learned to be as physically independent as possible in activities of daily living (mobilization, dressing, bathing, bowel and bladder care, etc.) and will see his or her self as a person who has growth potential and value *with* the injury and limitations.

It is important to realize that the stages described here do not, in reality, flow smoothly from one point to another and proceed in the precise sequence as outlined here. It is more likely that a person will move back and forth from one stage to another and this movement back and forth is an important part of the working–through process.

Self-Expression and Issues of Dependency

Many patients are frightened and hesitant to express directly the hostility and anger they experience. They are aware of their dependency on others around them; there is a concern that people might become unhappy and leave them, or worse yet, send them off to a nursing home or residential setting. Consequently, these patients may keep the negative feelings to themselves instead of confronting the feelings and working through them. In order to give practice in dealing with these issues, I have found the use of group meetings on the rehabilitation unit to be very effective. Patients on the unit are also sometimes frightened about confronting a nurse or therapist who may be having a bad day and who is irritable or disagreeable and inconsiderate. Giving patients the permission and training to express their feelings about these situations can be very helpful as they deal with similar situations after being discharged from the unit.

Family Consultation

It is also helpful to provide psychological consultation to family members.

Family members experience similar adjustment issues and stages as those described for the injured patient. The family often feels even more helpless, since they cannot work for the patient in physical and occupational therapy but must watch the patient struggle. The family frequently becomes overprotective and attempts to help the patient too much. For example, rather than watch a person struggle to dress the way he or she has learned in occupational therapy, a family member may go ahead and dress the injured loved one. The family must be confronted with the necessity of encouraging the patient to move toward greater independence, even though it is often easier and quicker for a family member to do something for the patient.

Sexual Functioning

The area of sexual counseling is one of extreme importance to the spinal cord-injured patient. Unfortunately, questions regarding sexual functioning following spinal cord injury are sometimes avoided, ignored, or answered in such ways as to shut off additional communication. The sexuality issue is best handled if it is integrated with the various other aspects of the rehabilitation process. It is ideal if some male *and* female rehabilitation staff members can be trained in sexual counseling. It is not necessary that the person who talks with patients about sexuality be a physician or a psychologist, although certainly the issue of sexuality emerges as the psychologist discusses emotional adjustment issues in his work with patients. It has been said that the first question asked by the newly injured spinal cord patient is "Will I live?" The second question tends to be "Am I going to be able to walk again?" The third question is "Will I be able to have sex?" (Heslinga, Schellen, & Verkuyl, 1974).

There are some excellent training programs at various universities across the country which are designed especially for helping persons who work with the spinal cord–injured to deal with sexuality. An example is the program at the University of Minnesota (Brenton, 1974). There is not space in this chapter to discuss in detail the various issues important to sexual counseling with the spinal cord injured. By way of brief overview, some of the areas of discussion include: (a) physiological issues relevant to erection and ejaculation in the male and lubrication in the female; (b) mechanical issues such as dealing with the catheter; (c) positioning, preventing bowel or bladder "accidents" during sexual activity; (d) communication issues such as the ability to talk about sexual feelings, sexual activities or options, the ability to say what one likes and what one does not like; and (e) exploring issues with a parent, spouse, fianceé, girlfriend or boyfriend. This list is by no means exhaustive, but it does suggest the range of issues which must be addressed for adequate sexual counseling to have occurred. Some references that are helpful in the area of sexual counseling include: Heslinga, Schellen, and Verkuyl (1974); Marinelli and Dell Orto (1977); Mooney, Cole, and Chilgren (1975); and Trieschmann (1980).

TREATING STROKE (CEREBRAL VASCULAR ACCIDENT) VICTIMS

Another type of patient a psychologist may be asked to see on a rehabilitation unit is the person who has suffered a stroke or cerebral vascular accident (CVA). The rehabilitation issues are similar to those already discussed for the spinal cord injured. Since the stroke is another type of sudden, traumatic injury, the process of adjustment following the injury is very similar to what has already been described. One difference is that, with a stroke, there may be more mental confusion which lasts for a much longer time. Aphasia (speech difficulties) may also be present.

Communication Dysfunctions

If aphasia is present, the communication difficulties can be immense. Aphasia may be expressive or receptive in nature. Expressive aphasia occurs when a person cannot express what he or she would like to say. Understanding may be present and the person can formulate what he or she would like to say, but the words will not come out. Some of these patients may repeat words or phrases over and over and sometimes profanity is either the only or the primary type of communication. This is often frustrating and embarrassing for both the patient and the family. Receptive aphasia means that the patient is unable to understand what is spoken to him or her. This is equally as frustrating for the patient and family.

Patients who experience a stroke affecting the right side of the body (right hemiplegia) are more likely to be aphasic than are left hemiplegic patients. This is because the center mediating speech functions is located on the left side of the brain. The left side of the brain is primarily responsible for right-sided body functions and, conversely, the right side of the brain is responsible for left-sided body functions.

The Need for Psychological Assessment

A careful intellectual and organic assessment using psychological tests can be very helpful in evaluating how the stroke is likely to affect the patient's ability to function independently. The psychologist can assess (a) judgment, (b) ability to comprehend and learn in a new situation, (c) mental confusion, (d) computational skills, and (e) ability to plan ahead—an ability which is very helpful to the patient in making appropriate plans after discharge from the hospital. How well the patient is able to function in these areas determines how much supervision is required in a living situation and makes the difference in determining if the patient can return to living at home or will require a more supervised setting.

The Need for Sexual Rehabilitation

As with spinal cord injuries, patients who have experienced CVA can profit from some sexual counseling. Erroneously, sometimes it is assumed that since the typical CVA patient is older, sexual functioning is not an issue; however, many people remain sexually active until they die regardless of their age, and stroke victims are no different. Both the patient and the spouse should have an opportunity to discuss their sexual options with a trained professional counselor or psychologist. Failure to do this may result in added pressure, confusion, guilt, anxiety, and uncertainty.

For example, one woman in her sixties made an appointment to speak with a psychologist working on a rehabilitation unit. Through many tears and in a session filled with anxiety and agony she revealed her predicament. She stated that she had never enjoyed her sexual relationship with her husband. In fact, she had never felt comfortable with her sexuality. She viewed intercourse as her "duty" but it was not enjoyable for her. After the onset of menopause, she and her husband had agreed that sexual intercourse would not continue.

Her husband, who was also in his sixties, then suffered a stroke. He was doing well physically and was now coming home on weekends in preparation for discharge from the hospital. He was aphasic both expressively and to some degree receptively, so he experienced severe communication problems. He now was much more impulsive, and was unwilling to postpone or delay gratification. In addition, some mental confusion was evident. He did not remember the arrangement he and his wife had made regarding their sexual expression with each other; he now was becoming insistent, sexually aggressive, and sometimes combative. He felt angry, hurt, and rejected by his wife's resistance to his sexual advances. The wife told the psychologist that she felt frightened because of the pressure he was putting on her. In addition, she felt angry and guilty. Her question to the psychologist was, "How can I get my husband to agree once more not to have any sexual contact?" This example clearly illustrates how complex the sexual issues can become.

Summary

Space does not allow continued exploration of various other medical problems which can profit from psychological consultation in a rehabilitation setting. The issues presented here provide some general guidelines as to what types of psychological issues may surface on a rehabilitation unit and how a psychologist can function in this setting.

Other types of medical conditions that can profit from similar psychological consultation include brain injury, amputation, heart disease, cancer, chronic pain, cerebral palsy, multiple sclerosis, severe arthritis, to name only a few. Each of these types of medical patients experience unique psychological reactions and must be dealt with accordingly. The attempt in this chapter has been to review a sample of the kinds of psychological issues which may surface and which need to be dealt with so that the physical rehabilitation process can proceed to the maximum level.

INTEGRATION OF FAITH

Faith can be either a tremendous asset to the person experiencing severe physical disability or a serious roadblock requiring intervention. Many persons who experience a serious physical disability ask the question, "Why me?" Some people feel that the illness or accident is due to God punishing them for some past sins.

They may feel that they missed God's will for their lives and the physical disability is the result. The problem with this type of thinking is that anyone can usually find something from their past that they either did or did not do that would make them wonder.

One young girl in a group therapy session on a rehabilitation unit expressed her thoughts on this issue. The group was discussing the fact that many of them were feeling that their physical disability occurred because they were not living the kind of life that God desired for them. The young girl replied, "I used to think that way too. But then I got to thinking. I didn't do anything *that* bad to deserve *this!*"

The psychologist may need to explore this essentially theological issue carefully with patients. This attitude can sometimes subtly, sometimes directly, interfere with the rehabilitation process by causing the person to feel that God is punishing him or her and he or she does not deserve to become more independent and functional. Obviously, an advantageous situation exists when the psychologist is a Christian believer; the subject can be addressed professionally *and* effectively in terms of Spirit-guided ministry.

Other people feel very angry with God and may require careful guidance through these feelings. They may feel angry that they tried to live a good life and the illness or accident happened anyway—so, what difference does it make if you live a good life or not? They may lose their faith in God and feel that God cannot be trusted to protect us or to intervene on our behalf. God is viewed as being uninterested and uninvolved in our lives. Family members and Christian friends have a very difficult time hearing these words and tend to shut off any further exploration of the feelings behind them. The psychologist must be willing to listen, to accept, and to explore these feelings and attitudes with the patients without a judgmental, condemning attitude. This will allow the person to face and work through the self-defeating feelings. By listening in a caring, understanding way, the Christian psychologist models the availability, care, and love of God. That God is long-suffering can be a source of challenge and encouragement to the rehabilitation therapist.

On the other hand, a person's faith can be an invaluable aid at this time of personal crisis. There may be a sense of strength that prevails and encourages the person through this very difficult time. The physical disability *can* provide an opportunity for great personal and spiritual growth. The psychologist can foster and encourage this growth by listening, guiding, and exploring with the patient various feelings, attitudes, and thoughts about the patient's personal relationship with God.

It is essential that the Christian therapist be willing to explore a patient's positive and negative perceptions of a personal God, a personal faith, and the physical disability. There are no easy solutions to these issues; no easy answers to difficult questions. If the therapist attempts to "preach," quote biblical passages, or give trite spiritual solutions to the patient, it is likely to be met with great resistance or passive compliance that will be too shallow to be of benefit to the person.

Kushner (1981) reminds us that a primary value of our faith is our awareness of our need for each other and our God. Each of us has value and worth and we need to express this and experience it with each other. God cares for us and grieves with us as we experience some of the heartaches of life. None of us is immune to the possibility of physical disability. We must encourage each other in order to build our faith together.

Many times the friends of patients who experience serious traumatic accidents resulting in chronic physical disability such as spinal cord injury or stroke have much difficulty relating to the "new" person. It is painful to see and live with the marked physical, psychological, and personality changes that may occur following traumatic injury. Consequently, many of the patient's friends do not remain friends. Some continue visiting the person for awhile but many become more distant. The patient often senses the discomfort of the friends and may themselves contribute to this pulling away and ending the friendships.

The church can provide a valuable ministry to the person with chronic physical disability if it remains sensitive to these issues. The church can make a point of encouraging the disabled person to become or to stay involved with the church and social activities. Church buildings could be designed or remodeled to be wheelchair accessible. Elevators can be installed so that the various activities such as Sunday school classes, church dinners, etc. can be attended by the physically handicapped. The transportation needs of the handicapped can be anticipated and provided for by church members. Church members can learn to transfer a person from the wheelchair to the automobile so that relatives will not always have to accompany the handicapped person. This ministry of the church encourages greater independence for the disabled person and fosters greater integration into the life of the church. This can be a very important source of spiritual strength to the person. The church can be a very vital social outlet as well. If church members who are peers of the handicapped person can display love and acceptance, it will foster a sense of personal worth and value. The social adjustment following serious physical injury is one of the most difficult adjustments the patient confronts. The body of Christ can play a very important role to assure that the disabled person continues to feel loved, accepted, important, and valued for who he or she *is*. In addition, by actively reaching out to touch, encourage, uplift, and fellowship with the disabled—perhaps physically unattractive—person, church members individually and collectively imitate the active, searching love and acceptance of God.

Select Bibliography

Alexander, F. (1950). *Psychosomatic medicine: Its principles and applications*. New York: W. W. Norton.

Bakal, D. A. (1979). *Psychology and medicine*. New York: Springer.

Basmajian, J. V. (Ed.). (1979). *Biofeedback—principles and practice for clinicians*. Baltimore: Williams and Wilkins.

Brenton, M. (1974). Sex and the physically handicapped. *Physician's World, 2*, 29-32.

Goldenson, R. M. (Ed.). (1978). *Disability and rehabilitation handbook*. New York: McGraw-Hill.

Grinker, R. R. (1973). *Psychosomatic concepts*. New York: Aronson.

Heslinga, K., Schellen, A. M. C. M., & Verkuyl, A. (1974). *Not made of stone: The sexual problems of handicapped people*. Springfield, IL: Charles C. Thomas.

Kushner, H. S. (1981). *When bad things happen to good people*. New York: Schocken Books.

Marinelli, R. P., & Dell Orto, A. E. (Eds.). (1977). *The psychological and social impact of physical disability*. New York: Springer.

Melzak, R. (1975). The promise of biofeedback: Don't hold the party yet. *Psychology Today, 2*, 18-22.

Melzak, R., & Chapman, R. (1973). Psychological aspects of pain. *Postgraduate Medicine, 53*, 69-75.

Mooney, T., Cole, T. M., & Chilgren, R. A. (1975). *Sexual options for paraplegics and quadriplegics*. Boston: Little, Brown and Company.

Moos, R. H. (1977). *Coping with physical illness*. New York: Plenum.

Neff, W. S. (Ed.). (1971). *Rehabilitation psychology*. Washington, DC: American Psychological Association.

Ruge, D. (1969). *Spinal cord injuries*. Springfield, IL: Charles C. Thomas.

Strain, J. J., & Grossman, S. (1975). *Psychological care of the medically ill*. New York: Appleton-Century-Crofts.

Task Force on Concerns of Physically Disabled Woman. (1978). *Toward intimacy*. New York: Human Sciences Press.

Trieschmann, R. B. (1980) *Spinal cord injuries. Psychological, social, and vocational adjustment*. New York: Pergamon.

Wittkower, E. D., & Warnes, H. (Eds.). (1977). *Psychosomatic medicine: Its clinical applications*. New York: Harper & Row.

9

DEATH, DYING, AND BEREAVEMENT

Raymond T. Brock

Death is a fact of life: "it is appointed unto men once to die, but, after this the judgment" (Heb. 9:27). Death has been defined as "an irreversible state that is characterized by the cessation of all those processes that sustain life" (Wilson, 1985, p. 282). It has been the concern of philosophers and theologians for centuries, but it has only been in recent years that behavioral scientists have given scholarly attention to the subject.

Attitudes toward death, dying, and bereavement differ, but the inevitability is always there—everyone will die unless the Lord hastens his return. That the apostle Paul found life and death equally attractive (Collins, 1969) is indicated in Philippians 1:21: "for me to live is Christ and to die is gain." Or, as Ken Taylor translated it in the *Living Bible*, "For to me, living means opportunities for Christ, and dying—well, that's better yet!" This same view can be shared by the Spirit-filled Christian coming to grips with life and death from a biblical perspective.

ANCIENT PERSPECTIVES ON DEATH

Egypt

Evidence that the ancient Egyptians believed the quality of life after death was contingent on preserving the body is revealed in the trappings of their funeral practices which survive today. They built huge pyramids and perfected the art of mummification. Relics of their funeral boats unearthed by archeologists bear witness to the practice of transporting the *sarcophagi* of the aristocrats to the islands reserved for burial. Found in the burial crypts are mirrors, utensils, furniture, and weapons for the dead to take to the world of the unknown. Slaves were buried alive in the tombs of the royalty to serve the Pharaohs in their afterlife, for the Egyptians believed the body would be resuscitated after death for an unknown type of existence. Unfortunately, some of our current Western funeral customs contain vestiges of this primitive view (Shipley, 1982).

Greece

The Greeks were more philosophical in their approach to death. It is from Greek mythology that we have the term *thanatology*—the study of death; *Thanatos* was the twin brother of *Hypnus* (sleep) in the Greek pantheon of gods (Shneidman, 1976a). The prevailing view of death in the ancient Hellenistic world was one of acceptance. It was best phrased by Socrates just before he drank the suicidal hemlock imposed by Athenian justice: "The time has come for me to go away. I go to die and you to live, but which of us goes to the better lot is known to none but God."

After his lifetime spent in the pursuit of wisdom, Socrates did not know if he would be better off dead or alive. Cleath (1970) observed that "for Socrates, death was the great liberator; it looses the soul from its prison in the body and led it back to its eternal home" (p. 4). But Socrates knew nothing of that home and shared the agnostic view which says of death: "Nobody still alive knows. The dead may, but dead men tell no tales" (Samuel, 1967, p. 32).

Plato, the student of Socrates and his successor as headmaster of the school in Athens, held a different view of death and immortality. He taught that although the body died and disintegrated, the soul lived forever. He said that after death the soul migrates to what he called "the realm of the pure forms." There it exists without a body, contemplating the forms. After a time, according to Plato, the soul is reincarnated in another body and returns to earth. In this view he was sharing ideas found in many African legends and the writings of Buddhism and Hinduism (Wilson, 1985).

Rome

In ancient Rome there were two conflicting views of death. On the one hand, Cicero, the famous writer, said, "After death we shall for the first time truly live" (Scherzer, 1963, p. 133). On the other hand, the Roman politician Gaius Caesar declared to the Senate, "Beyond this life there is no place for either trouble or joy." He was reflecting the fatalism of the barbarian tribes that were already invading the perimeter of the Roman Empire and influencing its thought with the paganism of the Goths and Visigoths from Central Europe.

Thus the conflict raged at the time of Christ. The Roman pantheon offered only a ritualistic approach to death with priests functioning as the masters of ceremony. The Romans believed in immortality, but could not comprehend resurrection. "Amidst this uncertainty Roman philosophers turned to the Orient for gods whose priesthood could reconcile man with the diety" (Scherzer, 1963).

JUDEO-CHRISTIAN CONCEPTS OF DEATH

The view toward the East focused on the ministry of Jesus who preached redemption and eternal life. It was Jesus who proclaimed the answer to the philosophical and spiritual quest of the ancient Mediterranean world, a message that is as relevant today as it was when he preached the good news of the gospel in the first century.

The Old Testament, a source for much of Jesus' teaching, did not separate the individual into body, soul, and spirit or body, mind, emotions, and will. The Hebrew language referred to a person as a *nephesh*, a whole being (Oates, 1973; Whitlock, 1983). This holistic concept envisioned the person as "enlived dust," an "animated body" which was a "unit of vital power" functioning as a "psycho-physical organism" (Doss, 1972, pp. 21, 22). Death marked the dissolution of this dynamic organism. The presence of death in the world was conceived as the result of sin (Gen. 2:7). An inevitable event (Josh. 23:14), death represented the cessation of natural life that came to individuals of all ages and all nations (Gen. 24:11; 2 Sam. 12:23). Death, which brought a release from pain, was no respecter of persons (Job 3:17–19). In death, humanity returned to the dust from which it was formed (Gen. 2:7; 3:19; Ecc. 3:10; 12:7).

To the righteous one, death was the introduction into a place of eternal good (Isa. 45:17; Dan. 7:14; 12:2), a glorious experience to be anticipated (Num. 23:10; Psa. 116:14). To the evil person, however, death led to everlasting torment (Isa. 35:10; Jer. 20:11; Dan. 12:2). In several messianic passages of the Old Testament was the belief that the Messiah would conquer death and remove its sting (Isa. 25:8; 26:10; Hos. 13:14).

The idea of the resurrection was not prominent in the Pentateuch and was totally rejected by the Sadducees of Jesus' day. Concepts of resurrection evolved in the writings of the poets and prophets, however, during the periods of oppression and suffering as God unfolded his plan for his people. It was from this portion of the Old Testament that the Pharisees drew heavily. The conflict between the Sadducees and Pharisees led to frequent debates over resurrection in the days of Jesus (Mark 12:18–27). In spite of divergent opinions, however, the overriding view of death in the Old Testament maintained confidence in Jehovah as Creator and Sustainer of life.

Job's affirmation of faith in life after death strikes a high watermark in Hebrew literature:

> For I know that my redeemer liveth, and that he shall stand at the latter day upon the earth: and though after my skin worms destroy this body, yet in my flesh shall I see God: whom I shall see for myself, and mine eyes shall behold, and not another; though my reins be consumed within me. (Job 19:25–27)

New Testament writers emphasized a concept of resurrection taken from the Jewish tradition. Jesus laid the foundation from which the apostles drew their ideas to illustrate the implications of death for both the believer and the unbeliever. Death, in the New Testament, is pictured as laying aside the body and taking down the tent of a temporary pilgrimage (2 Cor. 5:1) from which the spirit has departed (2 Tim. 4:6). Death is in the world as a result of sin and comes to everyone (Rom. 5:21; 6:23; 1 Cor. 15:56; Heb. 2:14; James 1:15). Death was conceived of as a temporary state and was frequently referred to as sleep (Matt.

9:18–22; Mark 5:35–43; John 11:4, 11–14; Acts 13:36; 1 Cor. 15:20–51; 1 Thess. 4:14).

Jesus implied that no correlation can be drawn between the manner of a person's death and God's verdict on the quality of his or her life (Matt. 5:45). First-century Christians maintained a contagious hope reflected in the terminal experiences of the Christian martyrs of the first century (Rev. 6:9–11; 7:13; 14:13; 20:4–6). In the New Testament, death comes to the righteous who go to their everlasting reward (Rev. 7:14). The death trauma was viewed as a glorious experience leading to union with Christ (1 Cor. 15:17–19; 2 Cor. 5:4; 1 Thess. 4:13–15).

New Testament writers maintained that unbelievers could anticipate eternal torment (Matt. 25:45; Mark 3:29; 2 Thess. 1:9; Jude 7), an event to be faced with dread by the unrepentant (Acts 1:25). Jesus, fulfilling the messianic hope of the Old Testament, conquered death and removed its sting (John 5:24; 1 Cor. 15:53–57; 1 John 5:20; Rev. 1:18), ushering the righteous believer into eternal rest (Rom. 7:24, 25; Rev. 14:13). The apostles taught that death is universal (Heb. 9:27), and resurrection will involve both the believer and the unbeliever, the righteous dead being resurrected a thousand years before the unrighteous dead with the millennium intervening (Rev. 20:4–6, 11–13).[1]

Paul's positive view of death demonstrated the hope of the Christian believer:

> I have fought a good fight, I have finished my course, I have kept the faith: henceforth there is laid up for me a crown of righteousness, which the Lord, the righteous judge, shall give me at that day: and not to me only, but unto all them also that love his appearing."
> (2 Tim. 4:7, 8)

---

[1] The Old Testament conceived the waiting place of the dead to be in the "bowels" of the earth. The Hebrew word *sheol* is used 65 times and is translated in the King James Version 31 times to read "grave," 31 times to read "hell," and 3 times it is translated "spirit." The *sheol* of the Old Testament was the waiting place of the dead with a special compartment, *paradise*, reserved for the righteous dead. Between Christ's death and resurrection, he was believed to have transferred the waiting place of the righteous dead to the Eternal City (Eph. 4:8). So the saints of the New Testament conceived of the wicked dead waiting in the Old Testament *sheol* but the righteous dead as awaiting resurrection under the altar of the heavenlies (Luke 16:22, 23; 2 Cor. 5:8; Phil. 1:21–24; Heb. 12:22, 23; Rev. 6:9–11).

The Greek word *hades* in the New Testament is comparable to the Old Testament *sheol*. It should also be noted that three Greek words are translated "hell" in the English New Testament. The "hell" of Luke 6:22, 23 is the Greek word *hades*; the "hell" of Matthew 23:33 is the Greek *gehenna* while the "hell" of 2 Peter 2:4 is *tartarus*. In each verse, however, the meaning is the place of departed spirits. Actually, these three Greek words have different root meanings in the original language. *Hades* is the *sheol* of the Old Testament and is the place where the spirits of the dead await their resurrection. *Gehenna* refers to the hell of eternal punishment. It is where the unrighteous dead will be consigned after the Great White Throne Judgment. *Tartarus* is used to identify the prison of the fallen angels referred to in Jude 6.

It is evident that the *sheol* of the Old Testament is the *hades* of the New Testament. This is vividly illustrated in Acts 2:27 where Psalm 16:10 is quoted. The Old Testament word for grave as a resting place for the body is *qeber*; the Greek word *mnemeion* means the same thing in the New Testament. The distinction between *sheol* and grave is consistent

Paul was not expressing a "morbid death wish" he simply recognized that the death question had been settled in Christ Jesus and the aged apostle could die in the confidence of his faith.

In comparison with other subjects, Scripture says very little about death, other than it is a stark reality which everyone must face. Jesus did not make death a central element in his teaching; neither did he regard it as an obstacle to faith in God. Rather, he emphasized the importance of life. It should also be noted that the New Testament writers did not attempt a speculative view of death (Doss, 1972, pp. 21, 22).

Wilson (1985) has effectively summarized the Judeo-Christian view of death:

> In the New Testament death is contrasted to life, so that time and eternity have different dimensions. In life, there is conflict; in eternity there is harmony. In life there is strife; in eternity there is peace. In life and eternity there are other contrasting qualities such as work versus rest, search versus discovery, suffering versus wholeness, faith versus strife, yearning versus fulfillment, and finally, imperfection and brokenness versus wholeness. In eternity there is no separation, and knowledge is complete. (pp. 283, 284)

CONTEMPORARY ATTITUDES TOWARD DEATH

Ours has been called a death-denying culture because many people try to deny death or pretend it will go away if they ignore it (Koteskey, 1980).

Death-denying Paradox

Shneidman (1976a) has used the term *oxymoronic* to describe the death-denying attitude of contemporary Western thought. "Death today is oxymoronic," he said, "a paradox made up of contrasting values, opposite trends, and even contradictory facts," such as "parting is such sweet sorrow" used by Shakespeare in *Romeo and Juliet* (p. xix.). To illustrate his point Shneidman (1976a) noted:

> At the same time we have created the most exquisitely sophisticated technological procedures for saving one individual's life, we have also created lethal technological devices, of at least equal sophistication, with the capacity of exterminating millions, of expunging cultures, of jeopardizing time itself by not only erasing the present but threatening the future. . . . On the one hand, marvelous devices for emergency surgery, kidney dialysis, and organ transplantations promise life; on the other hand, megadeath bombs constantly aimed from above the clouds and beneath the waves promise death. (pp. xix, xx)

Kastenbaum (1972) observed that we "isolate and punish the dying. We try to reclaim our consciences by purchasing elaborate funerals or we try to blink death out of our minds with skimpy memorial services. We forget the dead—and then we are haunted by them" (p. 6).

---

in both the Old and New Testaments. The body is never said to be in *sheol* or *hades* and the spirit is never said to be in the grave. So, *sheol* and *hades* are used consistently in the two Testaments to refer to the abode of dead spirits. The grave is just the depository where the body deteriorates, returns to dust, and awaits the resurrection.

The denial and repression of death by our culture was highlighted by Doss (1972) when he said, "Death has become the new obscenity and the literature of death the new pornography. The pornography of death seeks to deny the personal meaning of death by emphasizing that which is bizarre and dehumanizing" (p. 15). This attitude has erected an unhealthy dichotomy between life and death. Too frequently we picture life epitomized by youth, strength, prosperity, and health. Death is shoved aside by avoidance and the false assumption that it will only occur, as the old Pennsylvania Dutch proverb maintained, "to thee and to thee but not to me." This denial represents a secular view of death that is inconsistent with an awareness that Christ is Lord and the center of the Spirit-motivated personality.

Death Anxiety

Kübler-Ross (1969), the Swiss psychiatrist who has made the most significant contribution to the study of death in this century, noted the presence of death anxiety in her studies at the University of Chicago. She concluded:

> In our unconscious death is never possible in regard to ourselves. It is inconceivable for our unconscious to imagine our actual ending of our own life here on earth, and if this life of ours has to end, the ending is always attributed to a malicious intervention from outside by someone else. In simple terms, in our unconscious mind we can only be killed; it is inconceivable to die of a natural cause or old age. Therefore death in itself is associated with a bad act, a frightening happening, something that in itself calls for retribution and punishment. (p. 2)

The fear of death seems to be one of the few anthropological universals, a "frightening happening . . . even if we think we have mastered it on many levels" (Kübler-Ross, 1969, p. 5). Sociologically, the day when a person could die with dignity at home is almost gone. Yet, psychological studies have suggested that this is not so much a result of concern by loving families to prolong life as it is a function of a guilt-fear complex to remove the specter of death from the premises where the survivors will continue to live.

Wilson (1985, p. 284) observed that death anxiety is different from general anxiety. Death anxiety "occurs when it is impossible to discern meaning to death." He indicated that people who have a sense of purpose in life experience less death anxiety. Noting the difference between intrinsic and extrinsic religious motivation, he said: "Persons who go to church are no different from those who do not go, but those who are involved in their religion tend to have less death anxiety." He noted further that individuals who are likely to have high levels of death anxiety are (a) uninvolved with life, (b) have no well-defined purpose in life, or (c) are highly motivated toward achievement in life. Death anxiety can progress to despair: "one of the existential predicaments that human beings must face." This occurs if a person can not discern meaning when he examines life and contemplates the certainty of death.

Wilson's conclusion is consistent with the findings of Kübler-Ross:

> Religious patients seem to differ little from those without a religion. The difference may

be hard to determine, since we have not clearly defined what we mean by a religious person. We can say here, however, that we found very few truly religious people with an intrinsic faith. Those few have been helped by their faith and are best comparable with those few patients who were true atheists. The majority of patients were in between with some form of religious belief but not enough to relieve them of conflict and fear. (pp. 265, 266)

Kolb and Brodie (1982) have observed in clinical settings that when adolescents and adults have an awareness of death—their own or that of another—they experience a major emotional response. Such an awareness raises a basic anxiety about life—the sense of helplessness that accompanies a fear of the unknown. This is followed by a variety of fears: (a) loneliness, (b) loss of family and friends, (c) loss of one's body and identity, and (d) the loss of self-control. As a result, the coping and defense mechanisms of a lifetime are activated to confront the challenge of the terminal experience. Most frequently observed are the mechanisms related to dependency, aggression, sexuality, and identity.

There is a new surge of interest in allowing a person to die with dignity and not be arbitrarily subjected to artificial life-support systems to keep the body alive when the time for natural death has arrived (Shipley, 1982). Otherwise, death becomes lonely, mechanical, and dehumanized. Too often death comes in an impersonal, sterile emergency room or in unfamiliar surroundings. How different this is from the calm acceptance of the patriarch Jacob who gathered his children about him, gave each a blessing, and then slipped into the arms of his Creator (Gen. 49:33).

THE REALITY OF DEATH
Death is part of the plan of the universe revisited each year through the seasons: birth, flourishing, fading, dying, only to be born again the following year. From a Christian perspective, death is a multifaceted reality (Doss, 1972).

A Normal Event
Death comes to all and may be viewed either as the last enemy or as a friend who ushers us into the presence of God. When asked how he was at age eighty, John Quincy Adams replied, "John Quincy Adams is quite well. But the house where he lives in becoming dilapidated. It is tottering. Time and the seasons have nearly destroyed it and it is becoming quite uninhabitable. I shall move out soon. But John Quincy Adams is quite well, thank you."

A Personal Event
Doss (1972) emphasized that death is a "uniquely personal reality" in life. "It is the terminal event in infinite experience, the event that confronts a man with the meaning and purpose of that experience," for death "is not something which merely happens to me; it is that which I actively experience" (p. 19).

A Social Event
Death occurs within a community of friends and relatives—sometimes

strangers—who interpret the impact of the event and assess whether it has been a defeat or a victory. It is at this point that the church needs to be active in ministering to the dying as they face the inevitable and to the survivors who must go on living after the funeral is over and the family has returned to their homes.

A Mystery

Doss (1972) said that the contemporary mystery of death lies in humankind's inability to

> comprehend what the death of the self means. It was Freud who first noted that man protects himself in his contemplation about death. Even when a man imagines his own death, he is aware that he is the thinking subject. While we contemplate death and seek to understand its meaning, it is not possible for us to contemplate non-being. This led Freud . . . to conclude: "At bottom no one believes in his own death, or to put the same thing another way, in the unconscious every one of us is convinced of his immortality. . . ." Freud's observation is undoubtedly an important insight into the dynamics of denial in our culture. (p. 22)

Freud's conclusion is also a challenge to the Christian therapist who must develop his own psychology as well as theology of death.

A Liberating Experience

I have added this point to the outline of Doss (1972) because of my clinical observations that death is not necessarily a painful experience, as is often feared. Pain may precede death, but death brings an end to pain, anxiety, and tension. The fear of death, beyond the consciousness of sin, lies in guilt, loneliness, and fear of the unknown. These are not Christian concerns and need not cloud the death of the righteous. If they do, the expressed religious faith has been more extrinsic than intrinsic. For the intrinsically motivated Christian, as noted in the previous discussion of death anxiety, death frees one from all pain and fear; it merely transports one to another plane of existence to await the resurrection in the presence of God under the altar in the heavenlies (Rev. 6:9).

Paul expressed this liberation concept graphically in 1 Thessalonians 4:13–17:

> Brothers, we do not want you to be ignorant about those who fall asleep, or to grieve like the rest of men, who have no hope. We believe Jesus died and arose again and so we believe that God will bring with Jesus those who have fallen asleep in him. According to the Lord's own word, we tell you that we who are still alive, who are left till the coming of the Lord, will certainly not precede those who have fallen asleep. For the Lord himself will come down from heaven, with a loud command, with the voice of the archangel and with the trumpet call of God, and the dead in Christ will rise first. After that, we who are still alive and are left will be caught up with them in the clouds to meet the Lord in the air. And so we will be with the Lord forever. Therefore encourage each other with these words. (NIV)

Types of Death

That death is a reality is unquestioned, but how death is classified is a point of conjecture. Four modes of death have been recognized in the literature of thanatology and have been used to complete the U.S. Public Health Service

Certification of Death: natural death, accidental death, suicide, and homicide. Shneidman (1976b) found these labels inadequate and offered a new classification system that includes cessation, termination, interruption, and continuation.

Cessation. This refers to stopping any potential for any further conscious experience. "Only man, by virtue of his responsible introspective mental life, can conceptualize fear and suffer cessation. Cessation refers to the last line of the last scene of the last act of the last drama of that actor" (Shneidman, 1976b, p. 12).

Concerning cessation, Jackson (1983) observed: "Medically, a careful redefinition of death is taking place. . . . Is it when the heart ceases to beat, or when the flow of oxygen to the brain ceases, or when meaningful capacity for communication and relationships ends?" (p. 140).

Mant (1976) turned to Dr. Henry Beecher (1967) of Harvard for assistance and received three competing definitions of cessation:

1. The moment at which irreversible destruction of brain matter, with no possibility of regaining consciousness, was conclusively determined.

2. The moment at which spontaneous heartbeat could not be restored.

3. "Brain Death" as established by the EEG.

Beecher went on to say that any up-to-date determination of death would be a legal impossibility at this time, however theologically and scientifically sound it might be (p. 230).

Subsumed under cessation, Shneidman (1976b) listed four terms that denote varying degrees of conscious and unconscious involvement in effecting or hastening one's own death.

1. *Intentional death* applies "to those cases in which the individual plays a direct and conscious role in his own demise" (p. 15). The classical work on suicide has been written by Shneidman, Farberow, and Litman (1970) with Wekstein (1979) adding to the literature more recently. The Christian therapist will also profit from reading Blackburn (1982).

2. *Subintentioned death* refers to the "instances in which the individual plays an indirect, covert, partial, or unconscious role in his own demise" (p. 18). This includes such observed behaviors as being careless, imprudent, foolhardy, forgetful, and suffering from amnesia, or lack of judgment." These and/or other passive behaviors may be rooted either conscious or unconscious experiences. Shneidman (1976b) referred to these as the "psychosomatics of death" (p. 18).

3. *Unintentioned death* refers to occurrences in which the person does not deliberately plan a significant role in his death. "He is, at the time of his cessation, 'going about his business' (even though he may be lying in a hospital), with no conscious intention of effecting or hastening cessation and no strong conscious drive in that direction" (p. 20). Schneidman (1976b) emphasized that this includes death by disease or accident.

4. *Contraintentioned death* covers the behaviors of the person who threatens suicide but has no intention of carrying it out. "An individual who uses the semantic blanket of 'Suicide' with a conscious absence of any lethal intention

I shall term as one who has employed contraintentioned—advertently noncessation—behavior" Shneidman (1976b, p. 22) concluded. Such individuals may act out with no clear intention to commit suicide and have no intent to risk cessation. He described these as ones who "have remitted (in the sense of having 'refrained from') suicide" (pp. 22, 23).

Termination. Termination is defined as "the stopping of the physiological functions of the body" (Schneidman, 1976b, p. 12). This term distinguishes between cessation (the stopping of conscious experience) which may differ in time from the stopping of bodily functions. He coined the term "somize" to refer to the "demise of the soma" (p. 12).

> The operational definition (or criterion) for termination can be put as the stopping of the exchange of gases between the human organism and his environment; that is, an individual may be said to be terminated when, if a mirror is put to his mouth, there is no frosting of the glass—the subsequent growth of his beard or other activities do not matter. (pp. 12, 13)

Interruption. This term relates to cessation and is defined as the "stopping of consciousness with the actuality, and usually the expectation, of further conscious experience" (Schneidman, 1976b, p. 13). Sleep or altered states of consciousness such as being under an anesthetic, in an alcoholic or epileptic stupor, or a diabetic coma fall into this category as do such behaviors as fugue, amnesia, or dissociative states.

Continuation. Continuation is the term used by those who work with suicidal people and prepare "psychological autopsies." This refers to those patients who did not intend to die but experienced interruption in the stream of consciousness in a coma-like state that appeared to be terminal. "Continuation" can be defined as experiencing, in the absence of interruption, the stream of temporally contiguous conscious events. From this point of view, our lives are made up of one series of alternating continuation and interruption states (Shneidman, 1976b, p. 14).

Continuum of Consciousness

With a faith in Christ that is enhanced by the guidance of the Holy Spirit, how does the Christian therapist view death? Is the Christian view of death any different from the secular view? Is death lower than a comatose state or is it a transcendental reality beyond the highest peak experience or ultimate ecstasy? Here is where the therapist's view of conscious awareness comes into focus.

Without saying so, many people think of death as a level below the depth of a coma. Looking at the degrees of awareness on the continuum of consciousness, they see that in a coma an individual is totally out of touch with reality. Above this are the various levels of sleep, identified by the rapid eye movements (REMs) from deep sleep through dream sleep to awakening. Next comes the state of awareness in which a person is fully cognizant of what is transpiring around him. A more intense form of awareness is the raptness of a peak experience when a person is more aware of his potentialities and possibly views them in light of an eternal destiny. This is the point of religious experience that gives motivation to life and sometimes changes life's direction. It may be referred to as a "mountain-top experience" or ecstasy.

CONTINUUM OF AWARENESS

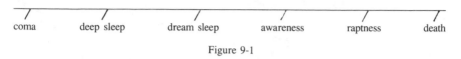

| coma | deep sleep | dream sleep | awareness | raptness | death |

Figure 9-1

My concept of the relationship between death and awareness was crystalized when my mother died suddenly from a stroke at the age of 70. In the solitude of viewing her lifeless form before the morticians had prepared her body for burial, I found it inconceivable to consider her as sleeping or even being in a coma. She was no longer in residence. Her spirit had taken flight. Death had brought the release of her spirit to transcend its earthly confines from that worn-out body to pass from awareness through raptness to total actualization with the Christ she had loved and served for almost 60 years. At that point tears would have been selfish and the product of my own self-pity and loneliness. I sensed in the tranquility of that moment that a saint had been ushered by the angels into the sanctuary of the redeemed, aware not of finitude but only of raptness and ecstasy in the presence of the Eternal Creator.

So, I perceive death for the Christian not as a state below the deepest coma, but as the point of maximum awareness beyond the ecstasy of life's most vivid peak psychological or spiritual experience. Admittedly, there is a curtain between raptness and death, but that is only the confines of finitude which Paul refers to as seeing through a "glass, darkly." This limited vision will be completed at the consummation of the age (1 Cor. 13:12). Such a Christian view of death

> affirms a faith in a personal, loving Creator who is working out his purpose with men. It affirms a view of reality which is dynamic and interdependent, where God's activity is interpreted not as coercive power but persuasive love. And it understands that temporality and finitudes are essential elements in defining what it means to be human. (Doss, 1972, p. 17)

No doubt the death experience of the non-Christian is qualitatively different because hope in resurrected living is contained in the good news of Jesus Christ and surrender to him as Lord and Master of life.

STAGES OF DYING

After extensive study of terminally ill patients, Kübler-Ross (1969) concluded that there are five stages in the process of dying when the patient is aware of his or her terminal condition. Wilson (1985), on the other hand, observed that subsequent investigators have not confirmed these stages but reported instead "two general responses to imminent death—despair and withdrawal" (p. 284). However, the sequence postulated by the Swiss psychiatrist remains a classical guide for the therapist when working with the terminally ill patient and offers a framework for understanding the dying patient and for devising strategies for interpreting the inevitable process.

Denial

Denial, the first stage of death, carries with it an initial shock, usually followed by withdrawal or isolation: "No, it can't be me. . . . There must be some mistake." Coleman and Glaros (1983) noted that denial can become a useful defense mechanism because it is difficult to move from the awareness of health to the realization of death as a personal experience. By denying the possibility of approaching death, an individual can developmentally progress in stages to cope with the reality of an impending terminal experience.

Anger

The anger may be directed at God because he is letting it happen, to the physician because he or she is the bearer of the bad news, or to the survivors because they are being granted an extension of life while the patient is being denied that privilege. Or, the anger may be directed toward all of the survivors.

Anger produces the question of why this "punishment" has been meted out and reminds us of Freud's view of the maliciousness of death noted earlier in this chapter. The patient often recites in his or her own mind, if not in verbal expression, his or her own exemplary life and unfulfilled dreams that make death seem so unfair. Too, there is the surrender of life to death and the sense of powerlessness that comes with facing the inevitable. Often this anger is focused indiscriminately and strikes without warning. Allowing the patient to express this anger through *appropriate* channels can be very therapeutic and removes much of the "sting" of the impending death. In fact, "the anger subsides more quickly when it is allowed to run its course with as little reaction from others as possible" (Davis, 1984, p. 93).

Bargaining

This stage of dying frequently involves quiet guilt and psycholgical negotiations for more time and another chance at life, such as Hezekiah (2 Kings 20:1-6), with promises to do a better job of living in the extended time. This bargaining can focus on physicians, families, God, or self. Some patients feel if they act more "correctly" they will win an extension of life. Not everyone bargains, but "the promise of good behavior in exchange for longer life may motivate a significant portion of the dying individual's behavior" (Coleman & Glaros, 1983, p. 116).

Depression

Depression may be intense or only a mood, depending on the patient's view of life and life after death. If it becomes too intense it can lead to a paranoid state. The depression can result from realizing that weakness and disability can no longer be ignored; it can focus on the sums of money being spent in treatment or on time lost from the job and away from family involvements. "An important source of depression results from our impending separation from the world and loss of all that is loved and dear to us" (Coleman & Glaros, 1983 p. 116).

Acceptance

At this point the patient accepts the fact that he or she is dying, puts personal affairs in order, but maintains hope for extended time. Acceptance is a final stage of rest before the terminal experience. Coleman and Glaros (1983) observed: "In essence we have said goodbye to the world and to our families and loved ones and now wish to die. Having detached ourselves from the world and from our important relationships, death becomes a great relief" (p. 116).

Observations

There appear to be two overriding concerns in these five stages of dying. First, at each stage in the process of dying there is a conscious or unconscious hope that there will be a remission, a healing, or a miracle that will bring an extension of life. Such hope is essential to mental vitality during a terminal illness. Otherwise, the patient disintegrates rapidly. In fact, medical authorities indicate that when they detect a patient has lost hope, they anticipate his death within 24 to 48 hours (Bowers, Jackson, Knight & LeShan, 1981).

Second, these stages are not mutually exclusive. The patient may vascillate from acceptance to momentary denial or anger and experience bargaining and depression. The patient *must* have worked through the earlier stages of his or her attitude toward death, however, if the patient is to maintain a positive acceptance as the end of life approaches.

The presence of hope in the acceptance stage of dying is not inconsistent. A patient may accept the fact that death is imminent, summon his or her family, make final legal arrangements, and maintain contact with reality until the body ceases to function and the spirit is transported to meet his or her Maker (2 Cor. 5:8). Acceptance of the will of God allows the believer to be open to either the miracle of extended life or the mystery of death. This surrender to the sovereignty of God makes the death of the believer a testimony to the world.

Christianity is not only a faith to live by; it is a faith to die by. One of the positive testimonies of the validity of Christianity is the attitude with which a person faces his or her own death and the death of loved ones and friends. It is not often emphasized, but funeral behavior is a vital facet of witnessing and evangelism, for it demonstrates the existence or absence of an intrinsic faith in the sovereignty of God.

As a former hospital administrator, I have observed hundreds of terminal patients and witnessed scores of deaths. It has been spiritually moving to witness the death of saints who slipped into the arms of their Maker. It has also been a grueling experience when the intrinsic faith was not present to sustain dying people in the hour of their death. This is consistent with the findings of therapists (Bowers et al., 1981) who have distinguished between the dying sequence of younger and middle-aged patients who still have "unfinished business" and that of older patients who have achieved what Erikson (1964, 1968) called "integrity" and Maslow (1968, 1971) called "self-actualization." (See the chapter on "Ministering to the Aging" in this volume.)

On one occasion I witnessed what I perceived to be the dialogue between the soul and spirit of a patient who saw the specter of death entering the room. She pulled at the side rails on her bed and said, "Don't let them take me. . . . I see them coming through the window . . . don't let them get me." As she strained to pull herself up in the bed, I assisted with assurance and touching. Then the tone of the voice changed dramatically to a deep guttural. I heard coming out of her mouth, "I can't let Maude go." I sensed that the soul and spirit were reluctantly parting company and the soul was holding fast to the spirit to maintain life. The struggle was brief and the subsequent coma lasting only a couple of hours until the signs of quiet death were recorded by the nurse in attendance.

MINISTERING TO THE DYING

Wilson (1985) noted that dealing with the dying is a delicate task. "When death is imminent, persons have needs which if not met can result in despair. These needs are (1) to control pain, (2) to retain dignity and self-worth as they participate in decisions that affect outcomes, and (3) to receive love and affection from others in the environment" (p. 284). Pain control lies in the domain of the medical staff, but maintaining dignity, enhancing self-worth, and giving love and affection are the opportunity of the family as well as therapists and ministers involved in caring for the dying patient.

Jackson (1983) concluded that the way a person faces death is a product of a lifetime of living: in facing death the patient confronts the realities of life. He listed 10 factors that make it possible for a person to face death with dignity (pp. 190, 191):

1. The ability to be guided by reality rather than by fear.
2. Long-term values.
3. A grown-up conscience.
4. Independence
5. The capacity to give and receive love.
6. A reasonable dependence.
7. A reasonable aggressiveness.
8. Healthy defense mechanisms.
9. Good sexual adjustment with acceptance of one's own gender.
10. Good work adjustment.

These factors are very similar to the qualities of the self-actualizer (Maslow, 1968, 1971) and the mature personality (Kolb & Brodie, 1982) discussed in the chapter on aging in this volume.

Caretaker Interventions

Coleman and Glaros (1983, p. 116, 117) have offered suggestions for easing the dying process. They noted first of all that caretakers should *treat the person, not a disease* (p. 116). Kastenbaum (1972) added that if the hospital, hospice, or home situation takes away the responsibility, credibility, and control of the aging or dying person from himself, "we also set up a situation in which much of his life has become the property of others long before the process of dying begins" (p. 110).

Second, caretakers should *be open with the dying person*. Dying people have the right to know what is happening to them. Acknowledging the impending death of the person can help both the sick and well cope more readily. In this regard Kübler-Ross (1984) noted:

> Until therapists learn that each person makes his or her own choices and lives through the consequences of these choices, they will not help one human being, no matter how many courses about grief they take and how many books they read. Therapists must understand that it is not the years that people live, it is how they have lived. If they live fully, they will feel that they have lived a hundred lives. (p. 8).[2]

Third, Coleman and Glaros (1983, p. 117) stated the caretaker should *ask what is needed*. The dying need an opportunity to get their affairs in order. This involves reviewing the will and making necessary arrangements for family and business affairs. The patient should also be consulted in the progress of his or her own treatment. Kübler-Ross (1984) illustrated this with the case of Jeffrey:

> When I walked into Jeffrey's room, I heard a young eager beaver physician who had just taken over the ward say to Jeffrey's parents, "We're going to try another experimental chemotherapy." He said this very casually, as if it were nothing." If he had looked at Jeffrey, he would have seen the child's face pale and his eyes tear up. He was so fragile, I blurted out, "Did anybody ask Jeffrey?" They shook their heads as if to say you do not ask a 9-year-old child if he wants more treatment. I said, "Yes, you do." He knows what he needs, not from his head, but from his heart. (p. 7)

THERAPIST PREPARATION

Kübler-Ross (1969) once observed, after months of interaction with terminally ill patients: "I believe that we should make it a habit to think about death and

---

[2] Kübler-Ross made her observations in reviewing a decade of working primarily with children who were dying, parents of murdered children, and parents whose children had committed suicide. She further observed:

> Although they may not recognize it intellectually, human beings are aware of their own impending death, whether it is a homicide, a suicide, a sudden death, or a slow natural death. If we would pay close attention, we would eliminate the grief work of our society— not grief, but grief work. Grief is a very natural emotion; it is really a God-given gift that allows us to come to grips with any loss of life, whether it is the loss of a valued item or death in the family. It is not necessary to work with grief; it involves shedding tears, sharing, and talking, but it will heal. Grief work, in contrast, is shame, guilt, and fear (Oh, my god if I had only done this or that!). The real grief work should be done before tragedy strikes. (p. 2)

This is the process that leads to acceptance in the fifth step in Kübler-Ross's (1969) stages of death discussed earlier.

dying occasionally, I hope before we encounter it in our own life'' (p. 5). In more recent years she has taken pains to show therapists—medical, psychological, and pastoral—how to prepare uniquely to minister to the dying patient. She stated:

> If people learn again to balance the physical, emotional, intellectual, and spiritual parts of themselves, they will become natural again and will begin to discover that they are very, very intuitive, very spiritual. The whole person is so intuitive that he or she is always at the right place at the right time. All things happen when the time is right, and there is no unfinished business. (1984, p. 3)

She concluded that this it true, even in what would appear to be an untimely death. She traced the developmental approaches of caring for infants and children and applied it to preparing to work with patients facing terminal experiences.

Physical Self

The physical self of the dying patient needs to be approached with the same care that was used to launch life in infancy. Kübler-Ross (1984) noted that physical care is the greatest need of terminally ill patients which includes ensuring that an incontinent patient is clean and dry before bringing in a visitor and making sure every terminally ill patient is touched, loved, and hugged.

Emotional Self

In relating to the emotional self, the psychiatrist stated that God created man so that his physical self is paramount in the first year of life while the emotional self develops between ages one and six. In dealing with the dying patient the therapist needs opportunity to deal with such emotional issues as fear, grief, and guilt (Hansen & Frantz, 1984).

The only *natural fears* are the fear of falling and the fear of sudden loud noises. Therapists who themselves have other fears need to become aware of them and work to eliminate them. Noting that *grief* is an important emotion, Kübler-Ross indicated that its ''natural expression is tears. . . . People who are not allowed to express natural grief as children have problems for the rest of their lives because life consists of thousands of little deaths'' (p. 5). Repressed grief, she concluded, is a contributing factor to many problems of the dying and to the therapists who work with them.

''*Guilt* can be overcome only by sharing it with a group of accepting, unconditionally loving people,'' Kübler-Ross (1984, p. 6) observed. But, guilt must be shared from the heart, not the head. The dying patient must be given the opportunity to shed tears, to enter into the process of grieving, and then to learn how to forgive both self and others—including God.

Kübler-Ross (1984) concluded that every unnatural emotion is a piece of unfinished business and illustrated the concept with *anger* which, she said, takes only 15 seconds in its natural state.

> Anger that is not expressed builds up until the individual explodes, and the explosion certainly lasts longer than 15 seconds. Repressed anger is the biggest killer of our society in terms of angry individuals' health and in terms of tragedy. It results in revenge. (p. 6)

The value of *unconditional love* in dealing with the emotional self must not be underestimated. Kübler-Ross (1984) noted that "Unconditional love helps keep natural emotions natural and flowing" (p. 6). She also observed that unconditional love has the capacity to say "no" when it is appropriate: "Unconditional love can say no in such a way as to give the child self-confidence. . . . Loving a child unconditionally does not mean total permissiveness. Firm, consistent discipline starts and ends between one and six. Once they have learned, parents need not worry" (pp. 6, 9).

Spiritual Self

The *spiritual self* develops in adolescence if the individual lives in harmony with his created potential. Yet thousands of pre-teen children die each year.

> These children lose physical abilities, but they find something that is better or more significant—they open intuitively and spiritually prematurely. Dying children are old, wise souls, as they are often called. It is an incredible experience to sit with dying children, and listen to them. They are unusual children who have a compensatory gift that can elevate them into a spiritual plane. (Kübler-Ross, 1984, pp. 6, 7)

Here Kübler-Ross was using a broad definition for "spiritual," speaking to the dimension of the person that goes beyond the instinctiveness of an animal to being alive as a human being, created in the image of God as a living soul (Gen. 1:26).

Therapists' Personal Struggles

Therapists must be open in dealing with the terminally ill patient.

> When the process of dying can be made a significant part of the life experience of an individual, the benefits are shared by those who die and those who confront the dying of another. A reduction of guilt, anxiety, and defensiveness is replaced by a sensitivity and understanding that enriches communication with genuine human concern. The counselor becomes less threatened as he becomes more humane; in the same way the human dimension of the dying person when properly supported becomes a resource for living during those last days—not merely regarded as a threat but also as a time of spiritual growth and a time for doing the important unfinished business of living. (Bowers, et al., 1981, pp. 3, 4)

Bowers et al. (1981) observed that physicians frequently hide behind masks to protect themselves from intimate contact with their dying patients. These masks include the professional medical language or jargon doctors use, cynicism, materiality, impersonality, ritualized action, the hospital routine, and the impersonal "it-it" relationship that emerges as barrier are built against personal closeness with approaching death. In addition to these masks, "there is the sedation which can be administered in order to take the patient and his unacceptable behavior away from any relationship that might exist between him and those around him" (p. 56).

The clergy also have masks they can hide behind, such as the "set-apartness" of the ordination ceremony, ritualized action, the special language of religious terms, clerical attire worn by the clergy from some formal churches, and the mask of business.

It is not enough to approach the dying patient with rituals and medical interventions that merely prolong the process of dying. The meaning of both life and death must be considered by the professionals who treat the patient, so that the patient can find personal fulfillment, a fuller self-realization even *in extremis*. This moves us quickly into an area beyond technique. This brings us into the naked confrontation of the existential values that can be achieved both in living and in dying. This obliges us to face our fears, and failures, and phantasies unmasked and with courage. (Bowers, et al., 1981, p. 73)

BEREAVEMENT

The process of bereavement involves mourning and grief. Davis (1984) has observed that "*Young's Analytical Concordance of the Bible* (1955) lists 350 references under the heading *death*, 135 references under *mourning* and 97 under *grief* and *grieving*" (pp. 89, 90). In ministering to the bereaved, the counseling pastor must be able to interpret the experience of grief biblically and therapeutically, as well as be able to offer guidance through the process of mourning.

Mourning

Kolb and Brodie (1982, p. 75) said that *mourning* is a broad term that denotes "the period of grief that follows loss through death or an important separation, or even the loss of a body part as from amputation." Mourning is best viewed as a stressful process of anxiety that involves recouping in the face of loss and reestablishing the personality to an appropriate life style. Mourning allows the person in grief to disengage psychologically from the lost object by reviewing past experiences and the meanings and emotional significance of a relationship that can never take place again.

Grief

Grief is a healthy experience that involves both cognitive and emotional processes in working through a significant loss (Larsen, 1985; Westberg, 1962). Kolb and Brodie (1982) noted that *normal grief* is different from depression. Grief involves sadness but is free from guilt or shame. While grief leads to a temporary withdrawal from activities and a preoccupation with the lost person, it is short-term and seldom leads to serious behavioral problems or psychological upheavals.

Therapists need to be alert to grief reactions in children as well as adults. In children, the sequence involves initial crying or aggressive behavior followed by a phase of helplessness, withdrawal, and inactivity which lead to detachment. In older children, the initial phase of anxious protest is accompanied by rage. Clinicians have observed that the

death of a mother before the child was 10 is found to have occurred more frequently in the history of schizophrenics than in the general population. Death of the father before the child is 10 also exceeds the expected frequency in the histories of those with schizophrenic and manic-depressive psychoses and the neuroses (Kolb & Brodie, 1982, p. 180).

Adults frequently experience a delayed reaction to grief. This can last from hours to several weeks. During this period the sufferer appears to behave as usual, but will frequently speak of feeling "numb." Thereafter the grieving person experiences periods of intense yearning and suffering that are associated with the reminders of the deceased person. These reactions are often accompanied by psychophysiological symptoms, especially gastrointestinal distress. In between the attacks of yearning, the bereaved person becomes apathetic, experiences a sense of futility, and may display signs of depression. Insomnia, anorexia, restlessness, and outbursts of irritability or even anger follow. There is a temptation toward overidealized thinking and rumination about the departed person. It is not uncommon to hear reports of the deceased person visiting the grieving person, especially at night (Kolb & Brodie, 1982). One of my patients reported this phenomenon for 10 years following his father's death when there had been "unfinished business" between the two men.

This period of yearning in normal grief lasts from one to six weeks. It usually subsides into a healthy "minimal yearning" after six months. It is seldom wise for a widowed person to make any major decisions involving selling the family home or moving to a new location until the intense period of yearning has subsided. Occasional, brief periods of yearning erupt for several years after the loss (Kolb & Brodie, 1982), so new attachments should be postponed until the bereavement has mellowed into realistic memory, usually a period of about two years.

Kolb and Brodie (1982) have also observed that

> bereavement caused by the death of a spouse is known to be followed by an increased mortality risk for the survivor. Young survivors and men are at the highest risk—the increased causes of death are due to such conditions as suicide, alcoholism, cirrhosis, heart disease, and the common respiratory infections. (p. 181)

It has also been noted that the anniversary of a death can bring heightened reactions including displays of grief. These include outbreaks of anxiety or other symptomatic defensive expressions that occur regularly on specific dates and may be reflected in a symbolic reenactment of an earlier period of bereavement. These have been observed to occur about the time the patient reaches the age of the parent at the time of a parent's death; sometime it occurs when one of the patient's children reaches the age the patient was when the parent died. Occasionally, recurrent attacks of anxiety have been observed to coincide with the anniversary date of the death of a parent.

Larsen (1985) described the most salient symptoms of grief as "acute psychological pain which includes emotional turmoil; wide fluctuations in mood; and feelings of hurt, guilt, depression, helplessness, anger, sadness, love, rage, loneliness, resentment, and hopelessness" (p. 473). Secondary symptoms include eating, sleeping, and sexual disturbances.

Following the work of Kübler-Ross (1969), many observers have noted that the stages of grief are not demonstrably different from the stages of dying: denial and isolation, anger, bargaining, depression, and acceptance. In the early stages grief might include shock, emotional release, depression, loneliness, distress, and panic. In its secondary stage grief may be displayed as guilt, hostility, and resentment, along with the inability to return to usual activities. Hope and the struggle to affirm reality come as the dimensions of grief are traversed successfully.

Abnormal Grief

Abnormal grief is sometimes observed in a variety of behaviors. The term *chronis grief* has been used to describe reactions in which the bereaved person prolongs grief reactions along with guilt and self-blame. Sometimes there is evidence of either partial identification with the deceased or aggressive behaviors. *Inhibited grief* displays itself in a lowering of responses to normal grief with the substitution of other behaviors that tend to mask the process of grieving. This is seen when grief is denied and the person disowns pain and proceeds with a "business-as-usual attitude" (Larsen, 1985, p. 473). *Delayed grief* involves repression of grief reactions for weeks, months, or even years and frequently resembles chronic grief long after the terminal episode.

Abnormal grief is sometimes observed when a person becomes psychotic and totally incapable of coping. Another form of abnormal grief is called "enshrinement" which occurs when a survivor leaves the deceased person's room and possessions untouched long after the death has occurred. "The creation of a 'shrine' becomes symbolic of the survivor's inability to let go of the loved one" (Larsen, 1984, p. 473).

Wilson (1985) also observed that abnormal grief can show itself in "persistent physical symptoms, angry withdrawal, intense loneliness, obsessing over the loved one, and lingering depression." He further noted that "if after a year to 18 months following a loss grief continues to interfere with one's overall function, professional help is indicated" (p. 473).

Grieving

Davis (1984) has wisely noted that "some people feel the expression of grief is a weakness, or a lack of Christian faith. Modern psychologists (both non Christian and Christian) tell us the expression of grief in a natural way is healthy and ought to be encouraged. It is, in fact, a kind of task to be worked through" (p. 95). Larsen (1985) concurred and observed:

> The Christian's spiritual experience is not unaffected by grief, especially when a tragic loss is involved. Some will react defensively with an over-devotion to God and the church, to the neglect of all else. Others will accuse God of being distant and will eventually leave the church. None of these individuals effectively mobilized faith resources in coping, because of a deep and unconscious anger toward God. So long as God-directed anger is unnamed, denied, and contained, spiritual paralysis is inevitable. In the healthy Christian response, all the pain typical of grief is present, and anger at God is recognized, accepted, and appropriately released. (p. 473)

Since death is not an ultimate tragedy to the Christian, the believer's grief is different from those who have no hope (1 Thes. 4:13). Caution must be taken not to hide behind denial as an expression of hope. The real pain of loss by death must be processed for healing to occur. "Christian faith, with its emphasis on

eternal life, in no way exempts one from the normal, human process of grieving"
(Wilson, 1985, p. 473).

Miller and Jackson (1985) observed that when bereaved people choose to talk
to someone about their grief, they frequently turn to their pastor. They offered
some guidelines that are good for psychological therapists as well:

> 1. Bereaved people often find it helpful to review the terminal illness that claimed their
> loved one. Often they want reassurance that everything possible was done, to relieve
> vague feelings of guilt by omission. It may be very helpful to involve the attending physician
> in this process if possible. Often the grieving person's contact with the physician was
> minimal and occurred during the period of numbness and confusion.
> 2. Allow crying if it occurs and use gentle reflective listening. If the person apologizes
> for crying, it may be a good time to explain that crying is healthy, part of the healing
> process, and not a reason for embarrassment.
> 3. During the initial period of shock it may be very helpful to assist the person in making
> day-to-day decisions, which tend to seem difficult and overwhelming to some at the time.
> The individual should be discouraged from making major decisions or choices about the
> future during this initial period.
> 4. If the person chooses to discuss the loved one who has been lost, it is often helpful
> to encourage him or her to talk about positive memories as well as painful ones. Some
> pastors have included this within the memorial service (for example, having those present
> say what they remember about the person). (p. 192)

Friends and relatives may express concern that a survivor is not grieving
"properly." It must be remembered that some individuals will proceed through
the grief process as the patient is in the process of dying. Others may have so
completely disengaged from the deceased that they have experienced no sense
of loss. Miller and Jackson (1985) suggested that "unless there is evidence of
a truly abnormal grief reaction, it is best to use reassurance and reflective listening
rather than conspiracy." For, they noted, members of the "family may be
projecting their own grief process onto the grieving spouse or may be operating
from mistaken assumptions as to how grief should or must occur. In the absence
of signs of abnormality it is usually best to trust the individual's own healing
process" (p. 192).

Dealing with loss requires effective release of grief. This involves expressing
the painful thoughts and feelings associated with the loss and working through
the grief, not devising strategies to avoid its pain, for there are no painless shortcuts
in the grief process (Larsen, 1985).

> Good models for handling grief, a strong faith, an understanding of what is involved
> in mourning, and caring support systems can facilitate the working through of a difficult
> loss. Because grief is a social event, it cannot be resolved in isolation. Those who grieve
> must be willing to risk sharing their pain, and those who minister must be willing to
> risk the discomfort of being with the persons in their pain. (p. 474)

CONCLUSION

Spirit-filled Christians experience loss, separation, and death just as other normal
individuals. They have the added advantage, however, of knowing Jesus Christ
as Lord and Master. In becoming submissive to his will for their lives, they learn

that nothing comes into the life of the believer without his presence (Heb. 2:18). So, when adversity comes, they look up and ask, "Lord, what new thing are you wanting to teach me today." Death then becomes an opportunity to explore new dimensions of God's grace. The Holy Spirit as the Paraclete is available to lead them into all the truth God wants them to know (John 16:13).

Spirit-filled Christians also know that God's wisdom is infinite and his ways of dealing with human problems unsearchable. Sometimes he deals miraculously, and the answer is instantaneous. Other times he heals over a period of time. There are times when he heals in direct answer to prayer; still other times when he allows the believer to experience medical interventions as an accompaniment to the healing process. Christians in medicine and pharmacy have been used tremendously as part of the healing team for both Christians and non-Christians alike, using the knowledge that was placed in the natural sciences by an all-knowing God for people to discover and utilize.

The ultimate healing comes in the form of death as the believer is ushered into the presence of God to spend the ages of eternity with the Father who created humanity for himself. (Unfortunately, unbelievers must spend eternity in a place that was not created for them, but for the devil and his angels because of their rebellion against the God of the universe.) This was the hope of the patriarchs and apostles of biblical times and is available to the believer today. It is the privilege of the Spirit-filled therapist to help searching souls find their peace with God.

For those who are bereaved, the Lord has left his word as a lamp to illumine the darkness that accompanies death (Psa. 119:105). Reading the Bible and meditating on its content bring healing and comfort to the dying as well as to the bereaved. It is in recognizing the sovereignty of God and becoming submissive to his will that ultimate peace comes into the life of the believer, whether he or she is the dying patient or the grieving survivor. The Spirit-filled believer has the added healing that comes by praying in tongues and receiving the comfort of the Holy Spirit when facing death or life after the death of a loved one.

Therapists who believe in the person of the Holy Spirit and allow him to operate in their therapy sessions should be more effective than their peers. They have the added dimension of spiritual insights into human problems since they are willing to treat the whole person—physically, emotionally, and spiritually. And, when it comes time for the spirit to be separated from the soul and body, they will not be at a loss for effective ways to minister therapeutically to the dying or to the survivors. For, they *know* that Calvary has left no unfinished business.

SELECT BIBLIOGRAPHY

Beecher, H. (1967, Dec. 12). *The Times*.

Blackburn, B. (1982). *What you should know about suicide*. Waco, TX: Word Books.

Cleath, R. L. (1970, March 27). Hope in the midst of horror. In *Christianity Today, 14*(13), pp. 3–5.

Coleman, J. C., & Glaros, A. G. (1983). *Contemporary psychology and effective behavior* (5th ed.). Glenview, IL: Scott, Foresman & Company.

Collins, G. R. (1969). *Search for reality*. Santa Ana, CA: Vision House Publishers.

Davis, B. C. (1984). *Teaching to meet crisis needs*. Springfield, MO: Gospel Publishing House.

Doss, R. W. (1972). Towards a theology of death. In *Pastoral psychology, 23*(224), pp. 21–22.

Erikson, E. H. (1964). *Insight and responsibility*. New York: W. W. Norton.

_____. (1968). *Identity: Youth and crisis*. New York: W. W. Norton.

Freud, S. (1959). *Selected works* (Vol. 4). New York: Basic Books.

Hansen, J. C., & Frantz, T. T. (Eds.). (1984). *Death and grief in the family*. Rockville, MD: Aspen Systems Corporation.

Jackson, L. M. (1983). *Coping with the crises in your life*. New York: Aronson.

Kastenbaum, R. (1972). *On the future of death: Some images and options*. Paper presented at the American Association of Suicidology: Third Annual Meeting, Detroit, MI: (March 30–April 2, 1972).

Kolb, L. C., & Brodie, H. C. H. (1982). *Modern clinical psychiatry* (10th ed.). Philadelphia: W. B. Saunders.

Koteskey, R. L. (1980). *Psychology from a Christian perspective*. Nashville: Abingdon.

Kübler-Ross, E. (1969). *On death and dying*. New York: Macmillan.

_____. (1984). Unfinished business. In J. C. Hansen & T. T. Frantz Eds.) *Death and grief in the family*. Rockville, MD: Aspen Systems Corporation.

Larsen, J. A. (1985). Grief. In D. G. Benner (Ed.) *Baker encyclopedia of psychology* (pp. 472–474). Grand Rapids, MI: Baker Book House.

Mant, A. K. (1976). The medical definition of death. In E. S. Shneidman, *Death: Current perspectives*. New York: Aronson.

Maslow, A. H. (1968). *Toward a psychology of being* (2nd ed.). New York: Van Nostrand.

_____. (1971). *The farther reaches of human nature*. New York: Viking.

Miller, W. R., & Jackson, K. A. (Eds.). (1985). *Practical psychology for pastors*. Englewood Cliffs, NJ: Prentice-Hall.

Oates, W. E. (1973). *The psychology of religion*. Waco, TX: Word Books.

Samuel, L. (1967). Answers to death. In *His Magazine, 27*(7) (April), pp. 32–34.

Scherzer, C. J. (1963). *Ministering to the dying*. Englewood Cliffs, NJ: Prentice-Hall.

Shipley, R. (1982). *The consumer's guide to death, dying and bereavement*. Palm Springs, CA: ETC Publications.

Shneidman, E. S., Faberow, N. L., & Litman, R. E. (1970). *The psychology of suicide*. New York: Aronson.

Schneidman, E. S. (1976a). *Death: Current perspectives*. New York: Aronson.

_____. (1976b). Orientations toward death. In E.S. Shneidman, N.L. Farberow, & R. E. Litman (Eds.), *The psychology of suicide*. New York: Aronson, pp. 3–45.

Wekstein, L. (1979). *Handbook of suicidology: Principles, problems, and practice.* New York: Brunner/Mazel, Publishers.

Whitlock, G. E. (1983). The structure of personality in Hebrew psychology. In H. N. Malony (Ed.), *Wholeness and holiness: Readings in the psychology/theology of mental health.* Grand Rapids, MI: Baker Book House.

Wilson, W. P. (1985). Death and dying. In D. G. Benner (Ed.), *Baker encyclopedia of psychology,* Grand Rapids, MI: Baker Book House.

SUPPLEMENTAL REFERENCES

Bowers, Margaretta K., Jackson, Edgar N., Knight, James A., & LeShan, Lawrence (1981). *Counseling the dying.* New York: Aronson.

Westberg, Granger (1962). *Good grief–A constructive approach to the problem of loss.* Philadelphia: Fortress Press.

Durant, Will (1944). *Caesar and Christ.* New York: Simon and Schuster.

Schaeffer, Francis A. (1976). *How should we then live?* Old Tappen, NJ: Fleming H. Revell.

10

GROUP THERAPY

Chuck Borsellino

Cast upon the shore of an isolated island, he alone had survived the wreck of his ship. The climate of this new frontier was comfortable, the food was plentiful, and the animals were no threat. He had seeds, weapons, and tools. Although he gave thanks to God for his good fortune in being saved from the sea, he denounced his solitary life. Robinson Crusoe was alone, no longer a member of any social group.

Undeniably, groups occupy a central position in the scheme of life—in work, play, education, and worship (e.g., Acts 4:31). In Romans 12, Paul described how each part of the body contributes to the whole. In essence, this passage speaks to us of our individual roles in reference to our contribution to the whole. There appears to be an unavoidable process whereby each member will not only modify the personality and performance of the group, but will reciprocally be sharpened by the group.

HISTORY

Groups have always existed, albeit in varied forms. Given that individuals have needed and relied upon others for survival, companionship, worship, and other areas of social interest, the formation of groups has been inevitable. The rise of political systems, through which people learned to govern themselves, is rooted in the phenomenon of "grouping." Genesis 11:1–9 records humankind's efforts to "group" and God's intervention to "re-group" the whole earth. He confused their language and thus scattered them into many smaller groups. Indeed, most of us have been confused ever since!

The rise of religious division and factions further illustrates the strength of our desire to form group loyalties and to exert influence upon our groups. It has been argued that culture itself, which is transmitted across generations through the process of enculturalization, reflects the cumulative ideas and values of chronologically successive groups (Belkin, 1984).

Many people have formed the impression that the fields of group dynamics and group therapy (GT) are well-formed, integrated frameworks for understanding human behavior. However, the literature demonstrates that only a token amount of research concerning group dynamics was conducted between the sixteenth and nineteenth centuries. The modern field of group dynamics—foundation for the discipline of group counseling—is strictly a twentieth-century development. This literature shows an increase in published papers from one article per year to 30 per year between 1890 and 1940. By the late 1940s, 55 studies were published annually, while 150 reports were published each year by the late 1950s. My own recent literature search revealed that about 125 group-oriented reports are now published annually.

Group counseling is a recently developed set of therapeutic techniques and procedures that emerged from a pressing and pragmatic reality (Ohlsen, 1970, p. vii). Individual counseling as the only means of therapeutic help became impossible as a result of the increasing demands for therapists' time during the middle part of this century. In particular, World War II produced a huge demand for psychotherapy which could not be met by long-term individual analysis.

Though it arose out of necessity, group counseling has grown into a specific science of its own. Ohlsen (1970) stated that group counseling will effectively change the lives of many people, from those experiencing anxiety and insecurity (neurosis) to those with continued ego dysfunction (psychosis).

Wertheimer, Koffkan and Kohler led early Gestalt psychologists in research that contributed greatly to the field of group dynamics and GT. However, Kurt Lewin, who studied under these pioneers, is recognized today as the leading authority in this new field. This is all the more impressive, given his early death in 1947 at the age of 57.

Lewin's research and trend-setting influence led to a recognition of the interrelatedness of group phenomena and the inescapable conclusion that changes in one aspect of a group will lead to changes in other group features. While emphasizing the complexity of groups and the interactions within them, group theory acknowledges the reciprocal nature of individual-group influence. In essence, GT is an approach to studying and modifying individual behavior; an approach which the church and other social, political, and vocational interests employ effectively.

DEFINITIONS

By definition, we see that group membership is inescapable. Cartwright and Zander (1968, p. 46) stated that a group is a "collection of individuals who have relations to one another that make them interdependent to some degree," while Shaw (1981, p. 454) defined a group as "two or more people who are interacting with one another in such a manner that each person influences and is influenced by each other member." Other definitions vary only slightly (see Bonner, 1959, p. 4; Hare, 1976, p. 4; Homans, 1950, p. 1; Sherif & Sherif, 1956, p. 144). Most definitions contain reference to three essential concepts: *association* (two or more individuals), *interaction* (communicating with one another), and *influence* (affecting and being affected by one another). Group membership in the church staff, board of elders, Sunday school class, home prayer group, and even families can be understood in light of these three constructs.

Because groups were originally formed for survival or social benefit, cooperation has always been integral to effective group membership and group functioning. As a group is formed, standards of behavior emerge, either implicitly or explicitly stated, and pressure builds for individuals to conform their behavior to the majority's standards in order to obtain the benefits of group membership. In fact, groups influence members' behaviors most powerfully through these "social norms" (Allport, 1954; McGrath, 1978).

Conformity is the tendency to modify one's behavior in order to comply with a group standard or norm. Conformity may be seen as being externally motivated (e.g., obeying orders) or internally motivated, in which the individual sincerely desires to do as the group does. Conformity by adolescents to their peer group is a clear example of this process of internalizing group norms. Members who fail to conform to the expectations of the group (often unstated) suffer its disapproval, sanction, and threatened expulsion from the group. Generally the milder forms of punishment for non-conformity are sufficient to maintain acceptable behavior.

THE NATURE OF GROUP COUNSELING

Group counseling may be a new approach or new resource to one's ministry, but the idea that healing occurs in small groups clearly is not new. The church's historic witness is that redemption and healing take place when one is reunited with God and with his people. We are instructed to bring healing to our relationships through repentance, acceptance, and behavior change; communion with God can then be all that he has designed it to be (Mark 11:25–26; 1 John).

Many behaviorists and social learning theorists believe that each group contributes to the individual's values, priorities, and developmental experiences. Knowles (1966) contends that one becomes a human being only in community context; the communities of family, neighborhood, educational facilities, church, and vocation actually "define" the individual. In other words, we discover our identities and fulfill our "life script" within the experiences of the community. As a result, we often esteem individuals who are involved, committed, and participating group members—those who are influenced by and who in turn influence other members of a given group. The recent trend toward a systems approach in family therapy further underscores the interlocking and interweaving nature of human relationships (see Hurley's chapter on "Family Therapy").

Group counseling as a therapeutic methodology acknowledges its foundation on the social reality of relatedness in small groups. Bandura (1977), a social learning theorist, stated that within the family and other significant social and developmental group situations, both healthy and unhealthy patterns of interaction are learned. The counseling group utilizes this understanding in providing a milieu for valuable *re*education, development, and experimentation with new behaviors.

Group counseling, then, offers an approach to healing within one's community;

it takes into account the communal aspects of human nature. However, it is essential to understand not only human personality but also the nature of divine healing when exploring the potential of group counseling within the Christian community.

We recognize the "pull" within each of us to "group" ourselves. Why, then, should we hold group counseling at arm's length within the church as a resource for healing, personality reconstruction, and behavior change? It is my belief that within the ranks of the "professional ministry" there are many who have the potential for counseling individuals in group settings. Some ministers already have adequate theoretical and experiential backgrounds in counseling via Clinical Pastoral Education (CPE) training, counseling coursework, practicums and on-the-job training; however, some may feel that they lack the practical framework or the support of professional personnel that they need to initiate group counseling. This chapter was written to assist qualified—and qualifying—pastor/counselors in their efforts to add group counseling to their repertoire of professional, ministerial, and therapeutic skills.

FORMS OF GROUP-ORIENTED HELP

Throughout this chapter, counseling is defined as a therapeutic experience for individuals who do not have severe pathological or emotional problems. Psychotherapy, in contrast, is defined as a therapeutic experience for emotionally disturbed individuals who seek assistance in resolving psychotic behavior, characterological disorders, or severe pathology (Ivey, Ivey & Simek-Downing, 1987, p. 19). In other words, psychotherapy provides major reconstruction of one's personality by uncovering psychologically repressed and denied (i.e., unconscious) issues. The group counselor, on the other hand, generally focuses on the "here-and-now" (i.e., present, conscious) issues related to normal human development. Group counseling is, however, an appropriate environment for individuals to discuss previously repressed issues which they may feel have a direct effect upon their present functioning.

A large number of group counseling models have been developed during the last two decades, including awareness groups, consciousness-raising groups, self-help groups, leaderless groups, sensitivity-training groups, and personal growth groups (Corey, 1981). Each type of group differs somewhat with respect to goals, techniques, focus (definition of the problem), role of the facilitator, group membership, and group process and duration. This variation results in a truly heterogeneous field, and an often bewildering array of terms and choices for the person seeking help in a group setting. The following discussion provides a brief overview of the major approaches to group counseling.

Group Counseling

Group counseling typically focuses on a specific or particular type of problem: personal, educational, spiritual, social, or vocational. It is carried out in various institutional settings, such as schools, mental health clinics, private counseling centers, and other human service centers. Examples of counseling groups include: divorce reaction groups, substance abuse groups, adjustment groups (death, relocation, vocational change, etc.), abused women groups, and premarital counseling groups.

As discussed above, the counseling group deals with conscious issues, is not aimed at major personality reconstruction, and is generally oriented toward resolving specific problems in a short-term intervention, rather than long-term treatment of psychotic disorders. It begins with the group members exploring their personal worlds to identify thoughts, feelings, and/or behaviors that are self-defeating. The group facilitator helps the group members to accomplish this by:

1. Assisting them in identifying counterproductive behaviors.

2. Moving them toward self-understanding through the process of uncovering psychological "payoffs" for these self-defeating behaviors.

3. Encouraging them to experiment with healthier and more productive responses and behaviors.

4. Providing them with feedback opportunities (from the group) to assist individuals in reality-testing as they incorporate these new behaviors into their world. (Corey, 1981)

The group counselor or facilitator will utilize a variety of counseling techniques in attempting to meet these counseling objectives. These techniques include *reflection* (mirroring the verbal and nonverbal messages of a group member), *clarification* (interpreting issues or feelings), *confrontation*, and *role-playing* (Corey, 1981, pp. 99–108). Further, the group counselor utilizes both structured and unstructured activities to facilitate the development of an atmosphere that is conducive to member interaction, mutual support, self-discovery, and behavior change.

Encounter Group

The encounter group, or growth group, offers an emotionally intense group experience. It is intended to assist relatively healthy people to gain self-awareness through self-discovery. The encounter group is growth-oriented, not treatment-oriented.

As Naisbitt (1982) has documented in his best-selling book, *Megatrends*, our society is moving in a materialistic and technological direction. We are subtly being told to value things and use people. The result is people alienated from themselves, from others, and from God. Therein lies the rationale for encounter groups—to combat this tendency by encouraging a "high touch" society in a "high tech" world.

Most encounter groups encourage non-sexual intimacy, self-disclosure, openness, and honesty. They emphasize feelings, experiencing, and intense, interpersonal sharing. There is an emphasis on self-expression, risk-taking behavior, spontaneity, and existential living. Members are encouraged to become increasingly aware of their feelings and to risk experimenting with behavior that they might have felt was not appropriate to their role: in short, to allow themselves to just "be themselves" (Corey, 1982, p. 4).

There are several types of encounter groups, ranging from unstructured groups where participants mutually shape the direction and goals of the group, to those which are structured by a facilitator who makes use of a variety of exercises to assist the members in fostering group interaction (Corey, 1981). The focus of such groups may be self-esteem and self-worth, identity formation, or role-clarification for both adolescents and adults. Most such groups are terminal in that they meet (by prior agreement) for a specific number of sessions—often 12 or more.

T-Groups

T-groups or training groups (also known as laboratory training groups) emphasize human-relations skills required for successful functioning in business, education or church management positions (Corey, 1982, p. 4).

The first T-group was initiated by Kurt Lewin in 1946. As part of a series of problem-solving workshops, Lewin arranged for his graduate students to observe and later discuss the dynamics of several work groups. These discussions were held in private until his graduate students requested the opportunity to discuss and interact openly with the observers and participants. The animated discussion that followed proved to be highly productive and educational. Lewin discovered that the individuals of the group were benefitting enormously from the interchange of open interaction, analysis, and feedback (Forsyth, 1983, p. 422).

Lewin subsequently developed the National Training Laboratory (NTL) at Bethel, Maine, which later flourished under the leadership of Leland Dradford. This center further developed the concept of special workshops or "laboratories," and during the sixties and seventies thousands of executives participated in programs offered by the NTL and other training centers (Bednar & Kaul, 1979).

In summary, the T-group approach is an experiential learning process. Proponents of T-group methods argue that essential group skills are most easily acquired by experiencing actual human relations. Hence, during laboratory training, members are encouraged to confront and resolve interpersonal issues actively with the goal of a greater understanding of oneself and others. While the long-term effectiveness of T-groups continues to be the center of debate (cf. e.g., Aronson, 1980; Bednar & Kaul, 1979; Kaplan, 1979), laboratory training groups that have focused on enhancing group effectiveness in task-oriented organizations through human-relations understanding have achieved positive results (Forsyth, 1983, p. 422).

Group Therapy

In response to the shortage of professionally trained therapists qualified to conduct psychological testing and psychotherapy during World War II, many therapists found themselves forced to abandon the traditional individual therapeutic model to work with small groups of clients who demonstrated similar pathological symptoms (Corey, 1982). Gradually, therapists began to experiment with various models, roles and therapeutic interventions. They discovered that the group setting offered unique therapeutic possibilities not found in the framework of individual therapy. The group provided mutual support, caring, trust, confrontation, reality testing, and many other advantages that are discussed in greater detail in the following section.

While some therapy groups are offered as a means to resolve specific emotional/behavioral disorders, the underlying goal remains the same—to transform or reconstruct personality structure. To accomplish this goal therapists focus on underlying and unconscious dynamics that are typically the root of pathological behaviors. Techniques that uncover unconscious dynamics are frequently used in order to promote greater understanding, personal insight, and eventually behavioral change.

Training requirements for group therapists are more stringent than those for leaders of personal growth groups. Group therapists are expected to have an earned degree or certification in psychiatry, psychology, or counseling. Further, they must have received clinical group supervision while leading therapy groups (Corey, 1982).

Because therapy groups often deal with serious behavioral disorders, they may meet more than once a week, and are of relatively long duration. Often, the group operates on the basis of individual rather than group termination dates. Examples of the problems treated in therapy groups are (a) eating disorders, (b) phobic disorders, (c) obsessive-compulsive disorders, (d) post-traumatic stress disorders, (e) psychosexual disorders—that is, gender identity, paraphilias, etc., and (f) impulse control disorders, such as kleptomania, pyromania, etc.

STAGES OF GROUPS: THE GROUP LIFE-CYCLE

The theories proposed by such developmental psychologists as Erikson, Piaget, and Freud suggest that throughout our lives we are constantly moving through systematic stages of development. We can see in the group process several developmental stages through which successful groups pass. While some groups are so stable that their basic processes and structures remain unchanged for months or even years, such groups are rare. As complex systems or interdependent human beings, groups typically are in a process of continual change.

Group therapists have developed well over 100 theories that seek to describe the kinds of developmental changes identified in most groups. Most of these models have taken one of two approaches: the Recurring Phase approach (Hill & Gruner, 1973) or the Sequential Stage approach (Shambaugh, 1978).

Recurring-Phase Model

This model suggests that certain issues tend to dominate group interaction during the various phases of group development and that these issues recur throughout the life of the group. For example, Bales's Equilibrium theory is based on the premise that group members strive to maintain a balance between task-oriented actions and emotionally expressive behaviors (Bales, 1965). Most groups tend to oscillate between these two concerns. Similarly, researchers examining therapeutic groups often describe three common themes woven throughout any group's development: (a) dependency on the facilitator, (b) pairing among the group members for security and emotional support, and (c) fight-flight reactions in which members either confront or evade issues (i.e., threats) within the group. To understand a group's development, one must identify its shifting position with regard to these three themes (Bion, 1961; Stock & Thelen, 1958; Whitaker & Thelen, 1975).

Although most of Recurring-Phase theorists agree that group development generally follows a sequential pattern with certain themes dominating at various times in the group's history, these same theorists suggest that these phases follow no consistent order. While one group may shift from a concern with leader dependency to problems in pairing and then to a fight-flight response, another group may display the reverse order. Thus, Recurring-Phase theories differ from Sequential-Stage theories, which attempt to describe common, somewhat predictable group stages.

Sequential-Stage Model

This model attempts to specify typical group stages which systematically appear during the development of the group. These stages are noticed as common themes that tend to surface during the life of most groups. While these stages collectively may be considered a road map through which most groups progress, it must be noted that the stages generally are not neatly separated discrete phases. It is also apparent that each stage does not conform to a theoretically preordained time schedule. The purpose and goal of the group, the orientation of the facilitator, and the population from which group members are drawn will account for difference among groups in their development. In spite of these differences, some general patterns can be identified which typically take place during the life of a given group.

Regardless of the theoretical orientation held, the group facilitator must have a clear grasp of the stages of group development. By educating potential leaders regarding these stages, the factors which encourage or interfere with the therapeutic process can be more effectively identified and understood. As they gain insight into the systematic evolution of groups, facilitators become aware of the developmental tasks that must be resolved successfully if a group is to move forward. Finally, knowledge of the developmental sequence provides the perspective which the facilitator needs to lead group members into healthier dimensions in their lives by reducing unnecessary group confusion and anxiety.

Several authors have analyzed and documented the stages of group process. It is clear that a wide array of opinions exist. For example: Schultz (1973) identifies three stages: inclusion, control, and affection. Gazda (1978) refers to four stages: exploratory, transition, action, and termination, while Mahler (1969) has expanded the process to include: formation, involvement, transition, working, and ending stages. To further complicate the issue, Rogers (1970) recognized 15 stages of group development and Shapiro (1978), outlined four general phases, but within this framework are 37 distinct stages!

From these descriptions, it becomes evident that, whereas the specific content of the group will vary considerably, the trends and process are more specific. Regardless of the nature of the group, some generalized trends become apparent over a period of time. The following figure offers several developmental orientations:

STAGES OF GROUP DEVELOPMENT

Tuckman (1965)
  Forming
  Storming
  Norming
  Performing
  Adjourning
Gazda (1978)
  Exploratory
  Transition
  Action
  Termination
Schultz (1973)
  Inclusion
  Control
  Affection
Berg & Landreth (1979)
  Precommitment Stage
  A. Testing of group limits
  B. Tentative self-
     disclosure
  Commitment Stage
  A. Heightened self-
     exploration
  B. Commitment to growth
     and change
  C. Increased personal
     effectiveness
  D. Preparation to leave
     group

Mahler (1969)
  Formation
  Involvement
  Transition
  Working Stage
  Ending Stage
Adler (in Corey, 1981)
  Establishing relationship
  Interpretation of Dynamics
  Development of Insight
  Reorientation
Rogers (Condensed, Shapiro, 1978
  Preparation
  Learning the Ground Rules
  Therapeutic Intervention
  Termination
Corey (1981)
  Orientation
  Transition
  Working Stage
  Consolidation

Hansen, Warner & Smith (1980)
  Initiation of the Group
  Conflict and Confrontation
  Development of
  Cohesiveness
  Productivity
  Termination
Levine (1979)
  Parallel Relations Stage
  Inclusion Stage
  Mutuality Stage
  Termination Stage
Yalom (1975)
  Stage 1:
  A. Orientation
  B. Hesitant participation
  C. Search for meaning
  Stage 2:
  A. Conflict
  B. Dominance
  C. Rebellion
  Stage 3:
  A. Increase of Morale
  B. Trust
  C. Self-Disclosure

Figure 10-1

While there continues to be widespread disagreement as to the specific developmental stages of group process, this in part is due to the fact that groups (and people) do not conform to any precise or preordained developmental sequence. The purpose of the group, the orientation of the facilitator, and the population of the group are all independent variables that will affect the nature and development of the group. In addition, there will always be "overlap" between the developmental stages that will complicate any attempts to package the group into neat and discrete stages. In spite of these issues, there does appear to be some generalized patterns or stages in the evolution of most groups. Following an extensive review, I have chosen to expand upon the developmental stages proposed by Corey, as they provide the essential framework that exists among the majority of the developmental theories: (a) pregroup issues, (b) orientation stage, (c) transition stage, (d) working stage and (e) consolidation stage (Corey, 1981).

PREGROUP ISSUES

If the group experience is to be successful, considerable time and planning must take place prior to the first group session. Planning may begin with drafting a proposal which would include:

1. Establishing the purpose and goals of the group.
2. Identifying the intended population to be served.
3. Developing plans to promote the group and to recruit group members.
4. Conducting pregroup individual interviews and screening for suitability for group membership.
5. Establishing the size of the group, its duration, and the frequency and time of group meetings.
6. Stating a theoretically determined group structure and format (e.g., open vs. closed group membership, voluntary vs. involuntary attendance).
7. Organizing plans for follow-up and group evaluation procedures.
8. Establishing fees (if any) and method of payment.

It cannot be overemphasized that leader preparation at this formative stage is crucial to the successful outcome of the group. If the goals, structure, and format are unclear or vague to the group facilitator, no doubt the group members will engage in unnecessary floundering. In addition to the compulsory preparation required for group leadership, the group facilitator must take time to address several personal issues: (a) motives for leading a group, (b) expectations of members, and (c) the spiritual direction for the group. The leader must spend quality time with the Lord in order to be spiritually prepared to be used by the Holy Spirit in ministry to the group members. Professional preparation will fall miserably short if one's spiritual responsibility to the group remains unattended.

After the selection of members is complete and the group is formed, I find it helpful to have one *pregroup session* as preparation for actual group activity. This meeting offers a great benefit to the members in that they can then most clearly understand the process and group experience, thus becoming more committed members. Unlike Yalom (1975) and Egan (1976) who advocate systematic and extensive group preparation sessions, I believe problems can arise with over-preparation and rigid structures which inhibit the group process (see Corey, 1981). While the lack of rigid structure may intensify members' fears, I feel it is helpful to discuss group goals and group functions in a spontaneous yet informative manner. Members thus learn that the group is a laboratory where experimentation and new behavior is encouraged, that the focus is on the here and now, that risk-taking and self-disclosure are expected, that giving and receiving feedback is essential to the group process, and that new behaviors learned within the group are designed for change outside the group.

In summary, the pregroup tasks that must be addressed before the first session should include:

1. Spiritual and psychological preparation for leadership tasks.
2. Developing a detailed written proposal.
3. Conducting individual screening interviews and selecting members.
4. Organizing the logistics (e.g., reserving the meeting room).
5. Securing parental permission (if appropriate).
6. Conducting a preliminary group session to clarify expectations, "ground rules," group confidentiality, etc.

ORIENTATION STAGE

Initially, most group facilitators recognize that a certain degree of anxiety and uncertainty prevail during the first few group sessions. Pastors will notice similarities between this phase and the experience of the church visitor. This typically results in members displaying their "socially acceptable" side; that is, they present dimensions of themselves they consider safe, secure, and protected.

Members begin to deepen their understanding of group functions and structure during this stage. In addition, it is a time of exploration with members defining their individual goals, clarifying expectations, discovering and testing group limits, determining group acceptance and their own willingness to risk becoming vulnerable. In essence, this is the stage of learning how new members become active group members. Active group membership will depend on answering the following questions (often asked silently during this initial stage).

1. Can I really trust these people?
2. How safe is it to risk?
3. How much can I reveal of myself?
4. Do I fit and belong here?
5. Will I be accepted by this group?

The group facilitator recognizes this phase as a passage to deeper commitment and involvement in the group; however, another major task must be addressed: the foundation of group trust. People will make a decision to trust or distrust a group. This decision will be based on the facilitator's ability to present the group as a safe place to reveal oneself. The leader should encourage members to share any factors that might inhibit trust; ironically they begin to thereby demonstrate an atmosphere of openness, honesty, and candor. It is a mistake to assume that people will "naturally" trust one another just because they have committed to being in a group, or because they trust the group facilitator. The importance of the development of trust is paramount to the continuing development of the group. Without this vital component, group interaction will become superficial, constructed, shallow, and unproductive.

During this initial stage the group's members will depend greatly on the facilitator, yet this should not be interpreted to mean that the tasks of identity-formation and trust-building are the exclusive providence of the group leader (while they can engender these vital tasks by their actions and attitudes). The successful resolutions of these tasks depends in large part on the members themselves— individually and collectively. This is why interviewing, screening, and selecting appropriate group members is so necessary and is designed to exclude individuals who might be perceived as limiting these two foundational building blocks.

In addition, (a) this stage is characterized by periods of silence and awkwardness (especially in unstructured groups). This tends to create even greater anxiety and ambiguity about how to behave in the group. Here members will flounder as they seek to discover "their place" in the group. (b) Issues dealt with will be safe as members discuss people outside the group (rather than themselves) or focus on past-tense historical issues in their lives. It is important to recognizes these early discussions as a testing ground for group identity and trust. As group members move toward revealing more of themselves to one another, the group will become a more cohesive unit. This emerging cohesion will strengthen the embryonic trust that currently exists and will create an experimental atmosphere which fosters self-discovery and self-disclosure.

The group facilitator must note that he or she will be verbally involved in the early stages of the group: setting the emotional tone, shaping the norms as a human relations expert, and modeling as a group participant. Corey (1981) proposed a number of personality characteristics that must be conveyed (or modeled) in order to facilitate an effective group:

1. Psychologically Present: paying total attention to the issues of the group and being sensitive to the verbal and nonverbal messages (body posture, gestures, voice quality, etc.) as well as being able to identify underlying messages.
2. Genuine: being congruent, not resorting to various roles to maintain artificial distance, and being willing to participate, self-evaluate, and self-disclose along with the other group members.
3. Empathetic: being able to understand deeply and subjectively the internal world of another's struggles and feelings; reliving and experiencing another's world as if it were one's own.
4. Unconditional Positive Regard: communicating a caring that is unconditional, nonjudgmental, and not contaminated by evaluation. It is a message of "I accept you *as you are*," rather than "I accept you *when. . . .*" (not to be confused with approval). It involves accepting the group members for who they are without necessarily approving of some aspects of their behavior.
5. Belief in the Group Process: believing in the effectiveness of group techniques as a treatment approach. (After all, how can group members have faith in a process that the group leader does not believe in?)

In summarizing the tasks of the orientation stage, we can identify the following elements:

1. Developing trust and identity for each member within the group.
2. Establishing ground rules and norms.

3. Modeling the facilitative dimensions of a therapeutic group.

4. Assisting members to develop general group goals and more specific and meaningful individual goals.

5. Displaying the essential therapeutic characteristics of being psychologically present, genuine, empathetic, and unconditionally accepting.

6. Educating members regarding their responsibility for the direction, outcomes, and personal change within the group.

7. Working toward decreasing leader dependency on the part of the members.

TRANSITION STAGE

The transition stage is typically characterized by an *increase* in member anxiety and defensiveness; this will normally give way to a deeper and more genuine openness to and trust in the group members. This openness and trust will develop if the leader understands and facilitates this process effectively. Anxiety often results from a number of fears and/or expectations the members experience: fear of being judged, misunderstood or unaccepted; and the felt need for more specific group goals, norms, and behavioral guidelines within the group.

Group members will test the group leader, the other members, and even themselves before they move on to the working stage of the group. The predictable defensiveness and resistance is quite normal and needs to be addressed and worked through. Most members are pulled by the need to remain safe and distant and by the desire to go beyond safety to risk becoming deeply involved in the group. As the participants come to trust the other members, both they and the leader become increasingly able to self-disclose and to allow the other members to see them as they really are. Here the facilitator's central task is to recognize that member anxiety, defensiveness, and resistance are normal; members must be encouraged to share these and other feelings that might keep them from full participation in the group.

Many researchers also discuss the roles that conflict plays during the transition stage (Yalom, 1975; Hansen, Warren, & Smith, 1980; and Schultz 1973). Negative comments occur more frequently, as well as criticism and judgmental opinions, which are a further sign of defensiveness, self-protection, and an unwillingness to trust the group. Yalom (1975) identified this process in the transition stage as a struggle for power and control. He stated that this struggle is an expected and integral part of each group: "It is always present, sometimes quiescent, sometimes smoldering, sometimes in full conflagration" (Yalom, 1975, p. 306). Characteristic group behaviors include competition, rivalry, a struggle for leadership, challenging group decisions, and behavioral resistance. In essence, this struggle for power and open conflict is an attempt to establish a social pecking order (Corey, 1981, p. 38).

Rogers (1970) proposed that members expressing negative and critical feelings are really testing the freedom and trustworthiness of the group. This discovering process is intended to ascertain if the group is a safe place to disagree, to express negative feelings, and to experience interpersonal conflict. If conflict is perceived to be unacceptable, the group will retreat to a safe and unproductive level of interaction, never moving to the working stage of the group process. If conflict is dealt with openly, honestly, and with concern for the individual, the members will discover that their relationships are healthy enough to tolerate honesty and individual differences.

Before conflict can be dealt with constructively, it must be recognized. Most leaders (and members), however, tend to ignore and bypass conflict with the understated assumption that conflict is indicative of negative personal characteristics or a negative peer relationship among the group participants. But when conflict is recognized and dealt with in such a way as to maintain the integrity of those concerned, the foundations of trust, honesty, and openness among the group members are established and deepened. In this manner, conflict actually facilitates trust and therefore reduces the probability that members will feel the need to escape from or avoid inevitable human conflict.

Conflict with and challenge of the group leader becomes an imperative issue in this stage. The group facilitator opens the door to both personal and professional challenges such as, "You're too distant," "you're too structured," or "you expect too much." It may be important at this time to distinguish between a challenge and an attack. While an *attack* may take the form of an angry hit-and-run judgment, *challenges* confront leaders with perceptions. The challenge will leave room for feedback, open dialogue, and exploration of the issue, the attack will not. It is also important to recognize a challenge as an initial step toward member autonomy. Most members struggle between leader dependence and independence. Fried (1972) noticed that groups initially focus on the leader and the leader's authority. If the group is led through this stage properly, the members become more autonomous, thus achieving a peer-leader unity. The manner in which a facilitator accepts and deals with challenges to personality and group skills will greatly determine the effectiveness of the group and its advancement into higher levels of development.

To summarize the key characteristics of this stage, I find the following distinguishing features:

1. Increased member anxiety, defensiveness, and resistance which gives way to deeper levels of self-disclosure and trust, if handled appropriately.

2. Heightened conflict and power struggles among the group members, serving as a testing ground for the establishment of freedom and trustworthiness within the group.

3. Conflicts and challenges directed toward the group leader that promote individual autonomy and peer-leader unity.

WORKING STAGE

The working stage is characterized by members realizing that they are responsible for self-disclosure, introspection, and behavioral change. Thus, the group members must decide for themselves the group issues. They must struggle to balance their efforts to become integral members of the group while retaining their personal individuality. Thus, members must filter the feedback received from the group as they attempt to integrate group responses and behavioral change into their individual, out-of-group lives.

The fulcrum of this stage is the members' sense of belonging, inclusion, and solidarity—in essence, the effects of *group cohesion*. It is in the working stage that group cohesion becomes a key element in the therapeutic process. If conflict, struggles for control, and leadership challenges have been successfully worked through, the group will pass through this testing period and will become a cohesive unit.

Although group cohesion is a prerequisite for self-disclosure and effective results, it is not in itself the magic element; it does become an indicator that most of the characteristics of healthy groups are evident to the participants. Cohesion fosters action-oriented behaviors such as self-disclosure, immediacy, mutuality, confrontation, risk-taking, and the translation of insight into action. While trust may be the forerunner to this stage, cohesion is a prime therapeutic factor and signifies movement to a deeper level of trust, i.e., from individual trust to trust in the group and its members.

Although group cohesiveness is necessary for effective group work, it can hinder the group's development if it is not accompanied by a challenge to move forward. The group members can stagnate in their newfound comfort and unity and choose to remain at a therapeutic plateau. This newly discovered cohesiveness should signal to the leader the beginning of a lengthy working process designed to accomplish the two main tasks of this stage: (a) development of personal insight and (b) transfer of insight into productive behavioral change. Therefore, we recognize this stage by its productivity.

Because the group members have at this stage developed feelings of trust, belonging, individuality, and autonomy, self-exploration can take place within the group setting. The remainder of this section will present an overview of the major therapeutic factors necessary to accomplish these tasks.

Empathy

As described earlier, empathy is a deep, subjective understanding of another's inner struggles and feelings. It is important to realize that the cohesion necessary in the working stage develops when the participants realize that they are not alone in their struggles and that others are empathetically "with them." As the group members empathize with the feelings of others (e.g., hurt, anger, sorrow, love, joy, etc.), they understand themselves even more.

Intimacy

According to Schultz (1973), after problems of control are resolved, the issue of intimacy begins to surface. Genuine intimacy develops in a group after the members have revealed a part of themselves with which others can identify. Intimacy grows within the group as the participants self-disclose, identify with one another, and recognize that they share certain needs, wants, anxieties, fears, and problems. Emotional guardedness and isolation quickly transform into identification and intimacy.

Commitment to Change

For change to occur, one must believe that change is possible; yet hope alone is seldom enough. Change requires that all members (a) identify areas of their lives they would like to reconstruct; (b) formulate a plan of action; (c) commit themselves to the plan; and (d) use the tools offered by the group process to explore methods of implementation.

Self-disclosure

During the working stage, most members risk disclosing personal and often threatening issues. They reveal concerns they would like to explore with the group, and share their ongoing reactions in a here-and-now perspective. It should be noted that self-disclosure is not an end in itself, but the means by which open communication, empathy, and intimacy can occur within the group.

Confrontation

Similar to self-disclosure, confrontation is a basic characteristic of the working stage. If it is absent, group stagnation will invariably occur. Meaningful confrontation occurs when a confronter shares his or her perception (not judgment) with a fellow member in a caring and sensitive manner. Confrontation, then, becomes an invitation to examine a discrepancy between words and behaviors, or between words and words. When confrontation takes place in a supportive therapeutic environment, it becomes a powerful act of caring.

Freedom to Experiment

Experimentation with new feelings and behaviors is a significant aspect of the working stage. The group is now a safe place in which to explore new approaches and restructured thoughts. Role playing is often an effective way to practice new skills in interpersonal situations while deciding how these skills and perspectives can be transferred to out-of-group situations.

Summary

During the working stage, the group will evidence the following characteristics:

1. The group leader will continue to be an active group participant while decreasing his or her leadership role.

2. The group members will assume a more participatory leadership role, taking greater responsibility for the direction and outcome of the group.

3. Group cohesion will take place and foster action-oriented behaviors such as self-disclosure, risk-taking, intimacy, and confrontation.

4. With cohesion serving as a springboard, the group members must then develop personal insight and transfer this insight into behavioral change.

5. The group will recognize the working stage by its movement towards

empathy, intimacy, commitments to change, self-disclosure, confrontation, and its experimental freedom.

CONSOLIDATION STAGE

From experience, I see the initial and final stages of a group to be the most decisive for the effectiveness of the group. While the orientation stage should permit every individual to establish his or her identity, goals, and trust within the group, the consolidation stage allows members to do the cognitive work needed to transfer the group experience, with its restructured behavioral changes, into the real world. This is the appropriate time to process unresolved issues and to apply the group experience to one's personal environment.

Shapiro (1978) has noted that this stage is often the phase of the group process most ineptly handled by group facilitators. Reasons for this finding include:

1. The leader's need for reassurance from the group members.

2. Resistance to termination by the group members.

3. Lack of training and inexperience of group leaders in handling this pivotal stage.

4. Isolation of group members in order to deal with separation anxiety.

Thus, it becomes crucial for the group leader to assist the participants in their efforts to develop a meaningful perspective of the group experience and its effects on the individual outside the group setting.

In order to accomplish this task, I find it a good practice to remind the members some weeks before the scheduled termination of a group that only a few sessions remain. This reminder facilitates termination: it also prepares the members to work actively on some of the unfinished issues they may have been dealing with throughout the group experience. Members will need assistance in facing the reality that the group will soon end. Feelings concerning separation and loss need to be explored and dealt with appropriately. During the initial stage of the group, members were asked to share their feelings regarding entering the group; they can now be encouraged to do the same concerning the termination of the group.

It is not uncommon to hear members share genuine bonds of intimacy, trust, safety, acceptance, and support. Also common are concerns of loss, a desire to "keep the group going," and fear that they cannot trust people outside the group. The leader should take this opportunity to acknowledge these special attributes of the group; noting, however, that they did not occur by chance. Each member made the choice to commit, trust, work together, and accomplish his or her goals. Therefore, they can now make similar choices, similar commitments, and set new goals in their relationships outside the group.

Toward the end of the group sessions, it is beneficial to give all the members of the group an opportunity to synthesize their group experience and to state in concrete and specific terms how they intend to apply this increased awareness and self-understanding to their outside world. This conceptualizing will increase the chances that their experiences will be retained and applied.

Finally, I allow time to deal with the various ways in which members might go further with the issues they have dealt with in the group. These may include participation in other groups, individual counseling, or other meaningful growth experiences. Because participation in a successful growth group often opens new doors of self-awareness that are not always worked through, additional therapeutic options for personal growth may need to be explored.

INTEGRATION

An understanding of the nature of group counseling commends it as a meaningful method of ministry to a wide variety of needs. The idea that personal and spiritual development occurs in communion and community (i.e., group) is not new. Indeed, the church's historic witness is that healing takes place within a reuniting, restoring fellowship of believers, energized by healing encounters with God and his people. Such interdependent (person-to-person) fellowships become the therapeutic settings, as we recognize that the mental and spiritual health of believers is largely determined by the experiences found in the church.

One of the cardinal concepts of the New Testament is that the church is the "beloved community." It is this *koinonia* that changes *a* church (organization) into part of *the* church (organism)—that redemptive, healing fellowship designed by God and established by Christ Jesus. Admittedly, this same church has not always functioned with the active love and acceptance Christ intended. In fact, some of the most painful, damaging experiences a believer can know occur not only in the "world" but also within this community of saints. I suppose if we, as his church, behaved toward one another as he desires (John 13:34), many of the technical aspects of this chapter would be of little use; however, until such time as the church instinctively heals instead of hurts, there will continue to be a need for structured, group-centered healing experiences.

Indeed, the church offers the context for the greatest healing and restoration. If there is any place in the world where broken, confused, and estranged people can find themselves, the church *must* be that place. Here, the love of God can be seen in fuller measure than any other setting. Here, the power of the Holy Spirit can be manifested via Spirit-filled people to confront sin (1 Cor. 5:2), to encourage those bruised and battered by life (Acts 12:5, 12), and to instruct in righteous (i.e., changed) behavior and thoughts. This Spirit-energized potential for changed lives may be greater than either the preaching pastor or the secular therapist have ever imagined.

One example of the mesh between the Scriptures and group counseling theory and technique will serve to illustrate further the dynamic integration which is possible. James wrote, "confess your sins to one another and pray for one another, so that you may be healed. The effective prayer of a righteous man can accomplish much" (5:16, NASB). Certainly, this admonition, and those surrounding it in James' letter, have a community focus. Certainly the confession of sin and faults to others (termed deep self-disclosure in group theory terms) opens the door to God's healing and change. In short, James 5:16 works! It makes sense both biblically and psychologically.

The only problem with James 5:16 concerns our inability to act it out! As indicated above, it is the rare individual who has self-disclosed to a friend or friends who has not had the disclosure betrayed at least once. We become cautious in self-defense, unwilling to risk unnecessarily. We become closed and alone, even within the church, because issues of confidentially, commitment to others, and trust are rarely addressed in truly practical ways in a Sunday morning service. These "group ground rules" are essential prerequisites to the self-disclosure admonished by James. When the ground rules are not understood and accepted by everyone concerned, most of us are not interested in risking—the very process that *can* bring us healing by the power of God.

Thus, an understanding of the group processes which lead to intimacy and loving confrontation and prayer can greatly aid those individuals committed to a people ministry. The small group may be the ideal place for the Holy Spirit to effect powerful and lasting changes in those who are fragmented in their relationship with self, neighbor, and God, so that—forgiven and whole—they can reenter these essential dimensions of community.

SELECT BIBLIOGRAPHY

Allport, G. W. (1954). The historic background of modern social psychology. In G. Lindsey (Ed.), *Handbook of social psychology*. Cambridge, MA: Addison-Wesley.

Aronson, E. (1980). *The social animal*. (3rd ed.). San Francisco: Freeman.

Bales, R. F. (1965). The equilibrium problem in small groups. In A. P. Hare, E. F. Borgatta, & R. F. Bales (Eds.), *Small groups: Studies in social interaction*. New York: Knopf.

Bandura, A. (1977). Self-efficacy: Toward a unifying theory of behavioral change. *Psychological Review, 84*, 191–215.

Bednar, R. L., & Kaul, T. (1979). Experimental group research: What ever happened? *Journal of Applied Behavioral Science, 15*, 311–319.

Belkin, G. S. (1984). *Introduction to counseling*. (2nd ed.). Dubuque, IA: Wm. C. Brown Publishers.

Berg, R., & Landreth, G. (1979). *Group counseling*. Muncie: Accelerated Development.

Bion, W. R. (1961). *Experiences in groups*. New York: Basic Books.

Bonner, H. (1959). *Group dynamics: Principles and applications*. New York: Ronald Publishers.

Cartwright, D., & Zander, A. (1968). *Group dynamics: Research and theory*. (3rd ed.) New York: Harper & Row.

Corey, G. F. (1981). *Theory and practice of group counseling*. Monterey, CA: Brooks/Cole Pub. Co.

_____. (1982). *Groups: Process and practice*. (2nd ed.). Monterey, CA: Brooks/Cole Pub. Co.

Egan, G. (1976). *Interpersonal living: A skills/contract approach to human relations training in groups*. Monterey, CA: Brooks/Cole Pub. Co.

Forsyth, D. R. (1983). *An introduction to group dynamics.* Monterey, CA: Brooks/Cole Pub. Co.

Fried, E. (1972). Individuation through group psychotherapy. In C. J. Sage and H. S. Kaplan (Eds.), *Progress in group and family therapy.* New York: Brunner/Mazel.

Gazda, G. M. (1978). *Group counseling: A developmental approach* (2nd ed.). Boston: Allyn & Bacon.

Hansen, J. C., Warner, R. W., & Smith, E. M. (1980). *Group counseling: Theory and process.* (2nd ed.). Chicago: Rand McNally.

Hare, A. P. (1976). *Handbook of small group research.* (2nd ed.). New York: Free Press.

Hill, W. F., and Gruner, L. (1973). A study of development in open and closed groups. *Small Group Behavior, 4,* 355–381.

Homans, G. C. (1950). *The human group.* New York: Harcourt, Brace & World.

Ivey, A. E., Ivey, M. B., & Simek-Downing L. (1987). *Counseling and psychotherapy.* (2nd ed.). Englewood Cliffs, NJ: Prentice-Hall.

Kaplan, R. E. (1979). The conspicuous absence of evidence that process consultation enhances task performance. *Journal of Applied Behavioral Science, 15,* 346–360.

Knowles, J. W. (1966). *Group counseling.* Englewood Cliffs, NJ: Prentice-Hall.

Levine, B. (1979). *Group psychotherapy: Practice and development.* Englewood Cliffs, NJ: Prentice-Hall.

Mahler, C. A. (1969). *Group counseling in the schools.* Boston: Houghton-Mifflin.

McGrath, J. E. (1978). Small group research. *American Behavioral Scientist, 21,* 651–674.

Naisbitt, J. (1982). *Megatrends. Ten new directions transforming our lives.* New York: Warner Books.

Ohlsen, M. M. (1970). *Group counseling.* New York: Holt, Rinehart, Winston.

Rogers, C. R. (1970) *Carl Rogers on encounter groups.* New York: Harper & Row.

Schultz, W. (1973). Encounter. In R. Corsini (Ed.), *Current psychotherapies.* Itasca, IL: Peacock.

Shambaugh, P. W. (1978). The development of the small group. *Human Relations, 31,* 283–295.

Shapiro, J. L. (1978). *Methods of group psychotherapy and encounter: A tradition of innovation.* Itasca, IL: Peacock.

Shaw, M. E. (1981). *Group dynamics: The psychology of small group behavior.* (3rd ed.) New York: McGraw-Hill.

Sherif, M., & Sherif C. (1956). *An outline of social psychology.* (rev. ed.). New York: Harper & Row.

Stock, D., & Thelen, H. A. (1958). *Emotional dynamics and group culture: Experimental studies of individual and group behavior.* New York: New York University Press.

Tuckman, B. W. (1965). Developmental sequences in small groups. *Psychological Bulletin, 63*, 384–399.

Whitaker, D. S., & Thelen, H. A. (1975). Emotional dynamics and group culture. In M. Rosenbaum and M. M. Berger (Eds.), *Group psychotherapy and group function*. New York: Basic Books.

Yalom, I. D. (1975). *The theory and practice of group psychotherapy*. (2nd ed.). New York: Basic Books.

11

COUNSELING WITH COLLEGE STUDENTS

John Goodwin

INTRODUCTION

Every semester, a new group of students enters college. If these students have (a) chosen the college wisely; (b) are college material; (c) don't become ill; (d) have a stable family background; (e) do not fall in love with the wrong person; (f) choose the right major; and (g) avoid drugs, alcohol, and other damaging pasttimes, then the work of the counselor in a college counseling center is simplified. If things begin to go wrong for the students, however, many will turn to counselors for guidance and assistance.

What type of problems do college students face? How serious are the struggles of a "typical" college student? The following six vignettes illustrate the variety of problems seen by college counselors.

Bob is a college freshman. His grades are poor, and his family does not accept failure. He does not feel in control of his present life or of his future. Lately, suicide has not seemed all that bad to him; at least then people would realize how much pressure he has been under.

Sue is a sophomore, unmarried, and pregnant. She knows the news will hit her family like a bomb. Surely a quiet abortion would be the best solution. No one would know, and it might save the relationship with her boyfriend.

Sandy *had* one of those quick abortions. Now when she sees a baby, she usually begins to cry. She wonders if she can ever be happy. She feels she doesn't deserve happiness.

Bill is homesick. Nothing exotic—just homesick. The only solution to this common problem *seems* to be just packing up, quitting school, and going home.

Tim is an "average" student with a reading problem: he reads too slowly. Consequently, he is behind in all of his classes and feels stupid. He is beginning to think that college is not for him.

Patty is a sophomore who still has not declared a major. Her grades are good, but she has now taken almost all of the required general education courses at her liberal arts college. Still, no one major appeals to her. She must make some sort of decision—and soon.

These six problems are fairly typical in a college setting. Some are very serious, life-threatening issues; others are not nearly so difficult. To the person who is struggling, however, any problem is serious business.

SOURCES OF STUDENT FRUSTRATION AND CONFLICT

Academic Advising

Often, the backdrop for one of these identified problems is some form of student frustration. In my experience, one major source of student frustration is poor academic advising by faculty members. Overworked professors, hurried and not-so-knowledgeable about graduation requirements, make disastrous mistakes. They may put together a schedule primarily based on the requirements of the professor's major field, or put several difficult courses on the schedule because "they meet requirements for graduation." For instance, some students can handle the science and math requirements if these courses are distributed over two or three semesters. Some overzealous advisors may push for 14 hours of these courses in one semester to "get it over with."

Other advisors might allow the student, semester after semester, to avoid all of the courses in the student's weak areas. Ultimately, however, the student may be faced with 16 hours of very difficult work in one semester. Still other advisors believe that "the student is an adult and should paddle his own canoe," and they resent the time spent in academic advising.

Loss of the Familiar

Most college students are away from home, many perhaps for the first time. Whether they realize it or not, they are making a definite step toward independence. Increasingly, home will seem like a place to visit instead of the place to return to permanently. Thus, the realization comes that a primary task is to establish a home for oneself. Whether acknowledged consciously or not, this realization often brings anxiety due to the loss of security that the family of origin represents.

Dormitory Living

Another problem area involves adjustment to new living arrangements. Many students simply are not ready for the give-and-take of dormitory living. Some feel forced into college by parental pressure; they may feel "showcased" by the college—as though they carry the family colors into battle and somehow must not fail. Others view college as a big party—a place to explore drugs, alcohol, sex, and other forms of self-indulgence. This approach is obviously full of pitfalls. It seems that the college system itself has situations built into it that produce student frustration and thus clientele for the counselor (Brunson & McKee, 1982).

Values Conflict: An Empirical Example

Another major source of student conflict and frustration is differences in interest, outlook, or philosophy with many others in the school. To illustrate, a study I conducted (Goodwin, 1972) examined the values of students at four different types of colleges. The variables investigated were college type, student values, gender, class standing in college, and satisfaction with the college.

The four colleges had different affiliations and statements of purpose; they were (a) a church-related college, (b) a state college, (c) an expensive private college, and (d) a college where students work out their tuition, room, and board via college-assigned jobs. Eighty students from each college, equally divided along class and gender lines, made up the total sample of 320.

The values-measuring instrument used was the Allport-Vernon-Lindzey Study of Values (Allport, Vernon & Lindzey, 1960). It measures theoretical, economic, religious, aesthetic, social, and political values. Personal data, the reasons students chose their respective college, and information pertaining to their levels of satisfaction/dissatisfaction were also gathered.

As expected, students at the four colleges differed in value patterns. The private school students were more political but less religious than the students from the other colleges. The church-related college students had higher religious values than any other students, and were lower on almost all the other values. The state-college students were more theoretically and aesthetically inclined than other groups, while the work-cooperative school students tended to be more influenced by economic matters.

It should come as no surprise that the church-related college students chose their school because of its religious emphasis. The state college and work-cooperative school students made their choice based on cost and location considerations. The private college students indicated they chose their college for its size and intellectual atmosphere.

Students who were dissatisfied with their college held significantly different values than their peers. In other words, they chose (for whatever reason) a school whose student population differed significantly from them in basic values. Also, the dissatisfied students were higher in political and aesthetic values and lower in religious values than were satisfied students.

This study indicates the need for counselors to be aware of the values held by most of the students in a given institution. An understanding of students' values would not only be useful in learning whether a student "fits in" with peers, but it might help the college in recruitment and in reflecting on and evaluating the image it seems to portray.

Summary

No matter how "home-like" the dorms are, how good the food is, how skilled the academic advisors are, or how well the counselors understand the students, problems will still arise. The potential for a college student to need therapy due to overwork, lack of sleep, laziness, romance, homesickness, poor grades, dorm or classroom conflict, and many other problems is very real. Students will still become depressed, will have their hearts broken, and will fail academically and socially. Thus, counseling is one student service that will be needed as long as there are colleges.

THE COLLEGE COUNSELING CENTER

Three Historical Influences

Today's college counseling center emerged from three basic sources. One was the vocational guidance movement, often said to have begun with the 1906 publication, *Choosing a Vocation*, by Frank Parsons. Parsons held that what young people needed in order to make intelligent choices for their vocational futures was knowledge about the characteristics of various occupations, as well as an idea about their own abilities. The vocational counselor's job was to make both types of information available and to help students use it effectively. Parsons' ideas were readily received; by 1915 there was a fully functioning National Vocational Guidance Association (NVGA) (Siegel, 1972).

The second source was the mental health movement. In 1908, Clifford Beers wrote a landmark book entitled, *A Mind That Found Itself*. "Mental health" came into vogue and various therapies emerged. Counseling became a profession and was generally linked with the concept of human development (Tyler, 1953).

The third source was the psychological testing movement that began in 1905 with Binet's individual intelligence test. Group testing grew out of the need to classify the great number of recruits flooding into U.S. Army camps in World War I. Testing grew rapidly, and names like Terman, Wechsler, Woodworth, Strong, Kuder, and Rorschach became well known among mental health professionals (Kendler, 1968).

Of these three early influences, perhaps the one having the most significance for college counseling was the founding of the NVGA. Many of the early "psychology clinics" at such colleges and universities as Pennsylvania, Michigan State, Minnesota, Harvard, and Cornell were active members of the NVGA by 1920 (Mortensen & Schmuller, 1959). The NVGA evolved into the American Personnel and Guidance Association (APGA) in 1951 (Norris, 1954). In 1984 the APGA became the American Association for Counseling and Development.

During this period, colleges became increasingly active in counseling. When America "discovered" psychoanalysis after Freud visited Clark University in 1909, colleges became even more of a focal point for counseling (Patterson, 1937). The early 1920s were prosperous years. Children were not needed at home to help with family finances and work. They were sent to high school and on to college in growing numbers. About this time the first group guidance courses were incorporated into college curricula (Feingold, 1947).

Through the end of World War II, much of the emphasis in college counseling centered on occupational choice, with mental health issues a distant second. Students who failed to adapt to the pressures of college life vanished from campus, so counselors dealt primarily with "healthy" students who were looking for their occupational niche (Miller, 1949).

Occupational choice is still a major student concern, as indicated by recent research (Pietrofesa, Hoffman, Splete & Pinto, 1978). Warman (1960) indicated that college students rated "occupational choice problems" as most appropriate for college counseling centers, while "adjustment to self and others" was rated as least appropriate. In my experience, many college counselors are so busy looking for "deeper problems" that they look past the basic issue many students worry about: "What am I going to be when I graduate—especially since it will not be so long before I do?"

Recently I had a conversation with the director of a counseling center at one of the largest universities in the South. He said: "Certainly job choice is a big reason students avail themselves of a counselor. However, the college counselor will encounter the whole gamut of problems during an academic year—from love to jobs to grades. In many ways, we are still '*in loco parentis*,' and often will need to operate in just that way." He was saying that we should at times resemble an intelligent and concerned parent.

As student clients come in to the counseling center, a useful procedure is for each counselor to keep a record of how many students he or she works with, the students' grade level, gender, and general type of problem. This will assist the center in making further adjustments to meet the campus need more effectively and in validating the ongoing work of the center to the college administration.

Reasons for Under-Utilization

If a student does have a problem and cannot handle it alone, the student may not come to the counseling center at all, for at least one of several reasons. First, in some situations, there is a stigma attached to a counseling center. Some people believe that if they go to a "shrink," they must be weird, crazy, or at least, very weak.

Second, the center is sometimes not adequately publicized—among either faculty or students. Faculty members need to know that there are qualified helpers available if they should have a personal problem or if they wish to refer a student or advisee. Dormitory and staff workers need the same information. Students need to be aware of the many kinds of help offered; academic advising, study skills, career counseling, dormitory conflicts, love problems, family troubles, and homesickness are all counseling center functions (Prola & Stern, 1984).

Third, some centers are too understaffed to handle the counseling caseload in a professional manner. Thus, some students fear that a counselor will only have time for a "once-over-lightly" counseling session. Counselors in this type of situation need to impress upon college administrators the crucial role a good counseling center can play in overall campus life and in individual student success (Lewicki & Thompson, 1982).

The Complexity of Program Development

Even those colleges with excellent counseling personnel who understand student needs can experience institutional roadblocks in developing innovative programs to assist students. I am familiar with one college that had an excellent study-skills program. Individualized "courses" were offered to increase reading proficiency, improve study skills and writing ability, and assist in career planning. After some time, it became evident to the counselors that most of the students enrolling in the courses were academically in the upper half of the student body. The more marginal students, those who needed the program most, were typically not involved.

An effort was made to provide more exposure for the program through articles in the school paper, reports at faculty meetings, and presentations at new student orientation sessions. To demonstrate the program's effectiveness to the administration, a pilot study was conducted which compared the grade point average (GPA) of probationary students who did and who did not receive exposure to the courses in study skills, writing, and reading. The "treated" group showed significantly higher GPA "survival rates" than "nontreated" groups. Armed with these data, the counseling staff sought to make the courses mandatory for all probationary students.

Although the idea was laudable, the college had just embarked on a crusade to cut rather than add programs in an effort to save money. Caught in this financial squeeze, the program as a requirement for probationary pupils never developed. At last notice it still operates on a voluntary basis, and as such is only partially successful.

Another college counseling center initiated a program of training psychology students as paraprofessional peer counselors. Training was given in basic counseling skills to a carefully screened group of good students. After a minimum of two semesters of training, the peer counselors began providing peer counseling services in the dormitories.

Two things resulted. First, the peer counselors reported good success, they made intelligent referrals as judged by the counseling center staff, and they received positive testimonials from those students who later came to the counseling center. Second, friction unfortunately developed between the counseling center staff and the dormitory staff. The dormitory staff felt their authority was being challenged by an independent organization. This friction was the result of the counseling center not laying the communication groundwork for the program by working with the director of student personnel and the dormitory staff *before* beginning training. Perhaps one solution would have been to put volunteer dormitory staff through the program first to see if the program would sell itself.

The basic conclusion we can draw from these examples is that no matter how worthy the idea or how skillful the training, no counseling program will work unless the "right" people are sold on the idea. Before any programs are initiated or publicized, however, a careful needs-assessment study of problem areas at the start is essential. Some problems will be very common on most college campuses, while others may be unique to only a few schools. Change for the sake of change may be self-defeating (Dagley & Gazda, 1984). All programs should be uniquely fitted to the college in order to maximize efficiency.

Research

In these times of shrinking college budgets, retrenchment, and program evaluation, counselors and counseling centers are being called into account as never before (Troy & Shueman, 1980). Increased use of counseling would benefit both the users and the counseling center: the users by improving the quality of their lives and the center by strengthening its position within the college (Altmaier & Rappaport, 1984). Nevertheless, recent studies indicate that students, even those with problems, often do not plan to use the counseling service (Carney & Barak, 1976; Friedlander, 1978). Tinsley and Harris (1982) reported that students believe that counselors are expert and trustworthy, but not necessarily *helpful*. Apparently counseling centers would do well to "sell" the worth of their services to the student population. Students who *do* visit counseling centers generally feel good about the service and are likely to use it again (Mathiason, 1984).

Since the gap between service awareness and utilization exist, several strategies of publicizing the center should be developed. At the School of the Ozarks, we print attractive brochures and distribute them to students, faculty advisors, and the college chaplain. We have sent news releases both to the campus newspaper and to the "underground" newspaper that appears from time to time. We have used the campus radio station (as have other colleges; Zwibelman & Rayfield, 1984), and have also released articles to the off-campus news media. Further, television has been used to good effect (see Shenk & Wiscons, 1984). Staff members schedule both off-campus and on-campus speaking engagements. We publicize the center at faculty meetings, during freshman orientation, parent orientation, and in selected classes such as introductory psychology classes. Freshman orientation programs are a useful tool for this advertising in other colleges also (Prola & Stern, 1984). Since freshman retention is an important area of counseling concern, several avenues of help have been under scrutiny. Dormitories have good potential for counseling impact—both in the training of resident assistants (Heppner & Reeder, 1984) and in direct service to students (Cooper & Sweeney, 1982).

Another area of help to students is academic assistance (Miller, 1984). This can come in an orientation course (Rogers, 1984), in career preparation courses (Gordon & Grites, 1984; Sherry & Staley, 1984), and in group counseling (Collins, Suddick, Brown, Brennan, & Grimsley, 1984).

Some successful programs have operated using peer counselors (Presser, Miller, & Rapin, 1984). At the School of the Ozarks we have used peer counselors during registration, in stress management work, and in study skills programs, all with good results.

I have mentioned ongoing programs in group and individual therapies in the areas of college adjustment, careers, majors, study skills, and retention. Needs also are evident in eating disorders (Kagan & Squires, 1984), stress management (Stevens & Pfost, 1984), athletic team efficiency (Gordon, Pfost, & Stevens, 1982), dating and marriage (Orzek, 1984), homosexuality (Jones, 1984), sexuality

(Kirkpatrick, 1980), minority concerns (Parker & McDavis, 1978), grief (Rosenthal & Terkelson, 1978), and alcohol and drug abuse (Ramsey, 1984; Seay & Beck, 1984).

Computer use by counseling services is continually expanding; recently an entire issue of the *Journal of Counseling and Development* (volume 63) was devoted to computer applications. Biofeedback is becoming another useful counseling center tool, especially as we realize the applications it can have in counseling, as well as in medicine (Crabbs, Crabbs, & Hopper, 1978).

As is evident, the problems on a college campus are about as varied as for any other group of people. Counseling centers not only try to reach students through their own staff, chaplains, and dormitory personnel, they may also work as consultants to help faculty to be more effective as advisors, lay counselors, and referral sources (Deming, 1984).

THEORIES OF COUNSELING

Even though the college counseling center sees a wide range of problems, the emphasis—at least in the centers where I have worked—is not on long-term counseling. Often situations can be handled in six appointments or less. Serious problems requiring long-term counseling should be referred to off-campus sources. Thus, the counselor must be as effective as possible in a short period of time.

The counseling approach currently emphasized in most student affairs settings contains contributions from many disciplines. The counselor's role is supported by a set of beliefs about people and life and assumes an active position relative to human growth and development (Mendenhall, Miller, & Wilson, 1983).

Regarding the general nature of psychotherapy, Matheson (1982, p. 306) stated:

> Psychotherapy is a general term referring to the use of psychological knowledge and techniques to treat behavior disorders. It covers a wide range of methods—analyzing a client's behavior, rewarding the client for appropriate behavior, hypnosis, and so on. A person need not be "mentally ill" to seek psychotherapy, but rather have only some behavioral difficulty requiring resolution.

As indicated in the quote above, "psychotherapy" is a very loosely defined term. "Therapy" is often defined as "any method for treating an illness." Adding psychological knowledge and techniques to that definition still leaves a very broad field. Since the range of psychotherapeutic methods is very wide, I will make no attempt to cover the entire spectrum. Instead, I will briefly summarize those methods having the most application to the college setting. More complete summaries of these and other methods are available in Gilbert and Brock, 1985.

Psychoanalysis

Though psychoanalysis has limited application to college counseling as practiced by most counseling centers, it has had an overall impact on the field that makes it impossible to ignore. After dealing with many people, Freud came to feel that most of our problems come from childhood, and stem basically from trauma, sexuality, or aggression. He held that humanity is basically evil, and without the laws of society and the church, humankind would soon destroy itself.

His concept of personality posited that there are two warring factions—the *id* (basic, animal-like desires), and the *superego* (moralistic, rules-making, conscience). Between these two stands the *ego*, which tries to satisfy the urges of the id without greatly violating the dictates of the superego (Daves, 1975).

This approach often required many, many sessions, but seemed especially effective for hysterical people. It continues to color many people's perceptions of psychotherapy. Many of the students who come to the counseling center at the School of the Ozarks expect to be "analyzed." Paradoxically, they often also expect to blurt out their problem and in 20 minutes have the counselor tell them what to do, as though dispensing a cold remedy!

Most theories will show flaws with the passage of time. This is certainly true with psychoanalysis (Durden-Smith, 1980). Indeed, Freud proves to be a faulty model for a Christian counselor.

> That Freud thought little of religion in general and less of Christianity in particular is an historical fact. He called himself a "completely godless Jew" and a "hopeless pagan." (Adams, 1970, pp. 15–16)

Still, psychoanalysis remains quite popular (Matheson, 1982), and many counselors with whom the Christian practitioner deals with will have this orientation.

Client-Centered Counseling

Another theory meriting attention is client-centered counseling, as developed by Carl Rogers, an American psychologist whose theories developed in the '40s, '50s and '60s.

Rogers believed (unlike Freud) that the individual is basically *good*. All the therapist must do is free clients from their hang-ups, and goodness will emerge. Thus, according to Rogers, we have within ourselves the power of self-healing. The therapist as an agent of change helps by guiding and clarifying (Hobbs, 1955).

Many counselors currently claim to be largely Rogerian. This model encourages the counselor to care for the client as an individual, but it poses the disadvantage of usually being a long-term treatment. However, in a more basic criticism, Adams (1970) argued that we really do not have within us the self-healing abilities that Rogers claimed. Further, Adams thinks the Christian counselor should not calmly accept hurtful attitudes on the client's part. If we could solve all of our own problems, we would have no need of God.

Rational-Emotive Therapy

One of the more directive of the current therapies, in contrast to client-centered therapy, is Rational-Emotive Therapy (RET), developed by Albert Ellis. He developed RET because he came to believe that his training as a psychoanalyst was not relevant in dealing with clients. His theory emphasizes disputing clients' irrational beliefs and substituting logical, rational beliefs instead (Ellis, 1973). It emphasizes putting newly acquired insights into action and experiencing the "here-and-now." It is a flexible model; it is easily adapted for group counseling (Ellis, 1979).

Ellis seemingly leaves no room for dependence on God (cf. Wessler, 1983); however, some of his ideas are very workable in the college counseling situation (Ellis, 1984), especially given that "rationality" is a lauded virtue on most college campuses.

Behavioral Counseling

One of the most rapidly developing methods is behavioral counseling. Simply stated, behavioral counseling conditions bad behaviors "out" and good behaviors "in." The therapist may at times use the same basic techniques used to train a puppy to "fetch." Based on Pavlov's concept of classical conditioning and Skinner's idea of operant conditioning, behavioral counseling has broad appeal to experimental psychology students and counselors alike.

The terms of behaviorism are becoming commonplace: *relaxation, desensitization, behavior modification, modeling, contracts,* and many more are becoming a standard part of counseling vocabularly. Success rates for some problems with behavioristic methods tend to be higher than with many other methods.

Behavioristic techniques have been applied and successfully used to (a) reduce test anxiety; (b) improve study behaviors; (c) develop assertive techniques, job-seeking interview skills, and decision-making skills; (d) control aggression; and (e) learn skills needed to relate to authority figures (Krumboltz & Thoreson, 1969).

Behavioral counseling deals only with observable behavior. There is no room in this model for a higher unseen power—God (Murphy & Kovach, 1972). Still, many of the principles of learning and counseling developed by behaviorists have proven very useful.

Transactional Analysis (TA)

One new counseling theory that is quite popular is Transactional Analysis (TA). Transactional Analysis is based on the work of Eric Berne, an American psychiatrist. According to Berne (1961), personality is made of three ego states: the *Parent*, the *Child*, and the *Adult*. Any of these ego states can be in charge of the personality at any time. Ideally, the Adult maintains ultimate control.

Practitioners of TA learn to recognize when they are interacting from Child, Parent, or Adult, and to recognize these ego states in others. This enhances good communication: the Parent in someone should not try to deal with the Adult in someone else (generally, this produces a "crossed transaction"). Both parties can realize which ego state is motivating them, and converse with each other accordingly. Transactional analysis can be used in individual counseling, but its primary application now often is in group counseling situations. Basically, TA is a way to analyze one's own behavior in social surroundings, and to find more effective behaviors. It may be particularly well accepted by college students because of its emphasis on self-analysis. Its concepts are often presented in a teaching format in a group setting—both aspects are a part of the student's way of life in college.

Reality Therapy

The last of the therapies chosen for this thumbnail sketch is William Glasser's (Glasser & Zunin, 1973) Reality Therapy (RT). Glasser's therapeutic goal is individual responsibility. He felt that unhappiness is the result of being irresponsible. The basic need all of us have, in whatever culture we are raised, is identity. Concomitant with this are the needs to love and be loved and to feel worthwhile to oneself and to others.

The focus in RT is on behavior, rather than emotion, and on the here-and-now (and, to a degree, the future), rather than the past. The therapist and client plan together a way to alter the client's behavior in order to live more successfully. Once the client has made a commitment to follow a certain course, the therapist will accept no client excuses for failing to follow through. If needful, he will help the client in devising a new plan, and will not dwell on the reasons the old plan was insufficient (Bassin, Bratter & Rachin, 1976).

Personal View

My own orientation is somewhat eclectic. Eclecticism is an orientation that requires studying many theories and then applying the one called for by a particular client and situation. Probably, most counselors begin a counseling relationship with a certain technique and then are eclectic (flexible) enough to change approaches if their initial strategy is not working.

THE COLLEGE COUNSELOR

Characteristics

What sort of person *is* a counselor and how is counseling a student population different from other types of counseling? Most discussions of counseling characterize it as a helping, warm, caring relationship. It is reasonable to believe, then, that a counselor would reflect these characteristics. Terms such as facilitative, accepting, and permissive are also used to describe effective counselors. In addition to these caring-type characteristics, some counseling approaches hold that the therapist has an obligation to society as well as to the client; thus counseling should do more than merely make clients satisfied with where they are. Further, the Christian must add to this belief the clear conviction that the counselor is responsible to *God* for *what* he or she does with clients and *how* he or she does it.

The effective counselor must not be shocked or become outraged in reaction to what a client says. The counselor must calmly hear, in a warm and caring manner, many disturbing accounts. That does not mean, however, that the counselor must forever refrain from providing some sort of helpful intervention. Paul expressed this basic concept of intervention in Romans 15:14 (emphasis added): "And I myself also am persuaded of you, my brethren, that ye also are full of goodness, filled with all knowledge, *able also to admonish one another.*"

Counselors are also advised to avoid becoming emotionally involved with the client's problem. It is often stated: "don't adopt *their* problem." This is wise advice, though difficult to follow. This imagines that a person who is by nature and/or training warm and caring can become somewhat cool, rational, and detached. The counselor is told that if he or she becomes as emotionally upset as the client is, he or she will not be able to be of much help. This is certainly true.

Counselors are also told that they owe to their *own* families openness, love, and involvement with them—not constant brooding over others' difficult problems. This is also true. Yet, it is not always possible to leave problems at work. Sometimes the burdens follow one home. To be truly Christian is to be like Christ, who "bore our griefs and carried our sorrows" (Isa. 53:4). Again, he is "touched with the feeling of our infirmities" (Heb. 4:15). One of the more difficult aspects of counseling is achieving this caring but not distraught mode of existence.

Some aspects of counseling students are a bit different from other forms of counseling. College counselors have themselves spent many hours in college classrooms. They are well acquainted with college pressures; the counselor and the client have, at the least, this common ground. In addition, the client is generally very bright, inquisitive, open to new ideas—in short, a very exciting, challenging person to work with therapeutically.

THE CHRISTIAN COLLEGE COUNSELOR

The Christian counselor is in a unique situation. More than counselors in many other areas of therapy, the college counselor must operate within constraints: institutional regulations, and local, state, and federal laws or regulations. Further, many counselors belong to professional organizations such as the American Psychological Association, the American Association for Counseling and Development, and the American Association for Marital and Family Therapy. These organizations have ethical standards with which the counselor must comply in order to remain in good standing.

In private colleges, the counselor may be relatively free to share personal faith. This same freedom exists in many state-supported colleges and universities, but on a greatly restricted level. (Even greater restraints are placed on counselors who work in public elementary and secondary schools.) Therefore, Christian counselors may find some real hindrances to sharing their faith. However, they certainly do not need to run ads in the college paper proclaiming their faith in order to be effective, Holy Spirit-guided counselors. Actually, for a counseling center on a secular campus to be widely known as a "hotbed" of evangelism may be counterproductive. This might prevent many hurting students from coming. Depending on the nature of the college, many students may be avoiding church or may have given up on religion. They may come to the counselor just wanting to get their "head on straight," not to hear a sermon.

Many counseling theories teach that the counselor should not moralize, lecture, or show much disapproval of a client. The idea, of course, is to avoid inhibiting the client and damaging the trust relationship between the client and counselor.

Anyone who has counselled knows that a drinking problem cannot be changed by a rapid-fire lecture on temperance. However, the Spirit-guided counselor can know how and when to allow himself to be used as an effective instrument of intervention, confrontation, and healing. Too often, spiritual values have been ignored by counselors (Russo, 1984; Theodore, 1984).

ISSUES OF COUNSELING—THEOLOGICAL INTEGRATION

A beginning therapist came to me one day and with a sigh of despair lamented, "My clients seem so desperate, yet so confident that I have the solution for them— that I can make it all right. I try to look calm, but sometimes I am frantic inside, fearing that I have no solutions for them. Am I to be a failure?" At that time I was also a beginner. My reply went something along the line that we had experience, training, theory, and smart colleagues. Since the client was going to talk to Uncle Charlie or the drunk on the next barstool or *somebody*, we were at least more qualified (probably) than they. Besides, I reasoned, a counselor's job is not to make decisions for clients; rather, it is to help clients see all the options and then allow them to make their own decisions.

Now after almost two decades of counseling, I have gained experience, more training, more theories, and more smart colleagues; however, I sometimes feel the same way my friend did years ago—as though I am fighting an unseen foe with a butter knife! And I know that I am not alone with this feeling; I receive similar feedback from other therapists. Over the years, however, I have learned to apply to counseling a source of strength and wisdom that I did not always have. This source is the Holy Spirit in full operation in my life and work.

The Holy Spirit

For the next few paragraphs, let us consider the Spirit and his function in and through believers. Our Lord promised, "Ye shall receive power, after that the Holy Ghost is come upon you: and ye shall be witnesses unto me" (Acts 1:8). Paul admonished the Ephesians to "be filled with the Spirit" (Eph. 5:18). In Acts 5:32, Peter said that God gives the Holy Spirit to those who obey him. Timothy was told by Paul to "stir up" the gift of God that was in him (2 Tim. 1:6–8).

Not only does the Holy Spirit empower the believers, but he gives instruction: "the same anointing teacheth you of all things, and is truth" (1 John 2:27). In John's Gospel, Christ said:

> But the Comforter, which is the Holy Ghost, whom the Father will send in my name, he shall teach you all things, and bring all things to your remembrance, whatsoever I have said unto you. (14:26)

In Luke 12:11–12, Jesus also said:

> And when they bring you unto the synagogues, and unto magistrates, and powers, take ye no thought how or what thing you shall answer, or what ye shall say: for the Holy Ghost shall teach you in the same hour what ye ought to say.

Thus, we basically are given the gift of the Spirit in order to be more powerful in our witness. The Spirit is much more pervasive in our lives than this, however. He is active in sanctification (1 Cor. 6:11–12; 2 Thes. 2:13–14; 1 Pet. 1:2). He is helpful in our day-by-day Christian walk (Mark 13:11; Acts 15:28; 16:7; Rom. 8:14). Most importantly, however, his presence in our heart is "God's guarantee of the consummation of his redemption" (Palma, 1974, p. 65). In this regard, Romans 8:11 reads: "He that raised up Christ from the dead shall also quicken your mortal bodies by his Spirit that dwelleth in you." Further, Paul stated in Ephesians 1:13–14:

> In whom ye also trusted, after that ye heard the word of truth, the gospel of your salvation: in whom also after that ye believed, ye were sealed with the Holy Spirit of promise, which is the earnest of our inheritance until the redemption of the purchased possession, unto the praise of his glory.

One of the most quoted Scripture verses is John 8:32: "And ye shall know the truth, and the truth shall make you free." How accurate and reassuring that is! But how does one arrive at the truth? Perhaps the Scripture speaking most directly to this is John 16:13. "Howbeit, when he, the Spirit of truth, is come, he will guide you into all truth." These and many other passages in God's Word are given to show that the Holy Spirit is of vital importance to born-again believers. Not only does he give power, wisdom, guidance, and direction for a righteous life (Ezk. 36:25–27; Luke 24:49; John 16:19), he is also our guarantee of future resurrection (Rom. 8:11; Eph. 1:13–14).

We are not automatically perfect after we receive the Holy Spirit, but we must grow in grace (2 Pet. 2:18). This growth is progressive (Phil. 3:10–14) as we yield increasingly to his leadership (2 Cor. 7:1; Rom. 8:13). Often we hear those in the world speak of a "sixth sense" or "intuition" or "instinct" or "ESP." In contrast, we *have* a Guide, Teacher, Power Source, and Comforter.

The Vital Role of the Christian College Counselor

Since the Spirit-led life can add so much to the individual, how important it is for a counselor of college students! Not only is the therapist dealing with another person, but that person is at a time and place in life where he or she can be greatly influenced for good—or for evil.

Webster, Friedman, and Heist (1962), found that student attitudes and values changed due to college. The type of institution attended makes a difference in the types of changes that take place. The change depends in part on the type of student who attends a school (Goodwin, 1972). The type of change is also influenced by the intent of the institution (Astin, 1968). Sanford (1962) said:

> [These] students are in a situation where they are virtually forced to consider alternative values and modes of behavior; and their chances of evolving a system of values that is more complex than that with which they began college, and that is increasing their own, would appear to be very good. (pp. 268–269)

Yamamoto (1968) agreed with this view in his statement: "The real test of the college is the amount of change it is able to bring about in students, whatever their level of ability" (p. 303). That change certainly occurs in college students is also supported by Keniston (1968) and Feldman and Newcomb (1969). The college counselor is in a unique position to help the student, the college, and the kingdom of God by caring for and standing with struggling, changing, maturing students.

CASE STUDY: DENISE

Denise was a wild freshman. She was sexually active and also had a drinking problem; however, her roommate persuaded her to attend a church. Through this contact, Denise found Christ. Still, problems arose—her busy schedule of courses and a weekend job kept her church activities at a minimum. Old companions kept calling for her to return to her former lifestyle. It was at this point, as a sophomore, that Denise was assigned to a counselor as an academic advisee. (All faculty members at this college had students assigned.) The counselor developed a good relationship with Denise, and by the end of the semester she was coming by weekly "just to chat." Up to this point no mention had been made of religion by either party. As they planned registration for the spring semester, the therapist felt led to share his faith; Denise had asked how he could remain unruffled during the chaos of registration.

This opened the doors that spring semester for Denise as a young Christian to be nurtured in spiritual as well as academic ways. She began to grow—to establish spiritual and moral priorities—to become involved in prayer and Bible study. She began to be committed to a good church, and began a life of Christian service that still persists. As a young wife and teacher, she remembers the "shepherding" she received at the crucial turning points in her Christian life. The important ingredient, she says, was her counselor's "consistent walk—it wasn't just a sometime thing with him." The counselor, who views himself in a much more frail manner, is thankful that the Spirit helped him both to live consistently before the girl and to know when to share.

SUMMARY

Each college is a unique environment. Each has its own goals, atmosphere, and rules, and each attracts its own special population. Thus, counselors need to study the institution as well as the students who attend it. They need to be certain that the programs they initiate fit the students' needs and are "sold" to those in authority.

Many counseling theories are in use today. Some of these theories have been devised by those who ignore the existence of God, but portions of them may still be utilized successfully by the Spirit-filled counselor. One's own theory is a reflection of one's own abilities and interests, but whatever theory one possesses as a base can be employed for God's glory.

Counselors must remember to keep their priorities straight. No matter how good many things may be, they need to refrain from being overloaded. How encouraging it is to remember that in their work they have the complete Teacher and ultimate Counselor—the Holy Spirit—from whom to receive wisdom, guidance, encouragement, and power.

College life can have a lasting impact on the lives of students, not only in terms of developing skills and intellect, but also as an environment in which to develop and refine adult values and beliefs. Christian counselors must be fully aware that they are agents of change in an institution of change. Whether the institution is a state university or a small, private college, Spirit-filled and directed counselors can be effective as facilitators of personal *and* spiritual growth.

SELECT BIBLIOGRAPHY

Adams, J. (1974). *Competent to counsel.* Philadelphia: Presbyterian and Reformed Publishing Co.

Allport, G., Vernon, P. & Lindzey, G. (1960). *Study of values: Manual* (3rd ed.). Boston: Houghton Mifflin.

Altmaier, E., & Rappaport, R. (1984). An examination of student use of a counseling service. *Journal of College Student Personnel, 25,* 453–458.

Astin, A. (1968). *The college environment.* Washington, D.C.: American Council of Education.

Bassin, A., Bratter, T., & Rachin, R. (Eds). (1976). *The reality therapy reader.* New York: Harper & Row.

Beers, C. (1906). *A mind that found itself.* New York: Doubleday.

Berne, E. (1961). *Transactional analysis in psychotherapy.* New York: Grove Press.

_____. (1964). *Games people play,* New York: Grove Press.

Brunson, B., & McKee, K. (1982). Crisis intervention and stress management. *Journal of College Student Personnel, 25,* 547–548.

Carney, C., & Barak, A. (1976). A Survey of Student Needs and Student Personnel Services. *Journal of Counseling Psychology, 26,* 242–249.

Collins, B., Suddick, D., Brown, S., Brennan, M., & Grimsley, H. (1984). The effects of a voluntary counseling program for students experiencing academic difficulty. *Journal of College Student Personnel, 25,* 360–361.

Cooper, M., & Sweeney, D. (1982). Residence hall personalization at the two-year college. *Journal of College Student Personnel, 23,* 543–544.

Crabbs, M., Crabbs, G. S. & Hopper (1978). Biofeedback in counselor education. *Counselor Education and Supervision, 18,* 130–137.

Dagley, J., & Gazda, G. (1984). Introduction. *Journal of Counseling and Development, 4,* 221–225.

Daves, W. (1975). *A textbook of general psychology.* New York: Crowell.

Deming, A. (1984). Personal effectiveness groups: A new approach to faculty development. *Journal of College Student Personnel, 25,* 54–60.

Durden-Smith, J. (1980). The second death of Sigmund Freud. In C. Berg (Ed.), *Annual editions, Psychology, 80/81,* 256–259. Guilford, CT: Dushkin Publishing Group.

Ellis, A. (1973). *Humanistic psychotherapy,* New York: McGraw Hill.

_____. (1979). Rational-emotive therapy. In R. Corsini (Ed.), *Current psychotherapies* (2nd. ed.). Itasca, IL: Peacock.

_____. (1984). Rational-emotive therapy and pastoral counseling. *Personnel and Guidance Journal, 62*, 266–267.

Feingold, G. (1947). *A new approach to guidance.* Chicago: University of Chicago Press.

Feldman, K., & Newcomb, T. (1969). *The impact of college on students.* San Francisco: Jossey-Bass.

Friedlander, J. (1978). Student ratings of co-curricular services. *Journal of College Student Personnel, 19*, 195–200.

Gilbert, M. G. & Brock, R. T. (1985). *Holy Spirit and counseling: Theology and Theory.* Peabody, MA: Hendrickson.

Glasser, W., & Zunin, L. (1973). Reality therapy. In R. Corsini (Ed.), *Current psychotherapies.* Itasca, IL: Peacock Publishers.

Goodwin, J. (1972). *Value patterns of students of four Missouri colleges.* Unpublished doctoral dissertation. The University of Missouri, Columbia

Gordon, V., & Grites, T. (1984). The freshman seminar course: helping students succeed. *Journal of College Student Personnel, 25*, 315–320.

Gordon, C., Pfost, K., & Stevens, M. (1982). Maximizing athletic performance: A consultative approach. *Journal of College Student Personnel 23*, 553–554.

Heppner, P., & Reeder, B. (1984). Training in problem solving for residence hall staff. *Journal of College Student Personnel, 25*, 357–362.

Hobbs, N. (1955). Client-centered psychotherapy. In J. McCary (Ed.), *Six approaches to psychotherapy.* New York: Dryden Press.

Jones, G. (1984). Counseling gay adolescents. *Counselor Education and Supervision, 18*, 144–152.

Kagan, D., & Squires, R. (1984). Compulsive eating, dieting, stress and hostility among college students. *Journal of College Student Personnel, 25*, 213 219.

Kendler, H. (1968). *Basic psychology.* New York: Appleton-Century-Crofts.

Keniston, K. (1968). Social change and youth in America. In K. Yamamoto (Ed.), *The college student and his culture.* New York: Houghton Mifflin

Kirkpatrick, J. (1980). Human sexuality: A survey of what counselors need to know. *Counselor Education and Supervision, 19*, 276–282.

Krumboltz, J., & Thoreson, C. (1969). *Behavioral counseling.* New York: Holt, Rinehart and Winston.

Lewicki, G., & Thompson, D. (1982). Awareness, utilization, and satisfaction with student services. *Journal of College Student Personnel, 23*, 477–481.

Matheson, D. (1982). *Introductory psychology: The modern view.* Arlington Heights, IL: Harlan Davidson.

Mathiason, R. (1984). Attitudes and needs of the college student client. *Journal of College Student Personnel, 25*, 274–275.

Mendenhall, W., Miller, T., & Wilson, R. (1983). *Administration and leadership in student affairs.* Muncie, IN: Accelerated Development.

Miller, L. (1949). Trends in guidance service for modern youth. In N. Farwell & H. Peters, *Guidance readings for counselors.* Chicago: Rand McNally.

Miller, E. (1984). The retention connection: The learning center and the community college. *Journal of College Student Personnel, 25*, n.p.

Mortensen, D., & Schmuller, A. (1959). *Guidance in today's schools*. New York: John Wiley.

Murphy, G., & Kovach, J. (1972). *Historical introduction to modern psychology*. New York: Harcourt-Brace-Jovanovich.

Norris, W. (1954). Highlights in the history of the National Vocational Guidance Association. *Personnel and Guidance Journal, 33(4)*, 205-208.

Orzek, A. (1984). Workshop on intimacy and trust in a loving relationship. *Journal of College Student Personnel, 25*, 83–84.

Palma, A. (1974). *The Spirit: God in action*. Springfield, MO: Gospel Publishing House.

Parker, W. & McDavis, R. (1978). An awareness experience: Toward counseling minorities. *Counselor Education and Supervision, 18*, 312–318.

Parsons, F. (1906). *Choosing a vocation*. Boston: Houghton Mifflin.

Patterson, D. (1937). *The genesis of modern guidance*. Paper presented at the University of Southern California. Los Angeles.

Pietrofesa, J., Hoffman, A., Splete, H., & Pinto, D. (1978). *Counseling: Theory research and practice*. Chicago: Rand McNally.

Presser, N., Miller, T., Rapin, L. (1984). Peer consultants: A new role for student professionals. *Journal of College Student Personnel, 25*, 321–325.

Prola, M., & Stern, D. (1984). The effect of a freshman orientation program on student leadership and academic persistence. *Journal of College Student Personnel, 25*, 472–473.

Ramsey, E. (1984). An intervention model for alcohol and drug problems on college campuses. *Journal of College Student Personnel, 25*, 346–348.

Rogers, C. (1984). Some new challenges. *American psychologist, 28*, 363–365.

Rosenthal, N., & Terkelson, C. (1978). Death education and counseling: A survey. *Counselor Education and Supervision, 18*, 109–114.

Russo, T. (1984). A model for addressing spiritual values in counseling. *Counseling and Values, 29*, 42–48.

Sanford, N. (Ed.) (1962). *The American college*. New York: John Wiley.

Seay, T. & Beck, T. (1984). Alcoholism among college students. *Journal of College Student Personnel, 25*, 90–92.

Shenk, P., & Wiscons, (1984). Career exploration groups: An outcome survey. *Journal of College Student Personnel, 25*, 368–370.

Sherry, P. and Staley K. (1984). Career exploration groups: An outcome study. *Journal of College Student Personnel 25*, 155-159.

Siegel, A. (1972). Fifty years of the P & G. In *Personnel and Guidance Journal, 50(6)*, 513–521.

Stevens, M., & Pfost, K. (1984). Stress management interventions. *Journal of College Student Personnel, 25*, 269–270.

Theodore, R. (1984). Utilization of spiritual values in counseling. *Counseling and Values, 28*, 162–168.

Tinsley, H., & Harris, D. (1982). Client expectations for counseling. *Journal of Counseling Psychology, 23*, 173–177.

Troy, W., & Shueman, S. (1980). *Individual accountability for providers of counseling psychological services*. Paper presented at American Psychological Association, Montreal.

Tyler, L. (1953). *The work of the counselor*. New York: Appleton-Century-Crofts.

Warman, R. (1960). Differential perceptions of the counseling role. *Journal of Counseling Psychology, 7*, 269–274.

Webster, H., Friedman, M., & Heist, P. (1962). Introduction. In N. Sanford (Ed.), *The American college*. New York: John Wiley.

Wessler, R. (1983). A bridge too far: Incompatibilities of rational-emotive therapy and pastoral counseling. *Personnel and Guidance Journal, 62*, 264–265.

Yamamoto, K. (Ed.), (1968) *The college student and his culture*. New York: Houghton Mifflin.

Zwibelman, B., Rayfield, G. (1984). An innovation in counseling outreach: Using the campus radio station. *Journal of College Student Personnel, 25*, 353–354.

12

CROSS-CULTURAL COUNSELING

David K. Irwin†

INTRODUCTION

The explosion of knowledge and technology in the twentieth century has brought the peoples of the world into such close proximity that we can no longer be content to study human behavior in isolation: we must be students of humankind universal. This highlights the necessity for dealing with individuals cross-culturally, as nations and cultures impact each other. The amount of data about human diversity is voluminous, but it seems to be more a collection of "findings" or observations than of solutions to problems of understanding each other. This sense of tentativeness is welcomed by those of us who are interested in the emerging field of cross-cultural counseling, especially as Christian mental health professionals.

It is too early in the development of this new discipline to be simplistic, dogmatic, or to limit ourselves to confining categories. Primarily, we must get to the issue of methodology, the interface of science and theology, and the relationship between Christian belief and human science. Beyond the methodological considerations a nagging question persists: How, and at what points, are anthropology-psychology and theology-missiology related?

Relationships and Methodology

The essence of research methodology lies in seeking answers to the following basic question: How can we find truly useful information about a particular domain of behavior? Most primary data in the social sciences come from three sources: (a) directly observed human behavior; (b) listening to and noting the contents of human speech; and (c) examining the products of human behavior (Pelto & Pelto, 1978). It is one of the goals of all scientific disciplines to link together low-order generalizations (propositions) into higher-order networks of propositions that will make possible the prediction and explanation of phenomena within the given domain (Meyers, 1978).

Methodology, then, refers to the structure of procedures and transformational rules whereby the researcher shifts information up and down a "ladder of abstraction'' in order to organize knowledge. What is important is to understand the difficulty of comparing and integrating two bodies of data at two different levels of abstraction (Felicou, 1983).

Cross-cultural testing of hypotheses requires standardization of research in such a manner that operationally equivalent observations can be selected and compared. The central methodological debates since 1970 have concentrated on the conflict between quantitative methods and more personalized humanistic qualitative scholarship. I would argue for a judicious mixing of both quantitative and qualitative research. The problem is not which mode of data-gathering to use; it is, instead, how to integrate both modes to build credible and effective cross-cultural counseling procedures.

Overreliance on personalized quantitative research can lead the missionary-counselor, a stranger to a host culture, to impose his or her culture's definitions on behaviors and events that may have quite a different significance from the insider's point of view. On the other hand, a people's point of view may be of limited usefulness (or even limited accuracy); an insider can be just as biased or unaware as an outsider concerning aspects of local behavior and culture (Pelto & Pelto, 1978).

If we are to understand why scientific and theological explanations need not be considered mutually exclusive, we must recognize that there are a variety of ways by which one might explain a given event, all of which can be simultaneously true in their own terms. A discipline incorporates knowledge from other, more elemental disciplines as phenomena are considered which transcend the more elemental understandings (Polanyi, 1961). Regarding the place of theology Polanyi stated:

> A universe constructed as an ascending hierarchy of meaning . . . is very different from the picture of a chance collection of atoms . . . . The vision of such a hierarchy inevitably sweeps on to envisage the meaning of the universe as a whole. Thus natural knowing expands continuously into knowledge of the supernatural. (p. 246)

A Starting Point for Synthesis

We can begin our integration effort by classifying Christian counselors as professional, pastoral-missionary, and peer. Cross-cultural counselors must not only master the science of psychology and the art of counseling, but they must also master the science and art of cultural adaptation. This is more than an ideal—it is an imperative. Too often pastors, missionaries, and peers are laypersons without professional training. The question persists: Are they, in fact, qualified to counsel? Obviously, they do provide counseling in a variety of settings, but they need both an educational background in two disciplines (counseling and anthropology) and the empowering of the Holy Spirit to function effectively as counselors in any location and any culture.

The fact that the Great Commission is a task that is incumbent upon all Christians is a presupposition for cross-cultural counseling. But ''task'' might be viewed as a rather exclusive term for a specific ministry such as cross-cultural counseling.

Gary Collins's (1980) designation of "people helping" is a corrective term for such broad categories. His emphasis recognized that the commission to evangelize and make disciples applied to all in the early church and equally applies to the modern counselor. However, one must not confuse "mandates" with "methods."

Often the Apostle Paul's pre-Christian training has been cited as a model of "directive counseling." It should be noted that Paul's counseling was to believers (often his own spiritual children) and tended to be autocratic and authoritarian. This perhaps was needed for those fledgling churches. His methods, however, do not serve as a cross-cultural model for our complex world today. Antithetical and often times clashing world views and culturally relativistic notions demand an eclectic approach.

I would posit that God's revelation in the Bible is complementary to his revelation in nature, and that psychology is complementary to theology and related areas of investigation. False integration, set forth as Platonic thinking, causes scientific psychology to lead to "nothingbutism" and "ratomorphism" (i.e., animal research with no apparent application of findings). Humanistic psychology leads to the illusion of mysticism and communication with nobody there. Both of these systems of thought lead ultimately to hopelessness.

During these pioneer years for cross-cultural counseling we must strive for a valid integrated model that unites psychology and theology into the wholeness of Truth. This synthesis must culminate in Christ—"the Word made flesh" (John 1:14). John Stott (1978) referred to God's special revelation in Scripture as *verbalized* and his general revelation in nature as *visualized*, and noted that both are combined in Christ.

Integration, then, as viewed by a Christian, affects three areas: (a) the relationship of Christian and secular concepts; (b) the way a Christian functions spiritually and psychologically; and (c) the way of thinking (i.e., thinking synthetically). In our study we should be focusing on the relationship between Christian and secular concepts so that a tentative transcultural model can be developed. What Niebuhr (1951) called the "Christ-transforms-culture pattern" has been explicated by Carter and Mohline (1976) as the "Scripture-integrates-psychology" model.

SOURCES OF THE DISCIPLINE OF CROSS-CULTURAL COUNSELING
Importance of the Individual in Culture

Anthropologists Barnet (1953) and Wallace (1956) shifted their emphasis from culture to the individual. Their insights concerning innovation and revitalization within cultures might heuristically serve as open-ended models for cross-cultural counseling. Counseling unbelievers must certainly have as a goal the conversion of the individual. In this regard, changes in a person's life which bring increased mental health, better interpersonal relationships, and self-actualization may occur both inside and outside the context of theology. Psychological healing, such as the removal of a phobia, is not the same as the restoration of the person's relationship with God via conversion (Johnson & Malony, 1982).

An often quoted truism about the nature of human beings is: every person is in certain respects (a) like every other person, (b) like some other persons, and (c) like no other person (Kluckhohn & Murray, 1953). Much of professional education in all the helping professions is necessarily devoted to teaching the scientific evidence and practical wisdom in reference to the first two propositions of this generalization, while affirming the importance implied in the third proposition.

Such complex and subtle knowledge offers the possibility of more flexible, adaptive, and responsive helping behavior. Ultimately, the counselor must test his or her knowledge through interaction with counselees. Therefore, they become teachers; they provide the counselor new information, correct misperceptions, and help refine counseling skills. The counselor must not only remain open to such teaching, he or she must encourage it; such dialogue is an essential component of helping people who are cultural strangers in a complex, changing society (Rubenstein & Bloch, 1982).

Functions within Culture

It is a basic assumption in ethnographic studies that all aspects of culture are interrelated in meaningful ways. In other words, no people's way of life is ever a haphazard jumble of unrelated parts. Furthermore, most parts must be so structured and function in such a way as to contribute to the continued survival of the sociocultural system as a totality. This, however, can be problematic. The proposition that every social usage has a function can then easily become the proposition that whatever *is* (i.e., exists) is *good*. Taken to the extreme, this would amount to a complete relativization of value. With regard to the theory of functionalism, it would be more appropriate to see it simply as a methodological precept that orients us to be aware of and look for the interrelatedness of cultural phenomena and the unintended consequences of cultural acts (Mair, 1964) It is helpful to note Merton's (1957) distinction between "manifest functions," as the conscious aims of people participating in some prescribed action, and "latent functions," which are apparent only to the observer.

Most functional studies of religious behavior have as an analytic goal the elucidation of events, processes, or relationships occurring within a social unit. The social unit might be a group of people who entertain similar beliefs about the universe, a congregation, or a group of people who participate together in the performance of religious rituals. Homans (1941) probably represents fairly the dominant line of anthropological thought concerning the functions of religious ritual:

> Ritual actions do not produce a practical result of the external world—that is one of the reasons we call them ritual. But to make this statement is not to say that ritual has no function. Its function is not related to the world external to the society but to the internal constitution of the society. It gives the members of the society confidence, it dispels their anxieties, it disciplines their social organization. (p. 172)

Religious Rituals and Movements

A major function of every system of beliefs and observances, therefore, is to offer its adherents a sense that they comprehend the forces that affect their lives and that by properly applying this understanding they can control in some measure the effect of such forces. Whenever natural phenomena and cause-and-effect relationships are explained in magical and religious terms, people logically seek magico- religious means of controlling them (Rappaport, 1967).

Religious ritual may be defined as the prescribed performance of conventionalized acts manifestly directed toward the involvement of nonempirical or supernatural agencies in the affairs of the actors. Religious rituals and the supernatural orders toward which they are directed cannot be assured *a priori* to be mere epiphenomena. "Ritual may, and doubtless frequently does, do nothing more than validate and intensify the relationships which integrate the social unit, or symbolize the relationships which bind the social unit to its environment" (Rappaport, 1967, p. 29).

Religious beliefs and rituals, in the widest sense of being "magico-religious," may be seen as having two sociological purposes: they are *instrumental* and they are *expressive*. "Instrumental" means that people use them to achieve particular ends; "expressive" implies that people use them to state and to symbolize certain social and cosmological relationships. Magical beliefs and practices are particularly significant in being mainly instrumental with little expressive content; by contrast, mythological and cosmological notions are almost entirely expressive and symbolic (Middleton, 1967).

Wallace's (1956) revitalization theory, alluded to above, assumed that all religious movements are variably confronted with corporeal and mental anguish for which immediate therapy is required, and it assumed disturbances in the orderliness of one's world view for which an ultimate redemption (via the religious movements) is necessary. Wallace argued that over time, movement would be dynamic in reference to these dimensions, and that the general movement or change in the course of modernization was from expressive to instrumental, nativistic to Christian, and therapeutic to redemptive.

H. W. Turner, the missionary scholar and historian of religion, classified African religious movements as neo-pagan, Hebraist, or Christian (Devereaux, 1956). Obviously the centrality of the pagan-Christian dimension is characteristic of most mission-oriented and theologically concerned counselors. However, while theological categories are characteristic features of Western religion, they are rarely so preoccupying in central Africa.

African religious movements have almost all developed in dialectical tension with missionary evangelization. Fruits of that tension are the valuable studies that have been done by mission-oriented scholars. The presence of mission, in one way or another, has alerted us to the sense of mission present in various analyses of these movements. One notes the natural tendency of missions-oriented scholars to pursue theological interests even though *theo*-logic is not a pronounced interest in African religious movements. *Socio*-logics, *psycho*-logics, and *ethno*-logics have also been imposed. What we instead point to here are approaches which are ontologic—they are grounded first in acts and images, and then embedded in the concepts of these movements (Horton, 1971; Mbiti, 1969).

While considering the regional perspective, it is relevant to note that some religious movements have difficulties in universalizing their communion beyond cultural frontiers. They tend to remain largely "ethnic communions." Generally, these can be summarized in the proposition that the more therapeutic, acculturated, and instrumental the movement, the more likely it is to recruit its membership from different ethnic groups (Fernandez, 1969, 1975).

Psychological Differentiation

Differentiation refers to the cognitive *structure*, rather than to the cognitive *content*, in an individual's psychological make-up. The psychological concept of differentiation is thus important in forming a cognitive "profile" of an ethnic population by students of both culture and missions. The opportunity to examine variations in cognitive function in a spectrum of naturally occurring variations may greatly enrich our understanding of the forces shaping cognitive development. Evidence now exists that individual differences in cognitive style are related to differences in family experiences while growing up. To the extent that cognitive styles are end-products of particular socialization process, they may be used in the comparative study of these processes (Witkins, 1967).

Perception may be conceived as "articulated," in contrast to "global," if the person is able to perceive items as discrete from an organized field when the field is analyzed (Segall, Campbell & Herskovits, 1966). By perception we can also *impose* structure on a field, giving it the appearance of being organized, when in fact the field has little inherent organization (structuring). Progress from global to articulated perception, which comes with growth, occurs not only in perception (where we are dealing with an immediately present stimulus configuration), but in thinking as well, where symbolic representations are involved. Articulated experience is a sign of developed differentiation in the cognitive sphere. The self is as much a source of experience as the world outside the self, yet it is adapted to the ecocultural setting in which it is located (Berry, 1976).

Karp (1977) hypothesized that on the one hand, more differentiated (i.e., field-independent) individuals, who experienced themselves and the world around them in a more articulated manner, were better able to analyze and organize aspects of their experience. They could be expected to function relatively effectively on their own with less need for information and guidance from others and to demonstrate detailed inner standards against which to evaluate suggestions from others. As a consequence, they would show less dependence upon external assessment for development and maintenance of their self-views. Less differentiated persons (i.e., field-dependent persons), on the other hand, who experienced themselves and the environment in a less articulated fashion and who had poorer abilities to analyze and structure their own experiences, might be expected to rely more heavily upon information, evaluation, and suggestions arising from sources other than themselves.

With regard to communication with others, field-dependent persons appear to be more willing to disclose information about themselves to others. They maintain less distance from the roles they are asked to play than field-independent persons. It is clear that field-independent individuals seem to think and behave in ways which suggest a commitment to maintain autonomy. They conform less to societal standards, view others in a more analytical (and thus distant) fashion, maintain more physical space between themselves and others, choose vocations oriented more toward objects or abstractions than people, and show more reserve in disclosing information about themselves. This distinction may functionally be seen as a potential way of penetrating the differences between some native peoples and expatriate missionaries.

In closing this section, I wish to assume here that my calling (as missionary-counselor and anthropologist) requires me to be called out of myself to live as close an approximation of the local culture and views as possible. It means being ever ready to abandon "centeredness" and look for what is revealed in "peripheries" (Hesselgrave, 1984, 1985). It is a calling which demands a tolerance of ambiguity amidst its strivings for a satisfactory method. For those who have lived in the complex interaction of religious cultures, there are, as Isichei (1970) has shown us, many varieties of ambiguity.

The Emic-Etic Distinction

The notion of cross-cultural counseling implies both cultural contact and cultural change. The question is: Change from whose perspective? Is it the perspective of the analyst or that of the host? Or, stated differently, is the focus on the view of the counselor or that of the counselee? Usually, unless we are informed to the contrary, it is taken for granted that the observer is being "objective." Yet, often there is a discrepancy between what the natives view as a "felt need" and the view of the analyst. And, it is entirely possible that the analyst may base his or her analysis entirely on the client/counselee's conceptions of what is and what is not problematic.

Harris (1968), borrowing from the psycholinguistics of Pike (1954), used the term "etic" (derived from phon*etic*) to refer to "culturally generalized." He used "emic" (from phon*emic*) to refer to "culturally specific." "Etic" approaches are thus dependent on the analyst's own observation of conditions, relationships, etc. Inherent in this construct is the tendency for verification to be sought from other analysts (theologians, missionaries, and/or counselors). Also, considerable disagreement may occur between the subjects/counselees as to whether a given practice is good or not!

Draguns (1976) seemed to miss the essence of the emic-etic distinction by trying to balance the culturally unique and the humanly universal in the counseling process. Emic-etic dyadic models are analytical, not ways of determining what is "unique" and what is "universal." Pedersen (1981) pointed this out in his essay on the "Cultural Inclusiveness of Counseling." It might be fruitful to think of emic-etic constructs as actually being a process of interaction and not as polar opposites or antithetical precepts. Could not there be a merging of insights from "insiders" from both host and expatriate cultures?

The Autoplastic-Alloplastic Dilemma

Draguns (1981) noted that "All of us respond to stimuli and situations by either changing ourselves (autoplastically) or the environment (alloplastically) and by combining these two operations in various proportions" (p. 22). Adapting the terms of the French social psychologist Vexliard (1968), Draguns (1976) said:

> autoplastic involves accommodating oneself to the givens of a social setting and structure [while] alloplastic . . . involves shaping the external reality to suit one's needs. Applied to the counseling situation, this dichotomy boils down to the question: How much should the counselee be helped to adapt to a given reality and how much should he be encouraged to shape and change that same reality? (p. 6)

Geertz (1965) maintained that culture is important in defining humanity. He stated that each culture is made up of a set of symbolic devices for control of behavior, for giving the individual a set of life goals, and for giving him or her a set of self-definitions. In short, he proposed, we need to look primarily for systematic relationships among diverse phenomena, not for substantive differences among similar ones. To do that effectively, we need to replace what he called the "stratigraphic concept of the relations between the various aspects of human existence with the synthetic one; that is, one in which biological, psychological, sociological, and cultural factors can be treated within unitary systems of analysis" (p. 106). To this I would add theological and missiological factors and suggest that this synthetic approach allows us the freedom necessary to create a uniquely Christian counseling model that combines both emic and etic approaches for the purposes of evangelism, edification, education (the training of trainees in small groups), and enculturation.

Word- vs. Spirit-Orientation

Stewart (1974) described basic Christian life styles as existing along a continuum between bipolar opposites of Word-orientation and Spirit-orientation. These bipolar opposites relate directly to ego-psychology's construct of cognitive and emotional styles (Higginbotham, 1979; Hsieh, 1981; Tanaka-Matsui, 1979). Christians who are primarily Word-oriented tend to be rational, articulate, and objective (i.e., cognitive). Those who are Spirit-oriented, on the other hand, tend to be experiential, emotional, personal, and interpersonally oriented (Ramm, 1974; Stewart, 1974).

Ramm (1974) provided additional distinction between the Spirit- and Word-orientations:

> Word suggests the truth claims of Christianity, the meaning of the texts of Scripture, and the formulation of the contents of Scripture into theology. It also includes the great historical (space-time) acts of revelation and redemption which are recorded in Scripture. The "Word" concept encapsulates the rational, articulated, objective aspects of the redeemed Christian life, whose lynch-pin is the unchanging standard of Scripture and

> its rationally-evolved theologies. On the other hand, "Spirit" speaks of the power of
> the Christian faith, of the richness of personal experience, of faith, of trust, of hope,
> of the ability to transform life, and the entering of the supernatural into our lives. (p. 12)

This quote clearly indicates the "Word" orientation generally held by the expatriate missionary/counselor. This, in turn, would most likely give a definite direction to his or her counseling methodology. This person would tend to emphasize a "Word"-oriented approach that reflects an Aristotelian, linear, sequential, logical/rational model, in contrast to the native's holistic, cosmic, intuitive/relational model.

Summary and Synthesis

There are some heuristically fruitful implications in these observations. First, there are two distinctively different orientations among Christians: Word vs. Spirit. Moreover, both Christians and non-Christians can be classified as field-independent or field-dependent. Second, there are predictable consequences for people whose cognitive style is not consistent with the dominant culture pattern, such as Spirit-oriented males or Word-oriented females. We are thus led to ponder the counseling outcome of a counselor-counselee orientation mismatch. For instance, what are the effects of such Word-oriented Christian counselors as Martyn Lloyd-Jones (1976) and Jay Adams (1970) or of Spirit-oriented Christian counselors as Hannah Hurnard (1975) and Ruth Carter Stapleton (1976) upon their counselees who have dissimilar orientations from their own?

In all probability, the superimposition of the Western cultural model would produce a counselee who is a cultural misfit, forced to live in a cultural no-man's land. Such a person would be rendered ineffective, at least in terms of potential cultural influence. What is needed is the development of a dialogical pedagogy which incorporates the *emic* view of the native with the *etic* (analytical) models of the expatriate counselor.

Farnsworth (1974) addressed this point quite effectively with his concept of "embodied integration." This integration is not a process of synthesis, whereby a combination of the two is "truer" than either one alone. It moves beyond substantial integration in that it is more than a verbal exposition—it is an actual *living out* of the integration. In effect, one lives two lives: one of academics and another of service (see also Carter & Mohline, 1976: Hseieh, 1981; McLemore, 1976). From a psychological, pedagogical perspective, these concepts would be starting points for developing meaningful and potentially long-range harmonious relationships between the native and the missionary-counselor, and between the national church and the mission.

Counseling may be described as a mixture of relationship and technique. "Relationship" is a helping, participatory construct while "technique" refers to a solving, acting-upon model. It is not clear to me, in an operational sense, how these constructs impact upon what is "constant" and what are "changes" in cross-cultural counseling. I *do* understand, however, that techniques do not remain immutable as they are applied across cultures. Hence, I take umbrage at the insistence of some psychologists that Freudian psychoanalysis (a Victorian, Western European typological system) could be employed universally. Malinowski (1960, 1961), Firth, (1961), and Hammond (1972), among others, found considerable non-Western anthropological data to prove otherwise. Bohannan (1963) discussed Freudian notions with the Tiv of Nigeria and found that, although they may have similar categories, they invest quite different meanings into them. Arguing from association is both bad science and illogical.

The weakness of superimposing a Western topology upon a non-Western pattern is the manipulation of the data by the analyst. This is the weakness of all systemics; something of value is invariably omitted. Obviously, a given system will only furnish data and conclusions which "fit" the schematic model. This is equally true both of scientific (psychological) and theological models. Thus, the challenge to the Western-trained observer is to be at home with and to live out the host culture so that its emic perceptions and cognitions direct the therapeutic system development.

CASE STUDY: MENTAL ILLNESS IN MALAWI

The Case

In September 1963, I received a frantic call from Wilfred Makhokho, the presbyter from Ncheu, Balaka District, Malawi. He implored me to come posthaste because Mrs. "T" was *zoipa zambiri* (very ill, implying activity of evil spirits). I rushed 65 miles through the mountains to help this wife of a local Assemblies of God pastor.

When I arrived, Mrs. "T" was incoherent, violently dangerous, and possibly, from my point of view, demonically oppressed. For the space of two days and nights she had shouted obscenities, scratched herself, and clawed any person who had gotten near her. She had retreated to a room and refused to come out, talk, or be consoled in any fashion. When I approached the window of the room, she went berserk, screaming and spitting on me. I was shocked (not angered) by her behavior because she had always seemed to be a typically passive, polite, and proper Achewa woman. My wife had often commented that Mrs. T was one of the brightest students at the Bible school in spite of the fact that she was illiterate.

I gathered the church people together, commented briefly concerning Christ's power to set us free from the power of Satan, and requested all to join us in prayer for her "deliverance." She did not calm down in the slightest degree. Rather, she began to scream (echolalia) back to us our very exact prayers in a cursing tone. She derisively shouted that we had no power and that we were helpless compared to the power of her village (i.e., resident magico-religious practices). Our prayer had no effect on Mrs. T.

Finally, we consulted among ourselves as to what might be the best procedure. There was no hospital nearby from which to obtain sedatives and, at that time, no mental hospital was available in the entire country! It was agreed that the best thing to do under the circumstances would be to take Mrs. T to her mother's village. She refused to move until a "sister" clansperson talked her into agreeing with our consensus plan. However, she refused to allow me to touch or talk to her and she refused to get into my car. After two hours of pleading by several church women, she was semi-restrained and put in the back seat of my car between two *Ankhoswe* (female elders). We drove to her mother's farm near Ntakataka.

Later I learned that the *singanga* (witch doctor) had "cured" her that night. But he would do nothing while I was there. I saw her several weeks later at a church conference and numerous times afterward. She apparently had been "cured" and seemingly had no lingering after-effects from the ordeal. I heard of no recurrence of this *zoipa* (evil) while I lived in this area.

The Conditions

To summarize briefly: the Achewa are a major tribe living along the border between Malawi (formerly Nyasaland) and Mozambique (formerly Moputo). They are primarily horticulturists with some cattle stock to supplement their subsistence farming. Characteristic features of their sociocultural and ideological stage of development are: (a) matrilineal/matrilocal inheritance and residence patterns; (b) polygynous and exogamous marital and sexual recruitment configuration; (c) preliteracy; and (d) mythico-animistic nature religion.

The Assemblies of God began frontier evangelism and church planting among the Achewa in the 1940s. The confrontational claims of the gospel of Christ had forced a radical reorientation on the part of those gentle peasants from a mythico-nature religious world view to a word-oriented, Aristotelian, linear sequential approach to reality. I was a missionary there from 1962 to 1967. It was a first-generation indigenous church that was being stressed by the acculturative process which daily challenged the traditional sociocultural religious system (not to be thought of as a theological system).

As animists, they held a holistic view of spiritual reality. Their ethnoscientific taxonomy placed all spirits on a hierarchial scale that included all dead ancestors and the yet unborn spirits which are "inside" every fecund female. Thus every effort was taken not to provoke the ancestors ("the living dead") lest calamity come upon the matriclan. This, in turn, provided a rationale which explained the causal relationships between good and evil within the clan entity. High spirits were the "ghosts" of great persons who were elevated to an intermediary position between the low spirits (the ancestors, the living, and the unborn) and the high god *Mulungu*, who is a projection of Achewa social stratification; that is, a godlike paramount chief who is over all the clans (peoples) of the world. We will be united in the spirit world ultimately, however, when present linguistic, cultural distinctions will have been transcended. Penultimately, we are created distinct from one another and, ideally, should not change and assume characteristics that agitate the "spirits" of our respective clans.

Below *Mulungu* is *Chiuta* (the bow, an implicit symbolism similar and analogous to the rainbow in the Old Testament which bespoke a native religion in archaic times). This god renews the earth each spring, causes babies to be born, and sustains life on the earth. He must ritualistically be placated to perpetuate good fortune and to deter misfortune. The Achewa hold a henotheistic hierarchial concept of cosmic spiritual reality.

It was quite difficult to explain the biblical teaching concerning the Holy Spirit as the Third Person of the Trinity to the Achewa. They apparently placed the Holy Spirit on a scale higher than the ancestral spirits. In other words, the Holy Spirit was honored but not recognized as God; he was understood rather as a very high (far away in a cosmic frame of reference) benevolent spirit/god. They would pray and make petitions to the Holy Spirit as a benefactor. Thus, they cognitively perceived a "blessing" as the result of appeasing one of the highest spirits.

In the subdiscipline known as the anthropology of religion, this practice would be referred to functionally as "magic," the manipulation of a god(s) for personal gain or merit. (It is probable that many contemporary Christians do something akin to this in seeking "formulas" or "techniques" with which to secure prosperity, material gain, etc., but who do not call it by its true name, "magic"). The penultimate function of "magic" for the Achewa is to guarantee the acquisition of protection by the clan spirits in this life. Consequently, the Achewa do not always distinguish between sources of healing, since they tend to attribute all good to favorable spirits. The ultimate function of "magic" is to guarantee one's place in the spirit world. This includes, here and now, clanspeople who will communicate with a person and eventually follow that person and thus perpetuate the clan which is preserved *kumwamba* (in heaven).

The Cure

In the case of Mrs. T, I failed as a cross-cultural counselor. This case occurred a few months after I had arrived in Nyasaland (now Malawi) and thus it was not possible for me to have known all the anthropological, sociocultural, linguistic, and ideological factors and traits required to "do" good diagnosis and counseling therapy. Also, at that time I was inadequately prepared to make distinctions between mental illness and demon oppression/depression.

It is my reflected opinion that most expatriates/missionaries are still unprepared to engage in meaningful cross-cultural counseling for several reasons:

1. Little or no emphasis has been placed on counseling as a ministry model.

2. Many evangelicals assume that a Christian's problems are spiritual, without refining aspects of *psyche, pneuma, soma*, etc.

3. Quite a few missionaries still are unconvinced of the demonic realm as a supracultural level of abstraction which might account for certain types of aberrant behavior.

4. Only a few missionaries who believe in the reality of demonic activity are experientially and theologically prepared to "test the spirits to see whether they are from God" (1 John 4:1, NIV). Mrs. T's behavior was directed generally

toward the mission (the agency of forced change) and specifically toward me (the immediate symbol of this change).

It should be obvious by now that I have designed this chapter to begin with the kinds of information one might need to know in order to develop a counseling theory that would include two world views, religious systems, psychologistic levels of explanation, and integrated concepts of causality. Mrs. T's behavior could be interpreted at both levels: demonic as well as psychological.

If all beliefs are included within culture, then no critical approach is possible; we are locked in our own respective groups and belief systems. Science, including anthropology, is not possible. There are no absolutes; the claims of Christianity are limited to the mind of its adherents. It can be demonstrated, however, that all beliefs are *not* cultural.

Concerning divine revelation, knowledge of this transcultural process may be gained by constructing a vertical continuum, placing God at the top and humanity at the bottom (in the sense of being a recipient). This continuum would include the following factors:

1. No one has seen God—he is approached only through the Spirit.

2. No one knows God by reasoning, yet knowledge of God is rational (Isa. 1:18–20; 1 Cor. 1:21–34).

3. Human beings must accept events in life by faith.

4. Humankind has received an invitation to have a relationship with God.

5. All people endure testings in everyday experiences of life.

6. While experience is personal, testimony is public and forms consensus.

7. Consensus is never the foundation of belief—it rests on an individual response to revelation.

8. Revelation is consciously and critically accepted.

9. Revelation requires dependence upon the word of God and acknowledgment of divine authority.

Science, on the other hand, is viewed as a continuum from humankind to things. Central to good science are the following considerations:

1. Approach is through the senses.

2. Observations are ordered by conceptualization and logic.

3. Science explains events in nature by intuition, models, and speculative thought.

4. Science demands the criterion of detachment from nature.

5. Science requires testing in experimental, controlled situations, and open publishing of discoveries.

6. Consensus is never the basis or proof of belief.

7. Science must be consciously accepted and critically held.

8. Science is dependent upon a published body of data, observations, and empirical tests.

9. Science carries logico-empirical authority.

At the interface of revelation and science is culture, the horizontal relationship between individual and individual, people and people. It is at this point that the dynamics of social interaction may be manifested in cognitive belief systems. Implicit in this construct are the following principles:

1. There is a pull of the human psyche to social interaction.
2. There are arbitrary conditions of group acceptance.
3. Tradition is self-proving (i.e., circular).
4. Group-enforced consensus affects everyone and is the basis of belief.
5. Beliefs are often unconsciously accepted and uncritically held.
6. People are dependent on the word of specialists in the culture.

What I have tried to do is set forth a matrix of factors that both impinge upon and interact with each other. This complex of data may be utilized as a backdrop upon which to state some critical observations that emerge in diagnosing and counseling in a case such as Mrs. T's.

First, the behavior of Mrs. T was not an uncommon manifestation in Achewa society. Periodically this particular type of hysteria (most common among females) was evidenced and reported by paramedics who worked in the medical clinics. Second, psychological anthropologists contend that mental illness is culturally conditioned; that is, behavior is learned and consequently cues the people that something is about to occur. It is important to both the distressed person and the community to understand that the signals or cues are actually calls for help. Third, the mental illness may be a way of coping with culturally determined stressors. In the case of Mrs. T, being separated from her matriclan due to her husband's pastoral assignment was probably the most prominent stressor. Cultural and social dislocation is often a precipitator of bizarre behavior among animistic people. Disorientation is sometimes manifested overtly by "disturbed" people.

Was Mrs. T demon oppressed/possessed? This question is both critical and difficult to answer. It is my belief that a Christian cannot be demon possessed. From all evidence I could observe, Mrs. T believed in Jesus Christ as Savior and Lord; however, it is most probable that her ideational beliefs included both biblical and animistic-mythical aspects. Whether a Christian can be oppressed by Satan is a moot point. Here I believe we must distinguish between (a) disease, illness, and calamity, which are common to *all* people and which may be explained causally by natural science, and (b) various forms of "mental illness," which may be explained by natural scientists, psycho-religious social scientists, and spiritual counselors. If Mrs. T was demon oppressed/possessed, by what power was she delivered or cured? Will Satan cast out Satan?

Asinganga (witch doctors) are still valued by the animistic Christian Achewas for their power over *Anganga* (witches). Witches place curses on people and this is the primary rationale for a causal explication of good and evil. This also poses some real problems. First, do witches have access to demonic power? Or, are they demonically controlled? If the former is true, do the witch doctors have power to exorcise demons? I find this to be seriously problematic. Second, if witches do not have demonic power, is their control over people merely based on fear, ignorance, superstition (native psychology)? If this is the case, is the problem really spiritual, or does it lie totally within the cultural-ideational system? In this latter event, what is the function of prayer by Christians? Were we praying spiritual prayers for a merely human phenomenon?

Were the Achewa Christians praying perfunctory prayers with little or no confidence that deliverance would come from a Spirit so far away? Stated in another way, did the Achewa Christians syncretize their Christian beliefs about God with the sociocultural religious systems that causally explain good and evil? I believe this to be the case. I failed to help Mrs. T because I was functioning in a traditional pastoral/missionary role that was not suited anthropologically, psychologically, or theologically to diagnose and prescribe a relevant cure. I somehow sensed this and realized the Achewa Christians did too. They respectfully cooperated in publicly praying for her, and then, without dissent, agreed that the best cure was to be found ''in her village.''

Was I wrong to have taken Mrs. T to her mother's village treatment? I did not know that a *singanga* (witch doctor) would be consulted. I have the lingering sense that the people involved thought I knew what was happening and respected me for taking her to her home. I also believe that this reinforced their belief in a syncretistic approach to revelation (Christ, the Word of God, etc.) and their primitive scientific beliefs which they employ to ''explain'' cause and effect. Such syncretism is manifested in a cultural system that fails to distinguish what is known about things through science. This is doubly painful to me.

If I were to work with Mrs. T today, the case would be different. First, as a missionary, I would help change our system of placing pastors in churches. We (the missionaries) thought it would be good to send pastors away from their wife's village (gardens, matriclan authority, etc.) in order to make them ''trust God and develop faith.'' It is my considered opinion that we programmed many of our Bible school graduates and pastors for failure. A truly indigenous church would have adapted to the social system of the Achewa.

Second, I would try to discover if there might be a physiological basis for Mrs. T's aberrant behavior. It seems evident that certain types of mental illness may be predisposed by nutritional deficiency and are manifested under stress. Among the syndromes noted by medical anthropologists are the Pibloctog, Susto, and Amok (Kaplan & Sadock, 1988, pp. 100-102). Further, venereal disease was present among the Achewa in Ntakataka district and it is quite possible that she suffered the effects of periodic recurring brain infection.

Third, it was a common practice for husbands and wives to be separated from each other for long periods of time due to the systematic recruitment of the Witwatersrand Mining Company of South Africa. This company contracted with labor pools in Malawi to hire laborers for South African mines, which meant a two-year period away from a peasant village style of living and placement in an urban development with its concomitant problems of culture shock, alienation, temptations of prostitution, alcohol, gambling, etc. It was this socio-economic situation that allowed me to begin understanding the fairly common incidence of hysteria among Achewa women. The writings of Michael Gelfand (1964), the Government Supervisor of Native Medicine in the Federation of Southern

Rhodesia, Northern Rhodesia, and Nyasaland, were especially helpful. He had obtained an intimate knowledge of and relationship with native paramedics who understood both native/tribal diseases and medicine as well as European (Western) medicine.

I would have held a meeting in Mrs. T's village so that all of the "sisters of her mother" could understand the problems of social changes incurred as a result of evangelism and building indigenous churches, and allow them to agree as to a proper procedure. A point of stress was that the "Western" church was completely controlled by men—both missionary and national. I would have suggested that the district presbyter place Mrs. T's husband in a church near (but not in) Ntakataka. That would have allowed her to put out her garden each spring (this ensures perpetual use of the land by the matriclan), and birth her babies at the home of her mother and the *ankhoswe* (female elders). Also, it would have allowed Mrs. T to remain in constant contact with her relatives in case of *maliro* (a word that means both funeral and tears), the most sacrosanct rite of the Achewa life-cycle. I found out later that Mrs. T had been separated from her matriclan for the birth of one baby and that this child may not be given a garden. Also, she was away from her husband when one of her aunts (*kazi wamkulu*—important old mother's sister) died and she missed the funeral. It was believed by the local people that these activities caused the ancestors to become angry, and they then punished the villages.

Finally, I would begin teaching the church members in such a way that the imposition of our "Western" theology and doctrine would be accepted by the innovators in this society rather than arbitrarily being forced on these gentle, passive, pre-literate people. It is my conviction that much stress was produced by our overt imposition of mission concepts and systems that acculturatively were too much and occurred too soon for the Achewa. In saying this I tentatively conclude that Mrs. T's case was primarily a culturally defined and induced reaction to several stressors that could be modified and thus not fall under the general concept of the demonic. In fact, other Christian families were at this time making the difficult transition from a primitive magico-religious animistic system to a Christian (albeit immature) indigenous church that could eventually develop into a mature body of believers.

Select Bibliography

Adams, J. (1970). *Competent to counsel.* Grand Rapids: Baker Book House.
Barnet, H. G. (1953). *Innovations: The basis of cultural change.* New York: McGraw-Hill.
Berry, J. W. (1976). *Human ecology and cognitive style.* New York: John Wiley.
Bohannan, P. (1963). *Social anthropology.* New York: Holt, Rinehart and Winston.
Carter, J. D., & Mohline, R. J. (1976). The nature and scope of integration: A proposal. *Journal of Psychology and Theology, 4,* 3–14.
Collins, G. (1980). *Christian counseling: A comprehensive guide.* Waco: Word.

Devereaux, W. (1956). Normal and abnormal: The key problems of psychiatric anthropology. In J. B. Casagrande (Ed.), *Some uses of anthropology: Theoretical and applied*, pp. 21–48. Washington, D.C.: Anthropological Society of Washington.

Draguns, J. G. (1976). Counseling across cultures: Common themes and distinct approaches. In P. Pedersen, W. J. Lonner, & J. G. Draguns, (Eds.), *Counseling across cultures*. Honolulu: East-West Center.

_____. (1981). Cross-cultural counseling and psychotherapy: History, issues, current status. In A. J. Marsella & P. Pedersen (Eds.), *Cross-cultural counseling and psychotherapy*, pp. 3–17. New York: Pergamon Press.

Farnsworth, K. E. (1974). Embodied integration. *Journal of Psychology and Theology, 2*, 116–124.

Felicou, C. J., (Ed.). (1983). *Cultural perspectives in family therapy*. Rockville, MD: Aspen Systems Corporation.

Fernandez, J. W. (1969). Contemporary African religion: Confluents of inquiry. In G. M. Carter & A. Paden, (Eds.), *Expanding horizons in African studies*. Evanston, IL: Northwestern University Press.

_____. (1975). The ethnic communion: Interethnic recruitment in African religious movements. *Journal of African Studies, 2*, 131–147.

Firth, R. (1959). Problems and assumptions in an anthropological study of religion. *Journal of the Royal Anthropological Institute, 89*, 129–148.

_____. (1961). *Elements of social organizations* (3rd ed.). Boston: Beacon Press.

Geertz, C. (1965). The impact of the concept of culture on the concept of man. In J. R. Platt (Ed.). *New views of man* (pp. 93–118). Chicago: University of Chicago Press.

Gelfand, M. (1964). Psychiatric disorders as recognized by the Shona. In A. Kiev (Ed.), *Magic, faith, and healing*. New York: Free Press.

Hammond, P. B. (1971). *An introduction to cultural and social anthropology*. New York: Macmillan.

Harris, M. (1968). *The rise of anthropological theory*. New York: Thomas Crowell.

Hesselgrave, D. J. (1984). *Counseling cross-culturally: An introduction to theory and practice for Christians*. Grand Rapids: Baker Book House.

_____. (1985). Christian cross-cultural counseling: a suggested framework for theory development. *Missiology: An International Review, 13*, 203–217.

Higginbotham, H. N. (1979). Culture and the delivery of psychological services in developing nations. *Transcultural Psychiatric Research Review, 16*, 7–27.

Homans, G. C. (1941). Anxiety and ritual: The theories of Malinowski and Radcliffe-Brown. *American Anthropologist, 43*, 164–172.

Horton, R. (1971). Ritual man in Africa. *Africa, 41*, 85–108.

Hsieh, T. T. Y. (1981). Cognitive styles and word versus spirit orientation among Christians. *Journal of Psychology and Theology, 2*, 175–182.

Hurnard, H. (1975). *Winged life*. Wheaton, IL: Tyndale.

Isichei, E. (1970). Seven varieties of ambiguity: Patterns of Igbo response to Christian missions. *Journal of Religious Affairs, 3*, 209–227.

Johnson, C. B. & Malony, H. N. (1982). *Christian conversion: Biblical and psychological perspectives.* Grand Rapids: Zondervan.

Kaplan, H. I., & Sadock, B. J. (1988). *Synopsis of Psychiatry* (5th ed.). Baltimore: Williams & Wilkins.

Karp, S. A. (1977). Psychological differentiation. In T. Blass (Ed.), *Personality variables in social behavior.* New York: John Wiley.

Kluckhohn, C., & Murray, H. A. (1953). Personality formation: The determinants. In C. Kluckhohn, H. A. Murray, and D. M. Schneider (Eds.), *Personality in nature, society and culture.* New York: Random House, Knopf.

Lloyd-Jones, D. M. (1976). *Spiritual depression: Its causes and cure.* Grand Rapids: Eerdmans.

Mair, L. (1964). The concept of function. In P. Hammond, (Ed.), *Culture and social anthropology.* New York: Macmillan.

Malinowski, B. (1960). *A scientific theory of culture.* New York: Galaxy.

_____. (1960). *The dynamics of culture change.* New Haven: Yale University Press.

Mbiti, J. S. (1969). *African religions and philosophy.* New York: Praeger.

McLemore, C. W. (1976). The nature of psychotheology: Varities of conceptual integration. *Journal of Psychology and Theology, 4,* 217–220.

Merton, R. (1957). *Social theory and social structure.* New York: Free Press.

Meyers, D. C. (1978). *The human puzzle: Psychological research and Christian belief.* New York: Harper & Row.

Middleton, J. (Ed.). (1967). *Magic, witchcraft, and curing.* Austin: University of Texas Press.

Nagel, E. (1961). *The structure of science.* New York: Harcourt, Brace & World.

Niebuhr, H. R. (1951). *Christ and culture.* New York: Harper.

Pedersen, P. B. (1981). The cultural inclusiveness of counseling. In P. Pedersen, W. J. Lonner, & J. G. Draguns (Eds.). *Counseling across cultures.* Honolulu: East-West Center.

Pelto, P. J., & Pelto, G. R. (1978). *Anthropological research: The structure of inquiry.* New York: Cambridge University Press.

Pike, K. L. (1954). *Language in relation to a unified theory of the structure of human behavior: Part A.* Glendale, CA: Summer Institute of Linguistics.

Polanyi, M. (1961). Faith and reason. *Journal of Religion, 41,* 237–247.

Ramm, B. (1974). The way of the Spirit. *His, 34* (5), pp. 12–15.

Rappaport, R. (1967). Ritual regulation of environmental relations among a New Guinea people. *Ethnology, 6,* 17–30.

Rubenstein, H., & Bloch, M. H. (1982). *Things that matter: Influences on helping relationships.* New York: Macmillan.

Segall, M. H., Campbell, D. T., & Herskovits, M. J. (1966). *The influence of culture on visual perception.* Indianapolis: Bobbs-Merrill.

Stapleton, R. C. (1976). *The gift of inner healing*. Waco: Word.

Stewart, V. M. (1974). Cognitive style, North American values, and the body of Christ. *Journal of Psychology and Theology, 2*, 77–88.

Stott, J. R. W. (1978). *Your mind matters*. Downers Grove, IL: InterVarsity Press.

Tanaka-Matsui, J. (1979). Cultural factors and social influence techniques in Naikan therapy: A Japanese self-observation method. *Psychotherapy, Theory, Research, and Practice, 16*, 385–390.

Vexliard, A. (1968). Temperament et modalites d'adaptation. *Bulletin de Psychologique, 21*, 1–15.

Wallace, A. F. C. (1956). Revitalization movements. *American Anthropologist, 2*, 264–281.

Witkins, H. A. (1967). Cognitive styles across cultures. *International Journal of Psychology, 2*, 233–250.

13

GUIDED IMAGERY AND INNER HEALING

Raymond T. Brock

My interest in inner healing as a counseling technique dates back to the early sixties, when Agnes Sanford (1947) lectured at Evangel College in Springfield, Missouri, and shared the story of Harry, my predecessor as professor of psychology at the college. His story is given succinctly in *The Transformation of the Inner Man* by Sandford and Sandford (1982).

> During World War II Agnes Sanford was a volunteer aide in a hospital. There she found Harry, a young Jewish-American soldier from whose leg three inches of bone had been blown away. Agnes prayed for him, taught him to pray, and rejoiced with him in the following weeks as those three inches grew back! During the time he received Jesus as his Lord and Savior. Later, he wrote to Agnes saying that he was just fine, studying to be a Christian psychiatrist, but could not understand why every once in a while he would fly into unaccountable rages and do awful things, like throwing his typewriter across the room. That drove Agnes to the Lord, who showed her a vision of Harry as a little boy being taunted and beaten by Gentile ragamuffins. The Holy Spirit revealed to her that the problem was not in the grown Harry but in the festering sore in his heart that had never been healed. Agnes prayed for the little boy to be eased and comforted and helped to forgive his tormentors. Harry wrote back amazed. What had she done? He felt lighter and freer than he ever had, and the rages seemed to be gone—and have been ever since. (p. 3)

Firsthand knowledge of Harry's testimony prepared me to be receptive to the concept of inner healing when I attended a seminar conducted by Ruth Carter Stapleton (1976, 1977) at Calvary Temple church in Denver, Colorado, in 1977. I watched with interest as she used guided imagery in her presentation. I began to explore the matter with Jerry Schmidt, Ph.D., then at the University of Denver and also in private practice. He was helpful in developing both theory and methodology from his own experience.

My experience has been further broadened through my association with F. Paul Kosbab, M.D., who has been long associated with Hanscarl Leuner (1969, 1977, 1973, 1984) in guided affective imagery and George E. Parkhurst, M.D., whose mother (Parkhurst, 1957, 1968, 1973) was influenced by Agnes Sanford and who has been effective in his own use of inner healing as a therapeutic technique in the City of Faith Medical and Research Center in Tulsa. My colleagues and I have witnessed some spectacular healings when we have felt impressed by the Holy Spirit to use imagery in counseling to effect whole-person healing (i.e., healing which blends spiritual, emotional, and physical dimensions of the personality).

HISTORICAL ANTECEDENTS

Guided imagery has had a long and cyclical history. Once honored by Wundt and the Structuralists, it was rejected by Watson and the early Behaviorists, only to reemerge early in this century as a viable therapeutic technique (Sheikh & Jordan, 1983). McMahon (1973) noted Aristotle's assertion that "images act as the sources of activation and guide behavior by representing the goal object" (p. 467). Miller, Galanter & Pribram (1960) suggested that "images are capable of representing situations or objects and, consequently, act as motivators for future behavior" (p. 393).

As early as the 1890s Freud was aware of spontaneous images experienced by his patients (Breuer & Freud, 1955). He said, "My therapy consists of wiping away of these pictures" (Quoted in Kosbab, 1974, p. 284), and he "abandoned the use of hypnosis in favor of an imagery procedure that was more under the patient's conscious control [and] gravitated toward verbal methods including free association and dream interpretation" (Sheikh & Jordan, 1983, p. 398).

Jung, on the other hand, regarded mental imagery as a creative process and noted that the psyche could be employed to attain greater individual, interpersonal, and spiritual integration. He utilized a method called "active imagination" and "discovered that the unconscious was in a sense constantly dreaming" (Sheikh & Jordan, 1983, p. 399). Jung was careful, however, to make a distinction between imagination and fantasy.

> A fantasy is more or less your own invention, and remains on the surface of personal things and conscious expectations. But active imagination, as the term denotes, means that the images have a life of their own and that the symbolic events develop according to their own logic—that is, of course, if your conscious reason does not interfere. (Jung, 1976, p. 171)

It appears that Pierre Janet (1898) first employed imagery as a therapeutic technique in Europe. Both he and Alfred Binet (1922) believed that pictures emerging during the use of the "dialogue method of introspection revealed diverse unconscious subpersonalities" of clients in therapy (Sheikh & Jordan, 1983, p. 396). Silberer's (1909; 1912) experiments supported the hypothesis that the psyche "has a spontaneous urge to repress itself in images in its visual fantasy" (Leuner, 1978, p. 12). About the same time Ludwig Frank (1913) explored the significance of deep relaxation and believed it to be cathartic in nature. As early as 1925 Marc Guillerey (1945) experimented with what he called "directed revery."

In 1905 Schultz introduced a self-generated and self-regulated technique called "autogenic training" which has significantly influenced the development of biofeedback. He encouraged his patients to imagine that they were having the same physiological feelings through imagery they had experienced under hypnosis (Schultz & Luthe, 1959). It should be noted, however, that the therapeutic use of imagery, especially as it is involved in guided affective imagery or inner healing, is not a form of hypnosis (Leuner, 1977).

In 1932 Happick introduced an unsystematic attempt to use imaginings as a psychotherapeutic technique in Germany. He encouraged patients "to employ muscular relaxation, passive respiration, and meditation." He speculated that there is a "meditative zone" between the conscious and unconscious where "productions that have matured in the unconscious become visible in the mind's eye" (Sheikh & Jordan, 1983, p. 396).

Leuner (1984) was influenced by the work of Happick (1932) and Heiss (1956). In 1954 he added depth psychology to the "imaginal consciousness" exercises of his predecessors and developed the concept of guided affective imagery. He traced his technique to Freud's early use of "directed daydreams." However, Leuner's approach is much more systematized and is supported by research dealing with therapy outcomes (Sheikh & Jordan, 1983). It appears that Ruth Carter Stapleton (1976) was deeply influenced by Leuner in developing her approach to inner healing (Malony, 1985).

IMAGERY RESEARCH

Three modalities of cognition and expression have been hypothesized by Horowitz (1978). The *enactive modality* is associated with the "corticalmotor regions and the limbic system of the brain." The *image modality* involves the right hemisphere of the brain and permits processing of information following perception that leads to the sensory character of cognitions and feelings. The *lexical modality* represents the linguistic mode and is predominantly associated with the left hemisphere of the brain and is "particularly effective in integrating extremely diverse phenomena into one language label and permits very rapid subsequent retrieval" (Shiekh & Jordan, 1983, p. 391).

Klinger (1971) concluded that imagery represented the central core of perceptual, retrieval, and response mechanisms. Referring to the works of Kepecs (1954) and Sheikh and Panagiotou (1975), Sheikh and Jordan (1983) stated that "imagery may be the main access to important preverbal memories or to memories encoded at developmental stages at which language, while present, was not yet predominant" (p. 393). It has also been demonstrated that imagery has the power to produce a wide variety of physiological changes (Simpson & Paivia, 1966; Yaremko & Butler, 1975). And, it has been suggested that solutions rehearsed through imagery during therapy can generalize to situations outside the therapy session (Klinger, 1971; Richardson, 1969).

Sheikh and Jordan (1983), conducted an exhaustive review of the research literature on imagery and observed that there is a plethora of claims supported by case histories to confirm the effectiveness of guided imagery by a variety of theoreticians. However, "there is no way to clearly determine whether some methods are better than others and whether some characteristics of the client (i.e., sex, age, cognitive style) make him or her a more suitable candidate for image-based therapies" (p. 423). They concluded:

> It is unfortunate that, although there has been a burst of interest in the clinical application of imagery, very scant experimental work has been devoted to the verification of the pivotal process assumptions that underlie these procedures. Behavior therapists, in contrast, have done a great deal of research, but they have neglected developing sufficiently broad theoretical foundations to support the research data on the effects of imagistic experience. (p. 423, 424)

They were almost prophetic in summarizing their findings (Sheikh & Jordan, 1983, p. 424):

> In conclusion, once again, we would like to strike a note of caution amid the rapidly growing enthusiasm for therapeutic imagery. It is true that creativity can be suffocated by a compulsion for rigid scientific methodology. On the other hand, however, roaming, unbridled fancy is unproductive. Overly enthusiastic image therapists perhaps should keep in mind that there was a time in history when the clinical significance of imagery was widely accepted, but that this period regrettably did not last. It is imperative that the creative surge be accompanied by sobering scrutiny, lest the future of imagery in the clinic be written in its past.

IMAGERY AND DIAGNOSIS

The use of imagery in diagnosis is a projective technique, for the instruction to visualize a particular thing, person, or event produces a type of projective stimulus similar to the use of the Rorschach or TAT technique. In carrying out such an instruction, the client would have to project "on the stimuli idiosyncratic perceptions that reflect his or her way of viewing life, his or her meanings, significances, patterns, and particularly feelings" (Sheikh & Jordan, 1983, p. 414).

Accumulating evidence suggests that images, both induced and spontaneous, are a rich and available source of information useful in diagnosis. Sheikh and Jordan (1983) concluded that three assumptions underlie this conclusion: There is inherent meaning in the images that relates to the individual's motivational system. If these images are a valid source of information, there must be some things in the perception and/or motivation of the subject which has been beyond conscious awareness. If the information in the image is accessible and intelligible to the counselor, there must be a set of "algorithms" from which interpretation is derived: (a) theory, (b) clinical and research evidence, or (c) empirical or actuarial findings. The first two sources have been the primary focus thus far, and most of the clinicians refer to "uncovering rather than diagnostic categorizing" (Sheikh & Jordan, 1983, p. 415).

The theory of representational systems recognizes that for any individual there is a difference between his/her world and any particular model or representation of that world (Bandler & Grinder, 1975, 1976). It also suggests that the world each person creates is individually different. A study of individual linguistic patterns appears to be the most efficient way of identifying a person's primary representational system. This linguistic analysis allows the therapist to use different sensory modalities and help clients by introducing "changes in their client's models which allow their clients more options in their behavior" (Bandler & Grinder, 1975, p. 18).

Guernsey and Bunker (1981) noted that therapists involved in inner healing have primarily emphasized visual (seeing), auditory (hearing), and kinesthetic (body sensations) modalities and relegated the olfactory (smelling) and gustatory (tasting) modalities to secondary importance. They pointed out that "identification of the client's primary representation system is a significant tool in therapy" and urged the study of a client's linguistic pattern as a vital clinical function (p. 4). This requires the therapist to accommodate to the kinesthetic and auditory/tonal person as well as the one for whom visualization is a primary mode of experiencing.

Some clients seem to be able to image with ease; others claim not to have the capacity. It has been my experience that those who use what Horowitz (1978) called the *lexical modality* claim—at least in the beginning stages of therapy—not to be able to image. However, as therapy proceeds, more interaction between the two hemispheres of the brain occurs and imaging becomes possible. When clients do begin to image, it is usually internal images rather than ones from remembered experience. Any reminiscence of previous events is pale and in shades of gray. With time and experience, and possibly lowered resistance, the images become more distinct. Ultimately, images can be created by the client, which indicates that another layer of repressed material is being exposed to scrutiny. In such a situation, "the image is a compromise between expression and concealment, and although it may incorporate many elements of camouflage, the impulse source must still be represented" (Sheikh & Jordan, 1983, p. 416).

One of my clients was encouraged to image a physiological pain she was reporting in her chest and abdomen. She struggled with words and gestures and then asked for drawing materials. With a crayon and note pad she produced the drawing of a bottle, colored it black, placed a cork in the top of the neck and indicated that the core of the bottle was solid. This is not unlike the "cartographic sketch" technique of Leuner (1984). The image in the drawing became the focal point of therapy in subsequent sessions as she examined the bottle, its possible contents, and how it could be removed from her body. The image became data with which the unconscious could work between sessions. Periodically I would refer to the bottle and the client would report it was becoming a lighter shade of gray and that the solid core was becoming less solid and more fluid.

It was an exciting day when this client opened a therapy session with the statement: "The bottle is gone!" So was the oppression of which the pain had been a symptom. This is consistent with what Rehyer (1977) called *emergent uncovering,* which allows valuable insight to be gained by the client through ongoing imagery even without interpretation by the counselor. Jellinek (1949) wrote of image production as a form of nonrational thinking that makes it possible to initiate a dialogue with the unconscious. The underlying assumption here is that "imagery is a mode of expression indigenous to the unconscious and that unconscious thought cannot be adequately expressed in words" (Sheikh & Jordan, 1983, p. 415).

GUIDED IMAGERY AND THERAPY

Since Leuner's (1969) concept of guided affective imagery (GAI) directly influenced the style of inner healing espoused by Stapleton (1976), his approach will be emphasized in this section, although it should be remembered that there are other theoretical approaches to the subject.

Imagination and Imagery

Leuner (1977) defined "imagination" as "the human capacity for visualizing mental contents which is a spontaneous manifestation of the psyche's urge toward self-representation and communication about itself" (p. 73). He based this on Freud's assumption that emotional processes are determined by a variety of interrelated conditions, which he used to explain slips of the tongue. Leuner called these "slips of the intelligence" (p. 73), a concept which he claimed predated Freud.

In therapy, imagination and imagery are seen as the visualization of mental contents that appear to be closely related to visual fantasies and daydreams and are a primitive form of thinking (Breuer & Freud, 1955). Leuner (1977) expanded this concept by saying, "The same unconscious motivations underlying Freudian slips are also the determining factors in bringing about and shaping the contents of imaginative experiences." (p. 74). He was referring both to affectively charged tension states and intrapsychic conflicts, which contribute to emotionally determined problems of an intrapsychic nature as well as the "imaginative experiences that tend to relieve and ease emotional tensions" (p. 74). Leuner pointed out further that under extreme emotional stress, people can have very vivid and highly precise imaginative experiences. For example, Viet Nam veterans who have been in acutely life-threatening situations report having vivid flashbacks of war-time experiences.

Relaxation Techniques

The use of relaxation techniques in preparing for the use of imagery varies with therapists. It is well known that clients relax when they feel secure, but it is also important to reduce sensory input from the environment. Alertness and attentiveness are helpful in focusing on inner events as is meditation which can "reduce the amount of varied sensory input yet allow, or in some instances promote a high level of cognitive arousal" (Richardson, 1983, p. 34).

The use of fantasy allows a client to process information creatively by combining and sometimes reorganizing its content. Thus fantasy can be the preparatory work by which imagination becomes the vehicle for understanding (Klinger, 1971;

Richardson, 1983). It has also been observed that those who seem not to be able to experience "imagination images" under the appropriate conditions may be using defensive strategies to inhibit awareness, while those who do experience the images may be more interested in and attentive to internal experiences (Foulkes, Spear & Symonds, 1976; Richardson, 1983).

Leuner (1977) does not emphasize relaxation exercises as a precondition to therapy. He found that after clients were given a few relaxation suggestions they could begin using the imaginative technique. He did note that the "image initially appears relatively pale, seldom in color, and must be 'held in place' by an act of the will because otherwise it will disappear or be replaced by the next image" (p. 77). He further noted that in a state of high relaxation the images become gradually clearer, have more color, and remain more vivid when the eyes are closed but the pale imaginative fantasies can also fulfill the purposes of the imaginative technique.

Leuner (1977) indicated that subsequent therapy sessions using relaxation with imagery led to more physiological signs of deep relaxation with more vivid images in progressive fantasies. "Imaginal consciousness" allows for "slumber images" to emerge and are similar to the experience of falling asleep. The more fully developed images he called "catathymic images," from *katathym* which means "caused by complexes. . . . having an effect on an emotionally laden (suppressed) complex on the psyche" (p. 78). Further, he said, "their special quality lies in the simple imaginings, which we have in everyday experience, when we recall a scene from the past or in our imagination" (1984, p. 13).

Imagery Production and Symbolic Content

According to Leuner (1977), two psychic functions are important in guided affective imagery: imagery production and symbolic content. The *imagery productions* are like slides projected on a wall as the unconscious emotions are projected onto the ego, which serves as a cognitive "screen." Such projections function as a normal and spontaneous activity that Leuner called a "creative urge." *Symbolic content* he equated with condensation: "multiple experimental elements, which frequently are contradictory with emotionally determined or tinged undercurrents and feeling tones, are unconsciously condensed in the symbolic 'token' " (p. 79). These tokens may have either positive or negative elements, but they possess an emotionally charged quality which holds significance for the client.

In response to the question, What should we look for in guided affective imagery and what can we conclude from it? Leuner (1977) emphasized content and reminiscence.

> First, of course, the therapist focuses his attention on the contents which, in imagination, he experiences together with the subject. Using his knowledge of symbolism in general, and the information provided by the subject's case history, he attempts to discover the possible meaning of the contents. Simultaneously he pays close attention to accompanying feeling tones and affective connotations indicated, for example, by the tone of voice,

pauses in the verbal description, or a deepening of respiration. Also, he observes the
subject's behavior within the context of imagined scenes and imagery sequences. (p. 80)

The content of imagery holds a message that works in two ways: one part of
the message goes from the client to the therapist and the other part of the message
is directed to the client's own ego. Since this kind of confrontation with one's
unconscious is not always pleasant, it may be disturbing to the point of resurrecting
forces of repression for defensive protection. Imagery offers a way of temporarily
suspending or circumventing the camouflage of the unconscious.

Reminiscence

Reminiscence in guided affective imagery is also of significance. Leuner (1977)
pointed out that old, almost forgotten memories can come into focus, and
regression to an earlier childhood experience can have a real impact on a current
event. "By means of reminiscences, the patient has an opportunity to re-experience
situations charged with childhood fears and anxieties and thus return to the roots
of basic conflicts" (p. 80). Release from these effects and feelings can be
dramatically therapeutic.

The therapist does not make it a point to interpret the contents of images on
the basic level of therapy but allows self-interpretation to occur. Leuner (1984)
recognized the contribution of Kosbab (1974) in "referring to the slow and gradual,
yet still clear, self-interpretation of the symbolic contents of symboldrama" that
emerge in therapy. He noted further that "the contents of every image and the
development of every scene or story (even if it is only made up of a stringing
together of scenic fragments) regularly convey elements of moods and emotions
and always make a certain statement" (p. 44). This brings about "image puzzles,"
which allow for the use of images with their diverse meanings, and
"suggestiveness," which Leuner believed is well understood by the preconscious
(p. 44).

Leuner's Research Discoveries

In the process of research and therapy, Leuner (1977) made several important
discoveries.

1. Some of the images appear to be fixed and are seen as stereotyped symbols.
They indicate emotional rigidity and appear in persons diagnosed as neurotic and
psychosomatically disturbed.

2. Some of the images are shifting and prove to be less problematic. They change
from time to time and show few contrasts or extremes and are not intensely charged
with feeling.

3. The changeable quality of imaginative projections reveals alterations in the
patient's communication with the therapist. Leuner called this "mobile projection"
and used it to account for "every minute inner change, every minor therapeutic
intervention, and every spontaneous emotional development [that] is almost

automatically reflected in subtle or marked changes of imagery contents''
(p. 82).

4. Centers of conflict exist and the flexibility of mobile projection is needed
to bring these areas into focus to provide valuable information for the therapist.

5. Operation on the symbol refers to the functional unity of imaginations and
emotional conflict. Leuner (1977) moved beyond the one-way process of Freud
and earlier theorists to explain projection and proposed a two-way process.

> The patient not only projects on himself "outwards," i.e., into the phantasied pictorial
> image, but the therapist or even the patient himself can also in turn influence the contents
> of such images or their part and this influence then has immediate repercussions on the
> inner emotional state represented in the image. This two-way process seems almost
> incredible and opens up infinite possibilities for resulting external behavior. This interwoven
> functional unity of imagination and inner emotional state can be tested at any time. We
> have designed the resulting therapeutic technique as "operation on the symbol." (pp.
> 85, 86)

6. The fulfillment or execution of "archaic" basic needs is a discovery that
is still under investigation. Leuner used the term "archaic" to refer to the content
and type of regressive experience in the guided imagery. He established a series
of standardized motifs to focus on potential neurotic conflicts in the client. In
using them, the therapist must be careful to interpret the images in the context
of the client's personal history, his present situation, and the patterns of his
emotional responsiveness.

LEUNER'S THERAPEUTIC MOTIFS

Leuner (1984) developed a system for teaching therapists to use the variety
of motifs he had discovered.

Basic Level

1. *The motif of the meadow* to set the stage for projection of current conflicts.

2. *The motif of the brook*, which can be followed upstream or downstream.

3. *The motif of the mountain*, which can be viewed from a distance and then
climbed for a panoramic view.

4. *The motif of a house*, which can be viewed from the outside and then from
room to room and from cellar to attic.

5. *The motif of the edge of the woods*, looking from the meadow, to let symbolic
figures (human or animal) emerge from the forest.

Intermediate Level

6. *Motif of referential figures*, which allows encounter with friends or relatives
who may be dressed symbolically.

7. *Motif for testing sexual attitudes*, such as car for a female or a rosebush
for a male. Sometimes the Garden of Eden can be used as this motif.

8. *Motif for exploring attitudes toward aggressive impulses*, such as a lion to
probe the capacity for self-assertion.

9. *Motif for determining the ego-ideal.* The patient is to think of a person of the same sex and then to visualize that person. Usually a person recognizes qualities the patient would like to have.

Advanced Level

10. *Motif to evoke "archaic" forms of the self*, beginning with symbols of the earth's interior such as a cave or swamp.

11. *Motif of a volcano*, a mountain spewing fire which has significance if a patient is experiencing strong aggressive impulses in a current situation.

12. *Motif of a book*, the use of an old illustrated book (such as a Bible) that is frequently filled with symbolism.

Leuner (1977) described guided affective imagery as a relatively short-term technique to be used over a period of 20 to 25 sessions, but no more than 50 sessions. The method has also been used in short-term therapy of from one to several hours as a form of crisis intervention. When imagery is used as short-term intervention, Leuner noted that the therapist "must be prepared to see the reappearance of symptoms and emotional reactions if and when the patient is again subjected to tension-producing, conflictual situations" (p. 89).

More recently Leuner (1984) has given special attention to the behavior of the therapist who utilizes guided affective imagery (GAI) as a therapeutic technique:

> The therapist can and also frequently will become so involved in his own imaginal world, which is controlled by unconscious impulses, that he is not at all, or only to a limited extent, able to observe and critically reflect upon his behavior as therapist. However, that is a basic requirement for guiding the patient in symboldrama. He must also be able to distance himself critically from his patient temporarily, to reflect on the catathymic productions and classify them within his store of theoretical knowledge and thus be able to continue his guidance to the patient's advantage according to clear cognitive and knowledgeable scientific conclusion. This is particularly important in critical situations within GAI, for which the therapist must be able to maintain the desired temporary distance. (p. 23)

Leuner (1977) also offered a note of caution in using GAI.

> Finally, I must point out the possible dangers involved in the use of guided affective imagery as a psychotherapeutic method. It is quite obvious that opening the gateways to the unconscious by giving free rein to fantasy can also have undesirable consequences: one only has to think of what may happen if a deeply emotionally disturbed person is suddenly confronted with highly charged, conflictual material from his unconscious. As a rule, the ego of the average neurotic patient is strong enough to protect and defend itself against such dangers. (p. 90)

Leuner (1977, p. 86) said in referring to the "operation on the symbol" technique of the strategy that the therapist using this technique is advised to be alert to the appropriate procedures as to "dosage" when he "steers the patient towards his problems by means of direct, deliberate intervention." A final caution by Leuner must be noted.

> *Initially the method described here of evoking and inducing fantasies may appear very simple; however, problems often arise when it is attempted by someone without sufficient*

general psychotherapeutic training and the special additional training required to gain adequate technical competence in the use of guided affective imagery. (p. 90; italics added)

INNER HEALING

Inner healing is as old as the biblical record (Sandford & Sandford, 1982; Seamonds, 1985). God's inner dealings with David as a result of his adultery, the murder-by-proxy of Bathsheba's husband, the death of the illegitimately conceived child, and other family tragedies are reflected in the writings of the poet-king (Psalms 32, 40, 41, 62). Paul also testified to the tremendous inner healing he experienced on the Damascus Road, which transformed him from a persecutor of Christians to an evangelist and missionary (Acts 26).

Definitions

In its contemporary form, at least in the form espoused by Stapleton (1976), inner healing has its roots in the guided affective imagery of Leuner (1969, 1977, 1984), whose contribution to the field continues to be perfected in West Germany. In the new *Baker Encyclopedia of Psychology*, Malony (1985) described inner healing as:

> a contemporary form of spiritual healing. As described by its advocates, it is a process wherein the Holy Spirit restores health in the deepest aspects of life by dealing with the root cause of hurt and pain. Basically it involves a two-fold procedure in which 1) the power of evil is broken and the heritage of wholeness that belongs to the Christian is reclaimed, and 2) memories of the past are healed through prayer. (pp. 579, 580)

Both Roman Catholic and Protestant writers have addressed the subject. Several have written from a charismatic perspective that seeks to magnify the role of the Holy Spirit in the counseling process. Frequently, however, they will take different approaches to the doctrine of sin and the role of exorcism in the healing process.

Francis McNutt (1974) and the Linn brothers (Linn & Linn, 1974) have approached the subject from a Roman Catholic perspective. The Linns appear to have been deeply influenced by American Indian mysticism with which they came in contact during their ministry among the Sioux. They postulated three basic steps in the healing of the memories and concluded that the process is time-consuming (pp. 64-67).

1. *Thanking God.* They equated "to confess" with "to praise God" in the tradition of the church fathers.

2. *Confessing what Christ wants healed.* Here they noted that we do not trust in a long list of sins, but in the power of Jesus Christ. And, they observed, reform best comes when concentrating on only one area at a time.

3. *Surrendering painful memories to Christ for healing.* This gives Christ the opportunity to bring about change so we act differently. This comes when, instead of just mentioning surface sins, we surrender to Christ for healing the root that causes those sins.

McNutt (1974) has been a major contributor to the inner healing movement.

He concluded that four types of human suffering can be dealt with through four types of prayers.

1. *Sicknesses of the spirit*, caused by personal sin, require prayers of repentance and seeking God's forgiveness.

2. *Sicknesses of the emotions*, which result from psychological hurts from the past, merit prayers for inner healing and are directed toward the healing of painful memories.

3. *Sicknesses of the body*, the result of disease and accidents, involve prayers for physical healing.

4. *Demon oppression*, which may involve physical, emotional, and spiritual sicknesses and their accompanying symptoms, requires prayers for deliverance or even exorcism of demons.

Protestant contributions have come from Agnes Sanford (1947), Genevieve Parkhurst (1957, 1968, 1973), Betty Tapscott (1975), Ruth Carter Stapleton (1976, 1977), David Seamonds (1981, 1982, 1985), Robert L. McDonald (1981), John and Paula Sandford (1982), and Rita Bennett (1982, 1984).

Sanford's Approach to Inner Healing

Sanford's (1947) method, illustrated at the beginning of this chapter, included four steps involving relaxation and meditation. First, she suggested, "*Choose the same time and the same place every day*, make yourself comfortable and relax" (p. 36). Then she introduced the concept of "happy visioning," picturing in one's mind the changes one would like to see occurring in life. In her words, "We see this picture in our minds, hold it up to the light of God's love and bless it in the name of Jesus Christ. Then we state with serene faith that it will be soon" (p. 263).

Second, "*Remind yourself of the reality of a life outside yourself*" (p. 36). This, she said, requires us to "forget the body so that we can quiet the mind and concentrate the spiritual energies on God" (p. 37). She then suggested methods and postures of meditation that involved some relaxation techniques. The person who followed her prescription, she predicted, would

> find that he is filled with such fullness of life that his spine will be free so that his chest can expand. He will notice as he relaxes that even his breathing is altered, becoming slow, thin and light, as if to leave room for the Spirit of God within. (p. 37)

Third, "*Ask that life to come in and increase life in your body*" (p. 37). Nerves, Sanford said, "are like children. They respond to suggestion better than command. . . . So we speak gently and soothingly to the nerves all the way up the body and in the head. And in the same quiet way we bid our conscious mind to be still" (p. 38).

Fourth, "*Make a picture on your mind of your body well*" (p. 37). This step allows the person to rejoice in a definite perception of increasing life within. Before we have learned to perceive these physical sensations, however, we will be conscious of Christ entering into us upon the footsteps of his peace (pp. 39, 40).

Healing of Memories

Treating the contribution of Betty Tapscott (1975) and John and Paula Sandford (1982) together, Malony (1985) noted:

> They suggest that "breaking the power of Satan" is the first step in any healing but feel that this is accomplished through spiritual healing, which means coming to know Jesus as personal Savior. This involves confession of sin, renunciation of occult power, being willing to forgive in the same manner that one has been forgiven, being honest, and being humble. Spiritual healing is the foundation for inner healing of the mind and physical healing of the body.
>
> The other side of breaking the power of Satan is reclaiming one's Christian inheritance, according to the Tapscotts. This means reaffirming what was true in creation and what has been provided in salvation; namely, that God wants people to be whole and has given many spiritual riches to his followers if they will but claim them. These acts of renouncing evil and reaffirming faith in God's goodness become the basis for inner healing, which is accomplished by prayer for the healing of memories. They are also the foundation for physical healing, which occurs through prayer for God to make the body whole again. (p. 580)

Prayer for the healing of the memories, then, is at the core of the inner healing approach to psychotherapy (Seamonds, 1985). These include memories of the recent past, those buried in the unconscious from early childhood, even "memories of being unwanted or neglected, or evil deeds or unexpected accidents, or even of events that happened while they were still in their mothers' womb" (Malony, 1985, p. 580).

Stapleton (1977) believed that there is evidence to support the belief that "children can be emotionally scarred during the period of gestation" (p. 21). She pointed out the trauma of the unwed mother and believed her experiences of shame and fear could be sensed by the unborn child. Adopted children, she said, "usually need Jesus to heal unremembered 'memories' of being born unwanted. They must be given the experience of a Jesus who can supply the love the unhappy mother was unable to give" (p. 22). Similarly, McDonald (1984, ch. 4) has elaborated on the function of the nervous system in memories, both prenatal and in young children. He concluded that memories are stored in the central nervous system of the unborn child that may influence subsequent behavior after birth. "Coenesthetic organization" is the process of memory recording until about the eighteenth month when "encephalization. . . allows memory to be recorded in the usual manner (p.34).

Malony (1985) concluded that the prime ingredient of inner healing is "breaking the power of unresolved and oppressive memories" (p. 580). He said:

> This understanding is the major diagnostic model for the prayer that releases persons from the tyranny of the past. It is presumed that the fears, guilts, lethargies, and depressions that result from oppressive memories are against the will of God and, as such, are susceptible to being remedied by him if the person is willing. Of particular import to the inner healers has been Hugh Missildine's *Your Inner Child of the Past* (1963). Inner healers feel that they are talking sound psychology because many models of psychopathology put similar emphasis on past experience. They see themselves as legitimate, even though they insist that they do not pretend to be psychologists. (pp. 530, 531)

Since some practitioners have entered into a ministry of inner healing through personal concerns and experiences rather than formal training in theology and the behavioral sciences, they have not achieved an adequate integration of biblical truth with scientific tenets. This has led to much of the contemporary controversy concerning the place of counseling in the Christian Community (Bennett, 1982, Hunt & McMahon, 1985; Malony, 1985; Sandford & Sandford, 1982).

As a result of their emphasis on the healing of the inner child of the past, many of the practitioners in inner healing either trace backward toward birth or begin their prayers with conception in the process of inner healing. The Tapscotts, for instance, request their clients to "visualize Jesus walking hand in hand with them back through every moment of their lives" (Malony, 1985, p. 581). Stapleton, on the other hand, began the group which I attended with prayer, focusing on conception and moving developmentally to adulthood.

Lack of love or feelings of rejection that lie deeply repressed in the psyche influence us (covertly or overtly) in later periods of life. This awareness lends credence to the emphasis that McNutt (1974) placed on love and belongingness. In this he is theoretically in harmony with Erikson (1968) and Glasser (1965), who are not related to the inner healing movement. According to Malony (1985), MacNutt began with the assumption that the basic need of life is for love. If anyone has ever been denied love, the ability to love and trust others may be seriously impaired and he or she may be left with serious psychological wounds. The first step towards inner healing, then, is for Jesus to be allowed to heal those wounds. Second, Jesus must be allowed to extend his love to meet the needs of the individual. He will heal the scars of past hurts and resentments and free the individual from the painful memories of the experience. Whenever one recognizes fears, anxiety, resentment, hate, or inhibition, it is time to seek inner healing.

Malony (1985) concluded that two questions need to be explored before the prayer for healing is offered.

> First, when can you remember first feeling this way? Second, what was happening that caused you to feel this way? If the person cannot remember an incident, then God is asked to reveal it. After the time and place of the hurt has been identified, a prayer for the healing of the hurt is offered. (p.581)

Guernsey and Bunker (1981), after studying the styles of several therapists, summarized their findings by saying that healing of memories

> refers to a prayerful process whereby Jesus is introduced into the painful memory as vividly as possible through the use of descriptive images or scenes in order that the particular painful memory or set of memories (such as a period of time which was particularly painful) may be reconstructed in a positive way. In a sense, it is reliving a painful event or period, but allowing Jesus to give the story a "happy ending." (p. 6)

MacNutt (1974) observed that Jesus is the Lord of time and can help bring to the foreground of consciousness the hurtful perceptions and experiences that were buried in the past. These can be consciously dealt with in the present through inner healing. "Now," MacNutt said, "I am discovering that the Lord can heal these wounds . . . and can bring the counseling process to its completion in a deep healing'' (p. 187). The Sandfords wrote of inviting the omnipresence of Jesus into the memory so the pain can be removed, ''basic trust'' restored, and ''slumbering spirits'' released. Malony (1984) noted that after the memories have been healed, the person prays for God to fill the void in his or her life with love.

Faith Imagination

Stapleton (1976) called her approach *faith imagination therapy* and shows the influence of Leuner's (1969, 1977, 1984) guided affective imagery. Malony (1985) noted that

> Stapleton is in accord with many practitioners of this technique in asserting that faith imagination is a way of inducing positive changes deep within the mind. According to Leuner, guided imagery attempts to replace aggressive and defensive mental habits with more mature, adaptive ego functioning. The core method in both guided imagery and faith imagination is that of suggestion. (p. 582)

Seamonds (1985) called it ''sanctified imagination.'' In my practice I have found it convenient to use the term *faith fantasy* when using guided imagery in inner healing as a psychotherapeutic technique.

Therapy in the faith imagination form is active rather than client-centered and requires what Malony (1985) called ''a great deal of intuition'' (p. 582), as the therapist *leads* the client in the fantasy being developed to bring about inner healing. He is quick to observe that ''neither faith imaginations or guided fantasies are hypnotic suggestions. . . . In inner healing and guided imagery the individual is encouraged to image the action and elaborate the basic situation in fantasy'' (p. 582).

As noted earlier, guided imagery incorporates Jungian understandings of the psychic structure which differ from the Freudian view by utilizing the *persona* and *collective unconscious* along with archetypes. Methods of contemporary therapists using the inner healing approach resemble basically two archetypical figures in the Trinity—the Holy Spirit and Jesus Christ. They encourage the individual to allow the presence of Jesus to be imaged in the reliving of these events and to heal them. Malony (1985) concluded that

> there is a common presumption among inner healers and guided imagists that something more than insight is needed for healing to occur. Both groups are action therapists in the sense that they agree that reexperiencing is the prime means of psychological change. In this they resemble both Gestalt therapists and psychoanalysts, although their presumptions of the dynamic processes involved are somewhat different. Gestalt therapists are more inclined to induce the reexperience of past processes, such as feelings, while psychoanalysts are committed to a spontaneous working through the transference with the therapist. (p. 583)

The Sandfords (1982), whose book *The Transformation of the Inner Man* is presented by the publishers as ''the most comprehensive book on inner healing today,'' treat initially the spiritual foundations essential for inner healing. They look specifically at sin, salvation, sanctification and transformation, and the necessity for forgiveness to break the sin cycle. Then they look at the developmental approach to inner healing, starting with infancy and coming through the developmental stages of the developing individual. They follow the sequences of Erikson's (1968) *Eight Ages of Man*, although they do not refer specifically to his work. Then they look at sexual sins, dating, and marriage. Their book and videotapes were prepared for laypersons and are replete with scriptures and personal illustrations.

Alsdurf and Malony (1980) have examined the strengths and weaknesses of the inner healing movement and explored its roots in guided affective imagery. Malony (1985) later concluded that there appears to be an "overreliance on semipopular authors such as Missildine" (p. 583) but that

> inner healing should be looked upon as a unique and powerful form of therapy currently held in wide respect by a large part of the Christian world. Christian psychotherapists should study it deeply and attempt to learn from its bold use of Christian resources in the helping process. (pp. 583, 584)

Seamonds (1987), on the other hand, lists Missildine's book as essential for the counseling pastor who wants to build a library on the Christian and emotions.

Criticisms and Critiques

Hunt and McMahon (1985), in *The Seduction of Christianity*, have objected vigorously to the use of guided imagery and inner healing in the Christian community by equating it with shamanism. However, Lantz (1986), director of counseling in a midwestern church, reviewed their book as a Christian therapist and found eight points where he felt their thesis was "unbiblical, anti-Christian, irrational, or inaccurate" (p. 55). Wise (1986) has compiled a rebuttal to the book from the contributions of a variety of Christian writers, some of whom were quoted in the Hunt and McMahon book. More recently Paulk (1987) wrote *That the World May Know* as a plea for unity among Christians who are divided on issues related to Christian counseling.

Given the controversy currently being generated, it may be time to go back to the early perspective of Genevieve Parkhurst (1973) in her autobiographical *Glorious Victory Through Healing of the Memories*. She referred to the conversion of Fritz Kunkel, M.D., a famous German psychotherapist with whom she was personally acquainted:

> Dr. Kunkel had no interest in Christianity, but one day he picked up the New Testament to see what the man Jesus had to say in the light of modern psychology. To his amazement, he discovered that Jesus was the greatest psychologist of all times, that he asked the right questions and always gave the right answers. Dr. Kunkel not only found Jesus, the great psychologist, but he found Jesus, the Savior. As a result Dr. Kunkel lectured and wrote a number of books in his effort to establish a firm foundation between modern psychology and the teachings of Jesus. (p. 7)

THE HOLY SPIRIT AND INNER HEALING

Spiritual Prerequisites

The presence of the Holy Spirit is essential if inner healing is to be a Christian form of therapeutic intervention. The Holy Spirit, as the Third Person of the Trinity, is available to make the Father and the Son real to the believer. As a result, this type of therapy is uniquely limited to use by the born again Christian therapist. If a client is not a believer in Christ Jesus, evangelism must precede therapy in order for the Holy Spirit to have free reign in the encounter. Some forms of guided affective imagery, such as Leuner's (1984) motifs, would not necessitate such a commitment, but inner healing, as it is addressed in this chapter, is predicated on the sovereign intervention of the Holy Spirit in the life of the believer.

According to the practitioners, inner healing must be preceded by the prayer of repentance (McNutt, 1974; Sandford & Sandford, 1982; Seamonds, 1985; Tapscott, 1975). Then the prayer for inner healing is appropriate. Dennis Bennett is quoted by his wife Rita (Bennett, 1984) as having defined inner healing as "simply cooperating with the Lord to let Him cure and remove from our psychological natures the things that are blocking the flow of the Holy Spirit" (p. 25). The person and presence of the Holy Spirit are essential in the healing process.

Rita Bennett (1984) used the term "soul healing," whereas McDonald (1981), from his background in psychiatry, preferred "memory healing" in discussing the importance of the Holy Spirit in the therapeutic process. He observed that *all* healing is by nature inner healing because "healing proceeds from the inside out. . . . The term memory healing is more accurate because in this process of change, memories, as a concept, are what actually undergo change" (p. 19). Referring to Romans 12:1, 2, he noted that Paul's reference to "renewing of the mind" basically refers to memory change. He noted further that

> There is "an opening" of one's spirit to permit contact with the Holy Spirit, resulting in a channel. Instead of speaking in an unknown tongue as the Spirit gives utterance (Acts 2:4), the memory is changed as the Spirit provides the creative energy. In both cases there is a releasing of the human spirit to provide access to the Holy Spirit for change. When this happens, the Holy Spirit changes the image being visualized by rearranging the chemical substance (this term is used loosely to describe simply the complex mental representation).
>
> Not only is the image often changed, the feeling tone is changed to one of neutrality, of peace and acceptance. No longer does one feel the anger, fright, rejection or physical pain. These negative feelings are released or neutralized. (McDonald, 1981, p. 39)

Memory Healing in Practice

One of the imaging techniques I have found helpful is to ask the client to imagine a pleasant place: a mountain scene, seascape, meadow, prairie, desert, or river scene. No sounds of civilization or movement of people should be included in the scene. Relaxation techniques may be used to encourage imaging and can also be used in the scene itself as the client is allowed to relax in the presence of God, to experience the release of tension and stress, and to feel at peace with the world of God's creation. Into this scene can be introduced individuals who are perceived as points of conflict, resentment, rejection, lack of love, or oppression. As this antagonist is brought into focus and closer to the client in the image, dialogue is encouraged in order to address the specifics of the problem as the client interprets them. At times the therapist can lead the encounter to set the stage, but ultimately it is the client who must verbalize the hurts that are to be healed.

As the dialogue progresses, Jesus can be invited into the scene in what Bennett (1984) calls reliving the scene with Jesus. The client can tell Jesus in front of the antagonist a personal perception of the fragmented relationship and ask Jesus to forgive each of them for their contribution to the hurtful situation. Then, Jesus is asked to love the antagonist in his own way until that individual can be reconciled with the Lord. Attention then turns to the client and a request is made for Jesus to love the client in those ways which have been missing so he can love others, including the antagonist, in a way that will bring honor to the Lord. Frequently, the antagonist will disappear from the image following the forgiveness during the love interaction between the client and Jesus. The sense of peace that usually follows such an encounter is beautiful to behold. It is not unusual, when working with clients of a Pentecostal or Charismatic persuasion, for them to break out in praise to the Lord, both in their own language and through speaking in other tongues.

But, as Stapleton (1976) observed, more than one such experience may be necessary to bring total healing to the client. This process may also be used with a number of individuals in a group setting if the atmosphere has been set appropriately.

Another technique I have found useful, especially with victims of sexual abuse (rape and incest), is to ask the client to re-live in imagery the beginning of a situation in which they were violated. When reviewing the setting, the client frequently resurrects not only the visual image but displays the emotional impact of the scene in bodily tensions. In this situation the client (a) is asked to confront the antagonist at the point of the original encounter, (b) is instructed to invite Jesus into the scene, (c) is to ask for his forgiveness for both the antagonist's actions and the client's bitterness or hatred, and (d) is to request that love from the Lord to be imparted to both of them. Again, the antagonist may disappear or may approach Jesus with the client as a personal encounter with the Master is experienced by the client in the presence of the antagonist in the faith fantasy.

In one situation, where a mother met Jesus in imagery at the coffin of her dead son in a mortuary, she found herself needing to forgive God for taking her young son from her and to ask for forgiveness for her selfish possessiveness. A flood of emotion came when she described to me how the coffin evaporated and Jesus was standing where the coffin had been. Before this session she had been in mourning for over a year and showed it in her dress and affect. After the inner healing encounter she returned to her usual fashionable style of dress, showed total contact with reality, and reentered the main stream of family and community life. Several months later she and her husband became members of a pastoral staff and are now ministering with others who are struggling with losses in their personal lives.

Another technique I have used in individual and group settings involves the metaphor of the Twenty-third Psalm in imagery. Allow the client to image himself in the pastoral setting of the Shepherd Psalm. Encourage him to become aware of the lush green grass, a stream flowing quietly nearby, the warmth of the sun, the coolness of the breeze, a precipitious mountain casting shadows a short distance away which indicates the opening to a gorge in the terrain. As the client images, lying or sitting on the grass, enjoying the peacefulness of the scene, and relaxing in it, Jesus can be invited to appear as the Good Shepherd with a rod in one hand and a staff in the other. As the verses are read and encouragement to be involved in the fantasy progresses, the client can release much tension and become open to the inner healing the Lord wants to perform.

Encourage the client to see Jesus as the Good Shepherd who meets all needs, allows rest in the lush green pasture, leads by still waters that are refreshing but not turbulent. Invite the client to acknowledge the peacefulness of the presence of the Lord. Looking at the precipitous cliff, encourage the client to see shadows falling across part of the valley and to receive the peace of the Lord to fear no evil in the valley of the shadow of death or in life's difficult circumstances because the Shepherd is ever present. The rod and staff comfort and protect from all forces that would impinge upon personality and life.

The Lord can then be invited to prepare a table before the client. Ask the client to see himself seated on the grass as a banquet table is spread out with Jesus at the other end. In one instance when I used this technique, the client saw a table so long she could hardly see Jesus at the other end. In another setting, the client said there wasn't room for a table; she imagined a picnic lunch between her and Jesus as they sat close together to converse.

Whatever the length of the table, the client can be encouraged to draw strength from the food on the table. Then the client can be instructed to invite an "enemy" to the table. This may be a person, living or dead, or an emotion such as fear or anger. The client then can be invited to draw strength from the food on the table which has been spread by the Lord and to address the antagonist and declare his defeat by the strength of the Lord. As the antagonist is allowed to retreat, the client is encouraged to rejoice in the victory that comes from drawing strength from Jesus to deal with the situation that was at the root of the conflict. One or more antagonists may be dealt with in a session, depending on the time and ego strength of the client.

When the antagonist has retreated, the client can be invited to stand and let Jesus approach from the other end of the table. The Lord is then invited to anoint the client with the oil of the Holy Spirit. As the client images the Lord standing close by with a horn of oil and pouring it over the head of the client, the oil can be seen in the fantasy to run down over the head and clothing of the client and drip off onto the grass. The closing affirmation of the Psalm is most appropriate: "Surely goodness and mercy shall follow me all the days of my life: and I shall dwell in the house of the Lord forever" (Psalm 23:6).

I discovered this technique while sitting at the bedside of a friend who had undergone surgery. He was in excruciating pain and it would be several hours before more medication could be administered again. I asked the Lord for a way to help ease the pain and the metaphor of Psalm 23 came to me. I took the patient's hand and invited him into the peaceful scene of the Shepherd Psalm. With eyes closed he imaged as I lead him in the way I felt led by the Holy Spirit. When it came to spreading the table in the presence of the enemy, I had him confront pain at the table. As my friend drew strength from the Lord to reject the pain, I felt the muscles in his arm and hand begin to relax. When I finished the Psalm, he was sleeping peacefully. Later I was informed that the nurses had to awaken him for the next round of medications.

THE COUNSELOR IN INNER HEALING

The role of the counselor in a ministry of inner healing is crucial. Beyond salvation and being Spirit-filled, McDonald (1981) observed, Spirit-led memory healing demands that the person yield himself to be Spirit-led. After observing that "memory healing is one of the most demanding of all ministries," he concluded:

> the counselor needs the same qualities as the person seeking memory healing. . . . motivation for change to occur, honesty, humility and forgiveness. Humility is the knowledge that Jesus is the Healer. . . . Forgiveness is the ability not to judge the other person who seeks your help. (p. 72)

The inner healing approach to psychotherapy emphasizes the operation of the Holy Spirit. He must have free reign in the personal life of the therapist if he is going to do his office's work of revealing Christ in all of his fullness. Sensitivity to the operation of the Holy Spirit comes through completely surrendering to Christ as Lord and Master of life and through opening the entire personality to be filled with the Holy Spirit. The fullness that comes with his presence heightens personal insights drawn from training and experience with the intuitive dimension of spiritual gifts as the Spirit is allowed to flow in the life of the counselor and in the counseling setting. When the client is also open to such spiritual intervention, therapy involves dimensions of the whole person—physical, emotional, and spiritual.

When the Holy Spirit is invited to permeate both hemispheres of the human brain, He brings insights that are both logical *and* intuitive, cognitive *and* aesthetic. The counselor then is able to follow the leadership of the Holy Spirit into exploring the inner being; in effect, he or she introduces a higher power to deal with the problems of the fragmented personality. The integration of the hemispheres under the influence of the Holy Spirit allows for the operation of the gifts and fruit of the Spirit. *Glossolalia* can be an expected to occur as a demonstration of this integrative process when the Spirit of God overshadows the spirit of the individual and speaks as the Spirit himself gives utterance, even as on the Day of Pentecost (Acts 2:4). When the client is also open to such operation of the divine in therapy, miraculous physical and inner healings can and do occur.

SUMMARY

It is the added dimension of the Holy Spirit in counseling that makes the Spirit-filled counselor an extension of the arm of God and brings healing to wounded souls. Because salvation is a part of the atonement, it brings forgiveness for sin and security in Christ. However, unless people are taught that the atonement includes healing of jaded memories as well as forgiveness for sin, they will not necessarily experience healing of some of their memories as part of their conversion experience. They need to be taught that as they are moving from the kingdom of the world into the kingdom of God, the Holy Spirit is available to lead them into a complete inner healing as part of the salvation experience which is their privilege because of the completed work of Christ for them.

When memory healing was not complete in the initial salvation experience, unresolved stress from the past may motivate a person to seek counseling. Remembering can help a person deal with conscious hurts, but there are times when the pain has been repressed so deeply in the unconscious that a more intense stimulus is needed to bring the painful memory content to the surface of conscious awareness so the pain can be dealt with. This is where the operation of the Holy Spirit in recall is efficient in bringing to the mind what is ripe for healing. The Holy Spirit, as the Paraclete, comes alongside the client to introduce the presence of Christ the Healer. Whether through guided imagery or personal awareness, an awareness of the presence of Christ to heal becomes the turning point as wholeness is effected, as sin and sickness are dealt the mortal blow by the power of the living Lord.

Thus the holy Trinity is involved in inner healing: the Holy Spirit convicts of sin and reveals its presence. Jesus Christ saves, forgives, cleanses from all sin, and reconciles the penitent with the Father. Christ also sends the Holy Spirit to lead the believer into all the truth the Father has available for his children. What a blessing to know that this power of the almighty God is available to aid the counselor who allows himself or herself to be filled with the Holy Spirit and to flow in the Spirit in each phase of the psychotherapeutic interaction.

SELECT BIBLIOGRAPHY

Alsdurf, J., & Malony, H. (1980). A critique of Ruth Carter Stapleton's ministry of "inner healing." *Journal of Psychology and Theology, 8,* 173–184.

Bandler, R., & Grinder, J. (1975, 1976). *The structure of magic,* 2 vols., Palo Alto, CA: Science and Behavior Books, Inc.

Bennett, R. (1982). *Emotionally free.* Old Tappan, NJ: Revell.

_____. (1984). *How to pray for inner healing for yourself and others.* Old Tappan, NJ: Revell.

Binet, A. (1922). *L'étude expérimentale de l'intelligence.* Paris: Costes.

Breuer, J., & Freud, S. (1955). Studies in hysteria. In J. Strachey (Ed. and Trans.), *The standard edition of the complete psychological works of Sigmund Freud.* London: Hogarth Press. (Original work published, 1905).

Erikson, E. (1968). *Identity: Youth and crisis.* New York: Norton.

Foulkes, D., Spear, P., & Symonds, J. (1976). Individual differences in mental activity at sleep onset. *Journal of Abnormal Psychology, 71,* 280–286.

Frank, L. (1910). Über *affektstorüngen*. Berlin.

_____. (1913). *Die Psychoanalyse*. Munich: E. Reinhardt.

Glasser, W. (1965). *Reality therapy*. New York: Harper & Row.

Guernsey, D. B. & Bunker, D. E. (1981). The use of representational systems in the healing of memories. *Journal of Christian Healing, 3*(1), 3–18.

Guillerey, M. (1945). Medecine psychologique. In *Médecine officielle et médecine hérétique*. Paris: Plon.

Happich, C. (1932). Das Bildbewusstsein als Ansätzstelle psychischer Behandling. *Zbl. Psychotherap., 5,* 663–667.

Heiss, R. (1956). *Allgemeine Tiefenpsychologie*. Bern: Huber.

Horowitz, M. (1978). Controls of visual imagery and therapeutic intervention. In J. L. Singer & K. S. Pope (Eds.), *The power of human imagination*. New York: Plenum.

Hunt, D., & McMahon, T. (1985). *The seduction of Christianity*. Eugene, OR: Harvest House.

Janet, P. (1898). *Nervoses et idées fixes*. Paris: Alcan.

Jellinek, A. (1949). Spontaneous imagery: A new psychotherapeutic approach. *American Journal of Psychotherapy, 3,* 372–391.

Jung, C. (1976). The symbolic life (F. R. C. Hull, transl.). *Collected works* (Vol. 28). Princeton: Princeton University Press. (Original work published in 1935)

Kepecs, J. (1954). Observations on screens and barriers of the mind. *Psychoanalytic Quarterly, 23,* 62–77.

Klinger, E. (1971). *Structure and functions of fantasy*. New York: Wiley.

Kosbab, F. (1974). Imagery techniques in psychiatry. *Archives of General Psychiatry, 31,* 382–390.

Lantz, W., Jr. (1986). The seduction of Christianity: Reviewed. *Journal of Psychology and Christianity, 5,* 55–58.

Leuner, H. (1969). Guided affective imagery. *American Journal of Psychotherapy, 23,* 4–33.

_____. (1977). Guided affective imagery: An account of its development. *Journal of Mental Images, 1,* 73–92.

_____. (1978). Basic principles and therapeutic efficacy of guided affective imagery. In J. Singer & K. Pope (Eds.), *The power of human imagination*. New York: Plenum.

_____. (1984). *Guided affective imagery: Mental imagery in short-term psychotherapy*. New York: Thieme-Stratton.

Linn, K., & Linn, M. (1974). *Healing of memories: Prayer and confession— Steps to inner healing*. New York: Paulist Press.

Malony, H. (1985). Inner healing. In D. Benner (Ed.), *Baker encyclopedia of psychology* (pp. 579–584). Grand Rapids, MI: Baker Book House.

McDonald, R. (1981). *God can renew your mind through memory healing*. Atlanta: author.

McMahon, C. (1973). Images as motives and motivators: A historical perspective. *American Journal of Psychology, 86,* 465–490.

McNutt, F. (1974). *Healing*. Notre Dame, IN: Ave Maria Press.

Miller, G., Galanter, E., & Pribram, K. (1960). *Plans and the structure of behavior*. New York: Holt.

Missildine, H. (1963). *Your inner child of the past*. New York: Simon & Shuster.

Parkhurst, G. (1957). *Healing and wholeness are yours!* St. Paul, MN: Macalester Park.

———. (1968). *Healing the whole person*. New York: Morehouse-Barlow.

———. (1973). *Glorious victory through healing the memories*. St. Paul, MN: Macalester Park.

Paulk, E. (1987). *That the world may know*. Atlanta: Dimension.

Rehyer, J. (1977). Spontaneous visual imagery: Implications for psychoanalysis, psychopathology, and psychotherapy. *Journal of Mental Imagery, 2*, 253–274.

Richardson, A. (1969). *Mental imagery*. New York: Springer.

———. (1983). Imagery: Definition and types. In A. Shiekh (Ed.), *Imagery: Current theory, research, and application*. New York: Wiley (pp. 3–42).

Sandford, J., & Sandford, P. (1982). *The transformation of the inner man*. South Plainfield, NJ: Bridge Publishing Inc.

Sanford, A. (1947). *The healing light*. St. Paul, MN: Macalester Park.

Schultz, J., & Luthe, W. (1959). *Autogenic training: A physiological approach to psychotherapy*. New York: Grune & Stratton.

Seamonds, D. (1981). *Healing for damaged emotions*. Wheaton, IL: Victor Books.

———. (1982). *Putting away childish things*. Wheaton, IL: Victor Books.

———. (1985). *Healing of memories*. Wheaton, IL: Victor Books.

———. (1987). Leadership bibliography: Emotions. *Leadership, 8*(2), 97.

Sheikh, A. & Jordan, C. (1983). Clinical uses of mental imagery. In A. Sheikh (Ed.), *Imagery: Current theory, research, and application* (pp. 391–435). New York: Wiley.

Skeikh, A. & Panagiotou, N. (1975). Use of mental imagery in psychotherapy: A critical review. *Perceptual and motor skills, 41*, 555–585.

Silberer, H. (1909). Bericht über die Methode, gewisse symbolische Halluzinationserscheinungen hervorzurufen und zu beobachten. *Jahrbuch für Psychoanalyse und Psychopathologische Forschung*, 1:1.

———. (1912). Symbolik des Ewachens und Schwellensymbolik überhapt. *Jahrbuch für Psychoanalyse und Psychopathologische Forschung, 3*, 621.

Simpson, M., & Paivio, A. (1966). Changes in pupil size during an imagery task without motor involvement. *Psychonomic Science, 5*, 405–406.

Stapleton, R. (1976). *The gift of inner healing*. Waco, TX: Word Books.

———. (1977). *The experience of inner healing*. Waco, TX: Word Books.

Tapscott, B. (1975). *Inner healing through healing of memories*. Houston: Tapscott.

Wise, R. (Ed.). (1986). *The church divided*. South Plainfield, NJ: Bridge Publishing.

Yaremko, R., & Butler, M. (1975). Imaginal experience and attenuation of the galvanic skin response to shock. *Bulletin of the Psychonomic Society, 5,* 317–318.

Scripture Index

Index of Names and Subjects